# BEST PRACTICE
## THE PROS ON ADOBE FLASH

# BEST PRACTICE
## THE PROS ON ADOBE FLASH

Douglas Easterly

**THOMSON**
**DELMAR LEARNING**

Australia Canada Mexico Singapore Spain United Kingdom United States

## Best Practice: The Pros on Adobe Flash

Douglas Easterly

**Vice President, Technology and Trades ABU:**
Dave Garza

**Director of Learning Solutions:**
Sandy Clark

**Managing Editor:**
Larry Main

**Acquisitions Editor:**
James Gish

**Product Manager:**
Nicole Calisi

**Marketing Director:**
Deborah S. Yarnell

**Marketing Manager:**
Bryant Chrzan

**Marketing Specialist:**
Victoria Ortiz

**Director of Production:**
Patty Stephan

**Production Manager:**
Stacy Masucci

**Associate Content Project Manager:**
Niamh Matthews-Schweitzer

**Art Director:**
Benjamin Gleeksman

**Technology Project Manager:**
Christopher Catalina

**Editorial Assistant:**
Sarah Timm

**Cover Design:**
Toni Toland

COPYRIGHT © 2008 Thomson Delmar Learning, a division of Thomson Learning Inc. All rights reserved. The Thomson Learning Inc. logo is a registered trademark used herein under license.

Printed in Canada

1 2 3 4 5 XX 11 10 09 08 07

For more information contact Thomson Delmar Learning
Executive Woods
5 Maxwell Drive, PO Box 8007,
Clifton Park, NY 12065-8007

Or find us on the World Wide Web at
www.delmarlearning.com

ALL RIGHTS RESERVED. No part of this work covered by the copyright hereon may be reproduced in any form or by any means—graphic, electronic, or mechanical, including photocopying, recording, taping, Web distribution, or information storage and retrieval systems—without the written permission of the publisher.

For permission to use material from the text or product, contact us by

Tel.   (800) 730-2214
Fax   (800) 730-2215
www.thomsonrights.com

Library of Congress Cataloging-in-Publication Data:
Easterly, Douglas.
  Best practice. The pros on Adobe Flash / Douglas Easterly.
     p. cm.
  Includes index.
  ISBN-13: 978-1-4180-5041-2
  ISBN-10: 1-4180-5041-5
  1. Flash (Computer file) 2. Multimedia systems. 3. Web sites—Design. I. Title. II. Title: Pros on Adobe Flash.
  QA76.575.E23 2007
  006.7—dc22
                            2007031977

### NOTICE TO THE READER

Publisher does not warrant or guarantee any of the products described herein or perform any independent analysis in connection with any of the product information contained herein. Publisher does not assume, and expressly disclaims, any obligation to obtain and include information other than that provided to it by the manufacturer.

The reader is expressly warned to consider and adopt all safety precautions that might be indicated by the activities herein and to avoid all potential hazards. By following the instructions contained herein, the reader willingly assumes all risks in connection with such instructions.

The publisher makes no representation or warranties of any kind, including but not limited to, the warranties of fitness for particular purpose or merchantability, nor are any such representations implied with respect to the material set forth herein, and the publisher takes no responsibility with respect to such material. The publisher shall not be liable for any special, consequential, or exemplary damages resulting, in whole or part, from the readers' use of, or reliance upon, this material.

## TABLE OF CONTENTS

### PREFACE

| | |
|---|---|
| About this Book | VIII |
| Intended Audience | VIII |
| Organization | VIII |
| Features | IX |
| Ingredients for Success | IX |
| E.Resource | X |
| About the Author | X |
| Acknowledgements | XI |
| Questions and Feedback | XII |

### CHAPTER 1   BASIC INGREDIENTS   1

| | |
|---|---|
| New Document / Multiple Documents | 2 |
| Workspace | 3 |
| Keyboard Shortcuts | 3 |
| Tools and Drawing | 4 |
| Layers | 8 |
| Creating Symbols | 10 |
| Keyframes and Motion Tweens | 11 |
| Guide Layers | 14 |
| Mask Layers | 16 |
| Shape Tween | 18 |
| Types of Symbols | 19 |
| Actionscript | 21 |
| Importing Media | 26 |
| Exporting | 29 |
| New Features | 31 |
| Key Concepts | 32 |

### CHAPTER 2   NICK FOX GIEG   33

| | |
|---|---|
| Digital Deconstruction: *The Option of War* | 35 |
| DIY: Drawing with Flash | 37 |
| DIY: Creating a Walk Cycle | 40 |
| Digital Deconstruction: *I Wanna Be Famous* | 43 |
| DIY: Rotoscoping | 46 |
| On Your Own | 48 |

| | | |
|---|---|---|
| **CHAPTER 3** | **RICARDO MIRANDA ZÚÑIGA** | **49** |
| | Digital Deconstruction: *Audiophile* | 51 |
| | Digital Deconstruction: *Dentimundo* | 52 |
| | Digital Deconstruction: *Fallout* | 54 |
| | Digital Deconstruction: *Vagamundo* | 55 |
| | DIY: Character Animation | 59 |
| | On Your Own | 72 |
| **CHAPTER 4** | **JESS LOSEBY** | **73** |
| | Digital Deconstruction: *Views from the Ground Floor* | 76 |
| | DIY: Movement and Texture with Actionscript | 78 |
| | Digital Deconstruction: *doc-u* | 83 |
| | On Your Own | 85 |
| **CHAPTER 5** | **MICHAEL TAKEO MAGRUDER** | **87** |
| | Digital Deconstruction: [ *Fallujah . Iraq . 31/03/2004* ] | 90 |
| | DIY: Controlling Color with ActionScript | 93 |
| | Digital Deconstruction: { *Transcription* } | 99 |
| | On Your Own | 100 |
| **CHAPTER 6** | **JULIET DAVIS** | **101** |
| | Digital Deconstruction: *Altar-ations* | 103 |
| | Digital Deconstruction: *Polystrene Dream* | 104 |
| | Digital Deconstruction: *Pieces of Herself* | 105 |
| | DIY: Loading External SWF's | 107 |
| | DIY: Scrolling a Movie Clip Inside a Mask | 110 |
| | On Your Own | 113 |
| **CHAPTER 7** | **CARLA DIANA** | **115** |
| | Digital Deconstruction: *Terranium* | 119 |
| | DIY: 3D Gadgetry | 122 |
| | Digital Deconstruction: *Repercussion* | 124 |
| | DIY: Adding Volume to Our Gadgetry | 127 |
| | On Your Own | 129 |
| **CHAPTER 8** | **AARON KOBLIN** | **131** |
| | Digital Deconstruction: *Flight Patterns* | 133 |
| | Digital Deconstruction: *The Sheep Market* | 136 |
| | DIY: Flash Drawing Recorder | 137 |
| | On Your Own | 144 |

## CHAPTER 9    ERIC SOCOLOFSKY    145

    Digital Deconstruction: *Vectogram*    149
    Digital Deconstruction: *Silly Walks Generator*    150
    DIY: *Silly Walks Generator*: The Inverse Kinematics Engine    152
    On Your Own    167

## CHAPTER 10    KRISTER OLSSON    169

    Digital Deconstruction: *Pretendster*    173
    Digital Deconstruction: *Zune-Arts*    175
    DIY: A Scaling Animated Line-up    176
    On Your Own    186

## CHAPTER 11    SANTIAGO ORTIZ    187

    Digital Deconstruction: *Sonido Y Energia (Sound and Energy)*    189
    Digital Deconstruction: *Mitozoos*    194
    DIY: Representing Life: 4 Studies    196
    Digital Deconstruction: *Microcosmos A Gaia*    204
    On Your Own    206

## CHAPTER 12    JEREMY THORP    207

    Digital Deconstruction: *Index for X*    212
    Digital Deconstruction: *Darwinstruments*    213
    DIY: Creating a Generative Particle System    214
    Digital Deconstruction: *Variance*    220
    On Your Own    222

## CHAPTER 13    JONATHAN HARRIS    223

    Digital Deconstruction: *WordCount*    229
    Digital Deconstruction: *10 × 10*    231
    Digital Deconstruction: *Phylotaxis*    233
    DIY: Databases and Flash    235
    On Your Own    252

## CHAPTER 14    DAN SHUTA    253

    Digital Deconstruction: *Audiorganic*    257
    DIY: Building a Custom Physical Interface for Flash    258
    On Your Own    279

## INDEX    281

## ABOUT THIS BOOK

When I first started experimenting with Flash back in 1998, the books available were far and few between. Now there are scores of Flash publications covering a variety of topics. So how is this book any different? While Chapter 1 provides a run-through of the environment and basic operations of Flash, the rest of the book focuses on talented artists and designers who have established themselves as some of the more innovative professionals in their respective fields. While many books on Flash simply reinforce the status quo, the artists in this book are known for breaking new ground, as is attested by the galleries, publications, reviews, and clients tallied across their lengthy CVs.

## INTENDED AUDIENCE

This book is intended for all levels of artists, designers, teachers, and students who employ Flash in their creative practice. Some of the chapters examine the simpler aspects of the featured artist's work, while other chapters dig deep, showing the most advanced techniques being engineered by these highly skilled professionals. But regardless of your current level of expertise, the methods covered in this book are sure to assist you towards achieving new heights of Flash mastery. Additionally, this book peers into the inspirations and creative minds behind the techniques—an invaluable perspective that supports the technical sections.

## ORGANIZATION

The first chapter can be thought of as an abridged version of a typical book about Flash. Such books tend to use the software as an outline for the content. *This* book recognizes that the general operations are important for someone completely new to Flash, and is thoroughly covered in this first chapter. But *Best Practice: The Pros on Adobe Flash* also recognizes that it is much more interesting, and educational, to learn by seeing what the pros are doing. So, each of the remaining thirteen chapters focus on just that—a thorough look at the creative practices of several creative professionals.

# PREFACE IX

## FEATURES

- The Digital Deconstruction section focuses on a particular project of the artist featured in that chapter. The project is analyzed both technically and conceptually.

- The DIY (Do It Yourself) exercises included in each chapter are step-by-step instructions for creating a certain technique or effect. These sections are related to, and inspired by, the work covered in the Digital Deconstruction sections.

- Concluding each chapter is the On Your Own section. Here, advice is offered on how to incorporate the chapter material into your own projects.

- Some chapters include FYI (For Your Information) sidebars that mention relevant protocols, standards, or advice that should be observed.

- Included as an insert on the back cover is a DVD. On it you will find video interviews and material referenced (such as Flash files) throughout the book, especially in the DIY sections.

Digital Deconstruction sections feature this vegetable peeler icon.

The DIY (Do It Yourself) sections are represented by a whisk icon.

Sections that feature basic information about an option or technique are marked with measuring spoons.

The On Your Own sections are represented by a spatula.

## INGREDIENTS FOR SUCCESS

For you newbies out there, make sure you stay organized while working through the book. Make a folder on your computer that corresponds to the chapter you are working through. Be sure to name your files in a sensible manner, like *mySQLtest4.fla* and not something like *untitled2.fla*. This is such a simple routine, but surprisingly not everyone follows it.

Creating artwork on a computer is not like carving on a $1000 block of marble. In other words, digital media is easily reproducible, manipulated, and saved. You should experiment, test, stretch, and even break what you are working on—without fear! But, as you do this, make sure you save your files with different names. If you get a Flash movie named *charAnim3.fla* working fine, but you want to try something new, immediately save it as *charAnim4.fla*. If you find yourself being attacked by ActionScript error messages, you can always go back to the previous version. Some of my projects have 40–50 stages of evolution, and a separate FLA file that represents every one of them.

# PREFACE

With each new software release, more and more "canned" creativity is built into the application. Be careful not to fall into the trap of relying too much on these gimmicky tricks. Every single contributor in this book shares a similar concern in this regard. Just by taking a look at their work, you can see that it is their creative vision and articulated ideas that resonate, not the mark of the software.

## E.RESOURCE

An instructor's guide on CD is available to assist teachers in planning and implementing their curriculum. It includes sample syllabi for using this book in either a 10- or 14-week course. It also provides PowerPoint and Keynote slides, which highlight the main topics as well as provide additional resources.

Order Number: 1418050423

## ABOUT THE AUTHOR

Douglas Easterly was born and raised in Anchorage, Alaska. After high school, he set off to Texas where he earned a BA from the University of Dallas and an MFA from the University of Texas at Austin. His teaching career began as an Assistant Professor at Southeastern Louisiana University. From there, he went on to earn an Associate Professorship with tenure at Syracuse University. Currently he is a Senior Lecturer of Interaction Design in the School of Design at Victoria University of Wellington, New Zealand.

In Louisiana, he was cofounder and proprietor of the Rhizomat—a gallery, design company and community education center. He is also a founding member of SWAMP *www.swamp.nu* whose artwork has been exhibited at ARCO in Madrid, SIGGRAPH in L.A. and Boston, published in numerous magazines such as *ReadyMade*, and won awards, such as first prize from the VIDA Art and Artificial Life foundation in 2004.

Doug's experience with technology began when his father taught him Morse Code in the late 70s. His family's first computer, a TRS-80, had a program that could translate the "dits" and "dahs" from this code into English, printing the results across the screen. His first creative experiments with the computer would come years later while studying at UT Austin.

When not preparing for class or working on his research, Doug enjoys a wide variety of music, reading books on new media and cultural theory, and surfing through Websites like boing-boing *www.boingboing.net*. He has even been known to go outdoors, usually to hike, camp, bike, or fish. He is also quite avid about exploring his new home of New Zealand.

## ACKNOWLEDGEMENTS

Working with the artists featured throughout this book was a real pleasure. Some of them I knew about before undertaking this project, others I discovered while curating the content for the book. What can be said of them all is that I became a much bigger fan of their work through the e-mails, phone conversations, personal meetings, and scanning of their Websites while generating their chapters. I am quite proud of how this book operates as a curatorial collection of these great artists and designers: thank you for your hard work and contributions!

I would also like to thank the additional people:

> Dylan Moore and Sarah Howell—two of my recent graduate students. Sarah provided graphics for Chapter 1, as well as other graphics and editing throughout the book; she is exceptionally talented with vector illustration and animation. Dylan applied his amazing programming talents to the DIY section of Chapter 13. Dylan also checked the technical accuracy of every chapter. In addition to doing a thoroughly professional job on this book, both of them are exceptional artists in their own right.

> Matt Kenyon is a good friend, Assistant Professor at Penn State, and my fellow collaborator with SWAMP *www.swamp.nu*. Working with Matt over the past several years has certainly influenced my curatorial eye, and his opinions assisted with who ended up being in this book. Thanks Matt!

> Mom and Dad — The best parents anyone could hope for. Thanks for supporting me, well, since I was born, but especially since I announced that I would no longer study accounting and economics, while taking up painting and philosophy instead. See—I ended up with a career after all!

> Harold Lehman and I collaborated on a variety of performance and multimedia projects in Austin back in the 90s. He produced the audio track for the DVD. Check out his Website at *www.sonicrabbit.com*.

**THE ARTISTS:**

Nick Fox-Gieg

Ricardo Miranda Zúñiga

Jess Loseby

Michael Takeo Magruder

Juliet Davis

Carla Diana

Aaron Koblin

Eric Socolofsky

Krister Olsson

Santiago Ortiz

Jeremy Thorp

Jonathan Harris

Dan Shuta

My partner Anne Niemetz—Not only did she help proofread, offer advice on curating and organization, but she also assisted with the DVD production. I will also use some room here to say thanks for being the first "away team" to report back from New Zealand. That assisted greatly with giving me the time to put the finishing touches on this book.

Finally, I would like to thank Thomson Delmar Learning, starting with Toni Toland, who recommended me for this book. Jim Gish, Niamh Matthews, and Nicole Bruno were great support, assisting me through phone calls, e-mails, and business meetings that resolved the countless issues that arise when undertaking such an enormous effort as this book. Thank you—I am looking forward to our next collaboration!

## QUESTIONS AND FEEBACK

The types of people reading this book will cover students, teachers, professionals, novices, pros, and too many others to list. Please lend your perspective by supplying feedback about this book. It will be carefully assessed and incorporated into my next work.

Thomson Delmar Learning
Executive Woods
5 Maxwell Drive
Clifton Park, NY 12065
Attention: Media Arts and Design Team
Douglas Easterly

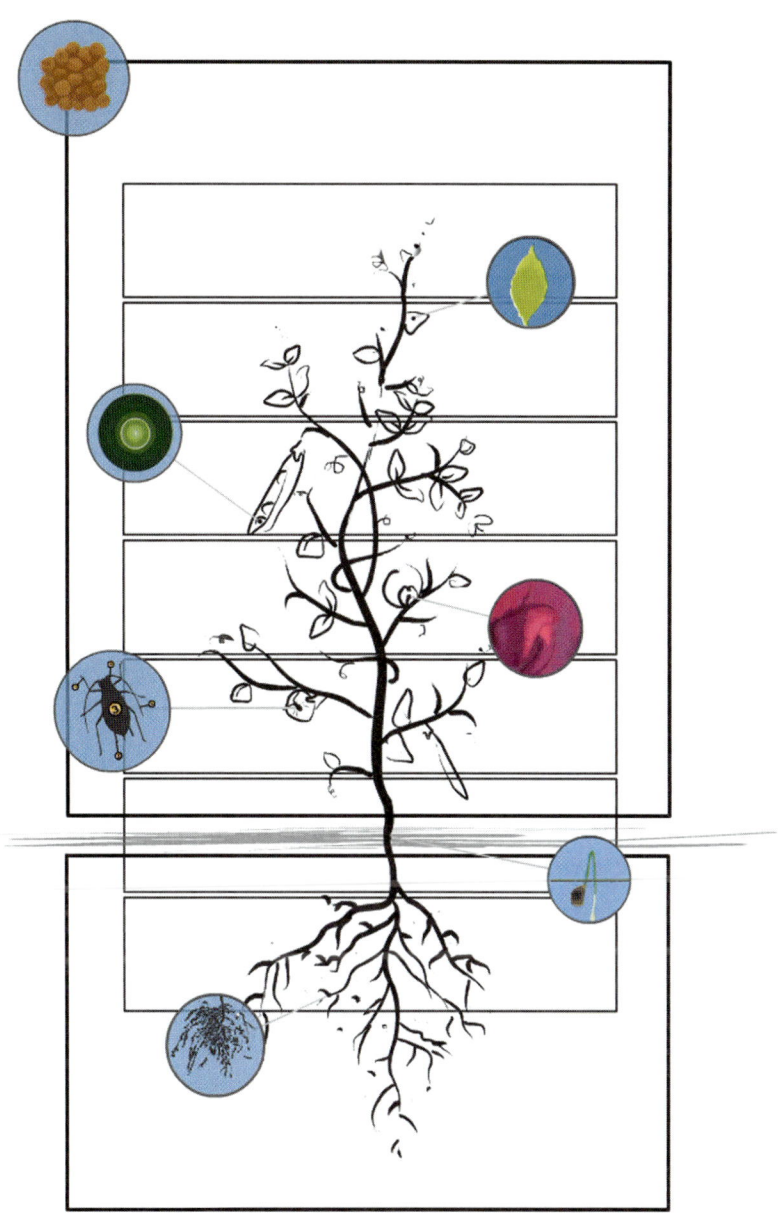

# 1 BASIC INGREDIENTS

New Document • Workspace • Keyboard Shortcuts • Tools • Layers • Creating Symbols • Keyframes and Motion Tweens • Guide Layers • Mask Layers • Shape Tween • Types of Symbols • ActionScript • Importing Media • Exporting • New Features

This chapter is designed to be an introductory course for those of you who are new to Flash, or just a refresher for those who have not worked with it in awhile. It does not include every aspect of the software, just the essential features in a nutshell. The proceeding chapters will cover more in-depth techniques as they pertain to each featured artist. Even if you are familiar with many of the topics listed here, you might still want to skim through this chapter for an item or two that you did not notice in your past experience using Flash.

## NEW DOCUMENT / MULTIPLE DOCUMENTS

Of course, to do anything in Flash, you must have a Flash file open. By default, Flash opens a Start panel whenever you first launch the program, or if you close a document while Flash is still running. From this panel you can choose to resume work on a recently opened document, or you can create a new one. When creating a new document, you will typically choose the default selection, Flash Document, but other file types are listed for advanced users.

You can also have more than one file open at a time. If you already have a Flash document open, and choose File ➡ New from the Menu, a similar window will open. Opening multiple files in Flash will conveniently place them in new tabs across the top of the Timeline, making it easy to flip back and forth between different projects (or the same project as we will do in Chapter 12).

New Flash Documents open up at a default setting of 550 pixels wide by 400 pixels tall, and 12 frames per second playback speed. You can change these settings by opening

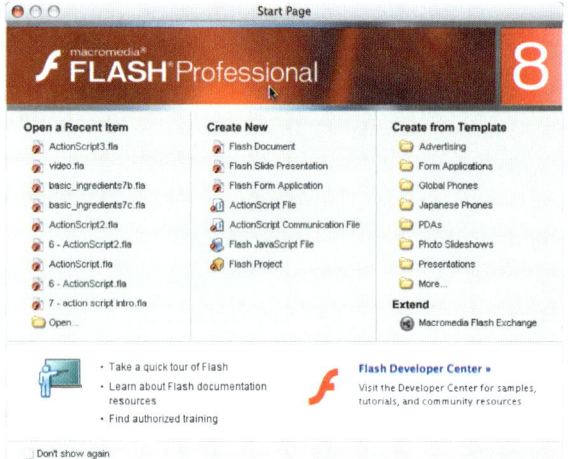

**Figure 1.1** A wide range of file types and templates can be selected from the Start panel. Typically you will be using Flash Documents. This page can also be turned on/off: Preferences ➡ General ➡ On Launch: No document.

the Document Properties window: Modify ➡ Document. You can also change the Background color and Ruler units in this window. Rulers are handy for creating a precise layout: View ➡ Rulers.

## WORKSPACE

Once a document is open, the workspace appears. The workspace may look different depending on what windows and panels were open during the last time Flash was running. At the very least, the main window will be visible, which consists of the Timeline and the Stage. The Layers section is also part of the Timeline, sitting in the upper left-hand corner. Usually, the Tools panel, Property Inspector and possibly a few others will be open too. If not, they are easily accessible from the Window section of the Menu. You can also reset your workspace to the default setting: Window ➡ Workspace Layout ➡ Default.

## KEYBOARD SHORTCUTS

While hovering your mouse over any of the items in the Tools panel, a brief pop-up label will appear, along with the keyboard shortcut for that tool in parentheses.

This is a great way to learn the shortcut for a certain tool or method that you find yourself using repeatedly. If this is not working on your computer, go to Flash ➡ Preferences ➡ General ➡ Show tooltips. Additionally, all of the keyboard shortcuts for Flash can be viewed by going to the Menu ➡ Flash ➡ Keyboard Shortcuts. From here, the shortcuts are grouped by workspace Menus and panels (like the Tools panel for instance). You can also save all of these shortcuts to an HTML file, where you can view them in a browser window, or print them out to tack up near your workstation.

**Figure 1.2** Tool tip: hovering the mouse over a tool will display its name.

## BASIC INGREDIENTS

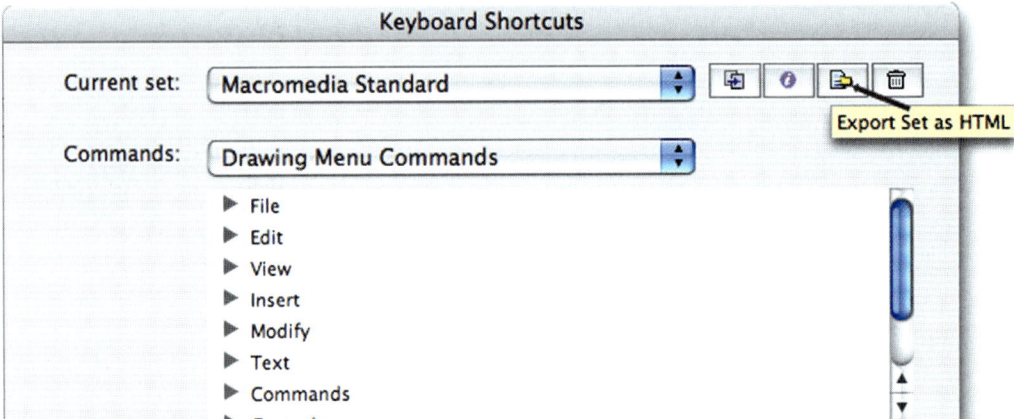

**Figure 1.3** It is a good idea to export all of the Shortcut Sets as HTML. Then you can open and print them from a browser, such as Firefox or Safari.

### TOOLS AND DRAWING

The Tools panel is the primary source for creating vector graphics in Flash; you will use it often, whether you are a novice or an expert. These tools are pretty standard, and indeed you might have seen them in other imaging/multimedia software, but Flash does have its own idiosyncrasies.

The best way to learn how to use these tools is simply to dive right in and see what they do. Here we are going to create some basic forms using some of the drawing tools found on the Tools panel.

1. Create a new document, and make sure the Tools panel is open (Window ➡ Tools).

2. Choose the Oval tool and then examine the Property Inspector (if this window is not open already, go to:Window ➡ Properties ➡ Properties).

# CHAPTER ONE 5

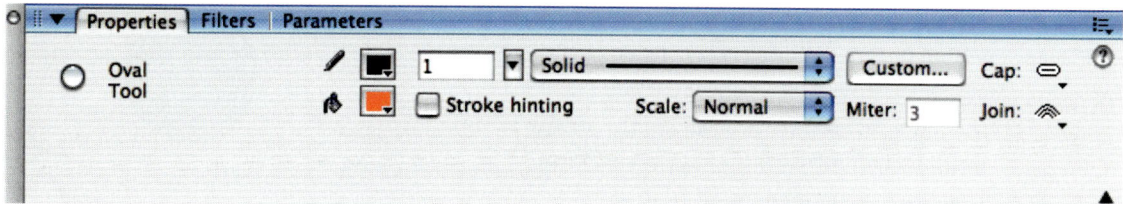

**Figure 1.4** The Property Inspector is variable in the sense that it displays different properties depending on what tool or object is selected.

3. In the Property Inspector, you can choose the fill color, the stroke color, and the stroke thickness. There is also a pull-down Menu for choosing other stroke styles (dotted, dashed, organic, etc.), or you can define a custom stroke by selecting the Custom button. Setting the stroke defines how the border around a graphic will appear. The fill area is the inner portion of a graphic. More refined color selection (for strokes and fills) can be made in the Color Mixer (Window ➡ Color Mixer). This window is especially important for making color gradients.

4. After choosing your color settings, draw a circle on the Stage by clicking and dragging (if you want a perfectly proportioned circle, hold the Shift key while dragging). Notice as you draw your circle that it uses the place where you first clicked as a registration point.

5. Undo the circle you just made (Edit ➡ Undo) and draw another circle, this time holding down the Shift + Option keys. The Option key places the registration point at the center of your form, so as you draw outward, the drawn form expands the same in all directions. This technique is really important when you want to draw something centered on a certain point.

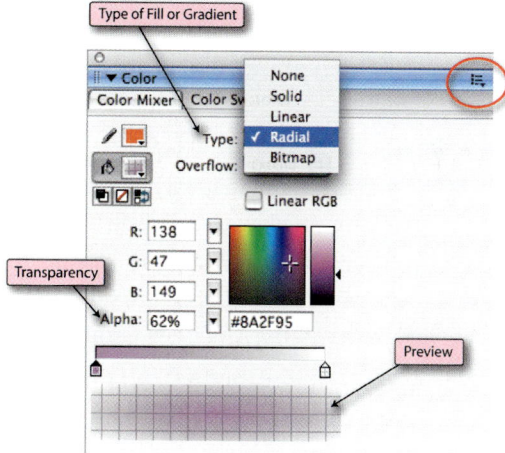

**Figure 1.5** A variety of adjustments in the Color Mixer can be used in tandem to make highly customized color gradients. The drop-down Menu in the far upper right-hand corner of the Color Mixer allows for even more options, including saving custom gradients to the Color Swatches panel for future access (Add Swatch).

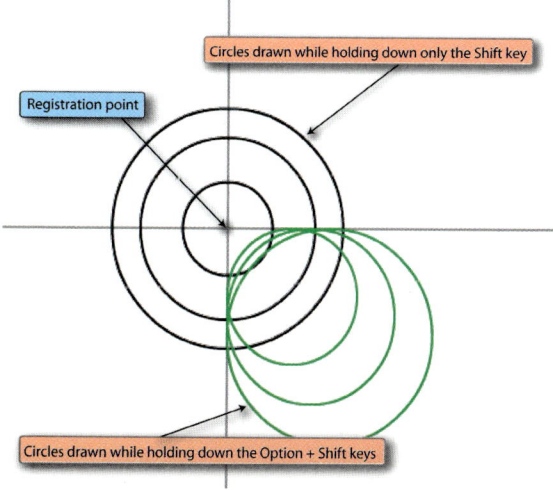

**Figure 1.6** Notice the different relationships between the circles and their registration points.

6. Flash highlights selected graphics with a bunch of tiny dots. Select the inside of the circle you just made and move it across the Stage. Whoa! We are leaving the stroke (outline) behind! Although these two forms were born at the same time, they will not naturally move together unless you select the stroke *and* fill before moving them. To do this, you can either click and drag across everything you want to select, click each graphic element in turn while holding the Shift key, or just double-click the object.

7. If you are going to be moving the fill and stroke of an object frequently, you might consider grouping them. Make sure all the parts you want grouped are selected; then go to the Menu, Modify ➡ Group.

You can even make groups of grouped objects together if you like . To ungroup, just go back to the Menu, Modify ➡ Ungroup or Break Apart (notice the Keyboard shortcut is also provided here in the Menu). To automatically group objects as you draw, you can toggle the Object Drawing box in the Tools pallet.

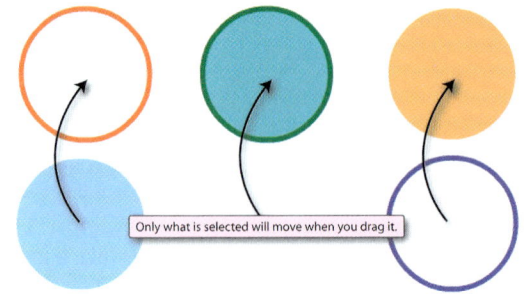

**Figure 1.7** You may think you have the entire object selected, but Flash treats strokes and fills independently.

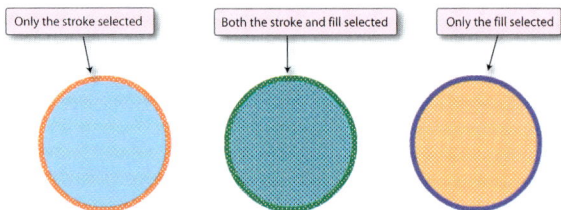

**Figure 1.8** Selected graphic material is indicated by tiny dots across the surface.

While getting the hang of these techniques, you should also be aware of how ungrouped objects can join and cut into one another just by overlaying them on the same layer. To try this, you may want to delete what you have drawn up to this point, or simply create a new Flash document. Then, prepare these three steps by drawing a circle somewhere on the Stage. Make this one with no stroke by choosing the little box with the red slash through it in the stroke color selector.

Next change the fill color and select the Brush tool. Notice the change at the bottom of the Tools panel. You can now change the mode, size, and shape of your brush. Also, in the Property Inspector panel you can adjust how smooth your line will be.

With this prep work done, let us take a look at the three steps involved with subtractive drawing.

1. Select a small brush size and draw a line over the circle. Be sure you selected a different color!

2. Using the Selection tool, click on the Stage to deselect the form you just made, then select your line form again and drag it off of the circle.

3. The line was used to cut a form away from the circle. This can be employed quite strategically for making subtractive decisions in a design.

**NOTE:** Inversely, try changing the color of the line form to the same color as the circle, and you will find that it becomes a single form: additive drawing! Many find this method of joining and cutting graphics on the fly a useful way of generating complex forms.

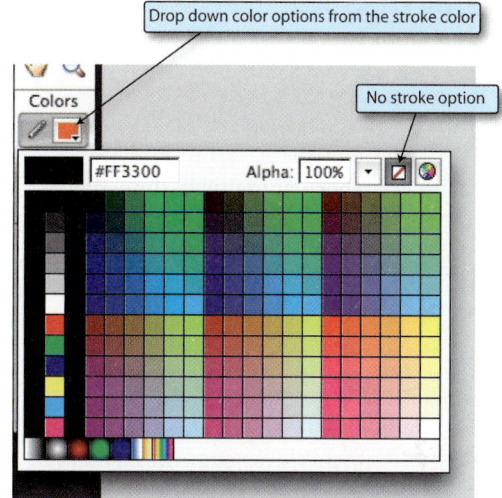

**Figure 1.9** Choosing fill and stroke colors, as well as disabling each one, is easily done from the Tools panel.

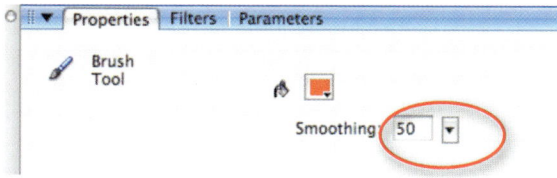

**Figure 1.10** The Smoothing adjustment for the Brush properties is a handy setting.

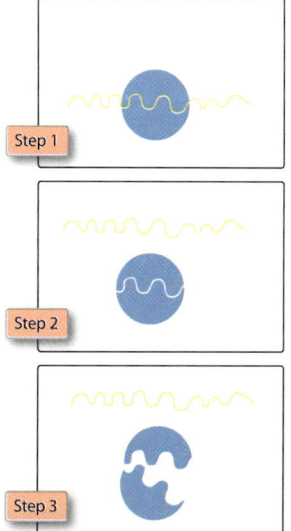

**Figure 1.11** In three steps, you can creatively utilize the subtractive nature of drawing graphics on the same layer.

**BASIC INGREDIENTS**

## LAYERS

Create a new document to make a clean space for working with layers and tweens—the next topics to be covered.

1. A new document will automatically have one layer called **Layer 1**. Double-click this text to rename the layer—call it **circleLayer** (we will use this layer later).

2. Now create a new layer by clicking the Insert Layer button. This button is located in the upper-left corner of your workspace. Name this layer **organicLayer**.

3. Click on frame 1 of the **organicLayer**. Use the brush tool to draw an organic shape on frame 1 of this layer. Be sure to spend some time choosing the settings for your brush, such as smoothness, color, size, etc.

4. Use the Selection tool to click and drag the edges of your shape to sculpt it into a form you are happy with. Modify ➡ Shape ➡ Expand is handy for "bulking-up" selected fill elements.

5. Once you have your basic shape, use the Color Mixer to create a gradient fill color. When you have a gradient you like, you can apply it to your organic shape with the Paint Bucket.

6. After applying your color, you can also save it for later as a custom swatch. Go to the pop-up Menu in the upper-right corner and choose Add Swatch.

7. Click on frame 1 of the **circleLayer**. We are now going to draw into this frame.

**Figure 1.12** Controls for adding and altering layers are conveniently located at the bottom of the layers area.

**Figure 1.13** The Selection tool is quite versatile; it can be intuitively used to change the shape of a form. Notice how the cursor changes depending on whether you are near the edge of the shape or directly over it.

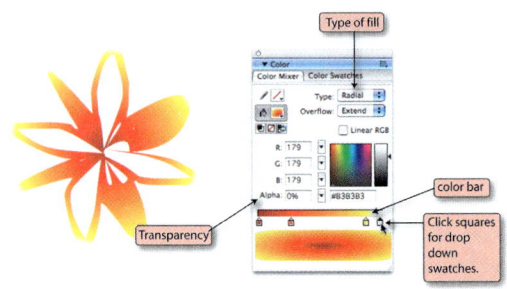

**Figure 1.14** The Color Mixer contains numerous settings for creating custom fills.

# CHAPTER ONE    9

8. Select the oval tool, and along with it, the stroke and fill color you would like to use. Draw a circle—I chose to make the diameter of the circle equal to the organic shape. Since the **circleLayer** is beneath the **organicLayer**, the graphics will reflect this hierarchy.

9. It is easy to reposition the layers in Flash. You simply do this by clicking and dragging the layers. Try swapping the **circleLayer** and **organicLayer** — you should see the circle eclipse the organic shape.

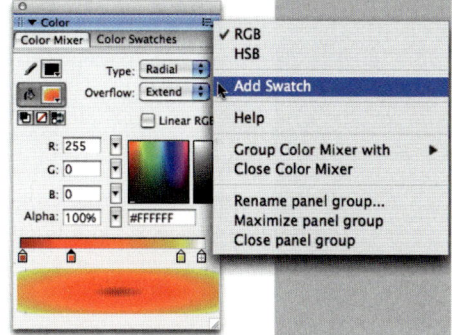

**Figure 1.15** If you spend a lot of time making a custom gradient fill, it is a good idea to save it.

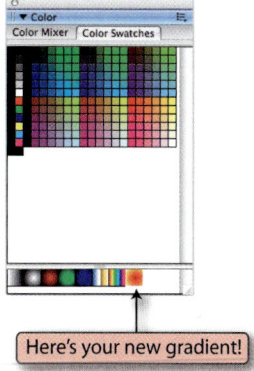

**Figure 1.16** In the future, you could easily access this swatch as you would the color red.

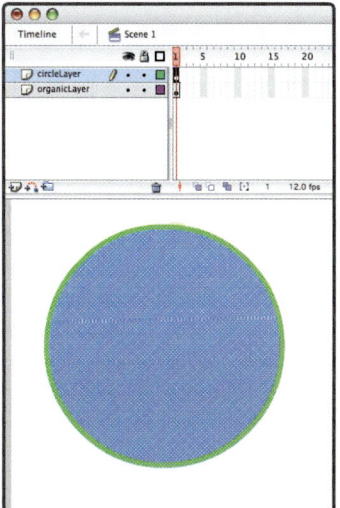 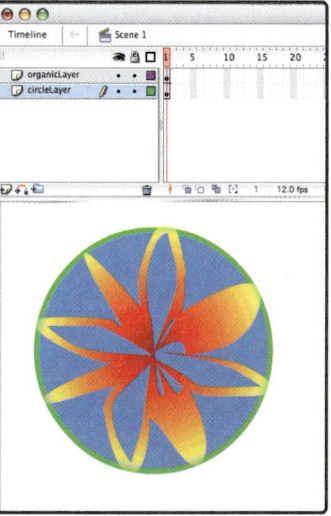

**Figure 1.17** This illustrates the hierarchy of layers in Flash: top layers will be shown as spatially above lower layers.

## CREATING SYMBOLS

One of the most important concepts in Flash is the use of Symbols. In fact, understanding the various ways to use symbols is crucial for becoming a pro with Flash. A symbol is a media element that has been converted into a reusable asset residing in the Library. Creating a Symbol from a graphic is quite easy.

1. Open the *creatingSymbols.fla* from the DVD. Select the entire organic shape by clicking on frame 1 of the **organicLayer**.

2. With your organic shape selected, go to the Menu and select Modify ➡ Convert to Symbol. This will bring up the Convert to Symbol dialog box. Keep the Type at the default setting of Movie clip and name it **organicShape**.

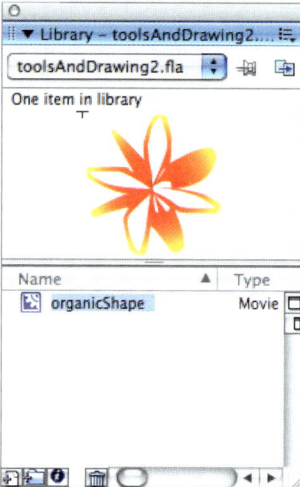

**Figure 1.18** When you create a symbol, you are also making a new Library asset.

3. Open the Library: Menu ➡ Windows ➡ Library. Notice the symbol you created has been stored there as an asset. Library assets can be added to your project as needed by simply dragging them to the Stage. It is generally a good idea to put assets onto their own unique layer for greater control.

## KEYFRAMES AND MOTION TWEENS

Creating a motion tween is one of the simplest things to do with a symbol. There is one other type of tween, a shape tween, but we will cover that later.

Use the same FLA that you have opened with your circle and organic shape (that has been turned into a symbol).

1. First, turn the circle on the Stage into a symbol: select the circle, go to the Menu item Modify ➡ Convert to Symbol, and name this symbol **circleSymbol**.

2. Now select frame 20 of the **circleLayer** and go to the Menu item Insert ➡ Timeline ➡ Keyframe. You will notice on the Timeline, that a keyframe was added in frame 20. Also, the organic shape will disappear. This is because there is currently no frame 20 for the **organicLayer**.

    A keyframe is a frame that is used to indicate some type of change of an object. Right now, there is no change—all we have performed is the initial setup. You can check this by clicking back and forth from frame 1 to frame 20, and indeed the circle looks exactly the same.

3. Making sure that frame 20 is selected, move the circle to the right. If you test your movie (Control ➡ Test Movie), you will see the circle remain in one spot, then suddenly pop to the right side of the Stage, then back to its original position.

The **organicShape** is doing some weird disappearing acts as well, but let us just concentrate on the circle for now. What is occurring is the playhead is moving across the Timeline, gets to frame 20 where we have altered the position of the circle object, and then automatically loops back to frame 1 to start from the beginning. Flash movies automatically loop, unless you explicitly set it to not loop, using the Publish Settings or ActionScript.

Instead of the circle popping to the position set at frame 20, let us have it tween over there.

**NOTE:** A Tween—short for "in between"—is a common process in the world of animation. Rather than drawing every frame in, say, a one-hundred-frame animation, you can define just a handful of "key"—or important—frames, and allow the computer to interpolate the motion "in between." This is what Flash is doing when you choose to tween a sequence of frames between keyframes.

Using the same FLA, let us go through the steps for creating a tweened animation.

4. Click on the keyframe for the circle on frame 1 of the Timeline. The Property Inspector panel changes to reflect the various settings for keyframes.

5. On the Property Inspector, change the tween setting from None to Motion. The sequence of frames in the Timeline for the circle will now have a blue bar with an arrow pointing from frame 1 to frame 20.

6. To shore things up a bit, select frame 20 on the **organicLayer** layer to add additional frames: Insert ➡ Timeline ➡ Frame. Now when you test your movie, you should see the organic shape remain static with a circle moving across the screen, then jumping back to Frame 1 as this movie is still set to loop. Open *motionTween.fla* from the DVD to see a completed version of this.

**NOTE:** Many beginning Flash users will try placing motion tweens anywhere they can (such as an ending keyframe). Motion tweens are always set on the first keyframe where you want the change to initiate—there is nothing to set on the ending keyframe. To remember this, I suggest thinking of tweens as pairs of keyframes, like bookends.

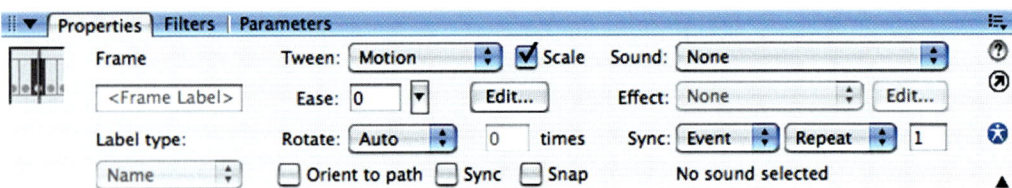

**Figure 1.19** The Property Inspector has special settings for frames too.

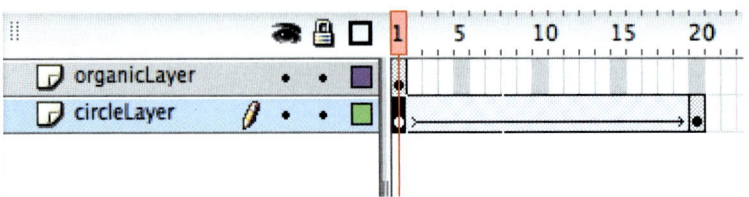

**Figure 1.20** A blue bar indicates a motion tween spanning between two keyframes.

7. In addition to position on the Stage, other properties of a symbol can be tweened. Let us keep working with the same file. If you accidentally closed it, simply open *motionTween.fla* from the DVD.

**NOTE:** If you try to make a Motion tween with non-symbols, Flash will automatically create symbols for you that will pop-up in the Library with generic names such as **Symbol 1**.

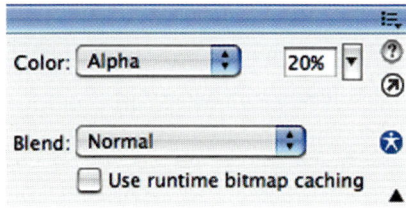

**Figure 1.21** This is another benefit of turning a vector graphic into a symbol: A wide assortment of properties can be adjusted and tweened.

8. Select frame 1 of the tween on the **circleLayer**. Go to the Property Inspector and give the Ease in setting a value of -100.

9. Move the playhead to frame 20 then select the circle on the Stage using the Selection tool; you will see the Property Inspector switch over to reveal the properties for this symbol.

10. Adjust the Color setting from None to Alpha then use the slider to adjust the value down to 20.

11. Now test the movie once more; you should see the circle starting off fast (and barely visible) then slowing down as it becomes visible. Take a look at *motionTweenAlpha.fla* if it is not working correctly.

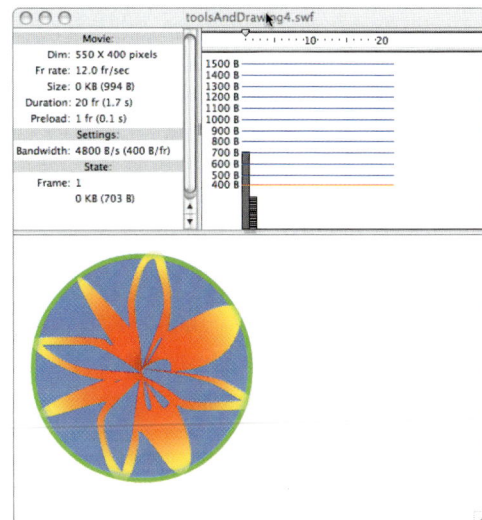

**Figure 1.22** Notice how you can tell what frame the playhead is on over time. Can you see it looping from 1 to 20 again and again?

**NOTE:** Whenever you test your Flash movie, go to View ➡ Bandwidth Profiler. This tool is a good way of checking the efficiency of your movie. The current file is too simple to give the Flash Player much of a problem, but when you begin to work on more elaborate projects, you will find yourself closely examining this window.

Probably the most valuable aspect of symbols is the ability to employ ActionScript to control them. ActionScript is the built-in programming language for Flash. Although we will be covering this topic in greater detail later in this chapter, here is a taste.

12. Click the **organicShape** object on the Stage then open the Actions panel (Window ➡ Actions).

13. Type the following code in the Actions panel:

```
onClipEvent(enterFrame){
      _y += 1;
}
```

This code is manipulating the lateral (`_y`) position of the **organicShape** symbol by increasing it by one pixel over time. While testing this movie, let it loop through several times. You will notice two things (besides the animation of course). First, the **organicShape** keeps moving, until it eventually leaves the Stage completely. As the movie loops, there is nothing telling the organicShape to ever go back to its original position. Second, the circle on the other hand, has a keyframe on Frame 1 with visual data and tween instructions that reset this portion of the animation.

### GUIDE LAYERS

Tweens do not need to occur across a straight line. By incorporating guide layers, organic and/or complex qualities can be applied to the motion path of tweened objects.

1. Let us start this new section by opening a new Flash document. From the DVD, open the *motionGuide_start.fla* from the Chapter_01 folder.

2. Change the background color: Modify ➡ Document ➡ Background color. Select the color #FFCCCC.

3. Rename **Layer 1** to **objectLayer**. Remember how to do this? Simply double-click the layer name and then type the new name once it is highlighted.

4. Drag and drop the **bird** movie clip from the Library onto the Stage. It will automatically go into frame 1 of the **objectLayer**, because this is the only frame and layer at the moment.

5. Now create a Motion Guide layer by clicking on the Add Motion Guide button located in the upper-left corner of your workspace, just below the Layers, next to the Insert Layer button. Change the name of this new layer to **pathLayer**.

6. Choose the Pencil tool, and from the Property Inspector select a dark color and set the stroke height to 1.

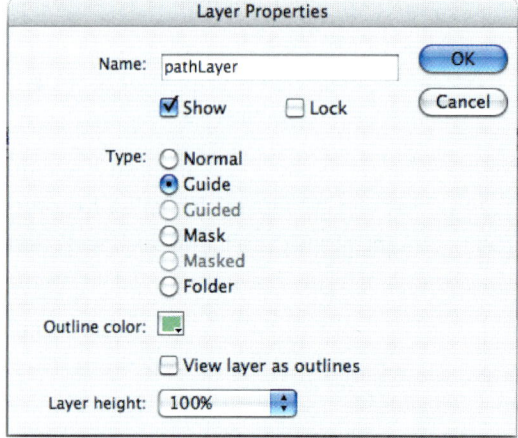

**Figure 1.23** In addition to the layer Type, the Layer Properties Menu allows access to several other items.

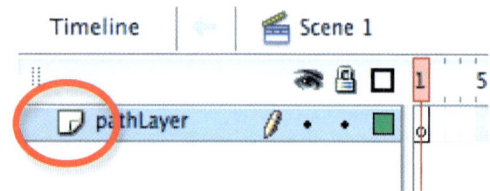

**Figure 1.24** You can also change the type of a layer by selecting the Layer Property button.

7. Click on frame 1 of the **pathLayer**, then draw a meandering line starting around the area of the bird and ending somewhere else across the Stage.

8. Double-click the layer icon of the **objectLayer** and change its type to Guided if it is not already. This will allow the motion tween on this layer to become subordinate to the path on the Guide layer above it.

9. To enable this action, however, you need to select frame 1 of the **objectLayer**, then select and move the **bird** symbol to where it snaps to the path at the start of the line. It helps if you move the symbol by its orientation point (the small circle in the middle of the symbol).

10. We need to extend the line drawing down the Timeline by inserting a frame on the **pathLayer** at frame 30. Select this frame on the Timeline, then Insert ➡ Timeline ➡ Frame (or F5).

11. On the **objectLayer**, we need our frames to stretch to frame 30 as well. But we also need a keyframe on frame 30 so that we can make a motion tween. We can do both by simply inserting a keyframe on frame 30: Insert ➡ Timeline ➡ Keyframe (or F6).

12. Select this new keyframe (keyframe 30 on the **objectLayer** layer). Reposition the bird somewhere on the end of the line-path, using the snap-to method described in step 9.

13. Now for the last step: click back on frame 1 of the **objectLayer**, look to the Property Inspector and change the Tween option to Motion and check the Orient to path box. Great! Test your movie by referring to *motionGuide_end.fla* for help.

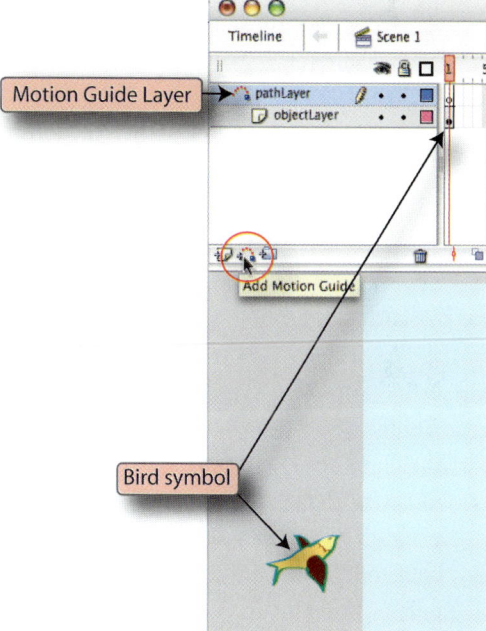

**Figure 1.25** Here is an overview of our workspace at this point.

## 16 BASIC INGREDIENTS

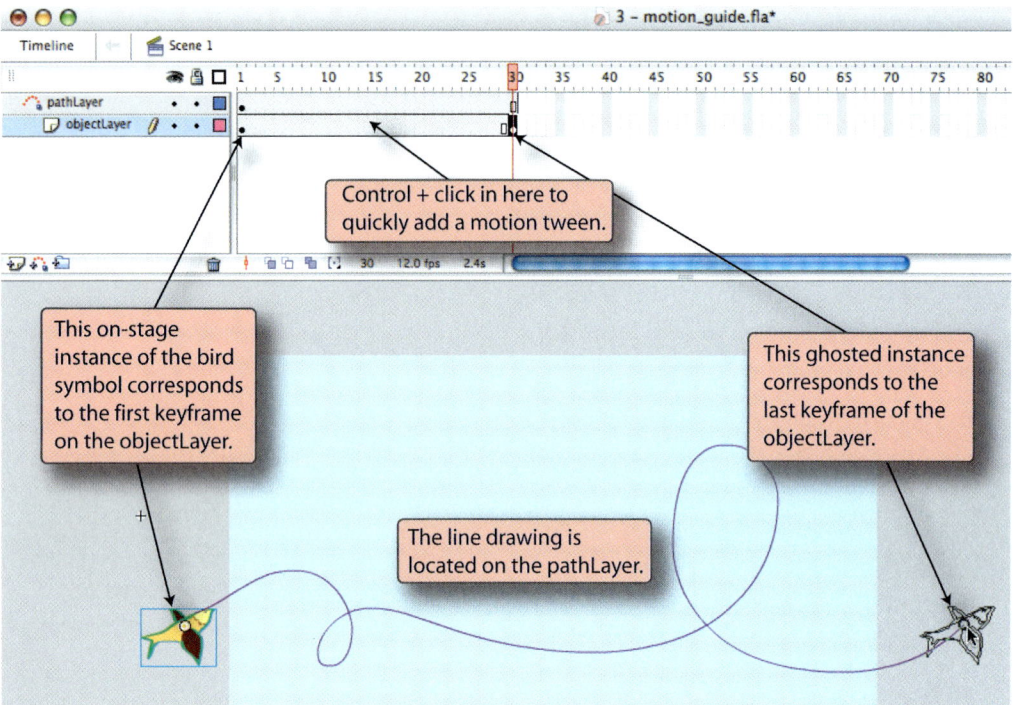

**Figure 1.26** Here is an overview of our guide layer animation.

Notice that whatever you see on a Guide layer will not show up when you export your movie. Instead, the graphics will be used to guide animated objects resting on any Guided layer beneath it. You can also use guide layers for backend layouts or alignments that will not be part of the final output (just for you and no one else to see).

### MASK LAYERS

Another type of layer is the Mask layer. It is similar to the Guide layer in that it works in tandem with other layers based on their order. The Mask and Guide layers are also similar in that anything visible on the Stage for that layer is not seen in the same way when you actually test your movie. But while the stroke on a

Guide layer disappears completely, fill colors on a Mask layer are visible in a way that is probably easier to see than to explain.

1. Create a new Flash document (File ➡ New ➡ Flash Document).

2. Rename the default layer (Layer 1) to **textLayer**. On this layer in the first frame, write some text. You can do this by either writing it out with the Brush tool, or typing with the Text tool.

3. Next, create a new layer and call it **maskLayer**. On this layer, draw some solid shapes using only a fill color (no stroke), such as vertical stripes for instance. Although it is not necessary, use a different color than your text. Also be sure that the shapes are positioned over the text so we can see the results of our mask effect.

4. Select these shapes and convert them to a symbol (Modify ➡ Convert Symbol). You can do this easily by simply selecting the keyframe containing all the shapes.

5. Control + click (or right click on a PC) on the **maskLayer**, and choose the Mask option. You will notice that Flash automatically changed the icons for each layer as well as locked them.

The Hide/Unhide, Lock/Unlock, and Outline toggle buttons for each layer can help you see what your mask looks like. Another thing to consider is that mask layers work with fills, not strokes. So, the Pencil tool will not work for this exercise, but the Brush tool will.

You can now animate either layer. Let us work with the symbol on the **maskLayer**. Create a motion tween on this symbol that glides the shapes across the text beneath it (refer to the

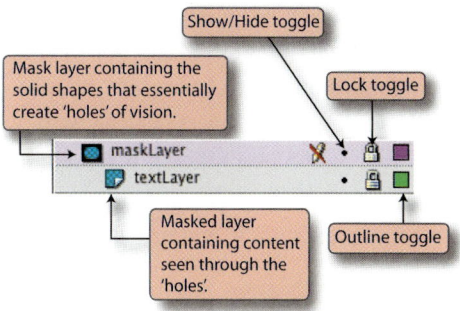

**Figure 1.27** Here is a breakdown of the mask layers.

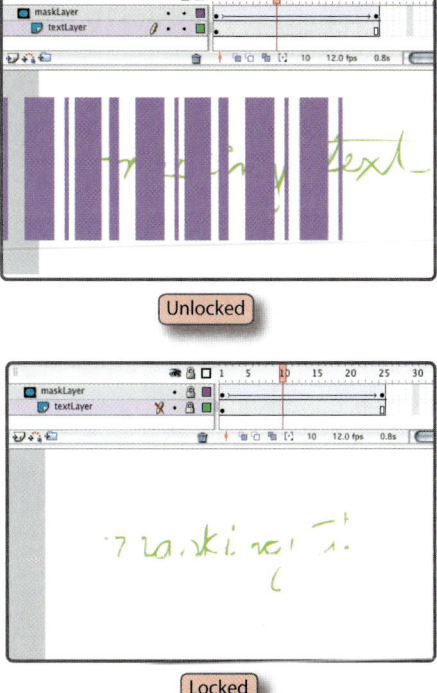

**Figure 1.28** By locking your mask and masked layers, you can observe the mask effects. SWF files will show this effect when you export your movie, whether they are locked or not.

# BASIC INGREDIENTS

tweening techniques covered earlier). Test your movie, or be sure both layers are locked and scroll back and forth to see how your Mask is functioning. If the layers dealing with your mask are not locked, then it will seem as if the mask is not working. See the *maskLayers.fla* file for an example if you need help.

## SHAPE TWEEN

While motion tweens can only occur between two keyframes containing the same symbol, a shape tween spans two keyframes containing a vector graphic (non-Symbol). Also, shape tweens appear as light green on the Timeline, while motion tweens are light blue. Remember that, when selected, a symbol appears with a blue line around it while non-Symbols exhibit small dots across the surface. If you open the file *shapeTween.fla* from the DVD, you can see several different shape tweens.

When working with shape tweens, it is often useful to enable the Onion Skin view. The controls for onion skin viewing are located directly below the Timeline. This viewing option allows you to see an outline of how the other frames of a tween will look. The brackets that appear directly above the Timeline allow you to select which frames you want to see in onion skin mode.

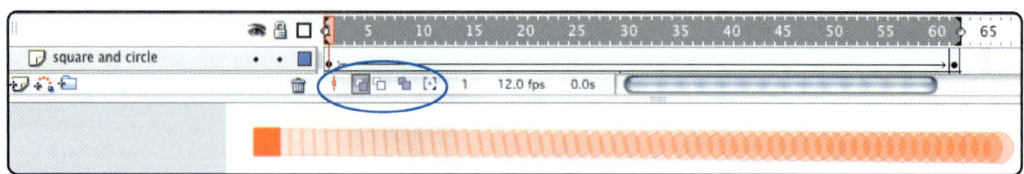

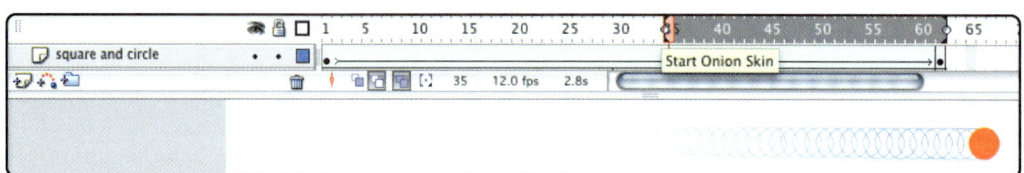

**Figure 1.29** The Onion Skin view provides a static preview of your animation. Since this is simply a feature to help aid your production, onion skinning view is not seen in the SWF.

# CHAPTER ONE 19

## TYPES OF SYMBOLS

You may have noticed in the Property Inspector, the Library, or perhaps in the ActionScript panel, that we have been working with the movie clip type of symbol. There are actually three kinds of symbols: buttons, movie clips, and graphics. Open *symbolTypes.fla* from the DVD and examine the three objects on Stage.

The clock is a movie clip, the hourglass is a button, and the sundial is a graphic. If you double-click any one of these objects, you will notice the main commonality between all forms of symbol: they each have a unique Timeline. Simply click the **Scene 1** button to return to the main Timeline.

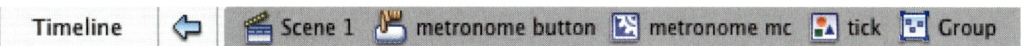

**Figure 1.30** The Timeline hierarchy allows for easy navigation among embedded symbols. Double-clicking a symbol will take you "down" a level into its Timeline, while selecting links in the Timeline control (displayed here) will bring you back "up."

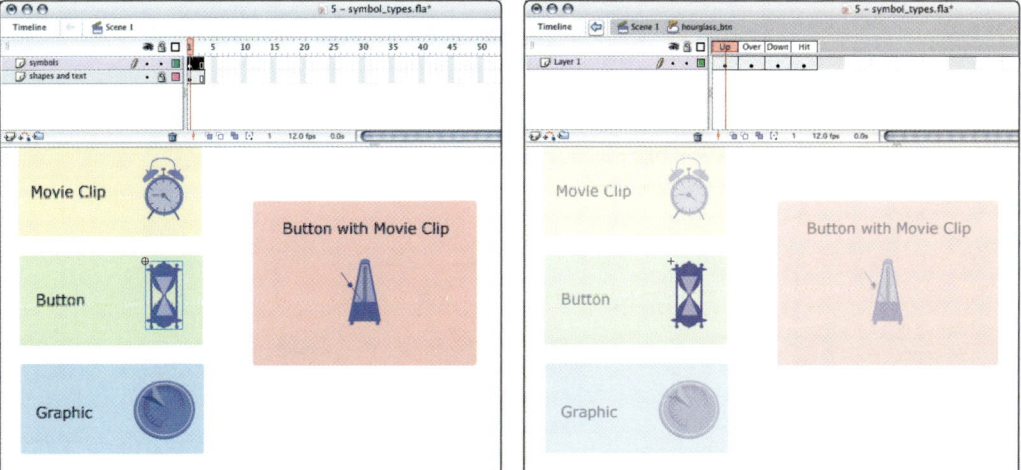

**Figure 1.31** Double-clicking a symbol will take you to its Timeline; the graphics from the main Timeline will still be visible on the Stage, but ghosted slightly.

The Flash movie acts as a "multimedia collage" when you test your movie: the internal animation for all symbols sitting on the Stage (or embedded in a symbol that is on the Stage) will be displayed together in the exported SWF. Let us take a look at each of the three types of symbols in more detail.

### Graphic

Graphic symbols are nice for grouping a collection of graphical content, while also adding a unique Timeline. Some imported media is automatically converted into a graphic symbol and stored as an asset in the Library—Adobe Illustrator (.ai) files for instance.

In the *symbolTypes.fla* example file you have open, the **Sundial** is a graphic symbol. It behaves a lot like a movie clip, except for one crucial difference: you cannot give graphic symbols an instance name (more on this later).

### Movie Clip

Also in our example file, we have a movie clip of a clock. Double-click this symbol so we can see what is "making it tick." On this Timeline you will see that it lasts 207 frames. This is of special note because our main Timeline (**Scene 1**) has only 1 frame! When we test our movie, we can see that indeed, the **clock** movie clip has its own little animation. The fact that it is sitting on **Scene 1** is simply allowing us access to see inside that nested Timeline.

### Button

And lastly we come to the button symbol. An hourglass represents this symbol type in our example. Go ahead and double-click the hourglass to see how it is composed. What is the deal? The Timeline for a button only has four frames; exposing its nature for detecting mouse events.

You should not think of a button's frames as being temporal. The Up, Over, Down, and Hit frames together form a series of state instructions: How will this button look when the user holds the mouse over it? What about when the mouse is clicking down on the button? The Hit frame acts as a mask of sorts; it defines the region where the mouse interactivity will be detected, sending the playhead to the appropriate frame whether the mouse is simply over the area, or clicking on it.

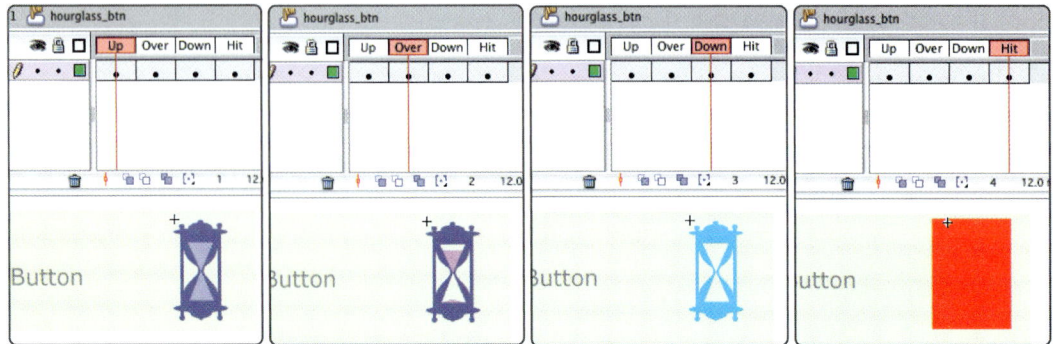

**Figure 1.32** Clicking on each of the four frames of the hourglass button reveals their differences. Each frame is meant to be part of an interactive animation.

Test the movie to check the interactivity of the **hourglass** button—move the mouse over and off of the button. Notice how and when the mouse changes from an arrow to a pointing hand as it goes from the Up state to the Over state. See how the defined Hit area (the now invisible red square) affects the mouse? Try clicking and holding on the button to observe the down state. Go back into the FLA and try changing the Hit area to see more closely how it functions.

### ACTIONSCRIPT

Open the *ActionScipt.fla* file from the DVD. It looks pretty much the same as the previous file that covered types of symbols. Test the movie and roll the mouse over the clock. You will see that the clock becomes slightly transparent when you move the mouse over it. How is this movie clip behaving like a button? ActionScript is the guilty party! If you close this SWF file and go back to the FLA, you can see how this movie clip has been rigged for reacting to mouse events.

The first thing you may notice is that I added an additional layer called **actions**. Also, click on the clock with the Property Inspector open. You can see how this movie clip has been given an Instance name: **clock**. This simple property illustrates the most powerful aspect of movie clips: the ability to connect them to the realm of ActionScript.

**Figure 1.33** Instance names are the glue that allows the ActionScript panel to "see" and control symbols.

Once a symbol has an instance name, you can refer to it inside the ActionScript panel. Open the ActionScript panel (Window ➡ Actions or Option + F9), then select frame 1 of the **actions** layer. You should see the following code:

```
clock.onRollOver = function(){
        this._alpha = 50;
}

clock.onRollOut = function(){
        this._alpha = 100;
}
```

**NOTE:** In addition to the code shown here, I also have a few comments. Comments in Flash begin with // (a line comment) or are bracketed like so: `/* this is a block comment */`. Comments are simply text that we can add to our code that we want Flash to ignore: notes for us, and others, to refer to when reading the ActionScript. Many people also use comments to add a signature/header giving information about the author and the date that the code was written or last edited. Several of the artist contributions on the DVD follow this form, like Jeremy Thorp in Chapter 12:

```
/*
Generative Art in Flash: Tutorial File
blprnt@blprnt.com
October, 2006
*/
```

### Statements

A statement is one single line of code, typically ending in a semi-colon. We can think of them as being the grammatical equivalent of sentences for programming.

```
The following is a statement
this._alpha = 50;
```

### Functions

Functions are usually a few lines (sometimes several or dozens of lines) of code characterized by a few different elements. First, it must be named and/or assigned; this happens in the first line. Secondly, it must have a body, delineated by curly braces ({}). Within the curly braces are usually a few statements known as body-code.

```
// The following is a function
// more specifically, it is an
Event Handler
clock.onRollOut = function(){
        this._alpha = 100;
}
```

If a statement is like a sentence of code, a function is like a paragraph. Or, using a more physical analogy, a function is like a machine, engineered to do a specific thing—like a blender, lawn mower, or oven. Like most machines, some sort of fuel, settings, and substance are introduced to allow the machine to operate in a certain way. In the real world, electricity allows a blender to run, on low, medium, or high settings, to make guacamole, or a milkshake, depending on what food we place inside. Likewise, many functions require an input of a certain type. We call them parameters.

Parameters go inside the parenthesis of the function: `function(parameter1, parameter2)`. And as you can see, these two functions in this example file do not require any parameters. These two functions are more accurately known as event handlers. They are different from a more general kind of function in that the name is predefined—they are built into ActionScript. By attaching them to our movie clip through dot syntax (`clock.onRollOver`), we are giving the clock movie clip all the powers of the `onRollOver` handler. This handler may be attached to any movie clip using the dot syntax. The statement inside of the body for this event handler is what Flash will do every time it detects that the mouse has rolled over this movie clip.

```
this._alpha = 50;
```

`this` refers to the movie clip where the code is occurring (the `clock` movie clip). `_alpha` is a property owned by all movie clips, and it refers to the level of opacity: 100 being fully opaque and 0 being fully transparent.

---

**NOTE:** When reading regular text (like this book) the form of the writing can be broken down into chapters, paragraphs, and sentences. Rules of grammar that we have learned since childhood have familiarized us with the organization of written language. Programming languages like ActionScript work in a similar, and far simpler way, just foreign to how we communicate person-to-person. Of course, communicating person-to-computer is going to be a bit different!

---

Let us explore more ActionScript fundamentals. Use the same FLA file we have been working with.

1. Above the two Event Handlers, type the following statement:

```
normal = 100;
```

2. Make a new keyframe on frame 10 of the **actions** layer. Select this keyframe by clicking on it, then type the following code in the Actions panel:

```
if(clock._alpha != normal){
        trace("the clock is
transparent");
        hourglass._xscale = 50;
} else {
        hourglass._xscale = 100;
}
```

3. Add frames through frame 10 for the other two layers.

4. Test your movie. If you roll over the **clock** movie clip, you should see how it affects the shape of the **hourglass** movie clip. The interaction is a bit flaky, and this is due to a few reasons—mostly because the newly added code is only checked when the playhead hits frame 10. This is when Flash *reads* this code!

If you get stuck, check out the *ActionScript2.fla* file on the DVD. We will let the pros in later chapters cover the more advanced implementations of ActionScript, but this is a start! Let us now digest this new code a bit more.

The first statement we typed on frame 1 of the actions layer, `normal = 100;`, introduces a third grammatical element of programming—the variable.

## Variables

Variables are like empty containers that can hold (almost) anything. While there are more accurate (and professional) ways of declaring variables, we are keeping it simple for now. This variable name, `normal`, is user defined. It could easily have been `value`, `spocksBrain`, or almost anything we want. Just make sure there are no spaces, you do not use weird characters (like %), and that the word is not already reserved by Flash (like `function` or `Math`). It will turn blue if it is reserved by Flash. Think of the variable name like a label on a folder: you can write anything you want on a label, but some things like "bills," "insurance," and "mortgage" make more sense, depending on what you are filing.

After declaring the name, we assign a value to the variable: `= 100`. Whenever we refer to this `normal` variable, we will be retrieving the value of `100` (unless it is changed—something very common to do with a variable). Collectively, this line—`normal = 100;`—is both declaring and initializing a variable. Later in the code, we will simply be accessing and changing the variable.

## Logic Statements

This chunk of code that we typed on frame 10 is called an If-Else statement. It may seem more like a function from what we said earlier (it has curly braces after all!), but this is yet another type of code structure.

There are essentially two parts to an If Statement. The first part is a Boolean expression (true/false) that is checked inside the parentheses. If the program determines this statement is true, the body-code is executed. The body-code is the second part of an If Statement.

There is also an optional *else* part of the code, with another set of curly braces containing code that is executed whenever the Boolean expression is determined to be false. The general syntax of an If-Else statement looks like this:

```
if (condition) {
    body-code
} else {
    else code
}
```

And, as you can see, this is an accurate model for the code we typed:

```
if(clock._alpha != normal){
        trace("the clock is transparent");
        hourglass._xscale = 50;
} else {
        hourglass._xscale = 100;
}
```

The only part that might be confusing is the `!=` operator in the conditional. This simply means "not equal." Speaking it out: "If the alpha value of the clock movie clip is not `normal` (and we defined normal to be `100`) then execute the body code. Additionally, our body code is executing a very handy `trace` function. This function takes whatever you place as a parameter, `"The clock is transparent"` in this case, and sends it to the Output window. You probably noticed this occurring when you were testing the SWF file. This trace function is very valuable for troubleshooting code, as we will see more of in later chapters.

## ActionScript Placement

ActionScript can be placed on any keyframe, on the main Timeline or in the Timeline of a symbol. ActionScript can also be placed *on* a symbol. Let us try that out before we wrap up this ActionScript lesson.

1. Make sure you are on the main Timeline (click the **Scene 1** button at the top if you are not sure).

2. Then click once on the **clock** movie clip. A bounding blue box should surround the movie clip. Take a look at the Actions panel. It should look like Figure 1.39.

    Notice how it says Movie Clip along the top, letting us know we are about to place code *on* the movie clip.

3. Now type the following lines of code in the Actions panel.

```
onClipEvent(enterFrame){
     this._rotation+=1;
}
```

This bit of code is another example of an event handler. The event being monitored in this case is when the playhead enters the frame of the movie clip. We do not have to use such a handler when we type code on a frame, because this event is just assumed. As the playhead continually triggers this enterFrame code, it causes the movie clip to slowly rotate by 1 degree.

4. For something a little more interesting, change your onRollOut handler on frame 1 to look like this:

```
clock.onRollOut = function(){
     this._alpha = normal;
     normal = normal - 5;
}
```

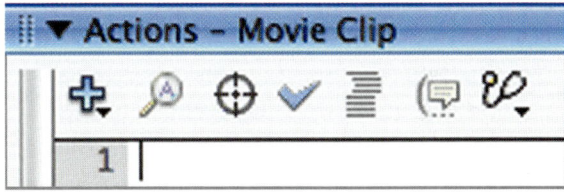

**Figure 1.34** You can alleviate some confusion about where your ActionScript is going if you simply examine the top of the ActionScript panel.

5. Also alter your frame 10 code to look like this:

```
if(clock._alpha != normal){
     trace("the clock is ↵
transparent");
     hourglass._xscale = 50;
} else {
     hourglass._xscale = 100;
}
gotoAndPlay(2);
```

6. Test your movie and see what happens when you roll over the clock a few times. Check out *ActionScript 3.fla* if you need help.

## IMPORTING MEDIA

Being the most popular interactive multimedia tool, Flash works with a wide range of imported media file types. Flash was originally oriented towards vector-graphics. Each new release has incorporated more and more capabilities for handling bitmaps, audio, video, and data files such as XML.

### Vector Graphics

Vector graphics are treated by the computer as geometry, possessing properties such as stroke color, stroke style, fill color, and fill style. Symbols, shapes, and certain cartoon styles lend themselves to being created with vector graphics, although a skillful use of the Color Mixer can yield images that look like 3D renderings or airbrushed images. Check out the Vectorkid *www.vectorkid.com*, and you will see what I mean.

### Bitmaps

Bitmap (raster) graphics are treated as a set of pixels, each with a certain color that can be broken down into the combined degree of red, green, and blue color (and sometimes alpha for transparency). Photos are saved in bitmap compression formats, such as JPEG and PNG.

Bringing bitmap images into Flash is as easy as going to the Menu, File ➡ Import. Flash can then import a variety of file formats. After importing a bitmap, Flash will place it in the Library with the other reusable assets. At this point, you can use the bitmaps in your document simply by dragging them onto the Stage. Chapter 3 covers this process in more detail.

### Supported File Types

Flash supports the following types of vector and bitmap based image imports: .eps, .ai, .pdf, .dxf, .bmp, .emf, .fh7, .fh8, .fh9, .fh10, .fh11, .spl, .gif, .jpg, .png, .swf, .wmf, .pntg, .psd, .pct, .pic, .qtif, .sgi, .tga, and .tif. While most people use Photoshop, Illustrator, and Fireworks for generating graphics to use in Flash, there are also some open-source software options that are multiplatform and free, such as GIMP *www.gimp.org* for bitmap images, and Inkscape *www.linkscape.org* for creating vector art.

### Audio

If your project is going to utilize audio, then you should consider the following when exporting your audio files from your audio program. Flash natively can import the following sound file formats: WAV (Windows only), AIFF (Macintosh only), and MP3 (Windows or Macintosh). If you have Quicktime 4 or later installed on your computer, you can also import the following audio formats: AIFF (Windows or Macintosh), Sound Designer II (Macintosh only), Sound Only QuickTime Movies (Windows or Macintosh), Sun AU (Windows or Macintosh), System 7 Sounds (Macintosh only), or WAV (Windows or Macintosh).

### Video

Flash supports a wide range of file formats for video. If you have Quicktime 7.0 or higher installed, you can import .avi, .dv, .mpg, and .mov. Windows users with DirectX9 or later can import .avi, .mpg, .mpeg, .wmv, and .asf.

There are some cases where Flash might successfully import the video, but leave out the audio that is embedded in the file. When this occurs, Flash will display a warning indicating the audio cannot be imported. You can continue with importing the video, but it will not have embedded audio.

When importing into Flash, the media is embedded into the FLA file and becomes an actual part of your movie when you export to SWF. The one exception is video, which happens to be the most expensive type of media you can use (in terms of bandwidth and file size). When importing video into Flash (File ➡ Import ➡ Video), you will come to the following screen. (Figure 1.40)

This interface gives options for how your video source will stream into your SWF file. Unless you have access to special server features, you will probably go with the first option, which coverts your movie into a Flash Video file format (FLV). This file will need to be uploaded to your server along with the SWF file. Other screens allow you to choose the quality used in the encoding as well as options for adding skins (pre-designed interfaces for controlling the video).

Once the FLM file has been added to your Library, you can add it to your Flash document like any other asset simply by dragging it to the Stage. Open the *video.fla* file from the DVD to see an example.

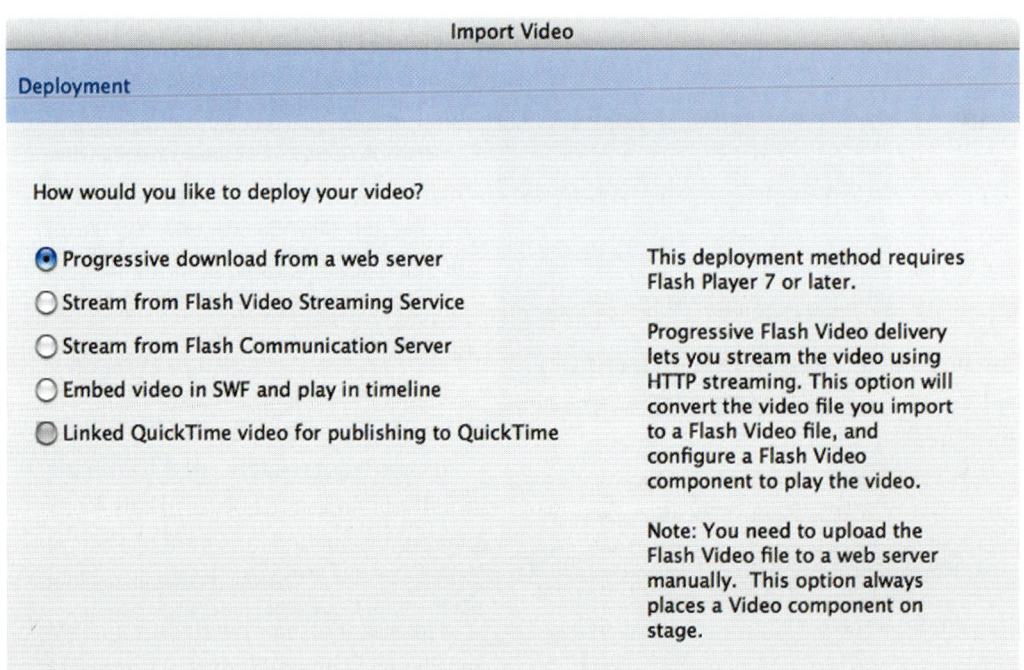

**Figure 1.35** Until you become more familiar with Flash and video, you should just keep this on the default setting.

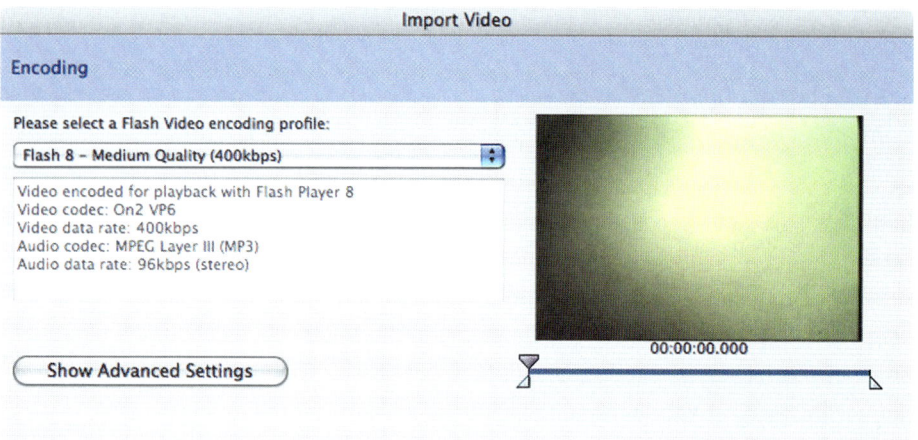

**Figure 1.36** A Medium Quality setting should be suitable for most cases.

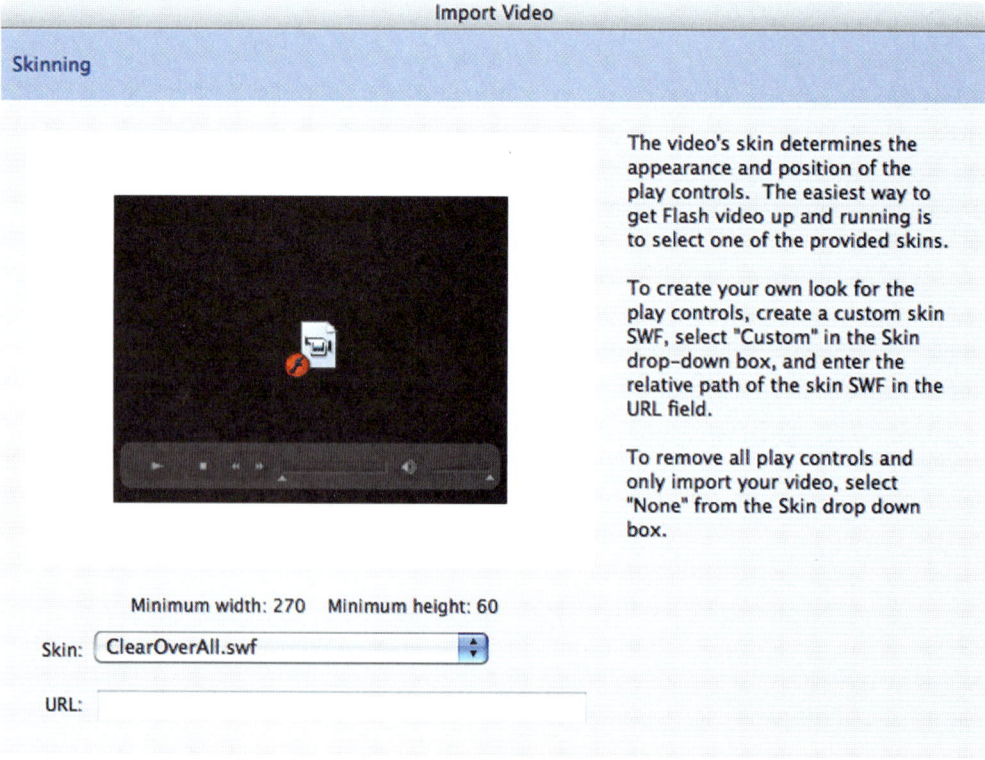

**Figure 1.37** A multitude of skins are available for styling the interface that will control the video.

## EXPORTING

When you are ready to share your Flash creations with the world, you need to either Export or Publish your Flash document. If your work is ready to place on the Web, you will want to use the Publish command (File ➡ Publish). The publish settings allow you to covert your Flash file into the format readable by Flash Players (SWF) as well as an optional .html file. Generally speaking, for a Web browser to read your Flash movie, it needs to be embedded in an HTML file. If you already have this know-how, and are preparing a document separately, you will probably want only to export the SWF, which by the way, happens each time you test your movie from the Menu with Control ➡ Test Movie. The Publish Settings give you greater control over the details of how your SWF file will be published. To open these settings, go to File ➡ Publish Settings. This will open an initial Formats window.

Here you can decide which, and how many, formats will be exported. Typically you will have just the Flash box or the Flash and HTML boxes checked. With each box checked, an additional tab will be available for specifying more details for how you want that particular format to be published. With this example, you can see that the Flash and HTML boxes are checked, thereby creating additional Flash and HTML tabs.

Selecting the Flash tab will bring up a window as shown here.

You should keep the Version selection the same as whatever Flash version you are running on your system. The Load order specifies how Flash will treat the layers of the SWF file. I always keep this set to the default setting of Bottom up.

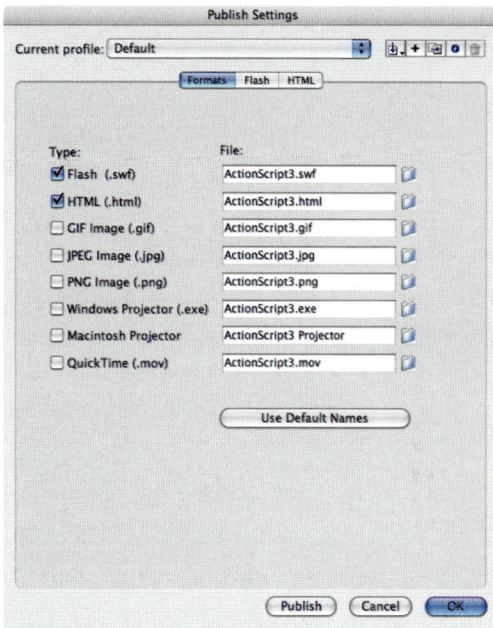
**Figure 1.38** Most of the time, you will just want the Flash and HTML settings or just the Flash settings.

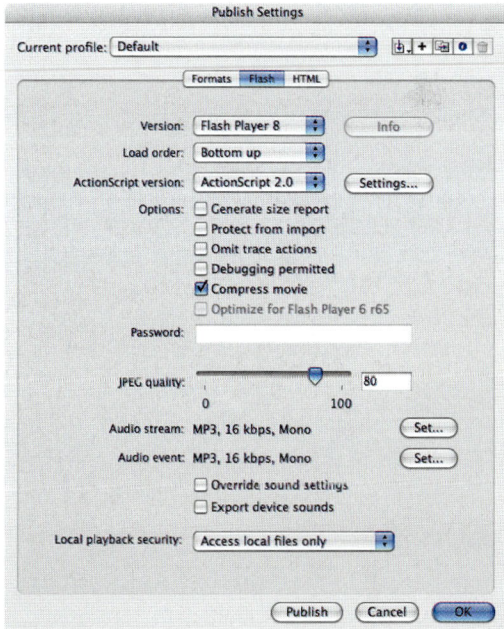
**Figure 1.39** Pay special attention to the Flash version and the ActionScript version. Everything in this book was published with the setting shown here.

The ActionScript version setting is very important. The code covered in this book is using ActionScript 2.0. Some examples might not work properly if this is set to ActionScript 1.0.

Another important feature to pay attention to is the JPEG quality. All JPEGS that are not given unique compression settings in the Library will be compressed according to this setting. This should be set as low as possible without seeing noticeable degradation upon export. A setting between 70 and 80 will be fine for most images.

The MP3 audio compression is a good general setting for most projects. If the sound is especially crucial, you may want to switch the Bit rate to something higher than the default 16 kbps. If the MP3 compression just is not cutting it, you can always select the Raw compression setting, which will not compress the audio at all. Carla Diana covers looping audio in Chapter 7. In this case she recommends using the Raw setting.

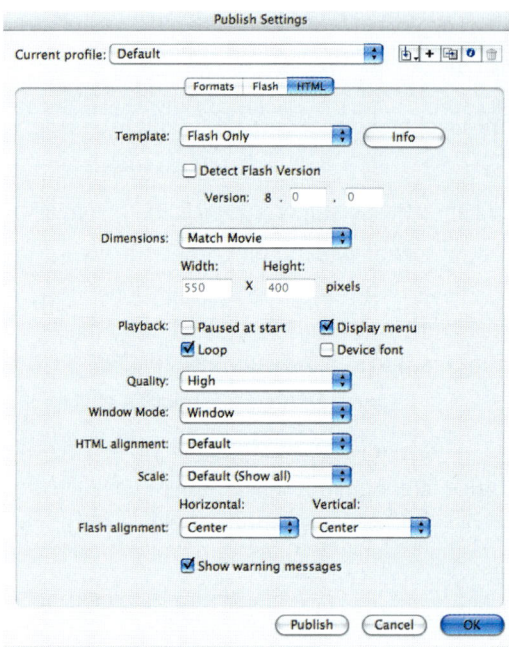

**Figure 1.40** The HTML Publish setting has some options for alignment, size, quality, and looping.

The HTML tab will open settings that will establish how the HTML file will look and operate.

For general purposes, keep the Template setting to Flash only. If you want the Web page just large enough to hold your Flash movie, keep the Dimensions setting to Match Movie. The rest of the settings in this window should also be kept to their default value, unless you have something really specific in mind. Notice the loop box that is checked (most people assume that Flash is going to naturally loop), and then use ActionScript to alter the stopping and running of the file.

### NEW FEATURES

- GRADIENTS: up to 16 colors can now be added; each gradient focal point can be adjusted independently.

- OBJECT DRAWING MODE: With the Object Drawing mode selected from the Tools panel, shapes can be drawn onto same layers without interfering with other shapes.

- RECTANGLE TOOL / OVAL TOOL: rounded corners can be given to rectangles by double-clicking the tool in the Tools panel and setting the Corner Radius setting; rectangles and ovals can be given exact width and height settings in the Property Inspector.

- STROKES: gradients can now be used on strokes as well as fills.

- TEXT BOXES: text can now be resized by dragging the edges of the text box.

- EASING: tweens are now more dynamic through Easing parameters located in the Property Inspector. Instead of simply making up the motion between two keyframes, the start or end may be adjusted to have a relatively faster or slower response.

- FILTERS: an assortment of Photoshop-like filters are now available for applying to texts and movie clips. The Filters window can be accessed through Window ➡Properties ➡ Filters.

- BLEND MODES: blend modes (similar to Photoshop layer blend modes) are now available on the Property Inspector for symbols.

- BITMAP CACHING: the Property Inspector for movie clips now has a "Use runtime bitmap caching" checkbox. Enabling this for static movie clips (perhaps acting as a background image) will greatly optimize playback efficiency.

- VIDEO IMPORT: the video import dialog windows have drastically changed, allowing for far greater control over streaming delivery and other options including quality and playback controls.

- VIDEO ENCODER: Flash 8 includes a video encoder application that can be installed on your computer alongside Flash 8. This program can batch process several videos into FLV format, while also performing some adjustments. This process can run independently in the background while you continue to work on other parts of your project in Flash.

- VIDEO ALPHA CHANNELS: alpha channels are now supported in videos used in Flash for working with transparency.

- VIDEO CUE POINTS: cue points can be added to FLV files. These can be utilized for synching to other media or triggering other events within a Flash movie.

## BASIC INGREDIENTS

### KEY CONCEPTS

- Be sure to separate animations and interactivity to different layers for greater control.

- Pay attention to Layers, Frames, the Stage, and the Property Inspector when working with objects and animation. If you are not achieving the desired results, these are the first places to look for the problem.

- Group drawn objects or convert them to Symbols for greater control and to avoid accidents when animating.

- Toggle the Object Drawing mode when you do not want drawn objects to have destructive influences on other objects.

- Check the status of the ActionScript panel before typing code. Is it being written on a frame or a symbol?

- Use the Onion Skin viewing mode when working with frame-based animation to see what is occurring across several frames.

- Utilize the Color Mixer for more unique and complex fill colors, including Alpha channels.

- Test your movie frequently to check the animation, interactivity, and ActionScripted elements and functionality.

- Use the Bandwidth Profiler to test efficiency of your movie.

 **NICK FOX GIEG**

Short Fiction with Flash

# NICK FOX GIEG

When it comes to creating fictional works with Flash, most people immediately think of the Web cartoons that are often the subject of forwarded e-mails. But Flash can also be used for making subtler narrative forms—multimedia stories viewed at festivals and alongside film. Nick Fox Gieg is an animator who is active in expanding Flash's visibility beyond Internet viewing. His animations have been shown around the world, at highly notable venues like the Rotterdam and Ottawa film festivals, the Centre Pompidou in Paris, and on Canada's CBC TV.

Fox Gieg has also worked with theatrical projection, video, and sound. This body of work has been shown in the Festival d'Avignon, a Broadway musical, Paridiso in Amsterdam, and the Redcat Theatre in Los Angeles.

The recipient of three state arts council fellowships in Pennsylvania and West Virginia, Fox Gieg currently lives in the Netherlands as a Fulbright scholar. During this residency, he has been producing new works (like the Foxhole Manifesto) while also being active in the European art community. You can view QuickTime versions of his films on his website *www.fox-gieg.com*.

It was actually in Amsterdam in 1998 that Fox Gieg was first exposed to Flash while studying at the Gerrit Rietveld Academie. At first, it appeared to be only a Web design tool, but later Flash's now popular abilities for drawing and animating became evident. From that point, Fox Gieg began creating a very successful series of short fiction animations, experimenting with a combination of Flash-based techniques that have found their way into the post-production environment of Adobe After Effects.

**Figure 2.1** Hot off the press! A still from what is perhaps Fox Gieg's finest animation to date—The Foxhole Manifesto (2007).

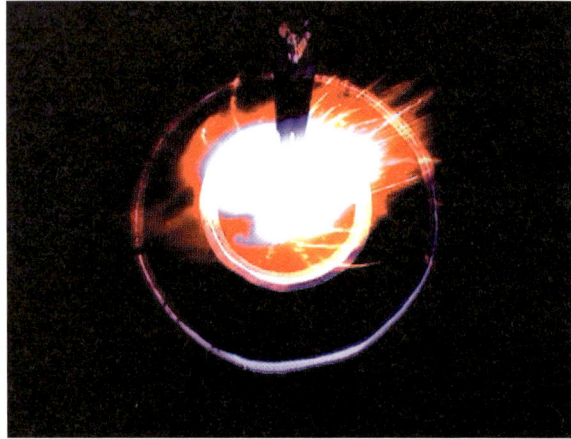

**Figure 2.2** A versatile artist, Fox Gieg does stage and theater design as well.

### DIGITAL DECONSTRUCTION: *THE OPTION OF WAR*

In 2002, while working in Oaxazo City, Mexico, Fox Gieg read a collection of short stories by Franz Kafka. During a long drive through a nearby desert, he was vividly reminded of the setting of one of the stories, "Jackals and Arabs." This work inspired Fox Gieg towards the concept and story behind his animation *The Option of War*.

**Figure 2.3** The jackals in *The Option of War* (2005) exhibit Fox Gieg's unique drawing style.

"The city's wooden statues of *alebrijes*, mythical monsters from the Zapotec culture of southern Mexico, inspired my version of Kafka's jackals. These initial powerful visual images provided me with the first spark of interest in adapting the story.

As I did more research, I learned that 'Jackals and Arabs' was a lesser-known Kafka work, and I decided that I wanted to share my own interpretation of it. I especially wanted to explore its powerful, but deliberately ambiguous, political message—a critique aimed not at the Middle East, as a modern reader might assume, but at the imperial ambitions of Germany, just then defeated in World War I."

A striking feature in *The Option of War* is how the jackals change their form from moment to moment. Fox Gieg purposefully animated this shimmering style by working his drawings over a series of frames in the Flash Timeline. In fact, all of the characters, forms, and environments that he illustrates in this adaptation result from a skillful command over a set of procedures he has perfected over the past several years.

**NOTE:** Fox Gieg's process for creating his short films can be broken down into six major steps.
1. Voice Track
2. Analog Drawing
3. Digitizing
4. Pencil Test
5. Digital Painting
6. Post Production

The production on *The Option of War* began with a voice track recorded from a written script. From there, Fox Gieg dove into the preliminary studies for the visuals by creating over 200 drawings, old-school style—pencil on paper. Many digital media artists still work quite a bit with these tools as well!

When the pencil drawing reached the desired look, they were scanned and imported into Flash. At this point, Fox Gieg brings out the Wacom tablet, a drawing surface that acts as an analog-to-digital converter. Digital artists who rely heavily on drawing often use these devices. No matter how skilled you might be with a mouse, it just cannot match the dexterity of drawing by hand.

With these drawings in place, Fox Gieg then creates what is known as a pencil test. This process figures out the general composition, timing, and sequencing of the animation. What a sketch is to a drawing, a pencil test is to an animation. Any issues with the general pace and composition should be worked out here. The pencil test is then brought into Painter, where color and detail are added to each frame.

**NOTE:** Corel Painter *www.corel.com/painterx* is a software application that is popular with many animators and digital imaging artists. As Fox Gieg's work shows, it can be a very good accompaniment to Flash.

While Painter's animation tools are crude by comparison to Flash, it offers a wider range of brushes and does a better job interpreting the unique hand gestures of drawing. Finally, Adobe After Effects is used as a post-production tool for compositing frames, adding final details, and exporting to HD video.

## CHAPTER TWO 37

### DIY: DRAWING WITH FLASH

Learning how to draw using Flash's GUI is a relatively easy task for someone just new to this software. Achieving good results rests largely on the shoulders of one's drawing abilities, not what the interface Flash provides. To get you started, Fox Gieg has put together some key points to consider when taking up the tools of a pen (or mouse) and Flash.

#### Software and Set-Up

Flash and a Wacom tablet make a powerful combination for hand-drawn animation. Flash is currently about US$250, and introductory tablets are under $100; add in a free sound-editing program like Audacity, and you have all your essential production needs.

I've noticed, though, that most beginning Flash tutorials do not take advantage of the program's best feature—its simplicity. After a few setup steps, you can literally just pick up your stylus and go.

1. The first thing you will need to do is choose a size for your document.

    Flash generally uses vector graphics (at least with the techniques covered in this chapter), so your finished movie can be exported at any resolution you like. All you need to worry about right now is the aspect ratio, the width and height of your screen. I would suggest using 640px × 480px for a 4:3 movie, and 640px × 360px for a 16:9 movie. You will notice that you can choose a frame rate too, although I usually leave that at 12 frames per second.

**Figure 2.4** It is amazing how many artists struggle to conform their drawing style to interaction with a mouse. Wacom tablets are relatively inexpensive–and ergonomic!

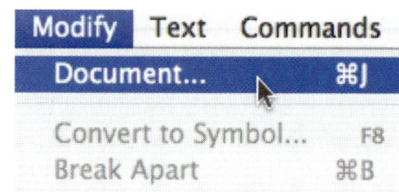

**Figure 2.5** You will find yourself using this Menu item often.

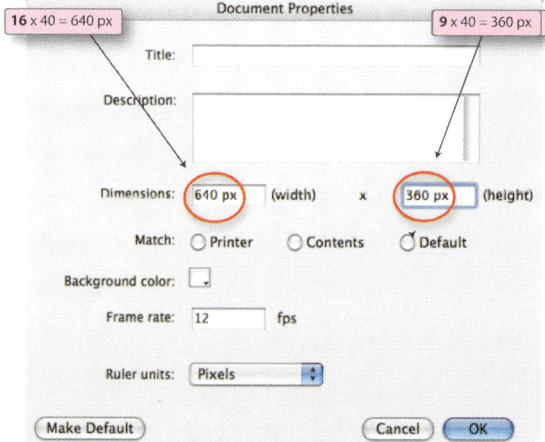

**Figure 2.6** If your Flash project is going to end up as video, you need to consider an appropriate screen dimension that follows standardized aspect ratios, like 4:3 or 16:9.

2. Next, pick the paintbrush tool from the tool palette. This drawing tool, unlike the pencil, responds to pressure from your tablet, painting thicker strokes the harder you press. Be sure to click the tablet pressure button to activate this feature. It is so useful that I do not know why it is not on by default.

3. Now we get to a slightly tricky part. You can not just start drawing into empty spaces on the Timeline in Flash. You have to create keyframes in which you want to draw. Fortunately, you can do a bunch at once. Select a group of frames:

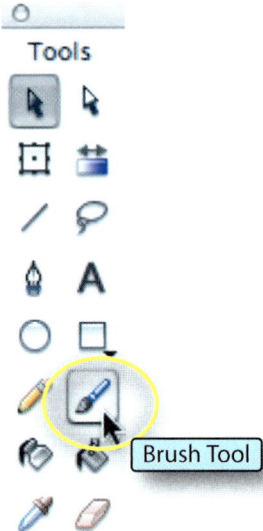

**Figure 2.7** Do you remember which tool is the Brush?

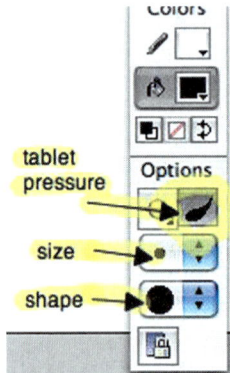

**Figure 2.8** If you are using a tablet, do not forget the tablet pressure setting!

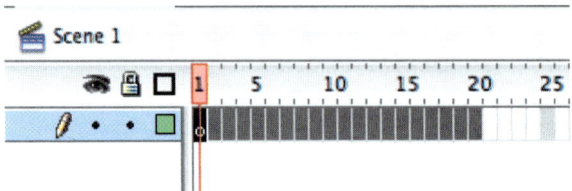

**Figure 2.9** To select a group of frames in the Timeline, just click and drag across them.

## CHAPTER TWO    39

4. Choose the rather well-hidden **Convert to Blank Keyframes** command from the Modify ➡ Timeline Menu. You will notice that it tells you the keystroke for this command is F7. That is handy to know, because you will actually be using this command often to create more frames as you go.

   The empty space you selected on your Timeline is now filled with blank frames in which you are ready to draw.

5. There is one more helpful concept to learn before you get to work. Onion skinning lets you see an overlay of the frames in front of or behind you, so you can keep a previous or future image in mind as you draw. You can drag the handles of the Onion Skin viewer to choose how many frames ahead or back you want to see. (I usually just keep one previous frame in view, to use as a reference; otherwise, I start to get confused.) Turn this feature on and off by clicking the Onion Skin button.

6. Draw away!

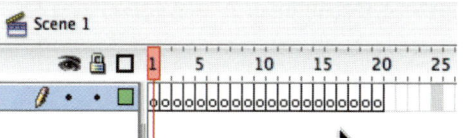

**Figure 2.11** Collectively, these keyframes are going to form our animation.

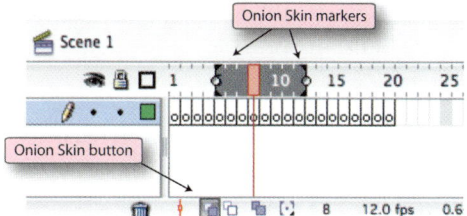

**Figure 2.12** Enabling the Onion Skin feature of the Timeline allows you to see frames other than the one you are working on.

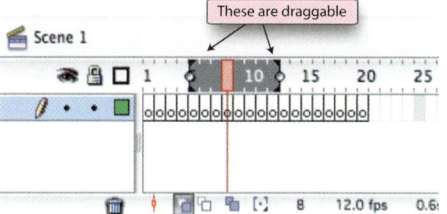

**Figure 2.13** The Onion Skin feature can be adjusted by dragging the markers that designate the beginning and end of the frames being viewed.

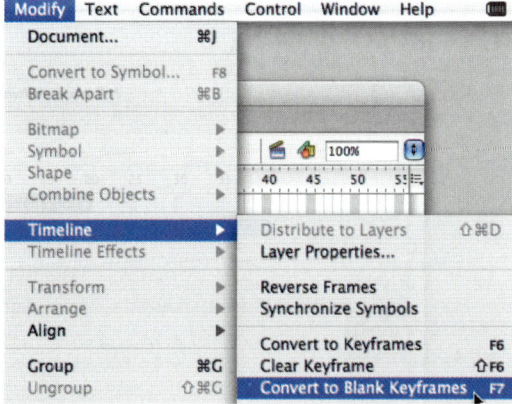

**Figure 2.10** Maneuver through that Menu a few times, and you will find yourself committing this keyboard shortcut (F7) to memory!

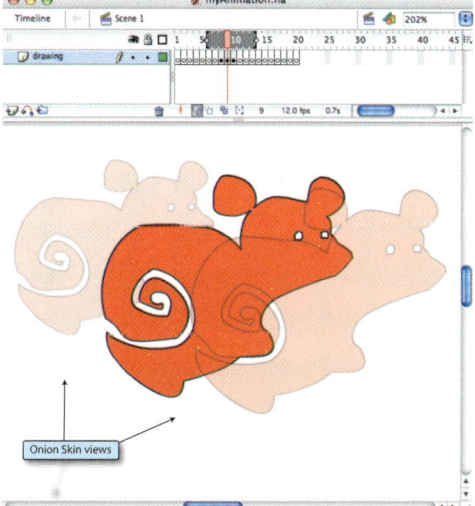

**Figure 2.14** The best way to find your own style is just to experiment–a lot!

### DIY: CREATING A WALK CYCLE

Now that we are prepped for drawing in Flash, it is time to put these skills to use. Whether working in 2D or 3D, one of the most essential tasks one does with character animation is the creation of a walk cycle. A walk cycle is simply a collection of sequential images that creates the illusion of a figure in motion. The walk cycle consists of several individual frames representing slight changes in position. It is actually quite an old, traditional animation technique. When the frames are played in fast succession, our eyes blend them together, and we see motion—in this case, walking.

1. Create a new Flash document. Resize the Stage to 640 x 480 in Flash Menu ➡ Modify ➡ Document.

2. Create 5 new layers so that you have 6 total. Name them accordingly: **front arm**, **front leg**, **head**, **body**, **back arm**, and **back leg**.

3. Drag from frame 1 of the **front arm** layer to frame 8 of the **back leg** layer. From the Menu, go to Modify ➡ Timeline ➡ Convert to Blank Keyframes.

4. Select all of the frames on the **head** and **body** layers and clear those keyframes: Menu ➡ Modify ➡ Timeline ➡ Clear Keyframe.

5. Select frame 1 of the **head** layer and draw—you guessed it—a head! Keep it simple for now. You can always go back and add more detail.

6. Go to frame 1 of the **body** layer and create a body.

7. Now, draw an arm on frame 1 of the **front arm** layer. Keep it on the side of the body as in a standing position.

8. Select this graphic and copy it (Edit ➡ Copy), then click on frame 5 of the same **front arm** layer and paste it *in place* (Edit ➡ Paste In Place). Be sure not to use the standard shortcut for pasting. This will paste the arm in a different location! Alternatively, you can control-click (right-click on a PC) the frame and choose Copy Frames, then Paste Frames.

9. *Paste in place* to frames 1 and 5 of the **back arm** layer.

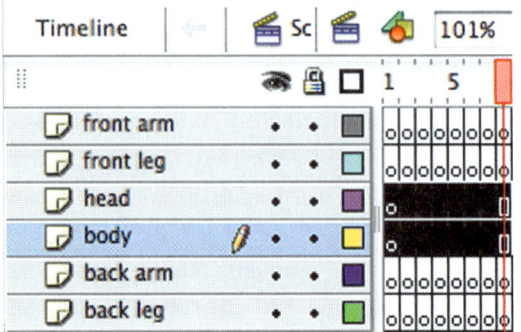

**Figure 2.15** Extra keyframes are not needed on the body and head layers.

10. Add a straight leg to frames 1 and 5 of the **front leg** and **back leg** layers using the same technique.

11. Turn on the Onion Skin view and use this to aid the placement of new limbs on empty keyframes. Instead of drawing each new arm and leg in a different position, you can copy and paste them from other layers, and rotate them slightly. To do this properly, you will need to select the Free Transform Tool and reposition the transformation point up towards the shoulder (by default, it will be in the center of the box). These slight rotations will be smoothly animated when we test our movie, creating our walk cycle.

12. Test the movie (Control ➡ Test Movie). If you have any problems, you can look at my example on the DVD, in the Chapter_02 folder, called *walkCycle_pt2.fla*.

13. If the figure seems to be speed walking, you can either alter the frame rate of the movie (Modify ➡ Document), or add an additional frame in front of each key frame. After selecting a whole column of frames, control click and choose the option for adding a frame (Insert ➡ Timeline ➡ Frame).

14. Of course, our figure should move when it walks. Create a new movie clip: Insert ➡ New Symbol, Name: **figure**, Type: Movie clip. Note that your drawing will dim, and your Timeline will look a little different. This is okay! You are now inside the new movie clip's Timeline. To get back to the main Timeline, click **Scene 1**, which is located at the top left of the workspace.

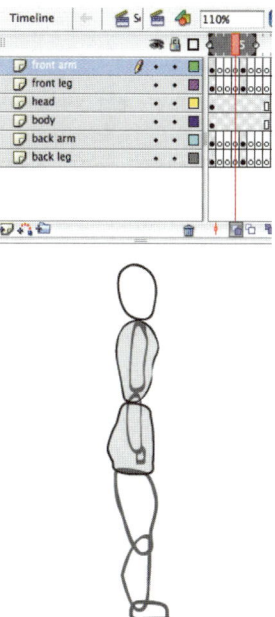

**Figure 2.16** Now that we have a basic body, it is time to animate it!

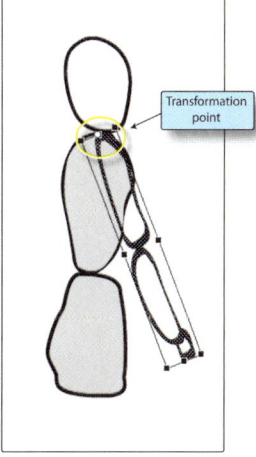

**Figure 2.17** The transformation point will determine how the graphic will rotate.

15. Select all of the frames by dragging from the top-left keyframe down to the bottom-right keyframe, then copy them, Edit ➡ Timeline ➡ Copy Frames.

16. Open the **figure** movie clip from the Library by double clicking on it. Select frame 1 in the Timeline and paste the frames you previously copied: Edit ➡ Timeline ➡ Paste Frames.

17. Return to the main Timeline, select all the frames and delete them: Edit ➡ Timeline ➡ Remove Frames. Delete all of the layers, except for one, and rename it **figureLayer**. Put a new keyframe on frame 1 (Insert ➡ Timeline ➡ Keyframe). Drag the **figure** movie clip from the Library to the left side of the Stage.

18. Make another keyframe on frame 40 of this layer, select this new keyframe, and move the figure to the right side of the Stage.

19. Select the keyframe on frame 1, open the Property Inspector (if not already) and set the Tween option to Motion.

20. Test your movie and watch the figure walk across the Stage. You can take a look at my final version on the DVD called *walkCycle_pt4.fla*. Sarah Howell (one of my graduate students who created many of the graphics for this book) made a more detailed version called *walkCycle_fancy.fla*; this is a good example of how you can extend these tutorials by making livelier, more personalized variations.

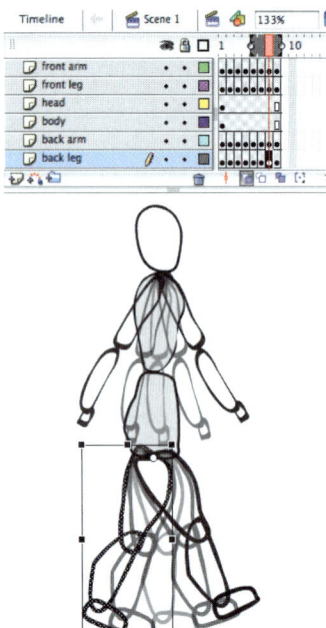

**Figure 2.18** Enabling the Onion Skin view is a good idea with this type of animation.

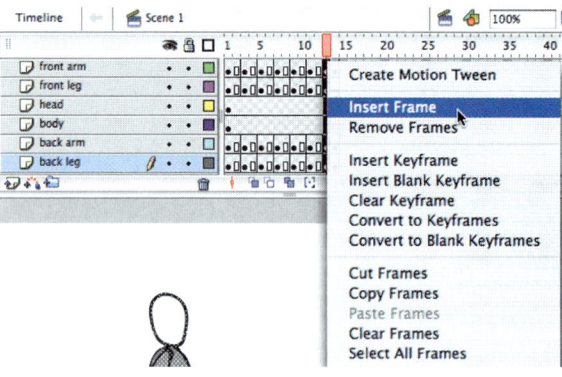

**Figure 2.19** Adding regular frames in front of each keyframe will cut the animation rate in half.

# CHAPTER TWO 43

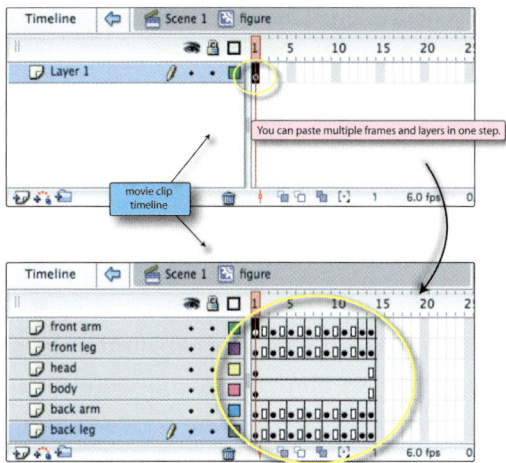

**Figure 2.20** When pasting multiple frames, Flash will bring the associated layers along too.

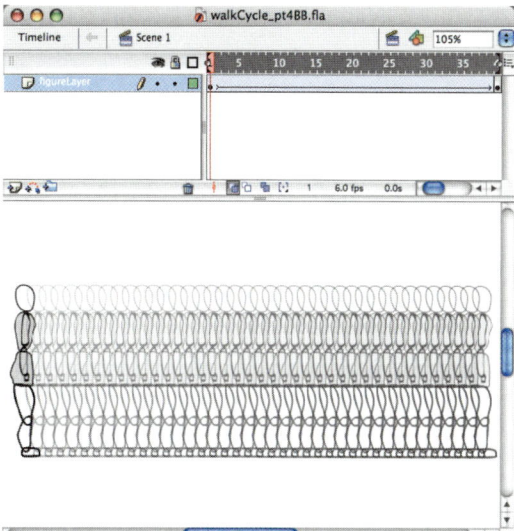

**Figure 2.21** If you turn the Onion Skin view on, you can see that Flash will display the changing frames of an embedded movie clip as well.

## DIGITAL DECONSTRUCTION: *I WANNA BE FAMOUS*

Creating a good film using Flash will take more than developing a unique drawing style and gaining mastery over tweens, keyframes, and scripting. From Fox Gieg's animations we can see that having a good story is essential. *I Wanna Be Famous* is a recent animation by Fox Gieg that illustrates a story residing in the lyrics of a song by Jessica Delfino. As with many artists, Fox Gieg finds that working collaboratively can be a great basis for creative invention.

**Figure 2.22** In collaboration with Jessica Delfino, Fox Gieg created *I Wanna Be Famous* (2006), a hilarious musical-short.

"I work collaboratively whenever I can—I'm always excited about experiencing other disciplines through the eyes of another artist I respect and admire. As far as Flash's particular advantages for collaboration, I think it has two: the small size of the files it produces, and the ease with which a work in progress can be revised and tweaked. Both of these become especially important when working with someone remotely."

While working with Delfino on *I Wanna Be Famous*, Fox Gieg also employed a collaborative partnership across his software tools, bringing audio tracks into Flash, importing Flash sequences into After Effects, as well as working Painter into the mix.

Figure 2.23 shows *I Wanna Be Famous* in the Flash animation stage. The characters, environment, and animation are complete, but lacking the textures, color correction, and special effects that will be added later.

Figure 2.24 shows the final version of the same frame in After Effects. Note the gun's muzzle flash; Fox Gieg carefully outlined this general form with a bright blue color in Flash, making it easy to key out in After Effects where he applied glow and blur effects.

**Figure 2.23** Here, we see some of the production within Flash. This scene depicts the crucial moment in which the main character puts aside her guitar and picks up a gun.

**CHAPTER TWO** 45

> "When you're dealing with bright colors of this kind—for explosions, lightning, fire, and so on—color keying in After Effects is a lot faster than exporting elements from Flash separately with their own alpha (transparency) channel."

While Fox Gieg is appreciative of many of the new features in Flash, including the ability to do certain After Effects-like effects, he still finds it limiting in this regard. He has certainly found a niche for incorporating the special abilities unique to each of the software programs he uses.

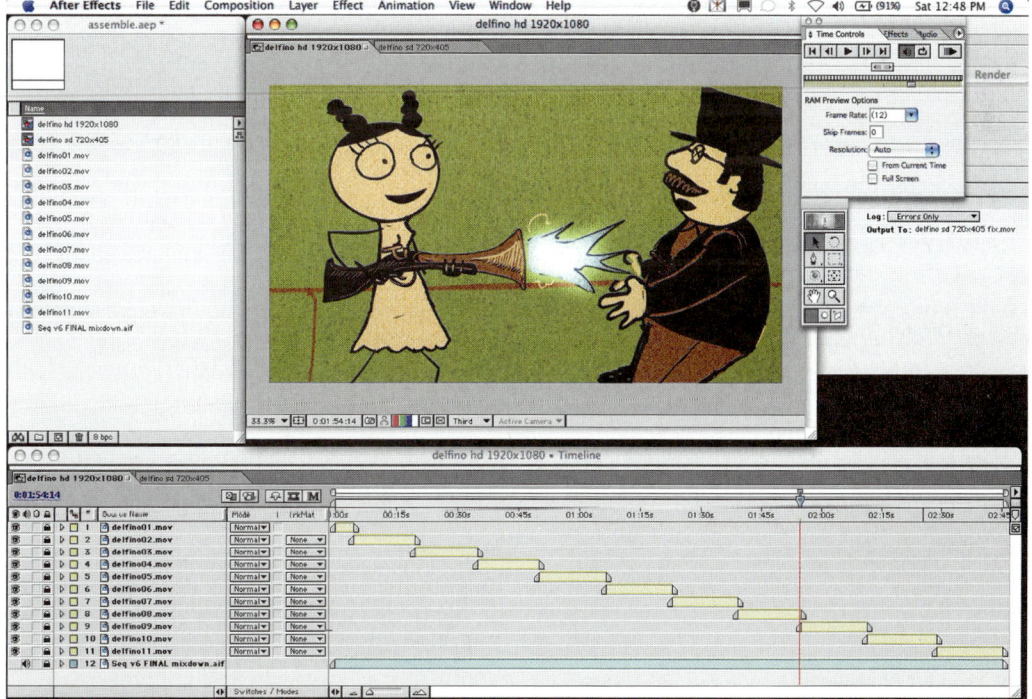

**Figure 2.24** After Effects can do a lot of motion-graphics work that Flash cannot.

### DIY: ROTOSCOPING

In addition to freestyle drawing, many people use a process known as *rotoscoping* for creating their animations. Rotoscoping uses photographed footage as a source to draw on top of. For a rotoscoped animation, you use the same techniques outlined in the other sections in this chapter, preceded by a few simple steps.

**NOTE:** Eadweard Muybridge is a seminal figure in science and art history. Using photography as a means of capturing animals and humans in motion, remarkable detail was recorded for a variety of biomechanical processes. His image sequences are great studies and resources for rotoscope experimentation.

Rotoscoping requires a few extra set-up steps.

**Rotoscoping (replacing Analog Drawing)**

a. Import a high resolution JPEG image (or series of images) onto the Stage.

b. Lock your JPEG layer, keeping it intact.

c. Create new layers above the JPEG and trace the form you want to animate using Flash's drawing tools.

d. Alternatively, you can use Modify ➡ Bitmap ➡ Trace Bitmap to have Flash automatically trace over your image. There are two settings to contend with here: Color Threshold and Minimum Area. These settings determine how closely Flash traces your bitmap.

**Figure 2.25** Most of Muybridge's photographs take a linear grid form, breaking down motion into frozen moments in time.

**Figure 2.26** With a new layer sitting on top of your JPEG layer, trace away!

e. Save this tracing as a new symbol in the Library.

f. Delete your work from the main Timeline, then drag these symbols from the Library into a new movie clip to assemble the animation.

Open the *horseInMotion.fla* from the Chapter 2 folder on the DVD if you get stuck or want to see the version I created.

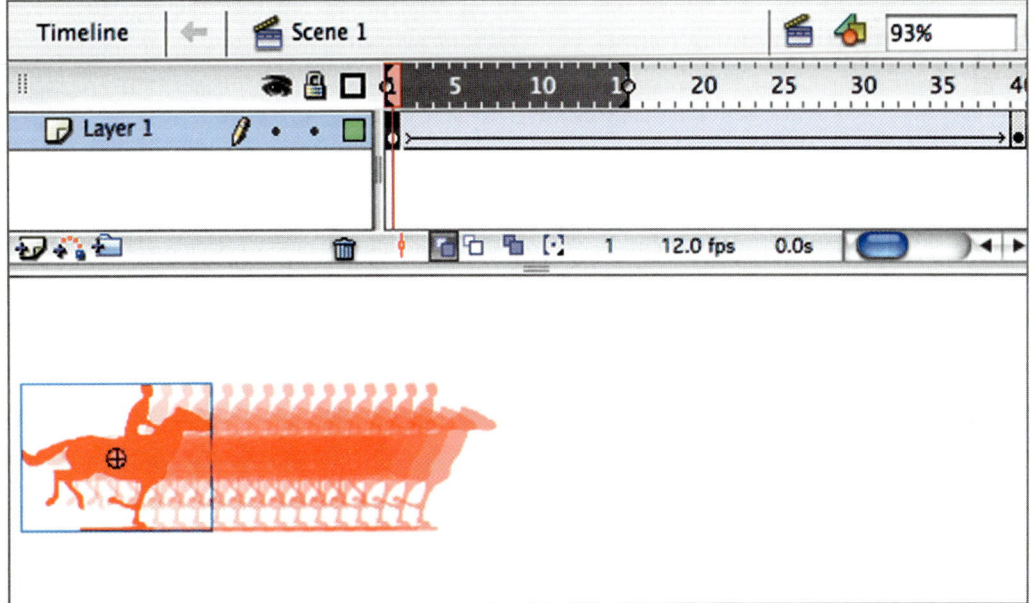

**Figure 2.27** As with our earlier examples, the Onion Skin view can help us see the animation in progress.

## ON YOUR OWN

The DIY sections in this chapter provided the basic layout for drawing with Flash and using tools such as a Wacom tablet. Something I really admire with drawing-based artwork is the level of stylization that can be achieved. Take the files you created in the tutorial sections of this chapter and spend some time adding color, form, depth, and perhaps even an environment behind the figures. If you have access to a drawing tablet, experiment fully with this tool, especially with adjusting the parameters for how it translates your unique style and gesture.

By employing coding techniques from the upcoming chapters, you can investigate the possibilities of dynamically controlling your animations. Through code and drawing style, a simple figure can soon become a character with traits, abilities, and behaviors. It can even respond to a user's input.

# 3 RICARDO MIRANDA ZÚÑIGA

Using Flash to Create Social Metaphors

# RICARDO MIRANDA ZÚÑIGA

**R**icardo Miranda Zúñiga is an artist and professor living in Brooklyn, New York. His expansive use of technology in his teaching and art practice frequently resources Flash as a principle component. Miranda Zúñiga's use of this software is quite different than mainstream practices, and is definitely not something covered in a software manual or the typical Flash book. Highly suspicious of gimmicks posing as "features" and "techniques" in software use, Miranda Zúñiga is interested in artwork that is rigorously dedicated to the exploration of concepts.

---

**Note:** All of Miranda Zúñiga's projects mentioned in this chapter can be found on his Website *www.ambriente.com*.

---

Miranda Zúñiga's professional career is highly influenced by his bicultural childhood. Growing up in the 80s between San Francisco and Masaya, Nicaragua, Miranda Zúñiga is equally familiar with the golden age of video games and sitcoms, as well as the Somoza dictatorship and the tragedies resulting from the Sandanista-Contra war. Although most young people have little concern for politics, as an eighth grader Miranda Zúñiga became very aware of the political corruption and scandals that linked his two countries. Being a politician was not in Miranda Zúñiga's future, but the seeds of becoming an artist communicating politically charged concepts were planted during these years.

Miranda Zúñiga's education framed his childhood experiences through a critical understanding of Western society—especially its imbalanced relationship with poorer countries such as Nicaragua. At UC Berkeley, his major was in English Literature with a minor in Spanish Literature, launching him into the literary histories of the cultures he still examines today. During this process, his focus was shifting towards visual art leading to a last-minute second major in Practice of Art. After graduation, he concentrated on painting and film while living in Oakland, Mexico City, and Nicaragua. This last destination brought Miranda Zúñiga to live on his uncle's farm, tending to chickens in the morning and creating artwork at night. It was during this stay in Nicaragua that he created the body of work for his graduate school applications.

In 1996, Miranda Zúñiga chose Carnegie Mellon University for his MFA studies because of its solid reputation, innovative interdisciplinary structure, and the incredible faculty there at the time. Through these studies, he developed skills spanning a wide range of media that supported his artistic perspectives on communication, technology, politics, and globalism.

# CHAPTER THREE

## DIGITAL DECONSTRUCTION: AUDIOPHILE

After receiving his MFA, Miranda Zúñiga landed a job at Oven Digital in the summer of 2000. Oven Digital was a dynamic and energetic Web design and development company that used Flash extensively. One of his first projects at this job was to develop a database-driven audio library to be used by designers for client Websites. The audio samples function as a vivisection of the aural environment of various cities.

> "I was given recording equipment and a great deal of freedom to traverse the city, recording its sounds, creating loops and a Flash application that would allow others to listen and download the sounds. Once I had the interface built, merely depositing new files into the audio library would generate the Flash buttons for that sound."

Oven Digital brought Miranda Zúñiga to Brooklyn, where he now lives and runs his studio. The winner of several awards and commissions, his artwork has been exhibited widely across the world. This success as an artist valuably influences his role as a teacher; he is also a tenured Associate Professor at The College of New Jersey where he teaches Fine and Digital Art.

Technology-based art is especially susceptible to the fixations of automated effects built into the software. To emphasize content, and encourage studio practices where software techniques are used as a means for enhancing theoretical issues, Miranda Zúñiga introduces students to artwork that exemplifies conceptual integrity over technical glibness—work that goes beyond the shallow "bells and whistles" that so often plagues multimedia art. He also formulates projects requiring more from his students than figuring out technical solutions, such as doing considerable research on a particular topic.

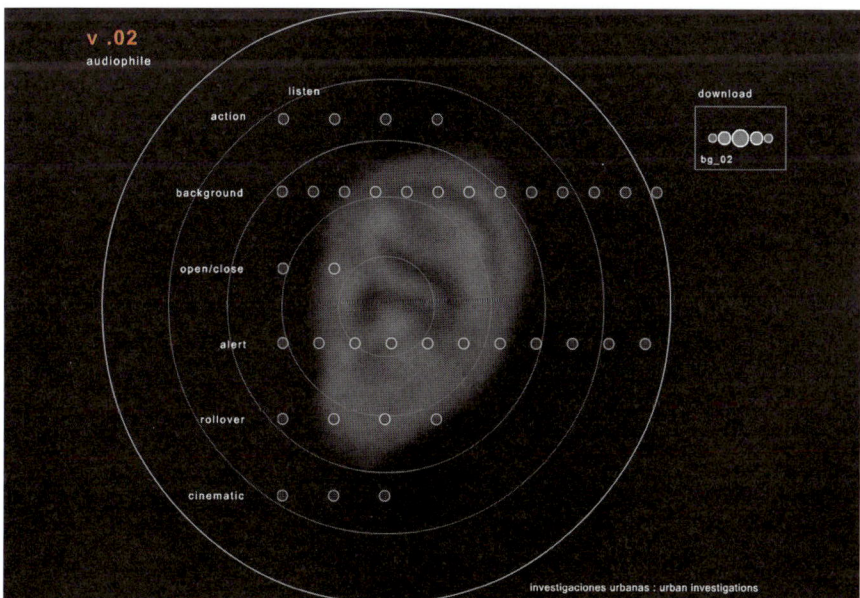

**Figure 3.1** *Audiophile* (2001) remixes sounds from Managua, Mexico City, and Manhattan.

## DIGITAL DECONSTRUCTION: *DENTIMUNDO*

*Dentimundo* is a recent artwork by Miranda Zúñiga that documents *border dentistry*, a trend that has a long history along the Mexico and U.S. border. This phenomenon represents a very particular element of globalization as Mexican doctors are moving their practices to border towns, attracting a migration antipodal to what is typically reported. Miranda Zúñiga's tour of the border discovered that thousands of Americans are flocking to these new offices where they can expect excellent dental service at ¼ the cost found in the United States.

The *Dentimundo* Website is a valuable resource for border dentistry, providing visitors a comprehensive set of tools for exploring this form of medical tourism in Mexico. The site's construction consists of a database that feeds data into HTML via PHP. This dynamic construction allows users to learn from *Dentimundo*, but they can also add to it by recommending dentists or recounting personal experiences.

The other principle component of *Dentimundo* is a series of Flash files embedded in the top of each page, controlling the multimedia content. When the site first loads, the background of this Flash movie plays a brief animation, explaining the concept of border dentistry while the background music, "Corrido al Dentista," begins playing. A *corrido* is a Mexican style of song used to celebrate and preserve a story or historical account. Miranda Zúñiga wrote the lyrics for this song composed and performed by Alejandro Espino Aldana.

**Figure 3.2** Dancing teeth accompany the intro to *Dentimundo* (2005), just in case you want to sing along!

After the introduction, the Flash movie turns into a navigation/slideshow—a unique blend of interactivity and motion graphics for the Web that can only be done with Flash. In the background, cascading images move and crossfade, taking the viewer through a photo tour of border dentistry towns and practices.

The tour guide then introduces the dentists whose interviews are featured on the site with accompanying caricatures appearing along the bottom. These types of vector drawings are a common feature on many of Miranda Zúñiga's Flash animations. In this case, they skillfully add a sense of personality and reality to these practicing dentists. While many Americans know about the savings that can be found across the border, a substantial degree of disinformation exists. *Dentimundo* excels at dispelling these feelings by showcasing actual border dentists and creating a forum for people who have utilized their services.

**NOTE:** In all of the work mentioned in this chapter, Miranda Zúñiga employs an interesting use of vector art that is influenced by a wide range of styles and artists he saw while growing up and while in school. These inspirations range from Caravagio and Gerhard Richter, to Batman and MAD comics.

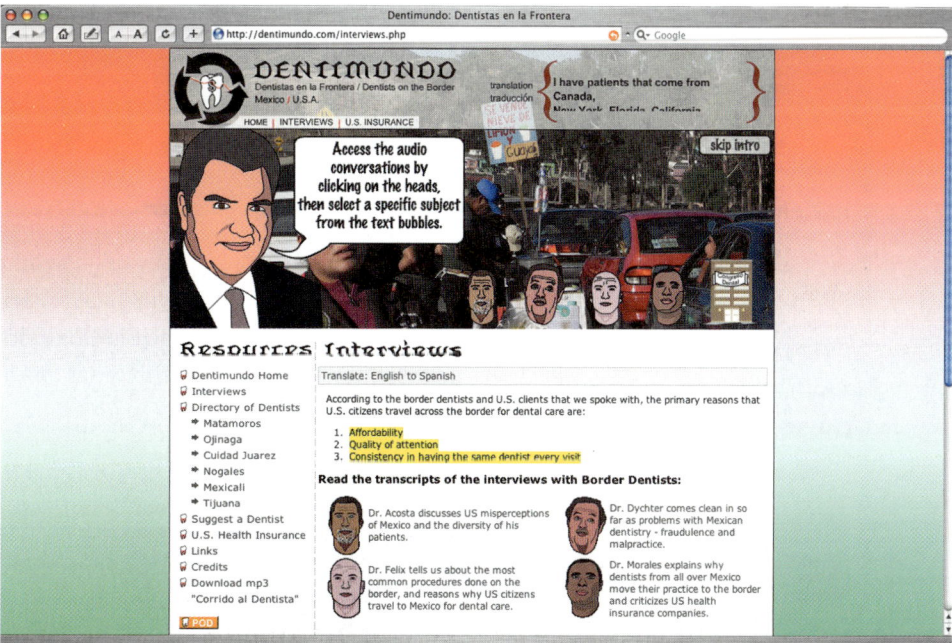

**Figure 3.3** Selecting one of the dentists will play an audio interview.

## DIGITAL DECONSTRUCTION: *FALLOUT*

*Fallout* is another of Miranda Zúñiga's Web-based artworks serving as a historical resource funded by New Radio and Performing Arts, Inc. (aka Ether-Ore) and hosted at *www.Turbulence.org*. Drawing from his childhood experiences, history, and interviews with natives and immigrants, this recent work serves as a dynamic space for discourse, inviting public response to the complex sociopolitical history of Nicaragua.

Like *Dentimundo, Fallout* begins with a Flash animation inspired by Nicaraguan painting, murals, and graffiti. A wealth of information regarding this country's tumultuous past saturates the Website, including an interactive Graphic History of Nicaragua. Selecting from a range of famous and notorious figures, the viewer can learn of Nicaragua's enigmatic history.

The main goal of *Fallout* is to draw together a collection of personal accounts of Nicaragua, creating a revisionist history that admonishes the way Western ideology represents this region in the media. Fueling this perspective is a Flash-based game called *Always Go Left*, linked within the Fallout Website. In this game, Miranda Zúñiga subverts the standard of side-scrolling games by having the character move from right-to-left. The game narrative establishes the

**Figure 3.4** Ancient and recent histories are juxtaposed creatively inside *Fallout* (2005).

hero as a champion of the people with the following goals: collect money while avoiding obstacles, distribute money to those in need, and buy weapons and radio equipment, all with the ultimate goal of overthrowing the corrupt government. Moving right at any point will bring death, as a pack of wolves are constantly prowling close by from that side of the screen.

## DIGITAL DECONSTRUCTION: VAGAMUNDO

*Vagamundo* was partially funded by Harvestworks *www.harvestworks.org*, a nonprofit organization in New York City. Similar to *Always Go Left*, this work references the side-view game genre to relay observations of migrant labor in the United States. These immigrants must overcome racism, a radically different culture, and physical danger (hundreds of people die each year trying to cross the border) in an effort to escape abject poverty.

Physically, *Vagamundo* is quite unlike most Flash games. Rather than simply residing on a Web server, this game is installed inside a cart similar to those used by *paleteros*—immigrant ice cream vendors whose presence has been steadily increasing in large metros across the U.S.

The game relies on traditional elements of game play such as enemies, obstacles, lives, score, levels, and a side-view environment. The main character is controlled with buttons and a joystick installed on the cart (or keyboard and mouse for the online version). The hero is a caricature of Cantinflas, the famous Mexican actor of the 1940s, somewhat comparable to Charlie Chaplan. The general premise sets Cantinflas as a newly arrived immigrant to

**Figure 3.5** Our hero found some money in the caverns. Hopefully he can continue without being devoured by the wolves.

**Figure 3.6** Who says Flash games need to be played on a standard PC?

New York City. The goal of the game is to help Cantinflas overcome the obstacles of each level, leading to a victorious conclusion where he becomes economically comfortable and successfully integrated into U.S. society.

When the game first starts, an introduction displays statistical information about the plight of migration attempts across the Mexican-U.S. border. This sets the stage for the educational content of the game: many U.S. citizens are not aware of the fatalities occurring under these circumstances. Animated vector graphics give the statistics with red pedestal markers and human figures donning fatality symbols. In the background looms a photograph from the border.

Following the introduction is a series of animated instructions for game play. The player is first shown how to wake up Cantinflas. Then, using the joystick (or keyboard controls online), the player makes him move, duck, or perform a somersault jump. Exiting the instructions screen brings up the first level, El Borracho.

### El Borracho: A Culture of Poverty

In the first level, El Borraacho, Cantiflas must avoid bottles being thrown at him while racing against the clock. This is the first introduction to the general mechanics of *Vagamundo*: the environment is a side-view style similar to *Street Fighter* (a classic arcade game from the 80s). A health display is located in the top left, and a clock sits off to the right. Bottles fly randomly from the side of the screen while the clock ticks a countdown. With each bottle smashing against Cantinflas, a substantial amount of the red health bar is reduced. If this happens often enough, Cantinflas is knocked out, and an FBI agent deports him off the

**Figure 3.7** Avoiding the bottles is not too difficult. But in this game, dexterity requirements are sacrificed in order to accommodate the delivery of content: it is challenging enough to be fun, but not so difficult that most players would be turned away on the first level.

screen (and presumably back to his home country). With this first level, it becomes quite clear how classic game references (*Mario-Brothers/Street Fighter*) can be used as a vehicle for delivering a more sophisticated, real-life quality of discourse.

Sustained success at bottle avoidance will keep the health bar up while the clock runs out of time, allowing the player to win the level. A small lizard (an Aztec symbol representing the most positive day of the week) flies down and ferries Cantinflas to the next level.

### The Green Grocer Bagger: A Culture of Assimilation

Level two has the hero now in front of a grocery store in the East Village. The pre-level text informs that Cantinflas now has a job as a grocery bagger. A gigantic cockroach wearing a wrestling mask descends onto the sidewalk, throwing menacing punches in the direction of Cantinflas. Our hero's goal is to defeat this stereotype-monster in order to continue his social status climb. Beating the monster, or surviving the clock, causes the lizard once more to swoop down and fly Cantinflas off to the final level. If you lose, the owner of the grocery store storms out and fires Cantinflas.

**Figure 3.8** Beating the boss of this level also defeats the negative stereotypes it embodies.

### The Head Waiter: A Culture of Prosperity

The third level shows a cleaned-up Cantinflas wearing a tux and working at a restaurant on the Upper East Side. Tip money appears randomly amongst the seated customers. Helping Cantinflas hustle and collect $180 before the clock runs out brings out the restaurant manager, who then promotes the hero to head waiter. Scrambling quickly in this level, fixated on chasing the dollars, one becomes acutely aware of the ignominious act of grabbing for money.

The real success behind *Vagamundo* is in how it summons more from the player than simple hand-eye coordination. Throughout the game, facts, information, and personal experiences are coupled with game play dexterity and anticipation, creating an experience that illuminates social issues in a unique form of dialog. After beating the game, a winning screen appears, asking the player if he wants to help future immigrants or discriminate against them. Selecting the former brings up a screen with several resources for finding out more about U.S. immigration. Selecting the latter sends Cantinflas to one more level of game play.

Starkly different than the other levels and considerably less humorous, this extra level depicts Cantinflas on border patrol with a menacing crosshairs moving along with keyboard input. Quite suddenly, bitmap images of young Hispanic men come running from the side of the screen. Shooting at them successfully kills the figures, but more and more come, leaving us with the prospect of a hopeless shooting game that will never end. The player is forced to face the most unfortunate of tragedies surrounding the issues explored in this game: violence and xenophobia associated with immigrant labor in the United States.

**Figure 3.9** Cantinflas is looking pretty spiffy, but also kind of pitiful when he starts running after the tips.

**Figure 3.10** Unlike the other levels, all fun disappears as the gravity of what this game is really about sets in.

**NOTE:** For those of you who are new to this terminology, Flash (and all multimedia software) can primarily work with two types of still images: **vector** and **bitmap**. Vector graphics are defined geometries where algorithms are responsible for the way the image looks. This way of displaying an image on the computer is ideal for line art, symbols, and illustrations—images that are generally simpler than photo-based images. Photos are usually saved as bitmap images. The individual pixels are assigned a certain color, and when the resolution is great enough, a photo-quality image materializes. Flash was originally a very strict program working almost exclusively with vector images, but each new Flash release incorporates greater ability with bitmap images. New to Flash CS3 is the interoperability between vector art, such as Illustrator files, and bitmap art, such as Photoshop documents. Both can be seamlessly imported into Flash for an easy integration of styles.

### DIY: CHARACTER ANIMATION

There are innumerable ways for animating in Flash, even with something as specific as character animation. In this section, we are going to cover a few of the techniques that Miranda Zúñiga has employed in his artwork.

Many artists working with Flash first create their vector art in Illustrator, (including Miranda Zúñiga ). While Flash contains an impressive set of drawing tools, drawing programs such as Illustrator have more features and flexibility. Working from a photo, memory, or raw intuition, Miranda Zúñiga draws his graphics using Adobe Illustrator before importing them into Flash. While building up the graphics for his projects, Miranda Zúñiga meticulously distributes the various elements of each drawing onto separate layers, allowing for more flexibility while deciding color, shape, and position.

### Working with Vector Files

In *Dentimundo*, all of the featured dentists on the Website have portraits that were first drawn using Illustrator before they were imported into Flash, where they were then made interactive. The image shown here is of Dr. Ramon Felix Landeros, a dentist from Tijuana.

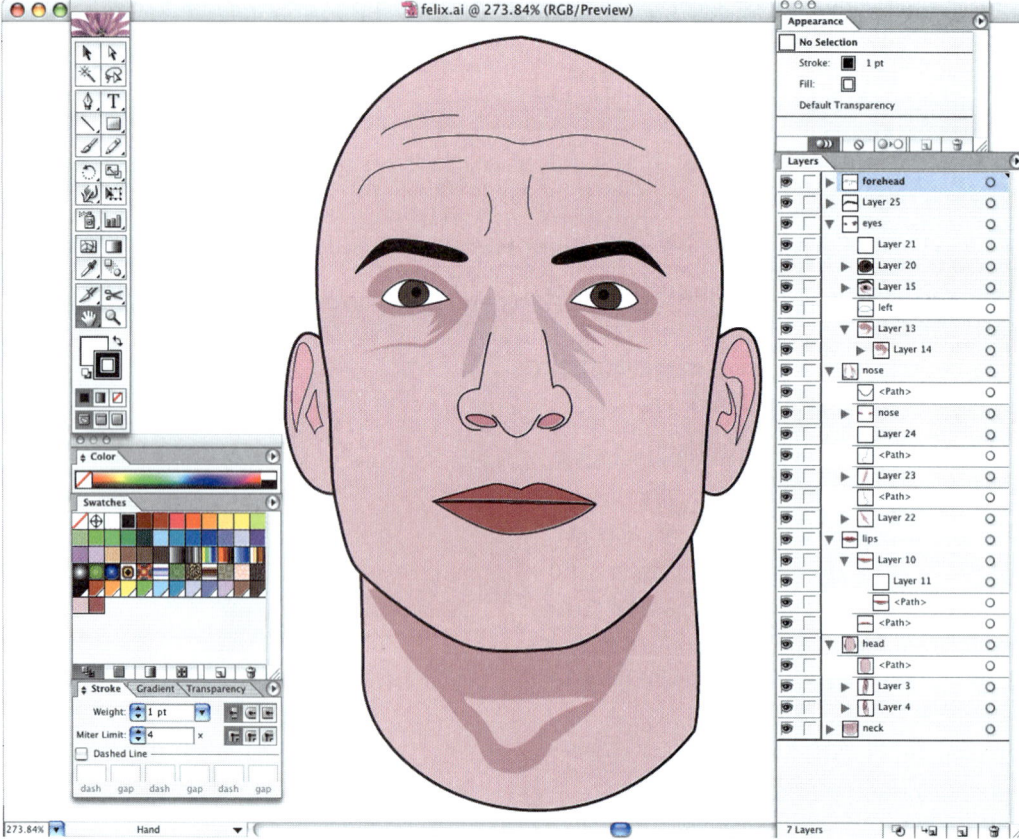

**Figure 3.11** A detailed use of layers will not only assist with keeping your drawings organized, but it will also prepare them for animation and interactivity in Flash. Luckily for us, Flash keeps Illustrator layers intact after importing them.

This Illustrator file is included on the CD. Try importing it into Flash. Make sure that Flash is launched and you have a new FLA file open.

1. First, let us resize our default Stage setting from 550 × 400 pixels to one that will match the file we are importing: Flash Menu ➡ Modify ➡ Document.

2. Change the Dimensions: width to 720 pixels and height to 480 pixels. Then click the OK button.

3. Now import the Illustrator file. Import ➡ Import to Library. This will bring up a dialog window. Find and select *felix.ai* on the DVD in the Chapter_03 folder. Then select the Import to Library button.

4. The Import Options dialog window will open. Choose the following in the window:
   - Convert pages to: **Keyframes**
   - Convert Layers to: **Layers**
   - Which pages to import: **All**

   Options: all of them should *not* be selected, except for the last one—Rasterize. You should see **felix.ai** in the Library with a Graphic icon next to it (Flash places imported vector art into graphic symbols).

### Working with Bitmaps

Importing a bitmap image is significantly different than importing a vector graphic. Since these types of images are defined by pixels, and not by algorithms, they are usually larger files in need of compression. Let us import a couple of different types of bitmap images and examine how they can be compressed in Flash for maximum run-time efficiency.

From the DVD, import the *grocery.tif* file and the *cart.jpg* files. Make sure they are in the

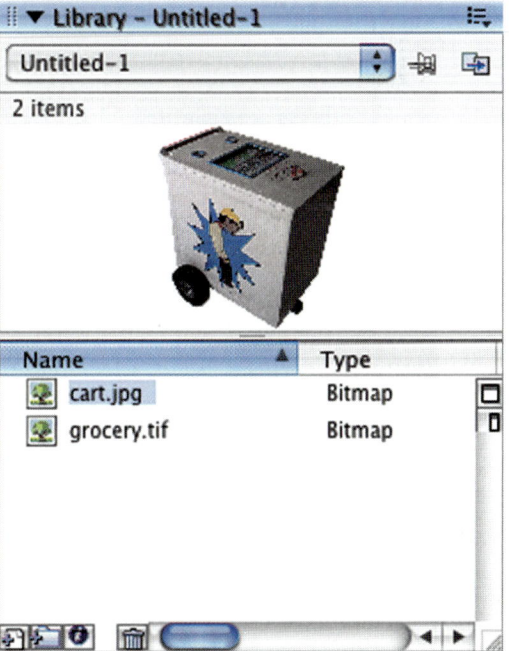

**Figure 3.12** Your Library should look like this.

Library when you are finished. Refer to the steps above for importing a vector image if you need to. The steps are the same, except the Import Option dialog will not come up.

The TIFF image (along with any other non-JPEG bitmap) will be compressed according to the general Publishing Settings.

1. File ➡ Publish Settings.
2. Under the Flash tab there are a variety of options, one of them being the JPEG quality slider.
3. Adjusting the JPEG quality slider will choose a global setting for how imported bitmaps will be compressed when your Flash file is exported (except for JPEGs). You will want to set this as low as possible, while reserving approvable quality.

For some reason, the global Publish Settings do not work on imported JPEG (.jpg) images. For adjusting the compression settings on imported JPEG images, follow these steps.

1. Find the **grocery.jpg** bitmap in your Library.
2. Double-click the icon for this asset, opening the Bitmap Properties dialog window for *this* bitmap.
3. The Compression pull-down should be set to Photo (JPEG). If not, select this option.
4. Uncheck the box for "Use document default quality." This will open the Quality option.
5. In the upper left-hand corner is a preview window. You can reposition the JPEG in this window to view a critical part of your image.

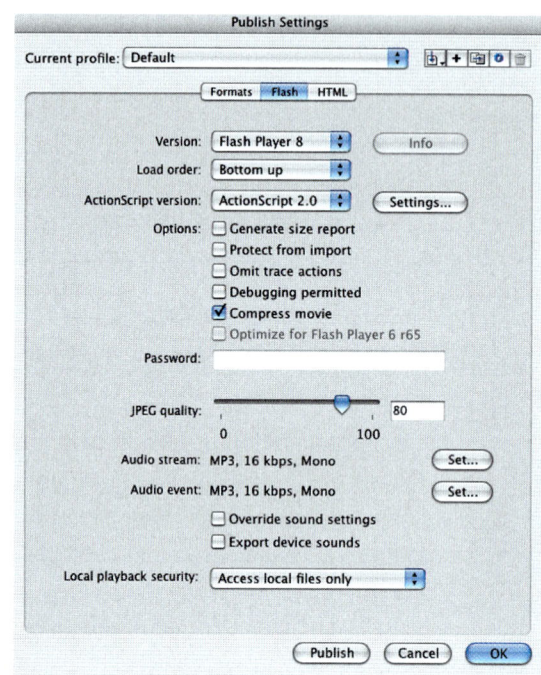

**Figure 3.13** The JPEG quality slider is found in the Flash tab of the Publish Settings.

6. Try putting different numbers between 0–100 in the Quality box and hitting the Test button on the side. Data regarding the original and compressed size of the file is displayed. Again, you will want the lowest number (translating into faster performance) while yielding a quality that is acceptable.

The Bitmap Properties dialogue can be really handy for finding the proper balance between quality and file size, a topic that eternally plagues artists working with interactive media. The only time you would want to use the Bitmap Properties dialogue with an image other than a JPEG would be when the quality of the image is crucial, in which case you will want to switch from Compression: Photo(JPEG) to Lossless(PNG/GIF).

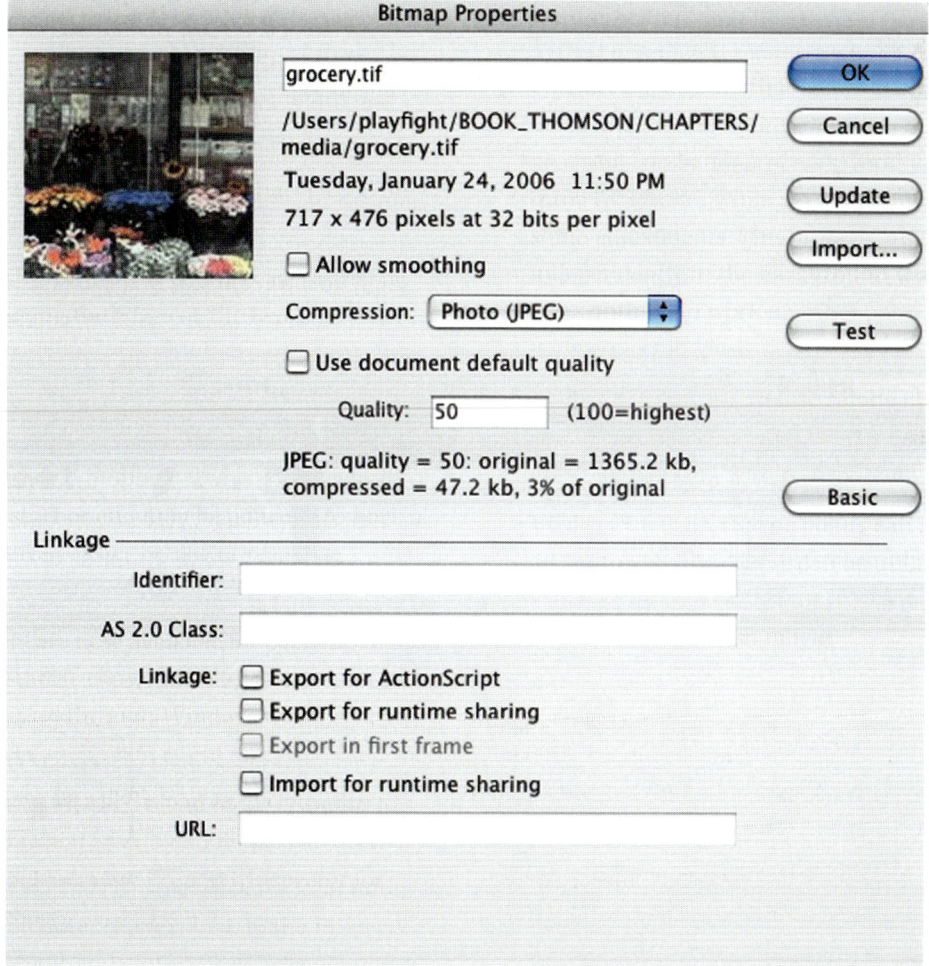

**Figure 3.14** Be sure to make use of the Test button. It is a lot faster than exporting a test movie over and over when simply checking bitmap compression.

## Working with Layers and the Timeline

Now that importing graphics and setting their compression has been covered, let us examine the imported vector image in more detail. Drag the **felix.ai** graphic symbol onto the main Stage.

If you click once on the face, you will see a blue bounding box around it. This is because it is imported as a graphic symbol. Symbols are a very important feature of Flash. It is a way to conveniently organize graphical content, and additionally, they are fundamental elements for adding animation and ActionScript control to your project. For right now, let us examine the hierarchal nature of the main Timeline and the embedded Timeline of symbols, while also briefly highlighting the Align window.

1. Window ➡ Align.

2. Click once on the face graphic that is on the Stage. A single bounding blue box should be around the head.

3. In the Align window, first click the To Stage button, then click the Align Horizontal Center button, followed by clicking the

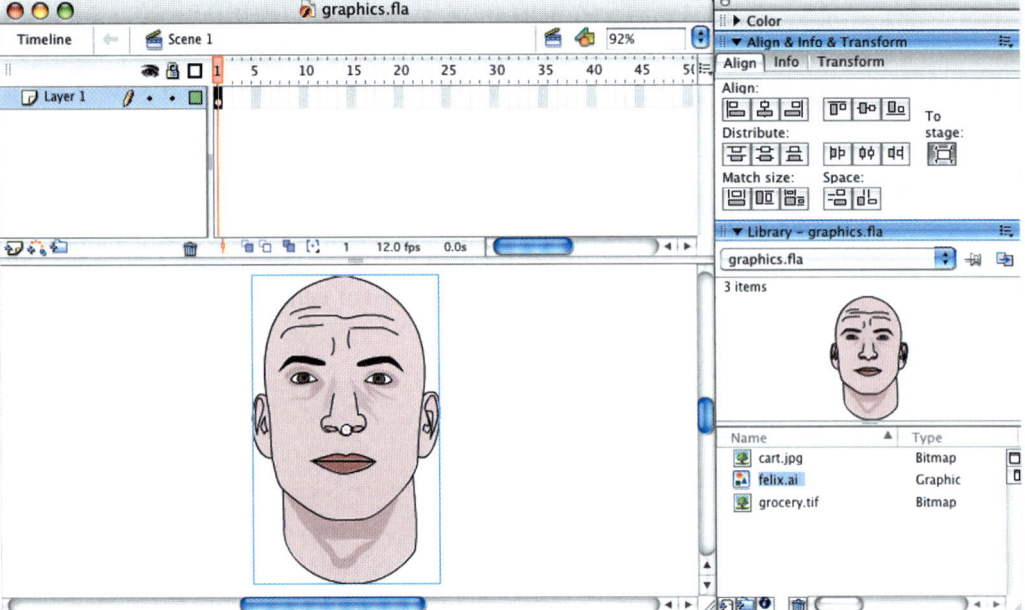

**Figure 3.15** The felix.ai graphic in the Library panel and on the Stage.

Align Vertical Center Button. Unless you placed the image exactly in the center of the Stage when dragging it from the Library, you will notice it shift slightly after performing these alignments.

4. Now, examine the **felix.ai** Timeline by double-clicking the face graphic on the Stage. You will notice a significant difference in the Timeline and layers.

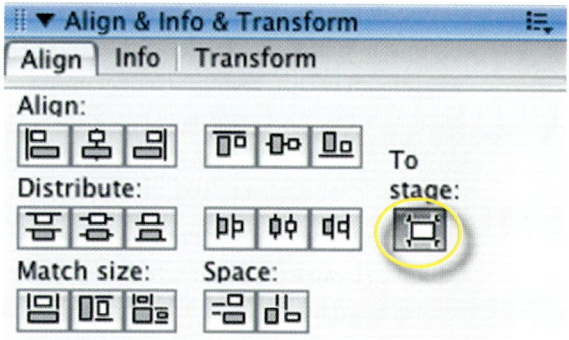

**Figure 3.16** The Align tool is handy for exacting compositions.

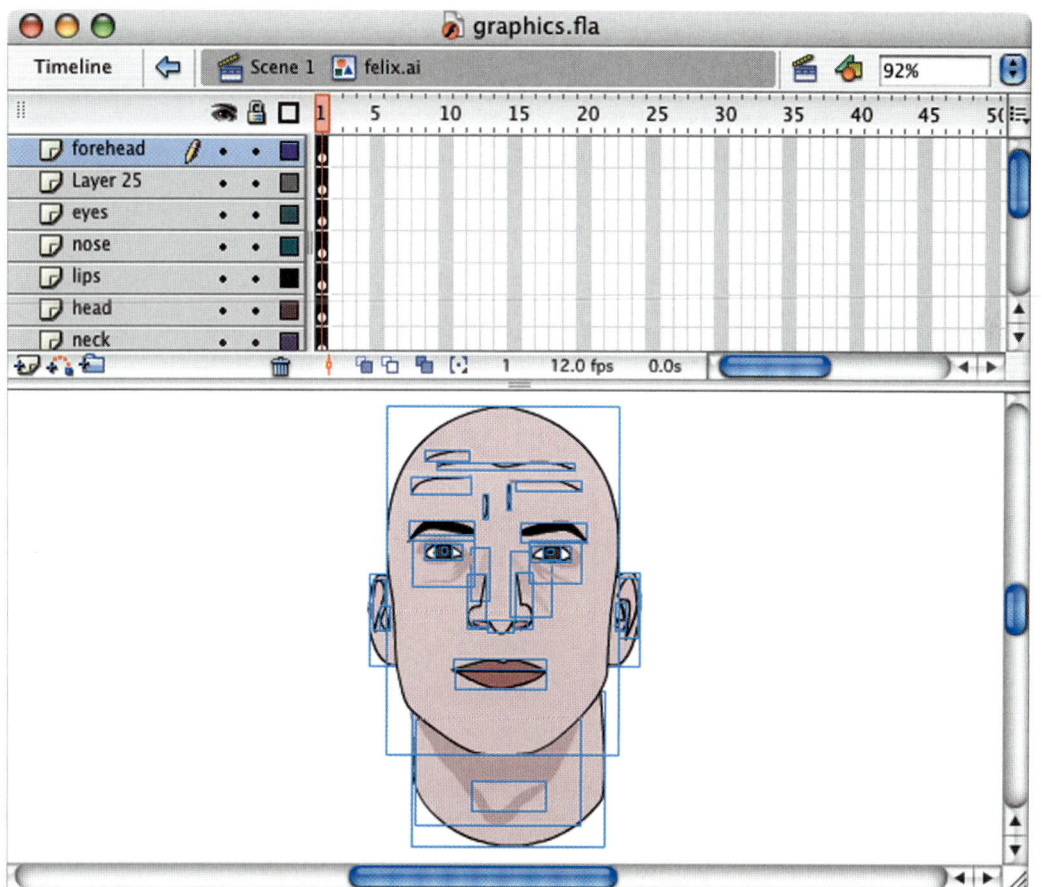

**Figure 3.17** The felix.ai graphic symbol has a Timeline with frames and layers, just like the main Timeline (Scene 1).

Notice all the layers and how they are named after prominent features of the face (nose, lips, eyes, etc.). This is a helpful strategy used to avoid accidentally merged graphics; it also helps to elicit greater control over individual graphic placement, shape, and coloring and lends to preparing images for animation. While this example shows how Flash retains layers that were created in an Adobe Illustrator document, successful layer use can be employed when creating drawings inside Flash. In addition to skillful layer usage, this figure also shows how a symbol actually contains a unique Timeline. All three types of symbols in Flash (graphic, movie clip, button) share this trait.

**NOTE:** The way Flash recycles screen real estate for different data and graphics may seem complicated at first. But imagine the confusion if Flash did not work this way; every symbol and the main Timeline would have their own windows floating around on the screen. You can easily flip back to the main Timeline by selecting it at the very top of your document (labeled **Scene 1**).

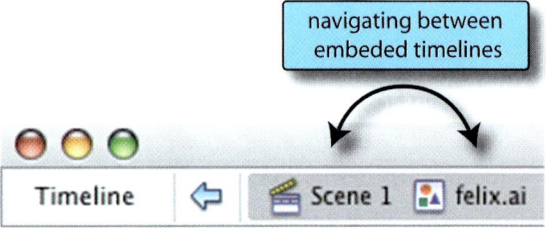

**Figure 3.18** Detail of the Timeline. Navigating between Timelines/scenes is easily done using these links.

### Motion Tween

One of the simplest types of animation in Flash is a tween. A tween is a term that describes the ability of Flash to gradually alter properties over a stretch of time that would be painstaking to do manually. Keyframes are special frames (indicated by a dot on the frame) intrinsically related to tweening and any type of animation. They alert Flash to pay special attention to data (code, labels, properties and/or graphics) occurring at that point.

There are two types of tweens in Flash: motion and shape. A shape tween can be employed on non-symbol vector graphics to alter the shape of an image between two keyframes. A motion tween works on symbols to adjust position, color, and/or transparency between keyframes.

Miranda Zúñiga uses motion tweens in several areas of *Vagamundo*. For instance, when each level loads, a background photo fades to a vector drawing of the same place. This visual effect works very well to enforce the reality of a place before taking the player into the familiar fictional world of a game level.

Try the basic form of this animation yourself. Create a new Flash document and Import *grocery.ai* and *grocery.jpg* from the Chapter_03 folder on the DVD, then do the following steps.

1. Rename **Layer 1** by double-clicking on its name. Call it **vector**.

2. Create another layer: Insert ➡ Timeline ➡ Layer. Rename this layer **raster**.

3. Resize the document to 720 × 480 pixels. Modify ➡ Document.

4. Select frame 1 of the layer named **raster** and drag **grocery.jpg** from the Library to the Stage. This will also place the image on frame 1 of the **raster** layer.

5. Use the Property Inspector (Window ➡ Properties ➡ Properties), to align the image exactly over the Stage. Set X to 360 and Y to 240.

6. Motion tweens only work with symbols. Click once on the image on the Stage, then: Modify ➡ Convert to Symbol. Set the Type to Graphic.

7. Select frame 20 on the **raster** layer. Insert ➡ Timeline ➡ Keyframe. This will make a grey bar leading up to Frame 20, which will have a solid dot on it. Keyframes are represented in Flash with dots.

8. With the keyframe selected on frame 20, click once on the image on the Stage. Use the Color pull-down menu in the Property Inspector and set it to Alpha. Then adjust the Alpha to 0%.

9. Select frame 1 on the **raster** layer. Use the Property Inspector to change the Tween pull-down to Motion. Scrolling the play head (pink box on the top of the Timeline) back and forth will reveal the tween effect.

**Figure 3.19** These two images are tweened to create a cross-fade effect in *Vagamundo*.

10. Select frame 1 of the **vector** layer and then drag the **grocery.ai** graphic onto the Stage. You may want to lock and/or turn the visibility off for the **raster** layer while working on the **vector** layer. Use the Property Inspector to align the image exactly onto the Stage.

11. Select frame 20 of the **vector** layer, then go to Insert ➡ Timeline ➡ Frame. Test the movie: Control➡ Test Movie. A SWF file will open and you will see the grocery store transform from a photo into a drawing. It will also loop, because Flash animations loop by default. That can be changed later with a little code.

**Figure 3.20** Moving the playhead into the middle of the tween will reveal the effects of the crossfade.

## Character Animation

This background tween is only a small part from a network of animations used to create *Vagamundo*. For animations to work within a game they need to be interactive: user input decides how the graphics change and unfold. In *Vagamundo*, Cantinflas walks, jumps, or ducks only when the user tells him to.

After creating a character, the best way to enliven it with animated behaviors (like a walk-cycle), is to first create a unique Timeline for that character, placing it in different positions across different frames. Open *cantinflas_start.fla* from the Chapter_03 folder on the DVD. Then open the movie clip symbol sitting on the Stage by double-clicking it. Notice how the layers are named according to position (jump, duck, flip, etc.). Scrolling back and forth across the Timeline gives a glimpse of how the character will move. There is also a layer containing frame labels and a layer that will hold ActionScript.

ActionScript is a programming language built into Flash that can lend powerful interactivity to your project. ActionScript is typed out as text in the Actions panel and usually resides on either frames or symbols (they can also be imported as an .as file).

On the **actions** layer add keyframes to frames 10, 17, 24, 31, 38, and 44. You can do this by selecting the frame. Then from the Menu: Insert ➡ Timeline ➡ Keyframe, or by selecting the frame and hitting the F6 key. Before we add the code, try testing the movie (Control ➡

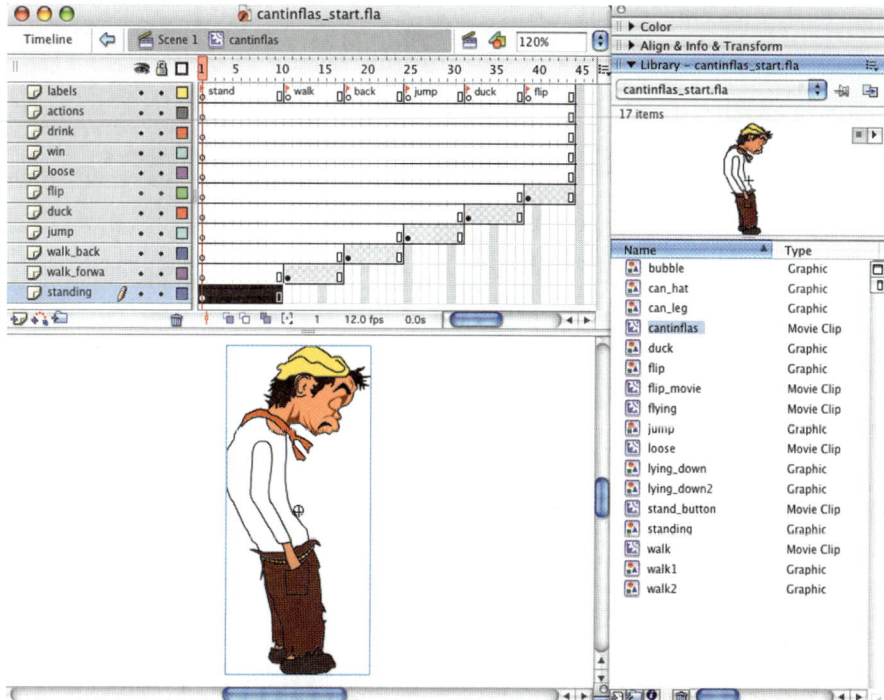

**Figure 3.21** With some tweaking, the same vector graphics can be reused in other symbols, setting the stage for character animation.

Test Movie). You will notice how the character simply loops through all of the motions. That is because it currently lacks ActionScript for controlling his movement, but you are about to change that!

Now we are going to add code to the keyframes.

1. Click on frame 1 of the **actions** layer.

2. Open the Actions panel: go to the Window ➡ Actions.

3. Type `stop();` in the window. Now try testing the movie. Cantinflas stays put!

4. Now click on keyframe 10 of the actions layer and type `gotoAndPlay("stand");` in the Actions panel. Do this for keyframes 17, 24, 31, 38, and 44 on the **actions** layer. This is setting up some other code about to be added.

5. Go to the main Timeline of this FLA by selecting **Scene 1** in the upper left-hand corner, just above the layers area. Now click once on Cantinflas on the Stage. There should now be a bounding box around him. Cantinflas is a movie clip symbol, so we can add code to it. Type this code in the Actions panel:

```
on (keyPress "<Right>") {
      this.gotoAndPlay("walk");
      this._x +=40;
}
on (keyPress "<Left>") {
      this.gotoAndPlay("back");
      this._x -= 40;
}

on (keyPress "<Up>") {
      this.gotoAndPlay("jump");
}
```

```
on (keyPress "<Down>") {
       this.gotoAndPlay("duck");
}
on (keyPress "<Space>") {
       this.gotoAndPlay("flip");
       this._x += 80;
}
```

For those of you who are new to programming, each line of code above that begins with on is referred to as a handler. A handler is a type of function that is designed to perform some action when a specified event is detected (it *handles* the event). In this example, user input in the form of keypresses are being handled. In the body of each handler, the movie clip where the code is being typed (referred to as this) is told to go to and play at a frame label name ("jump" for instance). In some cases, the movie clip is also told to reposition based on the _x property (_x controls the horizontal placement of a movie clip).

Try testing the movie and see what happens. Cantinflas stays at the default standing position, but if you use your arrow keys, or the spacebar, you will see him react according to the keyboard handlers you assigned with ActionScript.

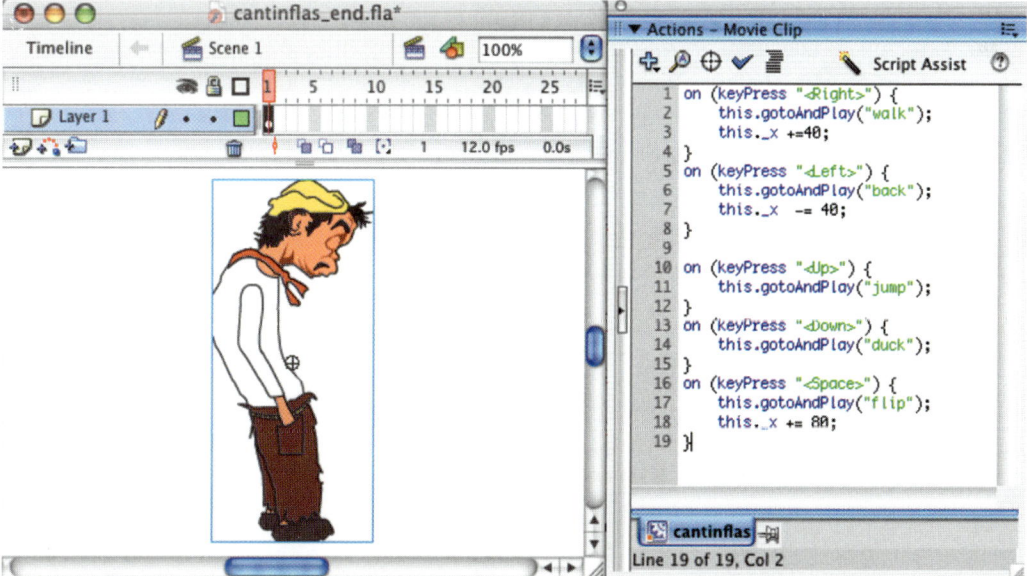

**Figure 3.22** Cantinflas has gone from illustration, to animation, and now—thanks to ActionScript—an interactive character.

Overall, *Vagamundo* is a great example of how artwork created with Flash can transcend the gloss and glam of interactive media—it can also resonate with valuable insight into social commentary. Miranda Zúñiga has a great talent for producing works that are not only visually intriguing and fun to interact with, but are also interactive tools for exploring vital content.

## ON YOUR OWN

ActionScripting can definitely have a steep learning curve for those new to coding. My experience has found that one of the best practices for learning code is to tweak and alter examples from others. For instance, in the handler event code that was written on the character movie clip above (several lines all starting with on), try putting in different numerical values than what was provided (e.g. switching the number 40 to 10) and test the movie. Or, instead of altering the _x value of the movie clip, try changing the _y value.

In this way, you can begin to understand how the code translates into action—with ActionScript!

**Figure 3.23** Miranda Zúñiga demonstrates how to play *Vagamundo*.

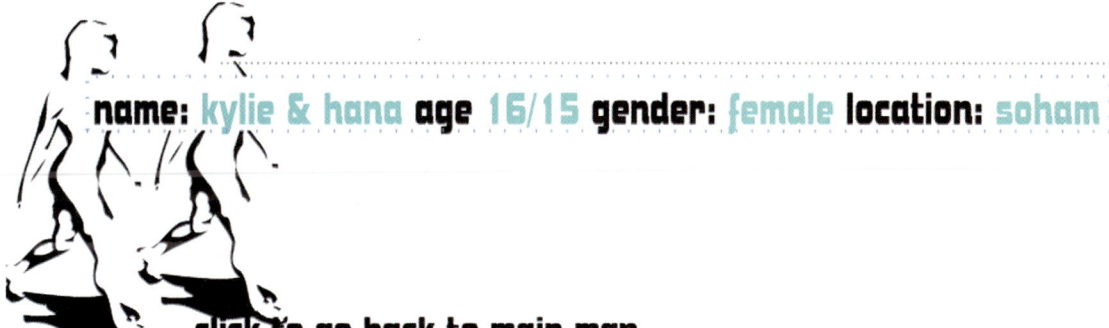

click to go back to main map

The Digital and the Domestic

# JESS LOSEBY

**J**ess Loseby is a digital artist working in the United Kingdom. Although her art usually targets the Internet, she also works with interactive installations, video, ubiquitous computing, digital imaging, and performance.

A thematic thread that runs through most of her work addresses ideas of "the cyber-domestic aesthetic." These works scrutinize the small and the domestic, while exploring notions of amplified reality and the various seams between the virtual and physical worlds.

Loseby's artwork is eclectic, ranging from a commission to teach children self-portraiture with mobile phones to digital set design for the Met Theatre in Hollywood. She was the first United Kingdom artist to undertake a totally virtual 6-month artist residency with Furtherfield.org. She has also exhibited in galleries and festivals nationally, and internationally, including London, Los Angeles, New York, Croatia, Spain, and Brazil.

A car accident at the age of 17 left Loseby paraplegic, and soon after she worked as a disability rights campaigner. Her university studies started at 26, where she completed a B.A. and an M.A. in Fine Art, with future plans for getting her Ph.D. Today, her focus is on furthering her successful art career and on building up her disability-friendly Web design company that she has just started with her husband.

Loseby reflects that her son was a meter of sorts for her progress with Flash, as she stumbled across this software after he was born in 2000. During this period she enthusiastically trawled through online resources and tutorials that were available, becoming immersed with

**Figure 4.1** The artist Jess Loseby.

**Figure 4.2** Some of the work Loseby creates on-screen ends up off-screen, as seen here in a stage production.

**Figure 4.3** Text plays an important role in most of Loseby's work.

net.art communities in the process. By the time her son was walking, Loseby was fully incorporating Flash into her creative processes.

Achieving a command over software and technology was a long and winding road for Loseby. Books, as well as a very supportive online Flash community, really supported her efforts in getting up to speed with using Flash (especially ActionScript). A disadvantage of not having formal digital training is that she was often told that she was "not using Flash correctly." This advice covered a range of topics from, "You shouldn't use Flash for manipulating video," to "You shouldn't make pieces larger than 500 pixels wide." But many people (myself included) view this as an advantage—especially with a tool whose "proper" use tends to produce generic work.

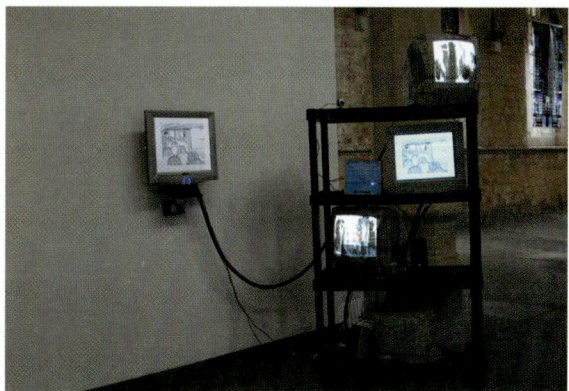

**Figure 4.4** *Position / Disposition* (2006) is an installation that uses Flash along with monitor displays to investigate how the realm of the digital comes to interface our domestic spaces.

**Figure 4.5** *The Cyber-Kitchen* (2002) is an on-line exhibition curated by Loseby. It features projects of several artists working from the conceptual premise of a domestic kitchen as a mixed technology interface, drawing comparisons to the endless cycle of consumption and elimination in a kitchen with technology-based processes.

> "My students love it when I tell them I couldn't find the off button on my first PC. It makes them realize that digital art doesn't necessarily mean being a computer wiz."

Loseby also spends one day a week converting unsuspecting fine art students to digital media at her local university, Chichester University in the UK. She humorously sums up her life as having "3 children, 2 wheels, 1 husband and 0 time."

## DIGITAL DECONSTRUCTION: *VIEWS FROM THE GROUND FLOOR*

*Views from the Ground Floor* was created with the financial assistance of The Daniel Langlois Foundation for Art, Science, and Technology in 2004. Using a combination of recorded audio, music, video, interactive Flash movies, HTML, and other media elements, the narrative of this net-film steers away from convention, finding a unique voice in the interactive blend of media that can be composed at the user's pace.

Spanning across the twelve interlinked scenes that compose *Views from the Ground Floor*, a meta-narrative unfolds that focuses on the digital conversion of domestic space. Further subcategories of repetition, creation, routines, and domestic rituals are further embedded within particular areas of the work.

*Views from the Ground Floor* relies on a technique that Loseby has really taken advantage of in her Flash work—embedding multiple Flash movies in an HTML page, rather than lumping everything in one gigantic SWF (which is the file type of a final and published FLA file). This allows for smoother interactivity as SWF files are ready on demand, but without a huge initial loading event. This technique also lends to the convenience of treating each

**Figure 4.6** A sample scene from *Views from the Ground Floor* (2004).

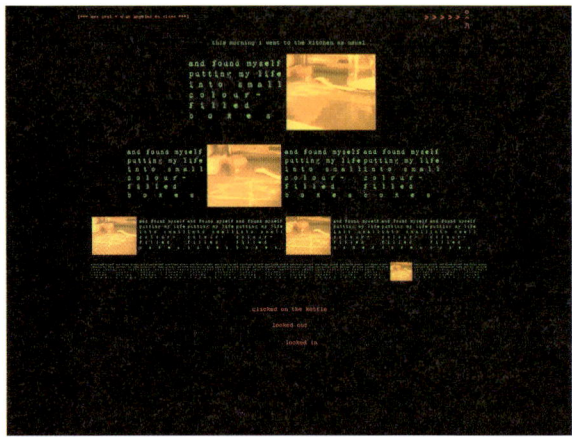

**Figure 4.7** *Views from the Ground Floor* (2004) organizes text as a structural composition element.

Flash movie independent in regard to frame rate, macro-color adjustments, and unique scale and positioning.

This project has been Loseby's most successful to date; not only being exhibited widely and receiving funding from the Daniel Langlois Foundation, but also in terms of creating connections and opportunities that have furthered her career. *Views from the Ground Floor* has also won the Premio Suzzara International Art Prize in 2005.

**Figure 4.8** Loseby's poetic narrations and compositions culminate in interactive spaces that live online.

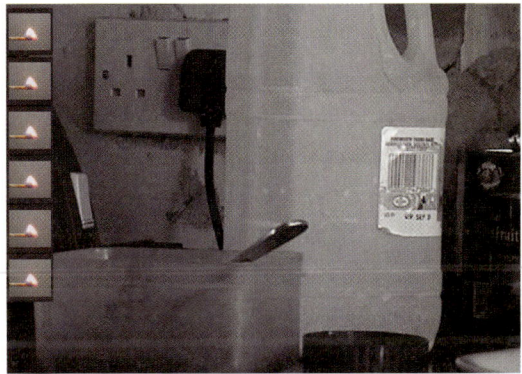

**Figure 4.9** Throughout *Views from the Ground Floor* (2004), Flash is used for interactive control and for supporting various embedded media. HTML is used as the cohesive binder for these SWF-based scenes.

**Figure 4.10** An exhibition at the Phillips Gallery realized a physical installation version of this work.

## DIY: MOVEMENT AND TEXTURE WITH ACTIONSCRIPT

Since 2001, Loseby has been using ActionScript for a number of dynamic elements in her Flash-based projects. One of these techniques involves programmed motion (sometimes constant, other times undulating), which can be witnessed in several of her projects. The following tutorial by Loseby explains the basics for how she created such effects.

### Introduction

If (like me) you will want to combine intensive video and sound in your pieces, saving size and processing power by animating via ActionScript wherever possible is vital.

Neither are particularly novel. I have seen variations repeated in numerous online tutorials and forums since the days of Flash 5. But both are quite useful in demonstrating how easily ActionScript can provide movement and texture and do so without appearing either formalized or tweened.

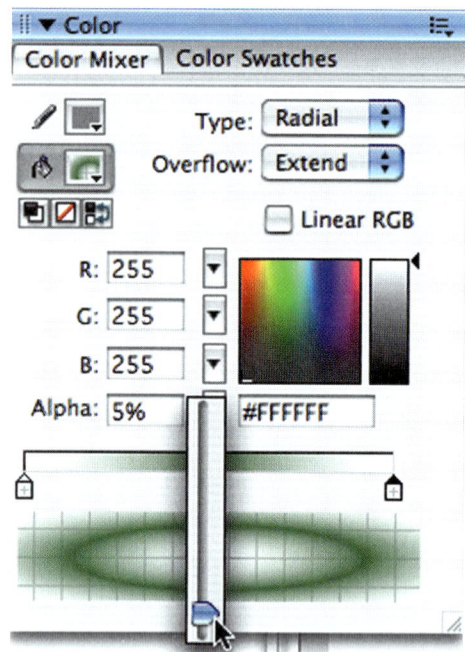

**Figure 4.11** The Alpha setting provides a greater degree of subtle control over color gradients.

1. Open a new Flash document and set the stage size to 800 × 600, frame rate kept to the standard 12fps.

2. Using the Color Mixer, set the fill style to a 3-color radial effect, using white at both ends with the Alpha set to 5% and a strong center tone (such as red, green, or blue) with the Alpha set to 100% in the middle.

3. Making sure the stroke color is disabled, create a small oval shape.

4. Modify ➡ Convert to Symbol to convert this shape into a symbol. Choose Graphic as the Type and name it **oval**.

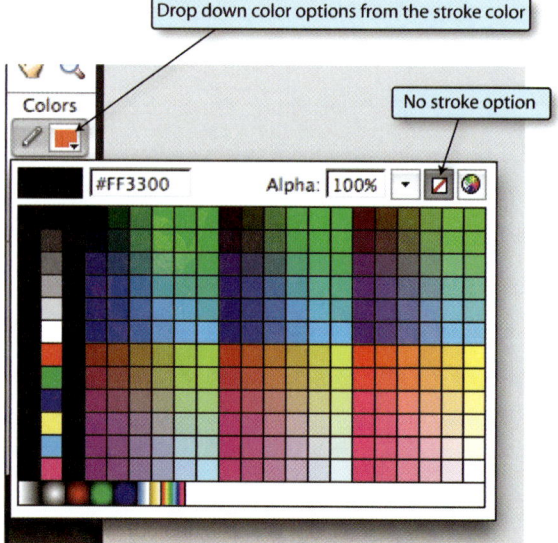

**Figure 4.12** The box with a red slash through it allows you to disable the color option.

5. Drag a copy of this graphic from the Library and place it over the first. Enlarge this top oval using the transform tool. Set the Alpha (using the Property Inspector) to 50% to create a nice little "eye candy" object.

6. Select both of these symbols, then choose Modify ➡ Convert to Symbol from the Menu, converting both of them into a movie clip.

7. Name this new movie clip **eyecandy**. Make sure you also select the advanced options and check "Export for ActionScript." Once you do this, you will be allowed to access the Linkage Identifier name. If you forget to do this when you first create the movie clip, open the movie clip's properties in the Library and add it from there.

8. Delete these symbols from the Stage. We do not need them anymore since they are in the Library. Further along, we will use the `attachMovie` method to access this graphic from the Library.

9. Change the name of our single layer to **actions** and select the first frame of this layer. Apply the following code in the Actions panel.

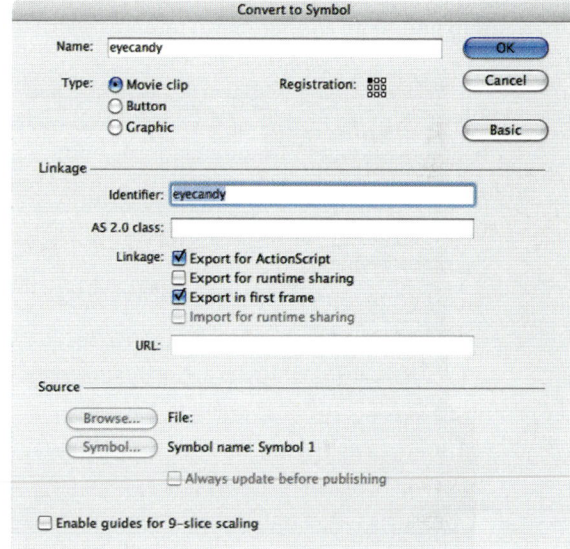

**Figure 4.13** If you want to use the `attachMovie` method, you must provide a Linkage Identifier, which is not the same as an instance name, found in the Properties Inspector. That will still be blank until you add a name.

```
function getdistance(x1, y1, x2,
y2) {
        var run, float;
        run = x2-x1;
        float = y2-y1;
        return (_root.hyp(run,
float));
}

function hyp(a, b) {
        return (Math.sqrt(a*a+b*b));
}
```

```
MovieClip.prototype.reset =
function() {
        var dist, norm;
        this.mwidth = 800;
        this.mheight = 600;
        this.x = this._x;
        this.y = this._y;
        this.speed = Math.random()
*4+2;
        this.targx = Math.random()
*this.mwidth;
        this.targy = Math.random()
*this.mheight;
        dist = _root.getdistance
(this.x, this.y, this.targx,
this.targy);
        norm = this.speed/dist;
        this.diffx = (this.targx-
this.x)*norm;
        this.diffy = (this.targy-
this.y)*norm;
}

MovieClip.prototype.move =
function() {
        trace(this.targx);
        if (_root.getdistance
(this._x, this._y, this.targx,
this.targy)>this.speed) {
                this.x += this.diffx;
                this.y += this.diffy;
        } else {
                this.x = this.targx;
                this.y = this.targy;
                if (!this.t) {
                        this.t =
getTimer();
                }
                if (getTimer()-
this.t>1000) {
                        this.reset();
                        this.t = 0;
                }
        }
        this._x = this.x;
        this._y = this.y;
}
movieHolder = new Array();
for(i=0; i<30; i++){
    movieHolder.push(_root.
attachMovie("eyecandy","
ec2"+i, i));
        movieHolder[i].reset();
        }
        this.onEnterFrame = function()
{

        for(i=0; i<30; i++){

        movieHolder[i].move();
}

}
```

These four functions are crucial for the system that will evolve once you run the movie (and we finish our ActionScript!). The first function, `getdistance`, takes four parameters, which are the X and Y values of two different objects, and returns the hypotenuse based on a function call to the second function: `hyp()`. The last two functions are prototypes; they extend the `MovieClip Class` by using the `MovieClip.prototype.nameOfFunction` syntax.

These two prototype functions are the main engines of these particles. The `reset` function establishes the X and Y coordinates for the movie clip and a target. It also figures out the distance between the target and movie clip and uses a little math to establish a velocity for propelling the movie clip toward its destination. The `move` function advances our movie clips to a random

## CHAPTER FOUR

target as well as resets them after a certain amount of time.

10. Now test your movie! Your Flash movie should look like some kind of micro-cellular activity. If you get stuck, go into the Chapter 4 folder of the DVD and open the file named *motion_end.fla*. In Chapter 12, we will investigate how to do something like this with OOP (Object Oriented Programming).

---

**NOTE:** Flash programmers cautiously use the `MovieClip.prototype.nameOfFunction`. Because all movie clips will inherit this method (whether calling it or not), `prototype` can be cumbersome in a complex Flash movie and drag down performance significantly. On the other hand, it is a fast and easy way to add customized functionality to the MovieClip class!

---

As you can see, this relatively rapid process allows a rather nice organic feel to these simplistic little clips. It is also worth adding alpha and rotation code to this sequence for a more dynamic animation.

Now we can add a secondary ActionScripted animation layer.

1. Create a new symbol (Insert ➡ New Symbol). Name it **linedance** and set the type to Movie clip. Be sure to check "Export for ActionScript."

2. From the Tools panel, set the fill color to none and select a red color for the stroke.

3. Make sure you are inside the **linedance** movie clip, select the first frame and using the pencil tool, draw the first stroke that will combine with others to make a large circle around the Stage.

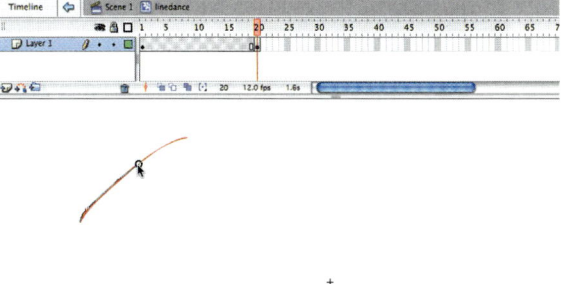

**Figure 4.14** Drag the end of each new line to snap to the end of the previous one.

4. Click on frame 20 in the Timeline. Go to Insert ➡ Timeline ➡ Keyframe. This will make a new keyframe including the graphical content from the previous keyframe on frame 1. From the end of that stroke, draw the same length (approximately) in a counterclockwise direction. If the lines do not quite touch, use the Selection Tool to merge the two lines.

5. Make keyframes every twenty frames up until frame 200, drawing connecting line segments on each one until you have made a complete circle. Now go back to each keyframe that you made and add a Shape Tween to each one using the Property Inspector.

6. Return to the main Timeline, create a new layer, name it **control**, and drag **linedance** from the Library onto this layer. Place it in the upper-left corner of the Stage.

7. Select the **linedance** movie clip again and convert it to another movie clip (selecting F8 or Modify ➡ Convert to Symbol) called **control**.

8. Open the **control** movie clip (double-click it) and change the only layer name to **actions**.

9. Select frame 1 of the **actions** layer and type the following code in the Actions panel.

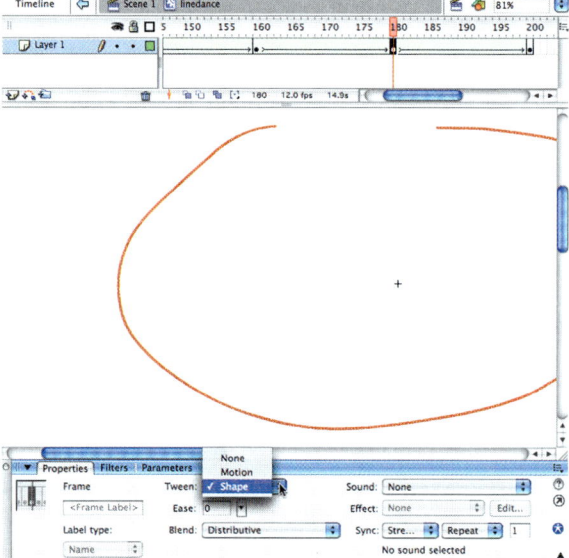

**Figure 4.15** Each line keyframe should be set to Shape Tween.

```
dir = 1;
sdir = 1;
var lines:Array = new Array();
for(x = 1; x< 50; x++){
        lines[x] = attachMovie
("linedance", "linedance"+x,x);
        lines[x]._xscale = 200-
((x*7.3)-1.05);
        lines[x]._yscale = 200-
((x*7.3)-1.05);
```

```
         lines[x]._alpha *=.95;
         lines[x]._x =200;
         lines[x]._y =200;
}
```

10. Create a new keyframe on frame 2 and add the following code to this frame:

```
for(x = 1; x< 50; x++){
         lines[x]._xscale *=
1.005*sdir;
         lines[x]._yscale *=
1.005*sdir;
         lines[x]._alpha-=(.5*dir);

if(lines[x]._alpha<10)dir*=-1;
if(lines[x]._alpha>100)dir*=-1;
if(lines[x]._xscale<10)sdir*=-1;
if(lines[x]._yscale>100)sdir*=-1;
}
```

11. Create another new keyframe on frame 3 and add this final code.

```
gotoAndPlay(2);
```

Since we are using an `attachMovie` method in the first frame, make sure that the **linedance** movie clip has `linedance` typed in for the Linkage Identifier.

12. Test your movie. If you get stuck along the way, open the *motion_end2.fla* in the *Chapter_04* folder on the DVD.

## DIGITAL DECONSTRUCTION: *DOC-U*

As with many of Loseby's projects, *doc-u* has two versions, a physical installation as well as a virtual screen-based interface. The work is the realization of a commission from the Babylon Gallery in Ely, UK. The commission was composed of a yearlong series of workshops where people were invited to create their own micro-documentaries (doc-us) using mobile phones which are now presented in online and onsite versions of the final work.

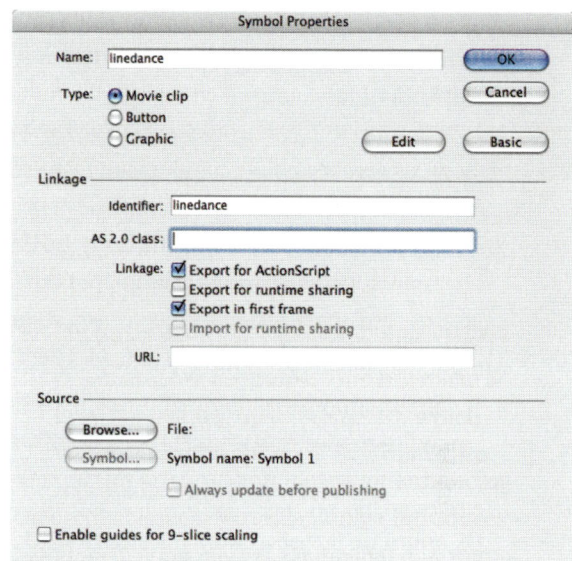

**Figure 4.16** The Linkage Identifier is how an `attachMovie` method knows what movie clip to look for.

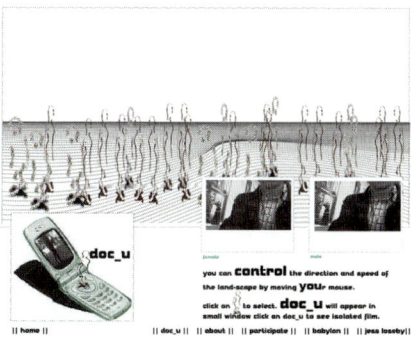

**Figure 4.17** The splash page for *doc-u* (2005).

Flash was integral to this work, providing the mechanics and delivery of the project. Participants as young as 18 months old (in toddler groups) to 70 (in workshops) were shown how easy mobile phone cameras can be used to build up a visual documentary of their lives. Loseby based this project on mobile phone photography because its ubiquity removed both the fear of "making art" and the perceived pressure to "take a good photograph." These mobile phone pictures were fed into Flash (which ranged from 5 to 200 images per doc-u) and animated to produce the documentaries. Users were able to click and freeze images as they flickered by.

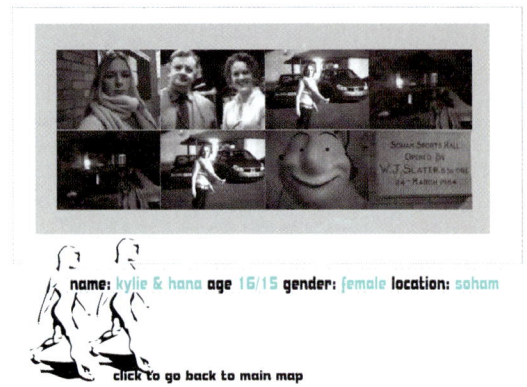

**Figure 4.18** In addition to the mobile phone images, each doc-u shows information about the participant.

The interface itself is a mixture of ActionScript and tween-based animation. The undulating landscape and walking figures were inspired by some tutorials Loseby came across early in her Flash

**Figure 4.19** The invitation for *doc-u* at the Babylon Gallery features several images from the project.

research. Each one acts as avatar-links for allowing the user to access the photo-documentaries. Loseby has since used similar animation techniques in creating a personal avatar.

## ON YOUR OWN

Loseby's DIY section covered some valuable techniques that combine ActionScript with drawn graphics for creating dynamic animation. To further these techniques, you can try multiplying the movie clips, offsetting them a bit, and perhaps rotating and altering their opacity. Loseby warns that adding too many movie clips can cause the Flash movie to behave erratically or play slowly.

To see how this will work on various connections, I recommend using some of the tools from the Menu of the Flash player. By going to View ➡ Simulate Download, you can bypass your personal computer's speed and see how a different system will handle your streaming file. Going to View ➡ Download Settings, you can choose different Internet connection speeds to simulate. Loseby also recommends that these effects be applied to other visual forms, such as text, vector drawings, or imported bitmaps.

Most importantly, I hope you will find inspiration from the themes and concepts surrounding Loseby's artwork. Anyone can plug away in the Actions panel and arrive at some cool looking generative animation. The key is then to provide a good concept with these experiments in aesthetics.

# 5 MICHAEL TAKEO MAGRUDER

Working with Color and Matrices

# MICHAEL TAKEO MAGRUDER

American artist Michael Takeo Magruder lives in the United Kingdom and works in the field of new, technology-based media. Many of his projects use the programming, networking, and media capabilities of Flash in conjunction with other applications and techniques. Just a sample from his diverse modes of production and presentation includes 3D worlds using VRML (virtual reality markup language), artwork for mobile phone/PDA display, stained glass windows, interactive Net art projects, and real-time data mining installations. Within this range of practice, a cohesive yet evolving vision has been guiding his work over the years, gaining much acclaim as his work has been exhibited widely on an international level.

**Figure 5.1** *Monolith[s]* (2006) uses Flash, VRML, and JAVA to create a real-time interactive 3D environment.

Most of the content driving Takeo Magruder's work deals with specific relationships between mass media and the individuals experiencing these forms of communication. Through experiencing these artworks, a variety of questions are raised: How do people construe reality from edited and censored news sources?

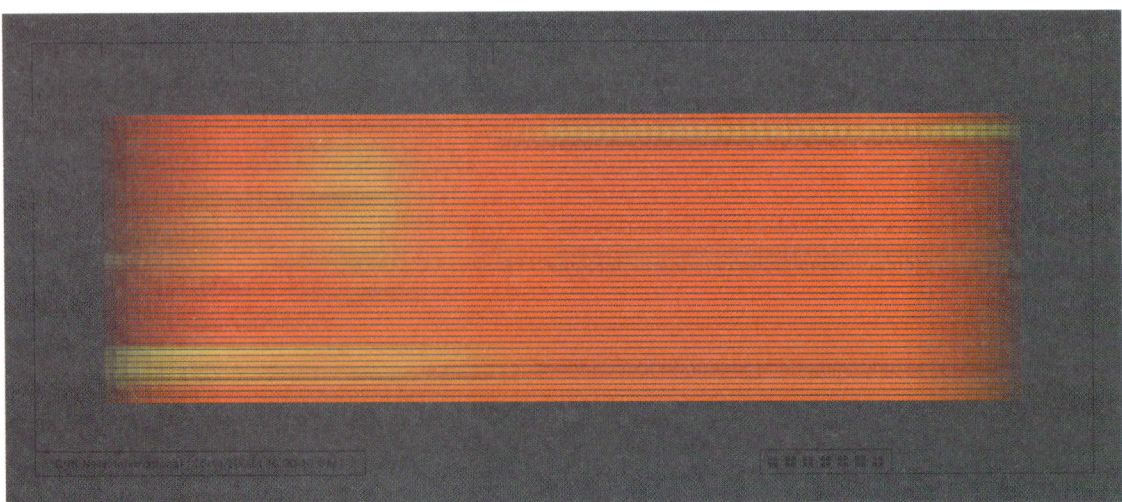

**Figure 5.2** *Codec* (2002) exemplifies how the human image is dissolved within the pixel matrix view of technology. While a beautiful image, this piece also alludes to the filtering process of mass media.

How do emerging information technologies redefine the way humans communicate? How does mediation by these technologies alter human perception and concepts of time and space? How do these questions affect both our personal and collective memories and world views? Takeo Magruder collects data from the Internet as a form of consensus reality, giving life to the symbols and forms in his work. Together, these elements stylize a visual metaphor for mass media and an alluring environment for interaction.

Considering Takeo Magruder's work <Event> as a specific example, the viewer is confronted with a series of compositions taken from events that were covered by international news networks. The artwork is constructed exclusively of images, texts, videos, and sounds from actual news data on the Internet in response to the events. The text sources become the rendering pixels for video of the same event. By layering the two media streams in this way, both the visual and text information are obscured; people, places, and facts are lost within the forces that create the revisionist histories woven by pervasive media networks.

<Event>, like the majority of Takeo Magruder's artworks, has been very successful within both the online art community and the traditional art establishment. His résumé consists of innumerable international exhibitions at highly reputable venues and festivals. A large number of these works have also been commissioned from notable organizations such as the Arts Council of England, the National Endowment for the Arts, *www.Soundtoys.net*, and *www.Turbulence.org*. Currently, Takeo is continuing a long tenure as an artist and researcher in King's Visualization Lab at King's College London.

**Figure 5.3** The intriguing formal elements of <Event> (2004) coincide with the artwork's substantive conceptual exploration of mass media's ability to obscure facts.

**Figure 5.4** Takeo Magruder works with whatever medium is best suited for a project. In this instance, *Communion* (2006), a site-specific installation in a deconsecrated church, features futuristic "stained-glass windows," constructed Duratrans, and aluminum.

With an undergraduate degree in biology, Takeo Magruder has no formal training using computer art software or techniques. He taught himself to use Flash, software he dabbled in for some time, but did not implement as a tool for making art until 2002.

As with many artists, career twists are not thrown away, but become incorporated as evolutionary stepping-stones that define their work. Biology provides a definitive influence in Takeo Magruder's work, made clear through a careful examination of human existence: how we communicate, conduct commerce, remember images and stories, and express our thoughts and emotions. Takeo Magruder's research explores how human biology (especially our means of perception) is now negotiated through the computer and its descendant technologies. In an interesting way, the formal aspects of his work find visual juxtaposition in referencing both the biological and digital realms.

## DIGITAL DECONSTRUCTION: [ FALLUJAH . IRAQ . 31/03/2004 ]

The "1st war for the Internet" is how Takeo Magruder refers to the current Iraqi war. He notes the recent changes in how news is created and told:

> "As a consequence of technological advances, the Media now generates a 'real-time' history in which the infinitesimal lag between subject acquisition, journalistic structuring, and public broadcast engenders a reflexive loop susceptible to subversive alteration. Considering the interpretive spectrum between ethical filtering of content and manipulative remixing of data, we must question the validity of the 'factual' information, which permeates our everyday, and consider the implications of its instantaneous dissemination."

**Figure 5.5** Peering into the depths of *Data_cosm* (2005): Is it a visualization of biological cell walls or digital firewalls?

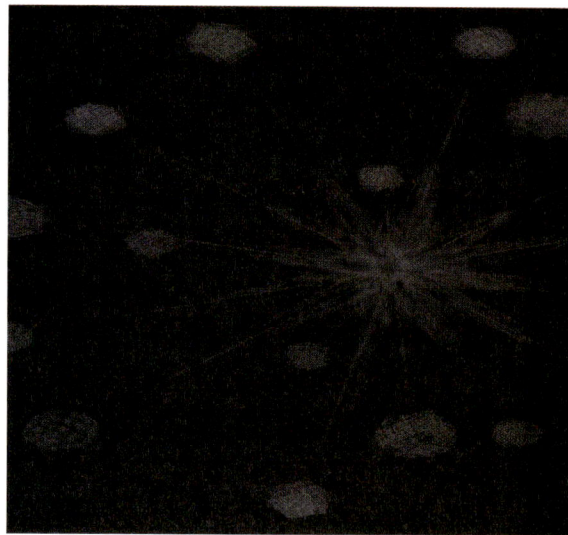

**Figure 5.6** *World[s]* (2006), oscillates between the micro and the macro.

Takeo created [ Fallujah . Iraq . 31/03/2004 ] as a response to the practices that now pervade all large corporate news organizations. Specifically, this work examines events that become emblazoned in the minds of those who read the popular news sources. The event in question occurred in Fallujah, Iraq, in March of 2004, when four civilian contractors were kidnapped, murdered, and their burned corpses were strung across a bridge. Research leading up to the actual artwork discovered that the greater portion of the event was filmed by an Associated Press camera crew, there was no intervention by coalition forces during the entire episode, the coverage of the event was highly censored on all international media networks, and the casualties were mercenaries employed by Blackwater Security Consulting of Moyock, N.C.

Takeo Magruder did not intend to enter into the discourse of '"the evil nature of war" with this work. The conceptual focus is more about questioning how and why we absorb perceived news items as fact. [ Fallujah . Iraq . 31/03/2004 ] also examines how conflict has become anesthetized in this new millennium. Heavily edited news items are crystallized into easily redistributable packets of pixels; they exist as icons traveling at light speed, being read simultaneously by millions of people at one time.

Technically, [ Fallujah . Iraq . 31/03/2004 ] was created by combining techniques from multiple software applications. Adobe After Effects was used for pre-production, mainly to clean up the quality of the pirate video Webfeed into something usable within Flash. A custom Java application performs the data mining of video, audio, and text. When the project first loads, we see images that are iconic to most people who regularly read mainstream

**Figure 5.7** [ Fallujah . Iraq . 31/03/2004 ] (2004) begins with a video that was used as historical marker, then layers of related news source text pours onto the screen.

**Figure 5.8** The video scenes from [ Fallujah . Iraq . 31/03/2004 ] quickly become overloaded with text.

Internet news sources: burned out cars, a sequence of mutilated bodies on the street, then presumably the same bodies hanging from a bridge. After the video/audio plays for a moment, text begins to load onto the page, piling up to the point of illegibility—a crescendo of the work's commentary on the opaque nature of the media. To achieve this, Takeo Magruder employed techniques working with loading random text. Flash is exceptionally good at working with external text files—several methods exist in ActionScript for accomplishing such tasks:

1. Create a new FLA file.

2. It all starts with a dynamic text field. To create one, you first need to select a keyframe to put your code on and open the Actions panel. Type in the following code:

```
_root.createTextField("myText",1, 100,100,200,100);
```

_root is typed before the function call, because in this example, we are placing the text field directly on the main Timeline (_root). Notice that there are six parameters ("myText", 1, 100, 100, 400, 100). "myText" is the instance name of the new text field. If we want to do anything with this text field in the future, we will access it through this instance name. The second parameter (the number 1) is the depth. The next two parameters (100 and 100) are the x and y positions that define where this text field will be placed on the Stage. The final two parameters are the width (400) and height (100).

3. Now to actually have text loaded into this text field, use a text editor on your computer (like TextEdit for a Mac, or Notepad on Windows) and type something like this:

```
quote1=Don't hate the media become the media - Jello Biafra&quote2=Any sufficiently advanced technology is indistinguishable from magic - A.C. Clarke&quote3=The street finds its own uses for technology - William Gibson&quote4=Every great advance in natural knowledge has involved the absolute rejection of authority - Sir Thomas Huxley
```

4. Be sure to save this file as a text file in the same location as your FLA, and name it *quotes.txt*. (The .txt extension is important—it means *plaintext*, or text without any special formatting marks. In TextEdit, choose format ➡ Make Plain Text before saving.)

5. Now, to load the text into your Flash file, you need to set up some more code. Add the following code after the previous `createTextField()` line.

```
quote = new LoadVars();
quote.onLoad = function(success) {
if (success) {
getRandom = Math.ceil(Math.random()*4);
randomQuote = this["quote"+getRandom];
myText.text = randomQuote;
}
else {
newQuote.text = "error";
}
}
quote.load("quotes.txt");
stop();
```

This additional code consists of three primary parts. First, create a `LoadVars` object called `quote`. Remember, creating an object may only consist as one typed line, but a whole lot more is happening behind the scenes. In this case, the `LoadVars` object `quote` is the recipient of all the methods and properties that exist within the `LoadVars` class. This is important, because the next line, `quote.onLoad`, is calling the method that will be executed when the `quote.load` function (towards the end of your code) has completed. Inside this method, you have logic statements that will handle two different scenarios: if the loading of your text has failed for some reason, `"error"` is sent to your dynamic text field; if successful, a random number is created and then concatenated with the string `"quote"` to actually pull the proper value from your loaded text file.

6. Be sure you save the FLA file and your TXT file in the same directory—then give it a try! More elaborate things can be done with dynamic text, especially using XML, and also working with other scripts using PHP. But this will get you started.

### DIY: CONTROLLING COLOR WITH ACTIONSCRIPT

Several qualities stand out in Takeo Magruder's work. While the conceptual content and techniques incorporating data mining have been the focus up to this point, people who interact with his work also frequently comment on his use of color. GUI (Graphical User Interface) tools in Flash deliver great freedom for working with color in an intuitive manner. But a much more articulate sense of control can be achieved when ActionScript is put into service. Takeo Magruder uses color objects extensively in his code. This section will cover some of the general groundwork for using color objects with ActionScript.

1. Start by opening the file on the DVD titled *color_start.fla*, in the Chapter_05 folder. The document will consist of a basic gray screen with some text arranged on it. We will use this text as a guide for placing the other media elements onto the Stage. You will also notice four layers, three of which are empty. Before we begin adding more elements, click on each of the four dynamic text boxes on the right side of the Stage—notice (in the Property inspector) that they already have variables assigned to them. This will reflect the current values of red, green, blue, and alpha when we adjust the sliders, which we will be adding next.

2. Drag the movie clip named **slider** from the Library onto the Stage. Center it between the **RB** text box on the left and the dynamic text box with the variable name `myRB` on the right. With this movie clip selected, go to the Property inspector and give this movie clip an instance name called `Slider_RB`. In the same window, move the Color selector from None to Advanced, then click the setting button next to it. This will open a pop-up window. Change the Blue and Green settings to –100.

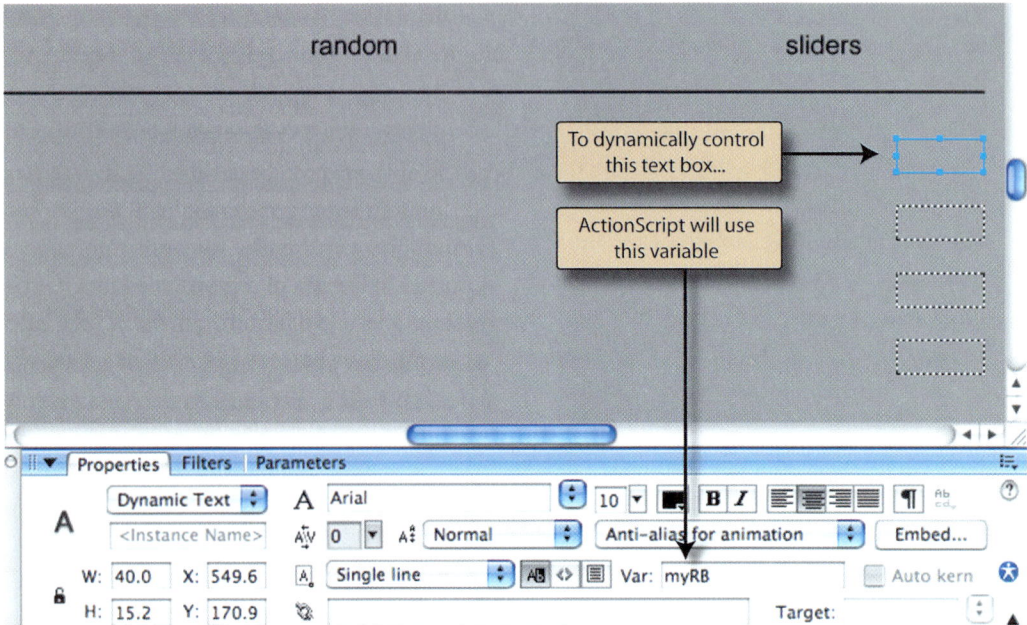

**Figure 5.9** When you select each dynamic text box, you can see the Var: box in the Property inspector change. These values will link directly to the ActionScript we are about to create.

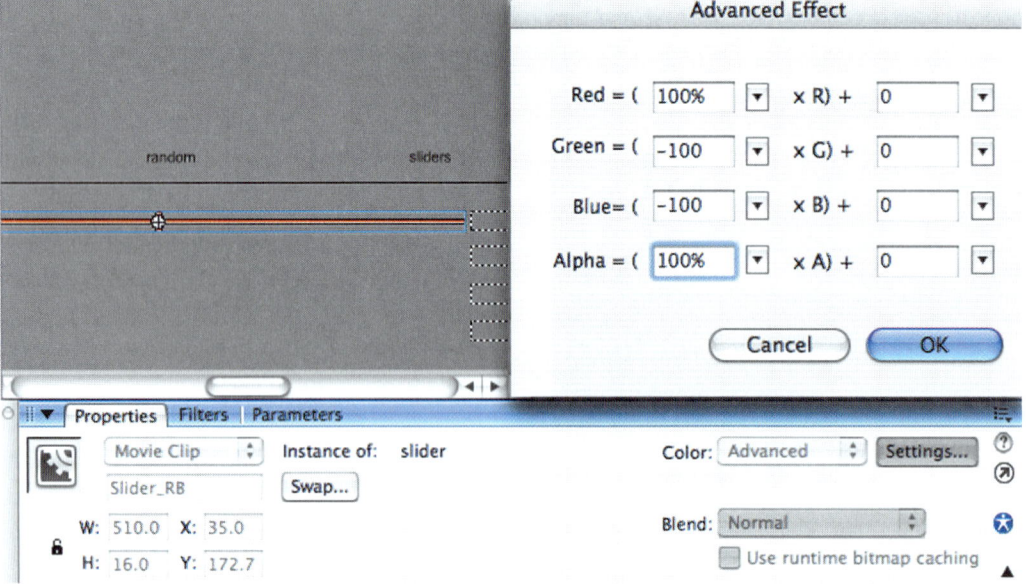

**Figure 5.10** You can change the color effects of a movie clip by adjusting the Advanced settings in the Property inspector.

3. Drag three more instances of the **slider** movie clip from the Library onto the Stage, making sure that the **Slider** layer is still selected. Center them in the appropriate place on the Stage. Perform the same alterations to these movie clips, creating instance names and adjusting the color effects in the Property inspector. For the movie clip with the instance name `Slider_GB`, change the red and blue channels in the advanced color settings to –100. For the `Slider_BB` movie clip, set Red to –100 and Green to –100.

4. Make sure the Actions panel is open, then select the red slider (the one you gave an instance name of `Slider_RB`). In the Actions panel, type the following code:

```
onClipEvent (enterFrame) {
    _root.myRB = Math.round
(_root.Slider_RB.knob._x);
    }
```

Now test your movie (Control ➡ Test Movie). If you move the slider back and forth on the red bar, you will see corresponding values appear in the dynamic text box to the right of it. But what is allowing the slider to move when dragging it? Double-click the red slider, then once inside that movie clip, double-click the small movie clip in the center (it has an instance name of `knob`). Now, click once on the small button in the middle of the slider, then look at the Actions panel—you will see that the following code was already placed there for you:

```
on (press) {
        startDrag("", false,
-255, 0, 255, 0);
}
on (release, releaseOutside) {
        stopDrag();
}
```

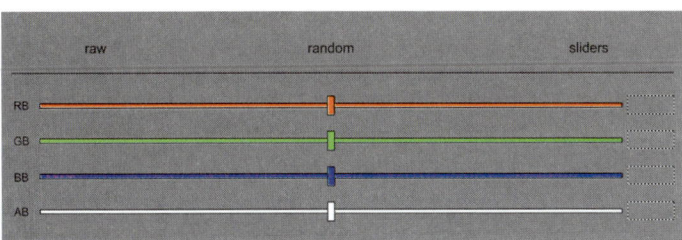

**Figure 5.11** All four sliders positioned with applied color effects.

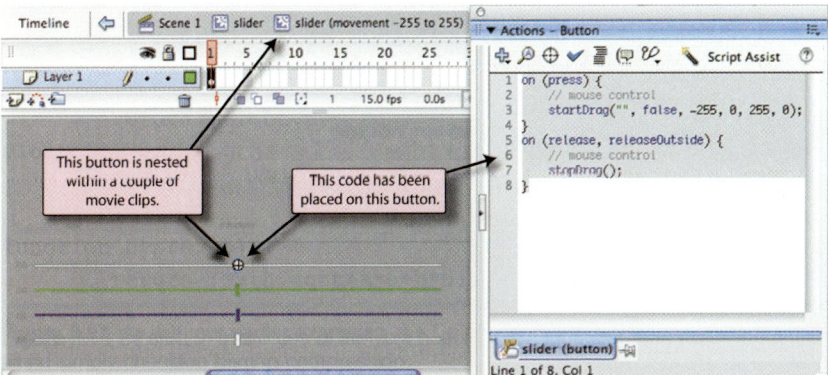

**Figure 5.12** This slider button is nested within a couple of movie clips.

5. Quickly return to the main Timeline (_root) by clicking **Scene 1** at the top of the Timeline window. Add similar code to the other slider movie clips by first selecting the movie clip, then typing the appropriate code for the selected slider into the Actions panel.

For the green slider:

```
onClipEvent(enterFrame) {
_root.myGB = Math.round(_root.
Slider_GB.knob._x);
}
```

For the blue slider:

```
onClipEvent(enterFrame) {
_root.myBB = Math.round(_root.
Slider_BB.knob._x);
}
```

For the alpha channel slider:

```
onClipEvent(enterFrame) {
_root.myAB = Math.round(_root.
Slider_AB.knob._x);
}
```

Test your movie again to make sure all of the sliders work and that they properly change the corresponding dynamic text box values.

6. For our sliders to alter something other than the dynamic text box, we need to bring in a movie clip from the Library. With frame 1 of the **Video** layer selected, drag the clip called **test clip-Movie** from the Library onto the Stage. Place this clip towards the top left, above the text that says **raw**. This instance of the movie clip will simply show us the raw video. Drag another instance from the Library onto the Stage (with the Video layer still selected) above the text that reads **sliders**. With the movie clip on the Stage selected, give this movie clip an instance name of `slider_mc`.

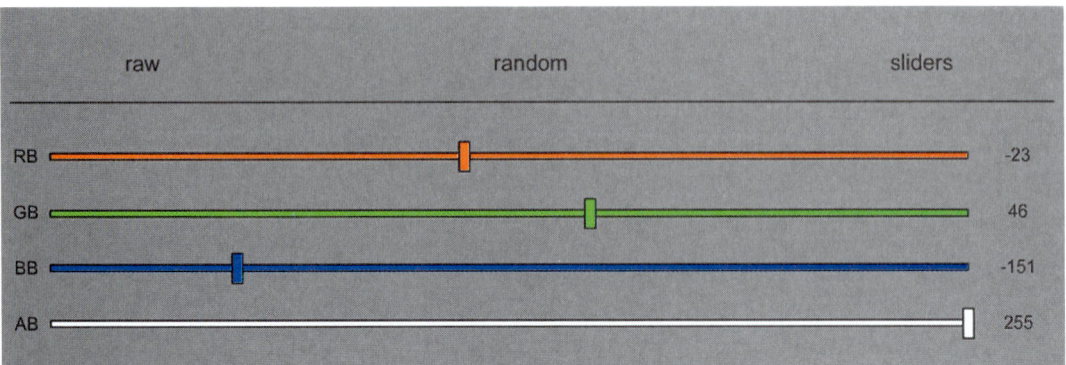

**Figure 5.13** All four sliders set to different levels.

7. The `slider_mc` movie clip is not going to change color according to the sliders on its own! With this movie clip selected on the Stage, type the following code into the Actions panel:

```
onClipEvent (enterFrame) {
    myColor = new Color(_root.slider_mc);
    myColorTransform = new Object();
    myColorTransform.ra = 100;
    myColorTransform.rb = (_root.Slider_RB.knob._x);
    myColorTransform.ga = 100;
    myColorTransform.gb = (_root.Slider_GB.knob._x);
    myColorTransform.ba = 100;
    myColorTransform.bb = (_root.Slider_BB.knob._x);
    myColorTransform.aa = 100;
    myColorTransform.ab = (_root.Slider_AB.knob._x);
    myColor.setTransform(myColorTransform);
}
```

This code you just put onto the movie clip is essentially doing three things. First, a custom color object, `myColor`, is created along with a generic object `myColorTransform`). The `myColor` object is set to the `slider_mc` movie clip, so anything we do to this color object will alter the color of that movie clip—a simple but very powerful line of code!

With `myColorTransform`, several new properties are established: `ra`, `ba`, `ga`, and `aa` are percentages for these channels, while `rb`, `bb`, `gb` and `ab` are offsets. The percentages can receive values from –100 to 100 and the offsets work with values from –255 to 255. To keep things simple, all of the percentages are kept at a default of 100, while the offsets are rigged up to receive values based on the slider positions on the Stage.

The last part of the code takes the `myColorTransform` object (along with its 6 properties) and applies it to the `setTransform()` method of the `myColor` object. Voila—the interface and display are hotwired together. Test the movie and try moving the sliders around.

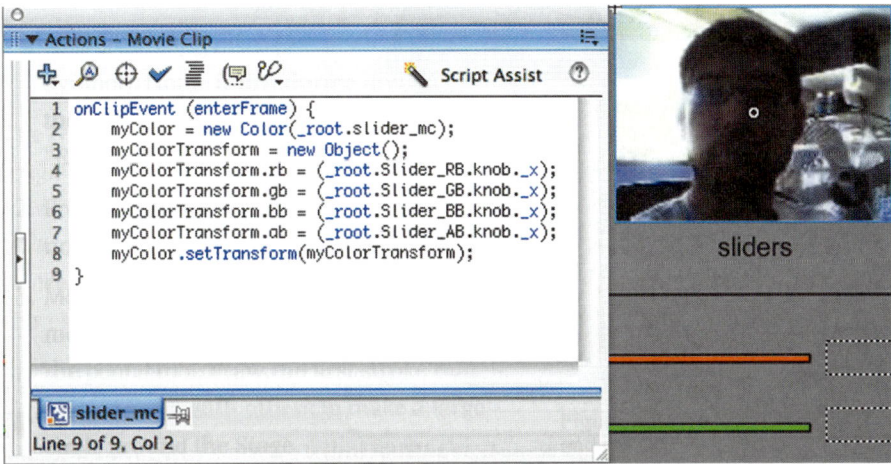

**Figure 5.14** Placing this code on the movie clip will link its color properties to the slider interface.

8. Drag one **more test clip-Movie** movie clip from the Library to the Stage (with the Video layer selected). Give this movie clip an instance name called `random_mc`. Now select frame 1 of the layer called **Code**. Type the following into the Actions panel:

```
function ColorChange() {
        myColor = new Color(_root.random_mc);
        myColorTransform = new Object();
        myColorTransform.ra = ((Math.floor(Math.random()*201))-100);
        myColorTransform.rb = ((Math.floor(Math.random()*511))-255);
        myColorTransform.ga = ((Math.floor(Math.random()*201))-100);
        myColorTransform.gb = ((Math.floor(Math.random()*511))-255);
        myColorTransform.ba = ((Math.floor(Math.random()*201))-100);
        myColorTransform.bb = ((Math.floor(Math.random()*511))-255);
        myColorTransform.aa = 100;
        myColorTransform.ab = 0;
        myColor.setTransform(myColorTransform);
}
ColorChange();
```

This code is going to work in a similar manner to the code we typed directly to the `slider_mc` movie clip. Here you can see that a function called `ColorChange()` is defined. Within this function, `Math.random()` is being used to calculate varied and unpredictable values to be applied to the color channels.

Try out your movie and see what happens. The `random_mc` movie clip indeed receives a random color assignment from the code, but then it does not change. This is because there is only one frame that loads, then remains static. The video movie clips keep playing because they have their own internal Timelines. Double-click one of them and you will see they have 120 frames in their Timeline.

9. Now add an additional frame to the main Timeline so the random color function will recursively reinitialize. Select all 4 layers of frame 2, then control-click (right-click on a PC) the highlighted frames. A pop-up menu will open, allowing you to select Insert Frame—you should now have an extra frame in your Timeline.

10. Test your movie now—notice how the `random_mc` movie clip now randomly switches color. This is because the Flash file is now looping back to execute the code sitting on frame 1.

Calling a function on the same frame where the function is defined is not exactly the cleanest way to code something: there is no reason to repeatedly rebuild the function each time we want to call it. But this illustrates the general concept.

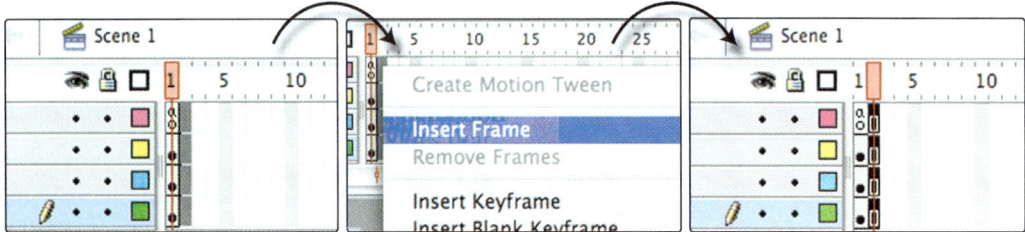

**Figure 5.15** After highlighting the whole column, insert frames for all of these layers.

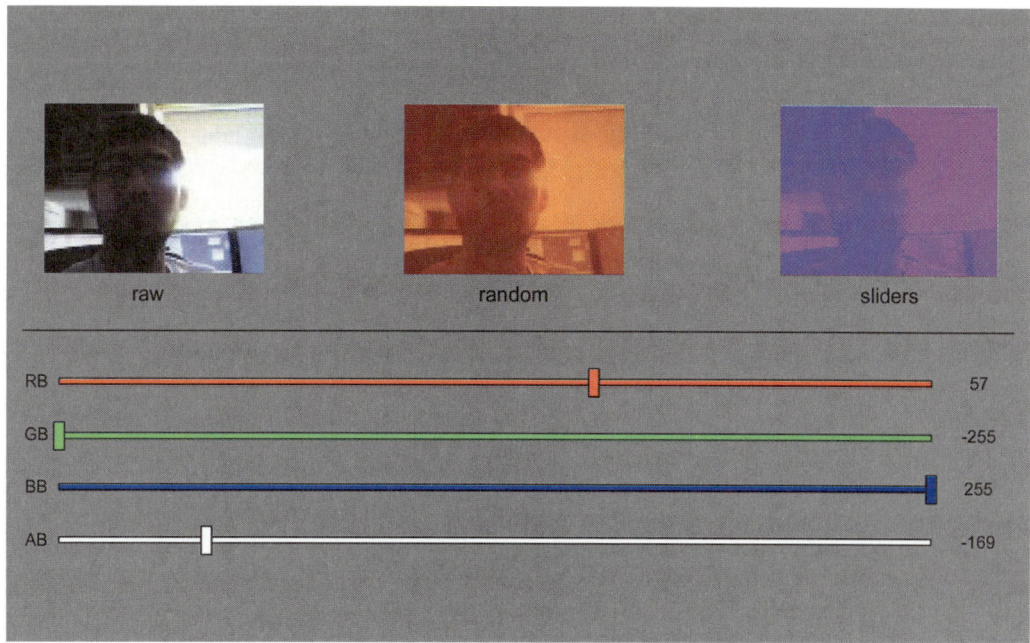

**Figure 5.16** The completed demo with random slider controlled colors.

## DIGITAL DECONSTRUCTION: { TRANSCRIPTION }

While most Flash work is targeted for the Web, some projects require on-site installation to successfully reveal the full scope of the work. Designed specifically for the Courtauld Institute of Art's six-level staircase, { *transcription* } is a real-time media installation that combines generative audio-visuals with wall-drawn elements. The digital projection spans across a screen using a back-projection system at the lowest level of the stairwell. Pulsing and morphing across this horizontal space are streams of images and text gathered from live BBC news sources.

Supporting the imagery from the news sources, while at moments completely obscuring them from recognition, are a matrix of cryptic symbols that reference machine code.

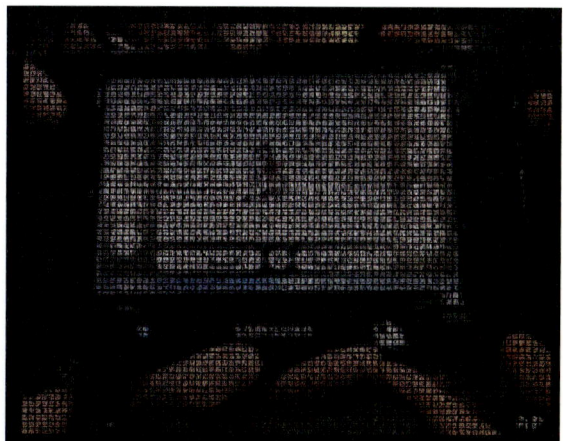

**Figure 5.17** A matrix of cryptic symbols generated from the re-assembly of BBC's news texts are the pixel source for the imagery, but also the cause for their obscurity.

Surround-sound audio of related news permeates the space—reinforcing the obfuscation of the media sources by fading back and forth between clarity and ambient noise. Overall, the work creates an eerie sense of mystique, as the news sources are familiar when they come into audio and visual focus, but when fading into abstraction, provide a form of opaque beauty. By obscuring the news data through this method of formal feedback, it helps us to reflect upon how it is hard to obtain a tacit feel or urgency for what is happening in the world around us. In this way, { *transcription* } is vital to the times we live in.

## ON YOUR OWN

This chapter provided some technical overviews for working with color mixing using the color object and importing text into Flash from an external file. More importantly, Michael Takeo Magruder's artworks were deconstructed as examples of where technical aspects of Flash were used as a vehicle for provocative and engaging theories and concepts. While the examples are meant to provide you with a solid understanding of how Flash can work with media and formal structures, you can easily evolve even these simple exercises into something more engaging and personal. Try finding three different news sources that portray mass media perspectives of a given event. Save the text and images from these sources into a directory on your computer. Then, produce a Flash document that uses this data in a visual and interactive design that conveys your feelings about the topic.

**Figure 5.18** Images come in and out of focus, allowing the viewer to recognize objects, then focus on curious symbols, and sometimes perceive nothing more than a diffused ambient field of pixels.

Interactive Environments

# JULIET DAVIS

**J**uliet Davis is a multimedia artist who has been working with Flash since 1999. Incorporating a methodology that positions concepts as both a starting point and a structural base, the interactive elements in her work are strategically added to engage the viewer far beyond the typical attention span for online interaction. Her career is highlighted by a collection of projects that generate dialogue around issues of technology, economics, gender, race, and other social issues. These works have gained recognition by a variety of renowned venues, including: SIGGRAPH, FILE, IDMAA, the Institute of Contemporary Art (London), and MAXXI Museum (Rome).

---

Although she grew up in the conservative environment of rural Indiana, Davis's mother and grandmother supported all of her artistic endeavors. Having such strong role models gave Davis the confidence and guidance to pursue a career as an artist and professor. When she entered college, Davis was drawn towards feminism and other social theories that question various power structures in society.

A diverse education in the liberal arts was crucial to Davis's artistic direction. She earned a B.A. in Honors English from Indiana University, an M.A.T. in English from Brown University, and an M.F.A. in Visual Art from Vermont College. At Brown she met Theodore Sizer, an early champion of interdisciplinary studies and nontraditional approaches to knowledge, an obvious influence for Davis who often references several disciplines in her artwork. Through Vermont College's unique partial-residency program, she was able to work with Faith Wilding, whose subRosa projects, and writing on cyberfeminism continue to inspire Davis.

Currently, Davis is a professor at the University of Tampa, where she builds Flash into her classroom practice. While software like Flash wields an enormous set of possibilities, her pedagogy stresses content; Davis is quite aware of how easy it is to be lured into the software features that can homogenize the creative process. To encourage students away from this entrapment, she advises them to think about their own passions and to actively bring controversial issues into their work.

## DIGITAL DECONSTRUCTION: ALTAR-ATIONS

In line with what Juliet encourages for her students, her own artwork is imbued with intriguing content and a wide range of visual and aural media elements. *Altar-ations* is a recent work that, upon first view, greets the user with what appears to be a retail Website for wedding accessories. In this way, the user is seduced into the semantics of commercial online culture.

In creating the splash page for this work, Davis made use of a Mask layer in Flash. Masks in Flash work in a manner similar to other programs; they only reveal exactly what is below them by using a tandem of Mask and Masked layers. This feature allows the artist to layout a variety of forms and graphics, but the final composition is largely dictated by this viewport.

Hovering over the navigational choices, the user is subtly introduced to the fact that the Website may not be what it seems. There are links for "Plan your WEDDING" and "Choose your ENGAGMENT RING" -supporting the notion that the site is the front-end for an eCommerce business. But what about "Make a better BABY" and "VIRGINITY management"?

**Figure 6.1** The splash page of *Altar-ations* (2006) appears to be a corporate Website.

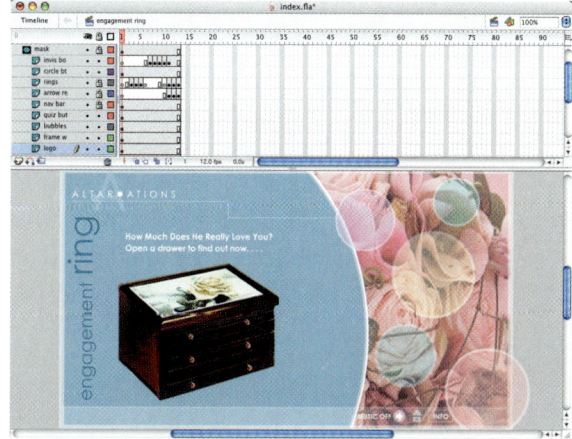

**Figure 6.2** Mask layers can be a handy way of adding depth to a composition.

These links begin to reveal the social issues that are further explored within the site. Selecting the "VIRGINITY management" link takes us to an interactive portion of the Website, where traditional beliefs regarding sex and marriage are challenged through audio clips of interviews. "Make a better BABY," similarly brings up the controversial topic of genetic engineering and the consequences of eugenics.

A complete navigation of *Altar-ations* is a cascading experience of discovery; each new scene yields topical information in a playful and engaging manner. At the end of each interactive section, external links lead to articles on the Web for further research.

**Figure 6.3** This section has audio clips expressing opinions on the topic of sex and marriage.

## DIGITAL DECONSTRUCTION: POLYSTYRENE DREAM

*Polystyrene Dream* is a Flash based artwork Davis completed in 2002. It takes aim at the social responses following 9/11 when patriotism, ethnocentrism, and military and religious fervor were (and continue to) run rampant. Barbie, the best-selling doll and target of mass criticism, plays the protagonist in each of the interactive scenes that comprise *Polystyrene Dream*. Each scene acts as a comical tableau; Barbie visits these historical events, representing certain demographics of thought through satire and social deconstruction. While this work utilizes Barbie as a cultural filter, it also exposes this toy's role in mediating belief systems through its enormous popularity.

When the site first loads, we are introduced to a splash screen with a glowing haloed Barbie head, surrounded by an animation of flowers and sparkling stars. Visiting the various links

**Figure 6.4** *Polystyrene Dream* (2003)—Barbie meets genetic engineering.

on the site, one can interact with a "9/11 Barbie," a "Last Supper Barbie," a "Fertility Clinic Barbie," and a "Barbie for President."

All of the scenes in *Polystyrene Dream* are organized in separate SWF files, loaded at the appropriate time with the versatile `loadMovie` command. This function is quite popular with artists working with Flash. It uses two arguments: the URL of the file and the target movie clip (where the SWF is being loaded into). Loading principle components of a project from separate SWF files has many advantages: it can help organize a complicated project, it allows for smoother streaming, and collaboration between multiple artists is simplified. The line of code that can splice these different files together looks like this:

```
loadMovie("home.swf", targetMC);
```

This assumes that `"home.swf"` resides in the same directory as the Flash file calling this function, and that there is a movie clip named `targetMC`.

### DIGITAL DECONSTRUCTION: *PIECES OF HERSELF*

*Pieces of Herself* examines feminine embodiment and identity in relationship to public and private space. A game-like interface invites the user to navigate through familiar spaces (kitchen, living room, neighborhood, etc.), hunting for pieces that can be dragged onto the body-silhouette on the side of the screen. The scrollable grayscale environments are explorative realms, encouraging the user to collect the bright pieces of self-identity that are distributed in spaces and on surfaces. Placing them inside the collection-zone body triggers audio interviews and sound effects.

**Figure 6.5** *Pieces of Herself* (2005) explores human spaces on a cultural and personal level.

After a period of exploration, a uniquely layered narrative unfolds, provoking thought, laughter, and self-reflection regarding domesticity and gender roles. It is interesting to see how the body becomes graffiti-ridden through the process of interacting with this artwork—an intended visual metaphor for how people become marked by their environment.

*Pieces of Herself* questions the typical way that domestic environments are regarded. Rather than a collection of common household items and spaces, we should consider the way that everything around us is interactive and effective.

Technically, *Pieces of Herself* is a reminder that multimedia is often a complicated business. This project uses over a dozen interconnected files, not to mention all of the layers, movie clips, audio files, and hundreds of lines of ActionScript. To organize and develop a plan of action, many Flash artists (including Davis) sketch things out by hand before even launching Flash.

Enabling all of these files to interact with each other inside Flash are the powerful gears of ActionScript. *Pieces of Herself* employs a fairly complex amount of ActionScipt; hundreds of lines of code exist throughout several SWF files that are incorporated into a singular functionality. For the sake of clarity, the following DIY section is focused on loading external SWF files, followed by making them scrollable.

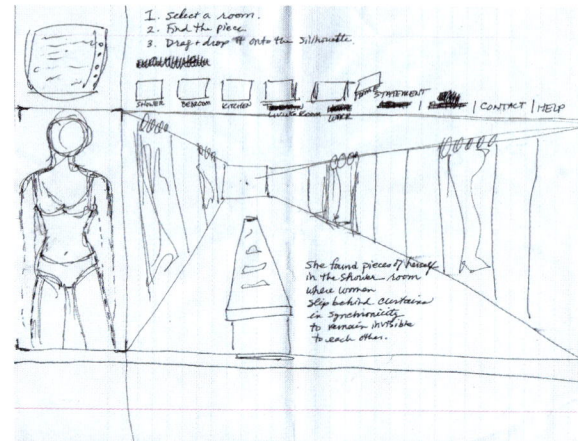

**Figure 6.6** Sketching things out by hand is often a good idea-even for digital artists.

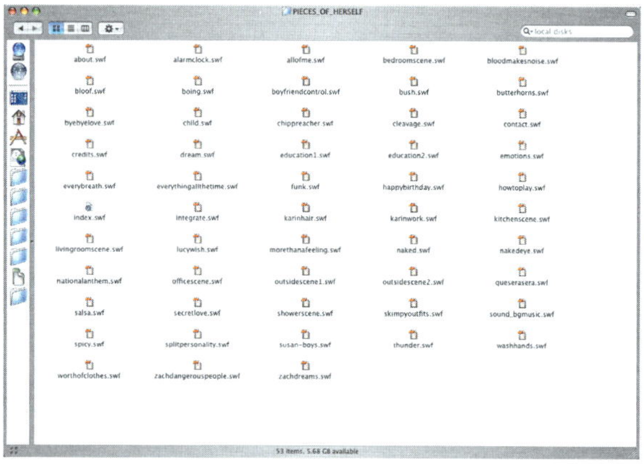

**Figure 6.7** Flash projects can often take the form of more than one SWF file.

# CHAPTER SIX    107

### DIY: LOADING EXTERNAL SWF'S

Let us try loading external SWF's into a Flash project. Launch Flash and insert the DVD that came with this book. You will be needing some files from the Chapter_06 folder.

1. Open the three files from the DVD titled *bathroom.fla*, *kitchen.fla,* and *bedroom.fla*. Flash 8 conveniently places these as tabs within the same floating window, making it simple to flip back and forth between them.

2. Spend some time looking at each of these files. If you open Modify ➡ Document, you can see they all have the same size, 1430 × 275 pixels. Each file also has a layer called **lines**, containing vertical lines spaced every 286 pixels across the image. Although the images are 1430 pixels wide, only 286 pixels will be displayed at a time. The user will have to scroll around the image to explore the rest of this visual space.

Export each of these FLA files into the same directory. File ➡ Export ➡ Export Movie. Give them the same name, except add a SWF extension (e.g. *bathroom.fla*

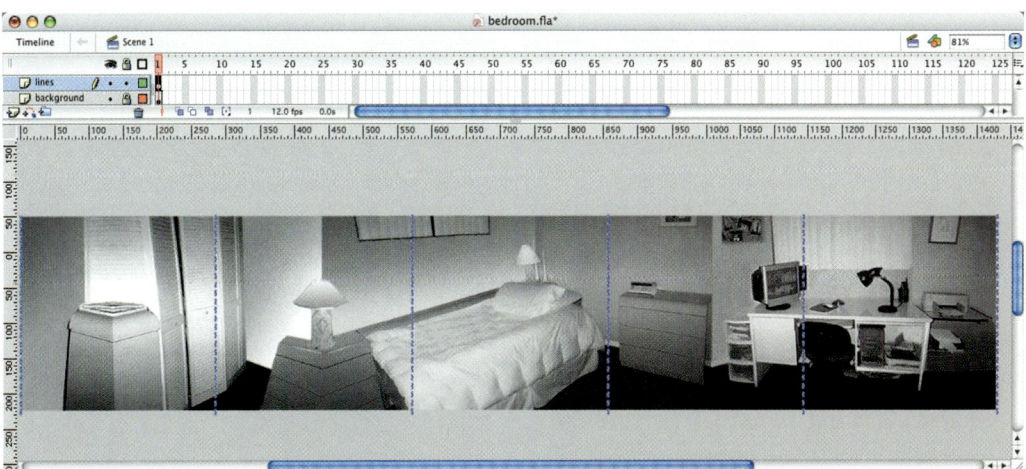

**Figure 6.8** This super wide SWF file will be loaded into a tiny window of 286 x 275.

should be exported as *bathroom.swf*). The naming is important because we are going to refer to these files with ActionScript. Leave the format to the default setting of Flash Movie.

3. Now open the *roomViewerStart.fla* from the DVD. Save it into the same directory as the other three files.

4. Take a moment to examine the graphics on the two layers named **mask** and **masked**. First, hide all of the layers by clicking the eye icon sitting above all of them. Then show each of the mask and masked layers so you can see that there is a gray rectangle on the *mask* layer and a movie clip containing a dotted "X" on the masked layer. The next step will be to convert these two layers from Normal mode to Mask and Masked mode, altering how the graphics contained therein will display in the final SWF.

5. Masked layers always work in tandem with two (or more) layers. First of all, there must be a Mask layer. To turn the layer named **mask** into a Mask layer, double click its icon (not the name, as this will just highlight the name, putting it into edit mode). This will open a dialogue window where you will see the option to put this layer into Mask mode. Do the same with the **masked** layer except select the Masked layer option. To see how Mask/Masked layers affect each other, simply lock both of them. Select the lock icons of both layers.

6. Click on the blue, orange, and green buttons that are sitting on the Stage. Notice in the Property Inspector that each button has what is called an instance name. Instance names are useful for controlling

**Figure 6.9** Be sure you are saving your SWF files into the same directory!

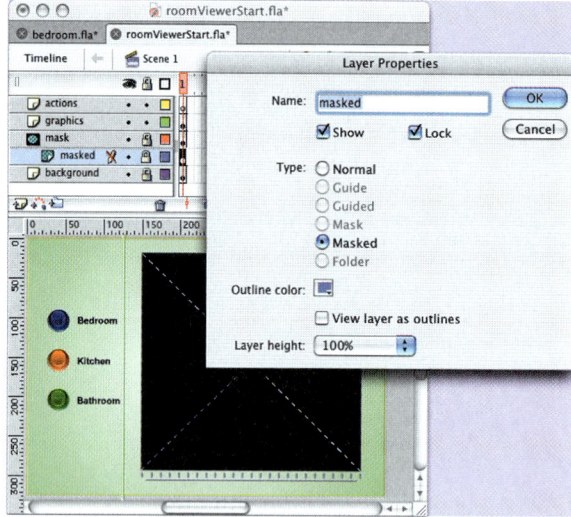

**Figure 6.10** Open the Layer Property Inspector by double clicking the layer icon you want to change.

symbols with ActionScript. Select the **roomViewer** movie clip (you may need to lock/hide layers) and make sure this symbol has an instance name - `viewer`.

7. Select frame 1 of the layer called **actions**. Open the Actions panel: Window ➡ Actions. Type the following in this window:

`loadMovie("bedroom.swf", viewer);`

8. Test this movie and see what happens: Control ➡ Test Movie. You should see the movie you have been working on with the *bedroom.swf* file loaded into the masked layer. If you don't see this, check the following: Was the code typed in correctly? Does the **roomViewer** movie clip have an instance name of `viewer`? This is the most common mistake. Check the instance name in the Property Inspector. Finally, check to make sure all four SWF files are in the same folder.

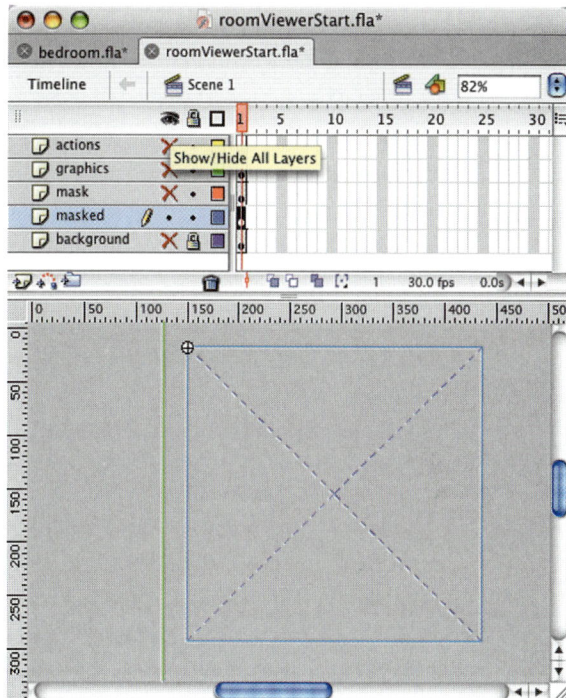

**Figure 6.11** The graphical content on a Mask layer acts as a "magic window" for the Masked layers.

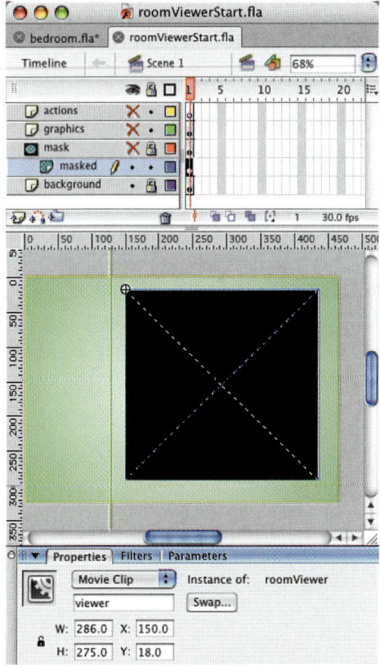

**Figure 6.12** Instance names are added in the Property Inspector of a symbol.

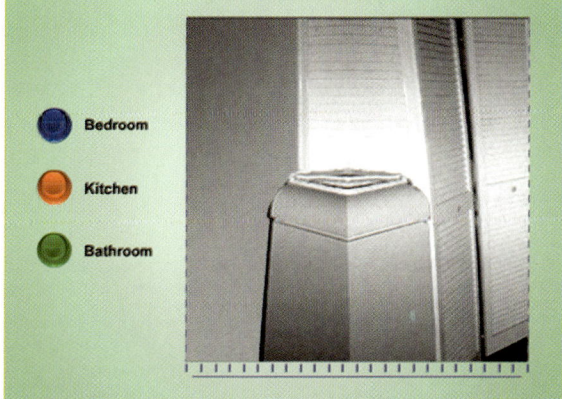

**Figure 6.13** Testing your movie should generate a SWF file that looks like this.

### DIY: SCROLLING A MOVIE CLIP INSIDE A MASK

While the last section got us started with masks and loading external SWF files, it is a bit limited because we cannot scroll around and view the entire 1430px width of our SWF file nor can we load other SWF files to replace the initial one. One of Davis's students, Liz Johnson, wrote the code in the original version of *Pieces of Herself*, allowing the viewer to navigate this space. Let's now fix our FLA by adding some code that allows us to navigate in a similar way.

1. With the **graphics** layer selected, drag the **scroller** movie clip onto the Stage from the Library. Center it over the **graph** movie clip (a bunch of vertical dashes beneath the mask). Give this movie clip an instance name: xScroller.

2. With the xScroller movie clip selected, open the Actions panel. The Actions panel should read "Actions - Movie Clip" across the top. If it does not, it means you have a frame selected for placing code. Make sure you have the movie clip selected instead! Type this code into the Actions panel:

```
onClipEvent (load) {
    initx = _x;
    left = _x-128;
    right = _x+128;
    top = _y;
    bottom = _y;
}
onClipEvent(mouseDown) {
    if (this.hitTest(_root._xmouse,_root._ymouse)){
                    startDrag(this, false, left, top, right, bottom);
    }
```

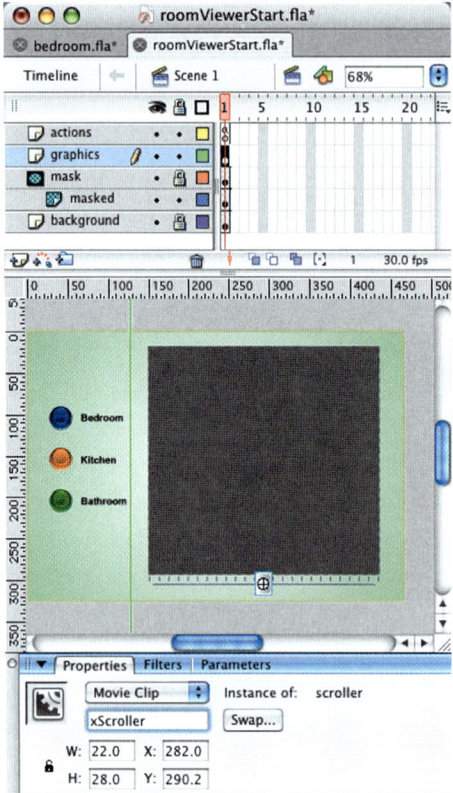

**Figure 6.14** Your setup for the xScroller movie clip should look something like this.

**Figure 6.15** The hitTest method rests inside the onClipEvent(mouseDown) handler.

```
}
onClipEvent(mouseUp){
      _x = initx;
      stopDrag();
}
```

Remember that ActionScript can be placed on frames as well as on symbols. Syntax differs somewhat depending on where the code is placed. When putting ActionScript on a movie clip as we just did, all code must go inside some type of *event handler*.

The above code is using three `onClipEvent` handlers. Event handlers (like most function calls) need arguments—some type of data that lends specificity to the function. For example, the `onClipEvent(mouseDown)` handler executes the code within its curly brackets (these are curly brackets- { }), whenever the mouse is pressed. This would enable the scroll button to move whenever the mouse is pressed, even if away from this movie clip. To make sure `scroller` only moves when the mouse is clicking on *it*, we have to add a method called `hitTest`.

**NOTE:** The `hitTest` method is very popular with Flash coders. Its purpose is to check the coordinates of two symbols (or one symbol versus specified coordinates) to see if they are intersecting. In this case we are seeing if the coordinates of the mouse are within the graphical boundary of the `scroller` movie clip.

3. Select frame 1 of the **actions** layer, then open the Actions panel (if not open already). Delete the code that you typed earlier, and type the following:

```
initx = viewer._x;
inity = viewer._y;

_root.onEnterFrame = function() {
      with (viewer) {
             _x += (xScroller.
x-xScroller.initx)/20;
             _y = 18;
             if (_x>initx) {
                    _x = initx;
             }
             if (_x< -994) {
                    _x = -994;
             }
      }
};

bedroom.onRelease = function() {
      loadMovie("bedroom.swf",
 viewer);
}
kitchen.onRelease = function() {
      loadMovie("kitchen.swf",
 viewer);
}
bathroom.onRelease = function() {
      loadMovie("bathroom.swf",
 viewer);
}
```

Do you have any idea what `onEnterFrame` is? You guessed it—an event handler! By prepending _root in front of it, we are asking Flash to run the code inside of this handler every time `_root` enters another frame. And `_root` just happens to be the way of referencing the main Timeline in ActionScript. But our main Timeline only has 1 frame. This might lead you to wonder: What is the use of such a handler if it is only executed once? Remember that Flash files default to automatically loop. So on every repetitive loading of frame 1 (12 times per second) this code repositions the `viewer` movie clip based on the positioning of the `xSlider` movie clip, as we drag it back and forth.

At the bottom of this code are three button event handlers loading new SWF's onto the Stage whenever they are pressed. Please refer to the *roomViewerEnd.fla* file on the DVD where I have added comments throughout the code, explaining in more detail what is occurring with each line

4. Test the movie again and see how it works now. You should be able to load new rooms using the buttons, as well as scroll around inside these spaces by using the slider on the bottom.

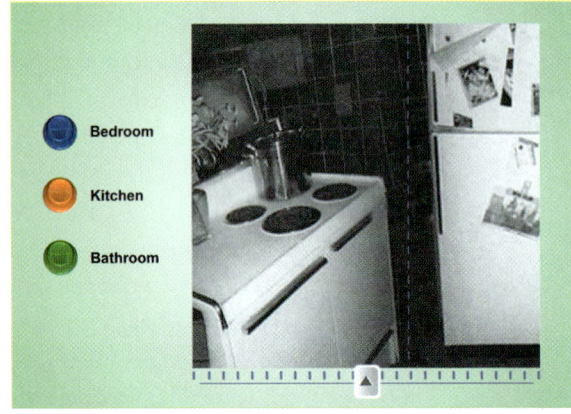

**Figure 6.16** Here is the fully functioning roomViewer demo.

You can see how crucial the use of the Mask/Masked layers are. If you put the **mask** and **masked** layers back into Normal mode, then test the movie again, the loaded SWF will simply sit on top of everything. By loading the SWF's into a movie clip that is on a masked layer, it creates a viewable "magic window."

There are many other ways of achieving this example. Coding can seem rigid for those who are new to it. But with a little practice, you can see that ActionScript can be quite malleable, and often times, a necessity.

## ON YOUR OWN

Following Davis's lead, try thinking of a series of spaces/environments that have inherent conceptual connections. Make separate SWF files that illustrate these spaces using imported images and/or drawn graphics. Using the files we have created in this chapter as a starting point, create an FLA file that will coordinate the loading of these SWF files. Unlike this simple example, think of more interesting graphics besides buttons that cause the loading of these spaces—recall Davis's use of TV monitors as buttons. For adding audio, you don't need to have expensive software—try downloading a free copy of the open source audio editor Audacity *audacity.sourceforge.net*.

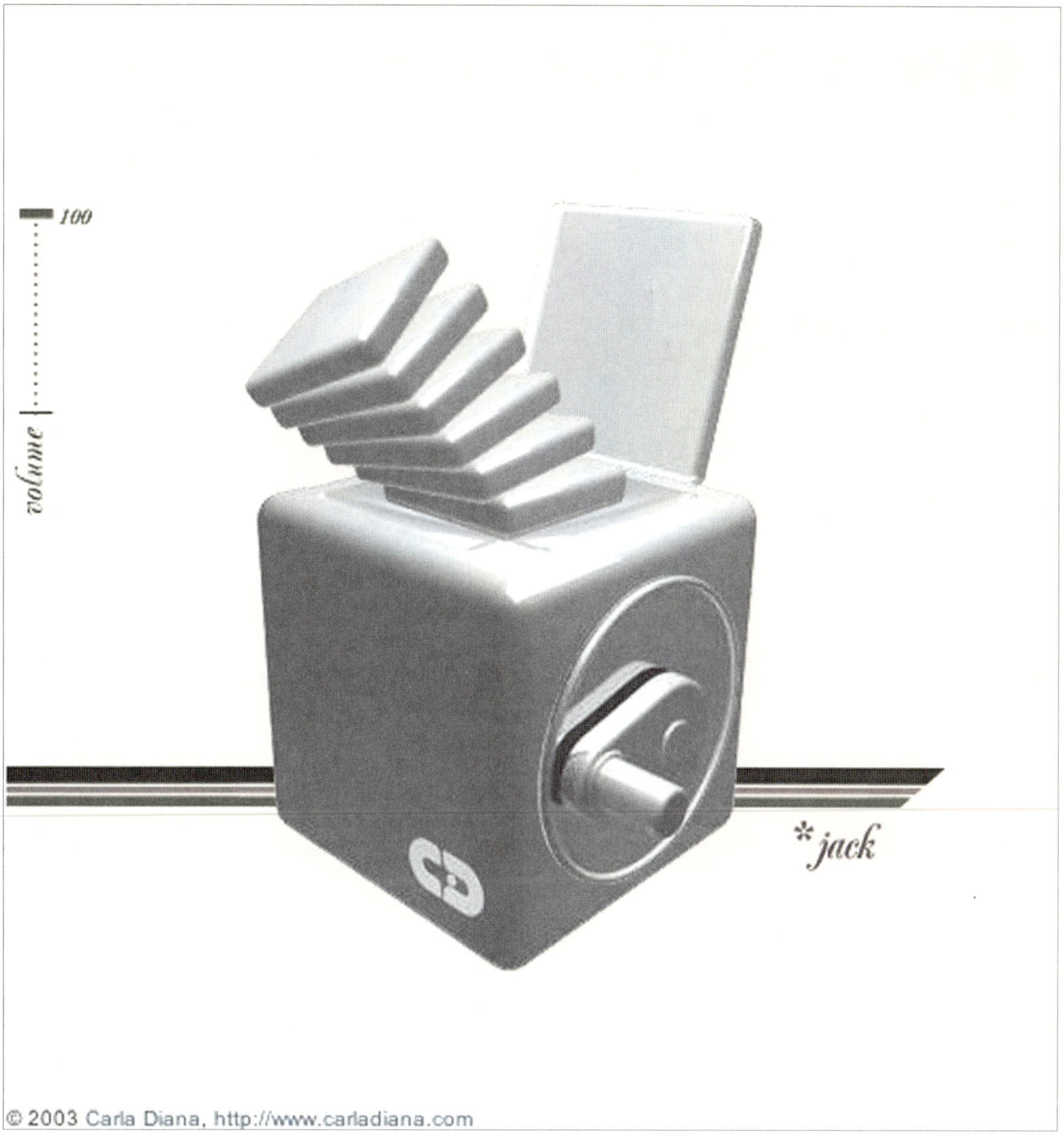

# CARLA DIANA

Expressing Musical Structures Through Interactive Objects and Environments

# CARLA DIANA

For Carla Diana, machines embody the perfect combination of motion and solid object. Her career as an interaction designer, programmer, and educator has explored machines through a remarkable series of projects. Clients like Mazda, Ford, and Atom Egoyan have featured Carla's real and virtual interfaces on the Web and at promotional events. Her experimental artworks have won awards with *Print Magazine*, the Art Director's Club, and the Flash Forward Film Festival. Additionally, her work has been featured in a variety of highly acclaimed international venues and several magazines, such as Korea's Impress, Japan's MacPower, and Print in the U.S.

**Figure 7.1** Diana's work was featured in the German magazine *Page*.

But even before Diana's impressive career, her knack for exploring machines, interfaces, and environments can be traced back to childhood. While many people were playing games with their Commodore 64s, TRS-80s and Apple IIs, Diana was learning how to program them with programming languages like BASIC, Pascal, and FORTRAN. While most people would simply buy and use various kitchen and household gadgets, Diana was dismantling them, trying to figure out how they worked. This excitement and sense of play is mirrored in Diana's art and design projects, where she hopes viewers interact with her work in a manner that is playful and exploratory—a concept she refers to as discovering "affordances" (coined by the cognitive scientist Donald Norman).

**Figure 7.2** A spider with interactive limbs guides the user through the Atom Egoyan website *www.egofilmarts.com*.

Diana's early college years built upon her nascent interests for machines. She absorbed her classes in Math, Mechanical Engineering, and Art, while focusing on Industrial Design as a way to combine all of these fields of study. After her bachelor's degree in Mechanical

Engineering (Cooper Union) and M.F.A. in Design (Cranbrook), Diana worked as an engineer, product design researcher, creative director, and professor; she is now an Assistant Professor at Georgia Institute of Technology.

Working for notable designers like frog design, Karim Rashid, and Sarkissian-Mason, gave Diana new perspectives regarding the relationship between the digital and the physical. These years in the industry also planted seeds for many of her digital processes, some of which ended up in her design work for clients, like Atom Egoyan (an independent filmmaker) and PLANETii (an educational technology company).

With such a dynamic professional career, Diana has developed an intuitive sensibility for how artists and designers relate to their tools and practice. She also holds a great enthusiasm for sharing her wealth of knowledge about ideation, process, techniques, and working with people and collaborators. Below are some points of advice she warrants to young multimedia artists and designers.

**Figure 7.3** Diana was the Creative Director and GUI designer for the eLearning company PLANETii *www.planetii.com*.

"1. Experiment! The beauty of working digitally is that you don't have too much to lose by experimenting with a number of different versions of a project—you can always 'undo.' Take as many risks as possible and try to look at your project in a unique way every time you revise it. It will get better.

2. Don't confound technical issues with design issues. It's important to have a design fully worked out before attempting to program details. In this medium it is very easy to fall in love with some little animation or trick and lose sight of the big picture. You must stay focused on the overall design and keep working on it until it is resolved and beautiful.

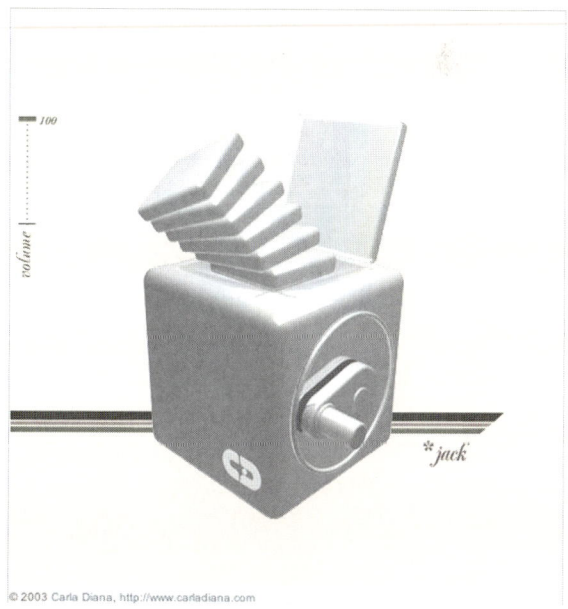

**Figure 7.4** *Jack* (2003) won the Special Sony Award with the Third Place Gallery (an online gallery sponsored by *Sony*).

You can have some programming tests going on at the same time, but don't combine the two until you are absolutely ready.

3. Draw! Draw! Draw! I see so many designers today who don't know how to draw and I really believe they are limiting their ability to develop fully. I like to tell my students that your idea is like a plant, and drawing is the water that the plant needs. Your plant may be alive if you don't water it, but it can only grow to its full potential if you feed it what it needs. It's the same thing with your ideas, they can exist, but they are only going to grow if you explore through drawing a variety of solutions. Too many people think that they can just go to the computer and design something right away without any planning. I don't think the drawing has to be in any way complete or refined (rough and quick sketches are often the best way to get ideas out), but should serve as a starting point for exploration.

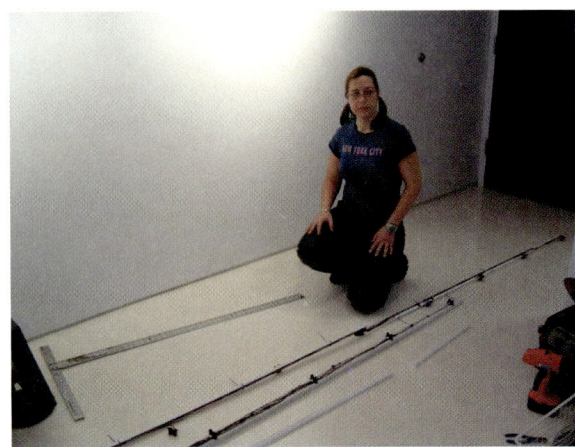

**Figure 7.5** Here is Diana setting up a project, which for her is much more than launching a software application.

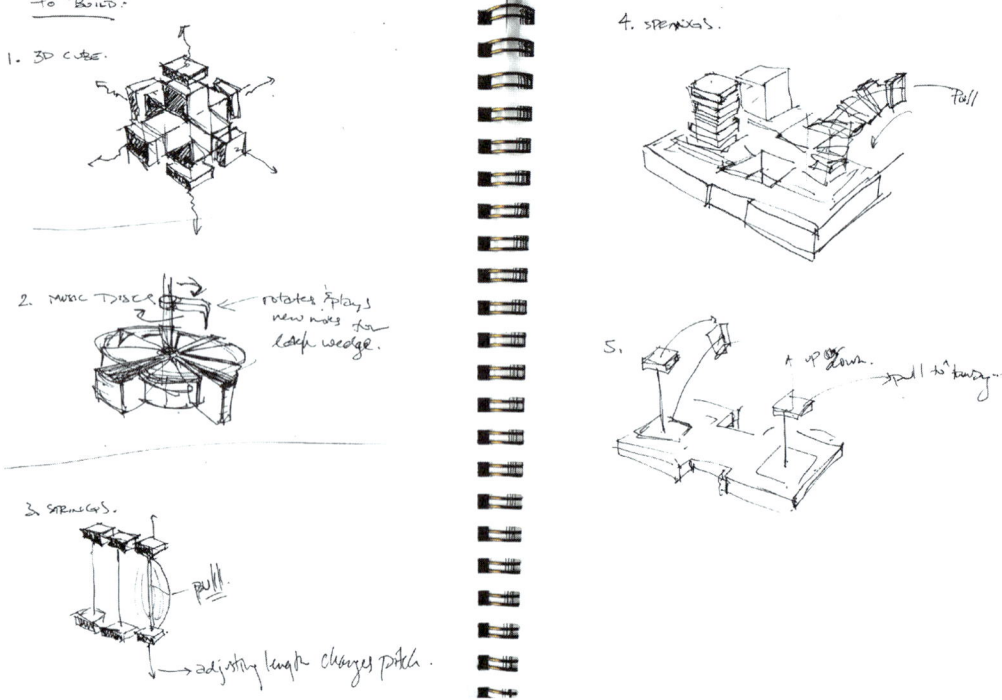

**Figure 7.6** All of Diana's digital work actually begins with pen, paper, and a rapid evolution of ideas.

4. Avoid the temptation to be competitive about using Flash tricks. It can take 2 weeks to build an effect of something zipping across the screen and in the end it may not even really work well in your interface. Be sure to have a well thought out concept that drives the rest of the project.

5. Pick two or three things that are your strongest points and keep working on those rather than trying to master everything at once. Interactive designers are often overwhelmed by their attempts to do every single aspect of the project from start to finish (narrative, graphic design, sound creation, programming, typography). Pick what you do best and do it well. For example, say to yourself, 'I will be good at design, typography, and programmed transitions,' or '... 3D, programming, and sound.' "

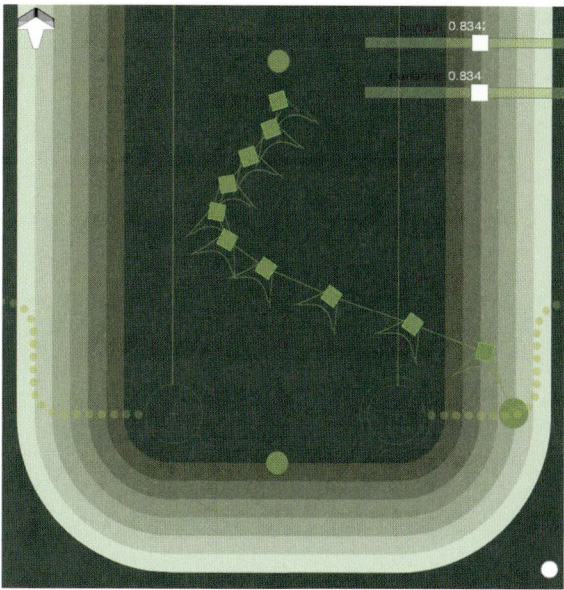

**Figure 7.7** *Terranium* (2003) employs organism-like elements, each inhabiting its own environment and producing unique sounds and animations as a form of behavioral expression.

In addition to the dynamic social environment it provides, Diana also enjoys teaching as a means to meditate on her own research. Over the past several years, an impressive range of experimental artworks has come out of her studio. These works explore visual relationships with audio through viewer interactivity, composing objects and environments in a way that references organisms, architecture, and other complex systems.

## DIGITAL DECONSTRUCTION:
### TERRANIUM

*Terranium* is a project that initiated a series of audio rich interactive environments that Diana is still exploring today. In this work, three levels of interlocking environments incorporate a wide range of playful interfaces, triggering animations and audio samples. Diana had actually worked with sounds and interfaces for many years before *Terranium*. These earlier projects involved sound loops with individual volumes that could be changed by manipulating the graphics on the screen. As these works evolved, they steered away from being a simple mixing board, targeting things like pitch, rhythm, tempo, and volume, while linking these sound properties to the graphics within a carefully crafted user-focused experience.

For precise control over sound, and composing audio-graphic correlations in the environment of *Terranium,* Diana employed the use of the Sound Object with ActionScript (rather than simply linking an audio file to a frame on the Timeline). The code below assumes that there is a sound file in the Library with its Identifier set to s1. Opening the Symbol Properties window for that Library asset will allow access to the Identifier.

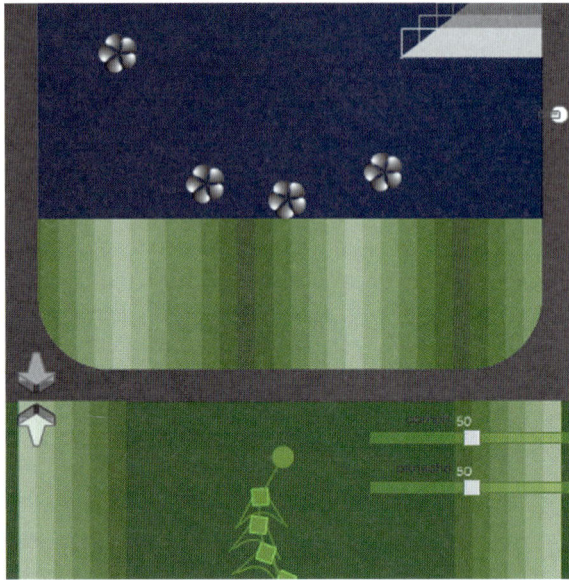

**Figure 7.8** The different levels of *Terranium* (subterranean, ground, and stellar) transition between one another when prompted by the viewer.

```
//make a movie clip - m1
_root.createEmptyMovieClip("m1",
_root.getNextHighestDepth());
//let us see m1
m1.beginFill(0xFF0000);
m1.moveTo(100,100);
m1.lineTo(150, 100);
m1.lineTo(150, 150);
m1.lineTo(100, 150);
m1.endFill();
//make a sound object - so1
so1 = new Sound();
so1.attachSound("s1");
//m1 detects the mouse rolling
over it
m1.onRollOver = function(){
    so1.start(0, 1);
    this._alpha = 100;
}
//m1 to detects the mouse rolling
out of it
m1.onRollOut = function(){
    so1.stop();
    this._alpha = 40;
}

m1._alpha =   40;
```

The first line of code creates an empty movie clip, followed by a few lines of drawing commands—so we can see this movie clip. Next we create a sound object while assigning it a name: so1. At this point, the sound object, ironically enough, does not have an actual sound. So the next line attaches the sound file (s1) from the Library and associates it with so1. The next several lines of code establish mouse handler functions for our movie clip, which are responsible for starting and stopping the sound object. You can open the file,
*simpleSound.fla* from the DVD to examine this more closely.

With *Terranium*, Diana builds on these principles of blending audio and graphics, achieving a higher level of complexity, craftsmanship, and artistic vision. Concentrating on organisms and their environments, various media elements are directed towards an implied narrative: the undulating form in the subterranean level is snake-like, the ground quadrant has some geometric flower forms, and the stellar level references planetary bodies.

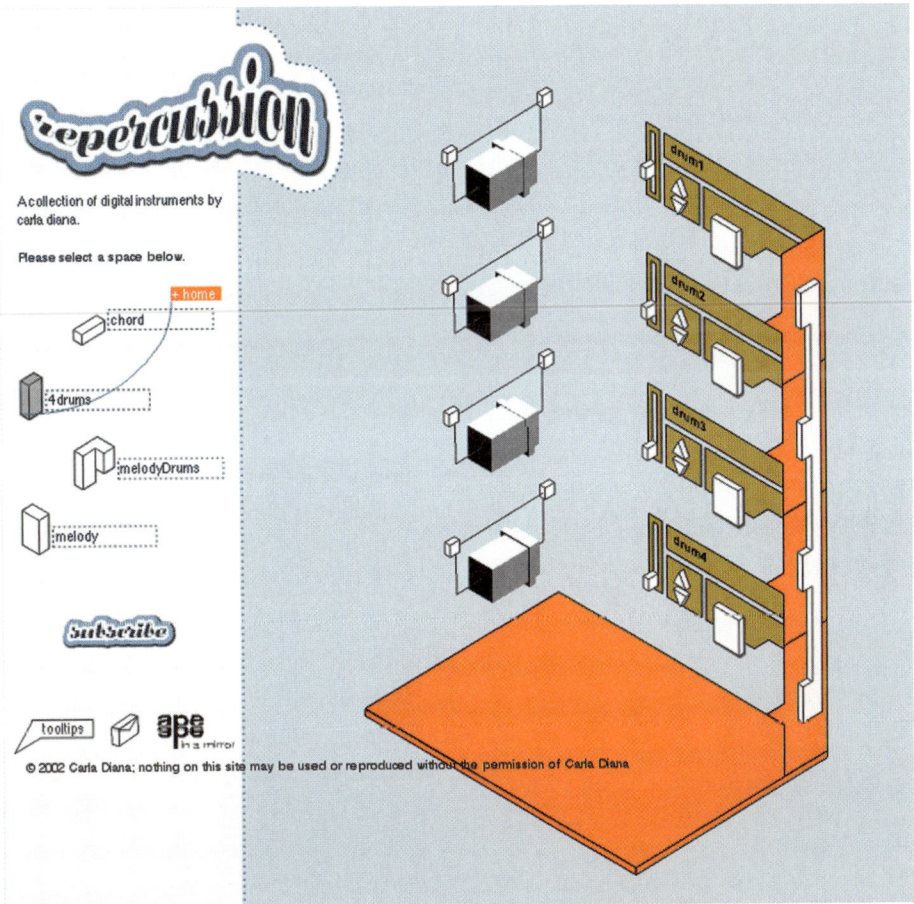

**Figure 7.9** A sample virtual instrument from the *Repercussion* (2004) collection.

## DIY: 3D GADGETRY

This tutorial outlines a strategy for how to create interactivity using exported stills from a 3D model. Diana has laid out these steps as a basic schematic for the more complex code acting behind the scenes of many of her works like *Repercussion*.

1. Open the file on the DVD titled *box_start.fla*. You should see a movie clip of a box on the Stage, as shown in Figure 7.10. Within that movie clip is another movie clip that contains just the box opening animation. (This was created using a 3D rendering program called Cinema 4D, but you can use this technique for any series of frames in an animation.) Note that the lid animation is separate from the static part of the box so that Flash does not have to redraw the entire box each time. There is a stop action at the first frame so it will not move past frame 1 if we do not want it to.

2. Next, let us give the user the ability to open and close the box lid using the mouse. The idea behind this is when the mouse is pressed, we will use a variable (startY) to remember the Y location where the user first started dragging, and then continuously monitor the mouse position using an onEnterFrame function. Type this function in the Actions panel, with frame 1 of the **actions** layer selected.

```
box1.lid.onPress = function(){
    var startY:Number = _ymouse;
    this.onEnterFrame = function(){
        var yMove:Number =
_ymouse - startY;
        trace(yMove/this.
totalframes);
    }
}
```

When you test your code, you will see the value for yMove in the Output Window. This number will get increasingly negative as you drag the lid up and more positive when you drag it down.

3. Write an onRelease function for the box1.lid instance so that the monitoring stops when the user stops dragging. Add the following code after what you just typed on frame 1 of the **actions** layer.

```
box1.lid.onRelease = function(){
    delete this.onEnterFrame;
}
```

It is always a good idea to also define the onReleaseOutside event when defining onRelease in order to account for those moments when the user lets go of the mouse while it is no longer resting on the graphic itself. This just means

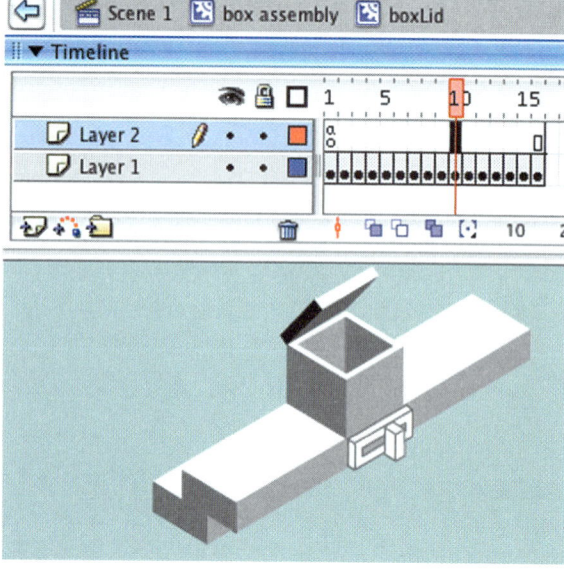

**Figure 7.10** Here are the initial movie clips sitting on the Stage.

adding the `onReleaseOutside` to the existing code as follows:

```
box1.lid.onRelease = box1.lid.↵
onReleaseOutside = function(){
       delete this.onEnterFrame;
}
```

4. While monitoring mouse position, we will send the box 1 movie clip to a new frame when there is enough change in position. Imagine that 200 pixels up is the most the user will move. This means that dividing 200 by the number of frames in the lid movie will give us a number that we can use to make the `box1.lid` movie clip go to a new frame. We can access the number of frames using the `_totalFrames` property of the `box1.lid` movie clip.

   To figure out the divider and save it in a variable, we will use the following code, added right before the `onEnterFrame` function.

```
var divider:Number = 200/this.↵
totalframes;
```

   To figure out the change in frames, we will want to look for this value: `yMove/divider`.

   We use `this` as the instance name because we are already inside a function scoped for the `box1.lid` instance. Because the above value is negative, we will want to multiply by negative 1 so that we make a positive change in frame numbers when the mouse movement is negative, and vice-versa. This means now we are looking for:

   `-1*yMove/divider`

   It is a good idea to round off this number because you are only interested in using it to send the playhead to a certain frame, meaning that you want only whole numbers. Use the `Math.ceil` method so that it rounds up.

   `Math.ceil(-1*yMove/divider)`

Your code for the `onPress` event should now look like this:

```
box1.lid.onPress = function(){
       var startY:Number = _ymouse;
       var divider:Number = ↵
200/this._totalframes;
       this.onEnterFrame = ↵
function(){
              var yMove:Number = ↵
_ymouse - startY;
              trace(Math.ceil↵
(-1*yMove/divider));
       }
}
```

5. Finally, we want to move relative to where the user first clicked, meaning that we are looking for the change in vertical movement, not absolute positions. In other words, a value of 2 will not send us to frame 2, but instead will send us to a frame that is 2 more than the frame we started on with the first mouse click. We will add a line to the beginning of the `onPress` function that lets us remember the frame we started on and store it in a variable called `startFrame`. The code now looks like this:

```
box1.lid.onPress = function(){
       var startY:Number = _ymouse;
       var startFrame = this.↵
currentframe;
       var divider:Number = 200/↵
this._totalframes;
       this.onEnterFrame = ↵
function(){
              var yMove:Number = ↵
_ymouse - startY;
              var newFrame:Number↵
 = Math.ceil(-1*yMove/divider) +↵
startFrame;
              this.gotoAndStop↵
(newFrame);
       }
}
```

6. The last bit of cleanup involves checking the limits of the new frame value to make sure we do not go lower than 1 or higher than the last frame of the movie. We can do this using an if-then statement or some clever use of the min and max Math methods.

```
newFrame = Math.min(Math.max
(1, newFrame), this._totalframes);
```

The above line of code will set `newFrame` equal to itself unless it is smaller than 1 or larger than the total number of frames. In those cases it will get set to 1 or the last frame number, respectively. Insert this line before the `gotoAndStop` command and you are good to go. Check out the *box_end.fla* file on the DVD to see it in action.

## DIGITAL DECONSTRUCTION: *REPERCUSSION*

The *Repercussion* collection is a series of virtual musical instruments whose design invites the user to perform compositions while exploring their unique morphology. While they behave like experimental musical instruments, these interfaces also bring to mind spatial relationships and achieve architectural significance.

Architectural impressions are especially clear when the real-time version of *Repercussion* is installed. In this version of the project, an immersive environment outfitted with microcontrollers and sensors invites participants to interact with the instruments by using their bodies. Performers can collaborate while controlling the tone or beat of a particular sound object and, subsequently, the visual interface.

Musical compositions are generated in real-time from a library of pre-recorded sounds, employing algorithms to map the on-screen

**Figure 7.11** *Repercussion Live* (2004) uses motion sensors to detect body movement. This data is routed through a TELEO microcontroller connected via USB to a computer running the Flash application.

**Figure 7.12** Some of Diana's students and colleagues interact with the installation version of *Repercussion* (2005).

graphics and input values to characteristics of the sound arrangement such as pitch, tempo, and volume. To keep all of the elements synchronized takes some coding that goes beyond the basic onEnterFrame function. The setInterval function has more elements to it, hence more control. The basic set-up includes three steps (although there are more advanced ways of using this function).

```
var interval_id:Number;
var c:Number = 0;
var end:Number = 4;
var duration:Number = 1000;
function execute_interval():Void {
        trace("execute_interval
interval_id: "+interval_id+"
count: "+c);
        if (c>=end) {
            clearInterval
(interval_id);
        }
        c++;
}
// parameters: (scope, "function",
milliseconds)
interval_id = setInterval(this,
"execute_interval", duration);
```

The first step is to establish a set of variables. interval_id is used for identifying this interval uniquely. c keeps track of how many times the interval is called. end is used as a conditional for clearing the interval after x-amount of times. Finally, duration is passed along to the setInterval function telling it how many milliseconds between each execution, in this case 1000.

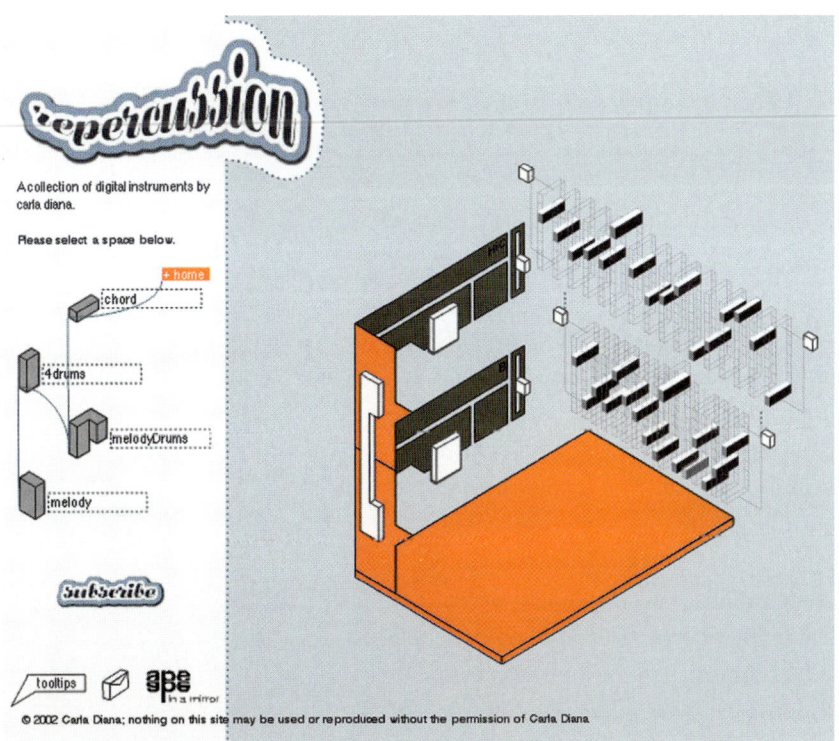

**Figure 7.13** This virtual instrument features several controls for multiple instruments.

Intervals require a function for the interval to call. This sample code has a function called `execute_interval`. This function does three things: First, it prints some text to the output window; Secondly, it checks to see if `c` is greater or equal to `end`, and if so, clears the interval; Finally, this function increments the `c` variable by 1 each iteration.

The last step is the simplest: calling the `setInterval` function, supplying it with the proper arguments and assigning it to `interval_id`. Setting the `interval_id` variable is crucial for later deleting this interval with `clearInterval`.

You can type the preceding code directly into the Actions panel of frame 1 of a new Flash document, and you will get the following output when testing the movie:

```
execute_interval interval_id: ↵
1 count: 0
execute_interval interval_id: ↵
1 count: 1
execute_interval interval_id: ↵
1 count: 2
execute_interval interval_id: ↵
1 count: 3
execute_interval interval_id: ↵
1 count: 4
```

Diana employed solid design strategies and paid careful attention to maintaining a fluid interaction experience in making *Repercussion* intuitive and whimsical. The graphics, and their controlled responses, were engineered with a wide audience in mind. Creating interesting compositions is not dependent upon musical training or expertise, yet enough detail and quality of sound provide limitless possibilities for creative exploration and jamming.

## DIY: ADDING VOLUME TO OUR GADGETRY

Open the file from the DVD called *box_end.fla*. We will continue with this file, adding some more code so we can use the same data controlling the playhead to control the sound volume. First, we need to create a sound object and get control of its volume, then we will link up the box lid value to the volume. We will be using a very basic tone, (which was created using Melody Assistant X *www.myriad-online.com*), and looping it so it plays continuously and sounds like one sound, rather than a series of beats.

1. Create a new sound object using ActionScript. In the sample file a new layer (called **sound**) was created for the actions that correspond to sound code. Here is the ActionScript for creating the sound object:

```
s1 = new Sound(box1);
```

Note the `box1` instance name in parentheses. It is a good idea to associate the sound with a movie clip because things like volume and panning are specific to each movie clip.

2. Attach a sound. In this case the sound has already been imported, but if you are starting from scratch you will need to import it yourself via File ➡ Import. Here is the ActionScript for attaching the sound:

```
s1.attachSound("C");
```

The `"C"` in parentheses is the sound linkage identifier. If you right-click (or control-click on the Mac) on the sound in the Library (in the **scale** folder, called **MiddleC.aif**, you will get the dialog box shown in Figure 7.14.

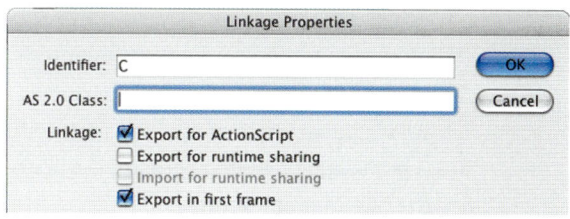

**Figure 7.14** The Symbol Properties window is where you can add `"C"` as the identifier for the MiddleC.aif asset in the Library.

3. Next, we will actually play the sound:

```
s1.start(0, 999);
```

The 0 right after the parentheses corresponds to a time offset in the start of the sound, and 999 specifies the number of loops. This is a short tone that we want to play continuously, so we will also want to make sure to replay the sound when it is done with all the loops (unfortunately, you have to give it a finite number of loops instead of just telling it to loop forever).

```
s1.onSoundComplete = function(){
        s1.start(0, 999);
}
```

4. Controlling volume: the syntax for this is

```
s1.setVolume(0);
```

For our box lid gadget we'll want the volume to be set to 0 when the lid is completely closed, and set to 100 when the lid is at the last frame of the animation.

If you have never worked with the sound object you might want to do some tests with the `setVolume` method to see how the different values sound. Just plug in different numbers in the parentheses, then do a quick Control ➡ Test Movie to hear the results, making sure the volume on your computer is turned up!

At this point we know how to control volume, and we know how to set up interaction to let the user control the box lid opening. All we have to do to get our gadget working is put them together by linking the action of the box lid to the volume.

The key to linking the two actions is getting the numbers to relate to each other in the correct proportions. One number is the frame number corresponding to the current location of the box lid animation, and what we will want to do is make the volume relate to this number. We can say that the two values need to be "mapped" to one another.

5. Calculate a fraction that describes how open the box lid is, taking its current frame location and comparing that to all the frames in that animation. From within the `onEnterFrame` function for the instance `box1.lid` (this is the code on the **actions** layer):

```
var howOpen:Number = this._currentframe/this._totalframes;
```

6. Next, multiply this fraction by 100 in order to scale the value to match the range of the volume (0 to 100). We can rewrite the code to look like this:

```
var howOpen:Number = 100*this._currentframe/this._totalframes;
```

7. Now that we have a number from 0 to 100, we can set the volume equal to it using the `setVolume` method. To simplify things, let us give it a whole number by taking a `Math.floor` value, rewriting the `howOpen` definition:

```
var howOpen:Number = Math.floor(100*this._currentframe/this._totalframes);
s1.setVolume(howOpen);
```

If you test this movie, there will be one small problem. When you trace `howOpen`, you will see that it never reaches 0, which means that even with the box lid closed, there will still be some volume. This is happening because the lowest the `_currentframe` value can ever be is 1, and the lowest fraction in this case will be 1 divided by the total number of frames, or 1/16. To resolve this, we can make the fraction into one that begins at 0 by subtracting 1 from the frame value. If we also subtract 1 from the total number of frames, we will wind up with the range we need:

```
var howOpen:Number = Math.floor(100*(this._currentframe-1)/(this._totalframes-1));
s1.setVolume(howOpen);
```

We could also have used the variable `newFrame` from Part 1 instead of `this._currentframe`; it indicates the same value.

You are done! Test out your file, and have fun! If you run into any problems, open the file called *box_volume_end.fla* from the DVD.

**NOTE:** The Publish settings for **Audio event** for this file are set to **Raw**, rather than one of the more common compression schemes like MP3. The reason for this is that with small looping tones it is essential that the sound loop seamlessly, and the compression will often clip the sound just a tiny bit. It is small, but very noticeable to the ear. In general, with special sound treatments like this one, it is often necessary to do a bit of trial and error testing to see how low you can go with compression before the sound quality gets degraded in some way that is no longer acceptable.

### ON YOUR OWN

Try combining a number of these gadgets and attaching a different tone to each one so that they can all play in unison. You can also take this principle of mapping volume to a value and use it with other mouse movements, or use it to match a movie clip property like `_alpha`, `_width`, `_height`, `_x`, `_y`, etc.

From an aesthetic viewpoint, you should pay attention to the cohesive nature of Diana's designs. The color, composition, shape, and element of play achieve a model experience in interaction design. When creating your own interactive objects and environments in Flash, consider the interplay between all of the applicable parameters.

 AARON KOBLIN

Creative Data Visualization

# AARON KOBLIN

Aaron Koblin is an artist/designer who works with several technologies for creating his work that draws inspiration from a variety of cultural phenomena. Born in Santa Monica, California, he received his M.F.A. from the Department of Design | Media Arts at UCLA, and his B.A. in Fine Art from the University of California, Santa Cruz. Aaron has also studied outside of the U.S., in The Netherlands and Japan.

**Figure 8.1** An installation view of Koblin's *Sheep Market* (2006) project.

Koblin's artwork has been shown internationally, including participation in festivals such as the Japan Media Arts festival, SIGGRAPH, and Ars Electronica. In 2006, his work *Flight Patterns* won a first prize award from the NSF's Science Visualization Challenge.

From the age of seven, Koblin has been intrigued by computer capabilities. Thanks to his stepmother's job at Disney Television, Koblin was allowed to play on their graphics processing computers. It was not long before he had a scary combination of computer-savvy and youthful mischief.

**Figure 8.2** *Flight Patterns* (2005) won an award from the National Science Foundation.

"By the time I was twelve I was spending hours morphing my family's heads together creating alien races and horrible genetic disasters. The intrigue and excitement of this process in some ways never left me, and I continue to use technology to investigate various alternative realities and the cultural and political ramifications of our society and humanity."

Koblin's precocious start with computers emerged from the once difficult processes of installing and running games on early MS-DOS based computers. Running custom scripts and other rigmarole eventually led to creating modifications on these games by altering parameters of the engine. These developing skills were soon articulated into a custom version of Duke Nukem, a 3D first-person shooter game from the '90s. Achieving this technical feat (even though still in high school!) helped Koblin land a job with a computer game publisher, creating character animations for the Game Boy console.

During junior high school, Koblin avoided a 100-page research paper by creating a multimedia project on the Civil War. The software he used for this project, Action!, was somewhat similar to Flash. So when he started to experiment with Flash a few years later, he was able to pick it up rather quickly. He was especially excited about its ability to transmit the final work onto the Web.

In addition to doing work in the videogame industry, Koblin has also taught game design and 3D design at UCLA, worked for the Center For Embedded Networked Sensing *research. cens.ucla.edu*, along with a plethora of other freelance creative work. Currently, he is working with data-driven projects at Yahoo's Design Innovation Group in San Francisco.

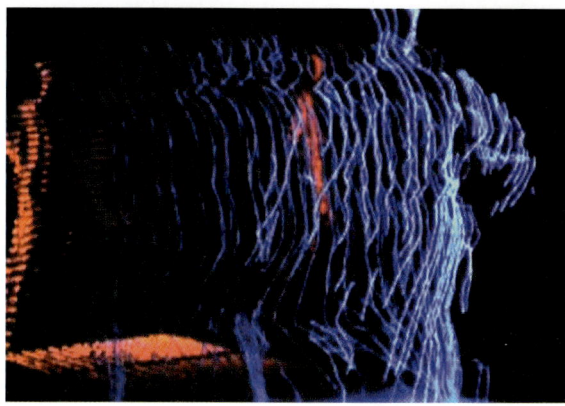

**Figure 8.3** Research at the Center for Embedded Networked Sensing uses lasers to digitize motion-captured forms.

## DIGITAL DECONSTRUCTION: FLIGHT PATTERNS

While Koblin was in graduate school at UCLA, he learned the importance of utilizing a wide range of media and methods. Since then, his work is often a choreographed effort of several techniques, software tools, and files of custom code.

> "I learned that it's important not to get caught up in the tools and implied limitations of the specific software and that the fusion of several tools usually produces the most interesting results."

Also during these UCLA years, Koblin studied under Casey Reas, who helped inspire his curiosity to pursue programming and data visualization. Professor Reas, along with Ben Fry at MIT, authored a programming environment called Processing, *processing.org*, which has many similarities to ActionScript. For instance, both can work directly with pixel data and raster graphics, as well as export Web-ready files viewable on most browsers. There are also many differences: ActionScript is nested within Flash's multimedia GUI and can easily tie into the wealth of vector drawing tools; Processing, on the other hand, has built-in 3D capabilities including openGL, a set of preconfigured libraries for efficiently rendering 3D objects and environments. There are a host of other comparisons and contrasts that can be made, but it is interesting to note, because most of the artists in this book experiment with both applications equally.

**Figure 8.4** *Memecry* (2004) is a reactive installation that builds a reflection of the user via corporate logos. Custom software, a pinhole camera, canvas, and a digital projector are used for this installation.

*Mood Threads* is a project Koblin created using Processing, along with PHP and MySQL. At the essence of this artwork, abstract drawings animate on the screen while data is mined in real-time from LiveJournal, *www.livejournal.com*. LiveJournal is essentially a blogging service; many people who use it often list their current emotional state. Koblin used this data to control the parameterized properties of the generative animations running at the core of *Mood Threads*.

Koblin also used Processing in his project called *Flight Patterns*. Working with data from the Federal Aviation Administration, he was able to create procedural animations that reveal the patterns of North American flight

**Figure 8.5** *Mood Threads* (2005) uses images and emotions determined from the data mined from LiveJournal.

traffic. After Effects, Maya, and a bit of PHP were other tools used in creating the project.

*Flight Patterns* is amazing in its capacity to reveal elements that are hidden to unaided human perception. When the animation first plays, patterns emerge as the flights accumulate and streak across the screen. Even more interesting is the topology of the North American continent that is revealed due to the pervasiveness of current-day flight activity. We also see the busier and more populated regions of North America more prominently, as lines from the data-driven drawing tend to coalesce in the Northeast and West Coast.

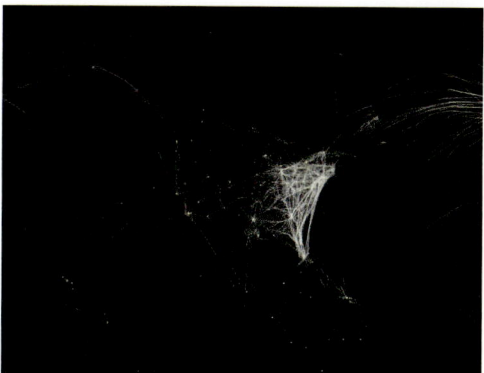

**Figure 8.6** *Flight Patterns* (2005) shown here in mid-animation.

**Figure 8.7** Population density is revealed as a subset of the flight pattern activity.

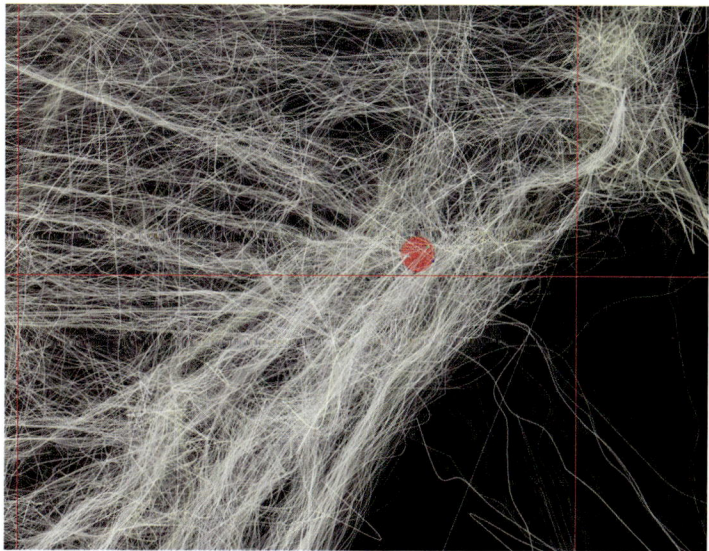

**Figure 8.8** A detail of flights arriving and departing around New York City.

## DIGITAL DECONSTRUCTION: *THE SHEEP MARKET*

The Sheep Market, *www.thesheepmarket.com*, consists of 10,000 images of sheep drawn by online workers. For this project, Koblin contacted thousands of workers through Amazon's Mechanical Turk Web service *www.mturk.com*. They were paid two cents to draw a sheep facing to the left. Their drawing actions were recorded, and the final renderings were saved in a database. Viewers can experience the sheep collectively, arranged in a grid, or singularly, through animations that replay every stroke of the drawing process. Visitors are also able to share and purchase the sheep directly through the Flash-based Website.

The cool thing about using code to create artwork is how it allows you to do things that would be impossible to do manually. For instance, what if you wanted to know what the average sheep out of 10,000 drawings would look like?

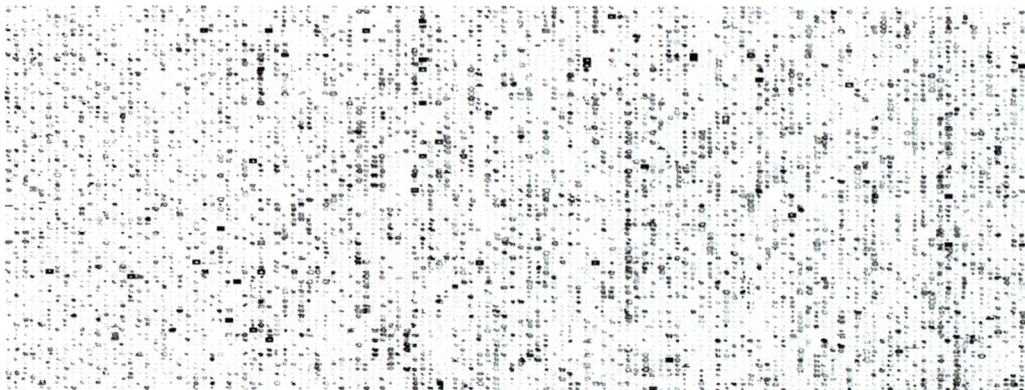

**Figure 8.9** That is a flock of sheep!

## DIY: FLASH DRAWING RECORDER

A prominent feature of *The Sheep Market* is the ability to record the process of user interactivity through drawing and recall these processes later as animations. Koblin put together the following tutorial as a way to present the fundamental steps required to create a drawing application that will record user input through a Web browser.

### Setting Up the Tool

First we will set up the scene and create the tools for drawing.

1. Open the file *drawingTool_Start.fla* from the Chapter_08 folder on the DVD.

2. Select the black circle on the **mouseCursors** layer and give it an instance name of `pencil_MC`. This movie clip will be dragged by the user to create the illusion of a brush.

3. Select the white area within the black border on Stage. Give this clip an instance name of `drawMask_MC`. This clip is located on the mask layer and will be used as a mask to visually restrict any drawing content to the canvas area. Lock this layer.

4. With the mask layer locked, click the white area again selecting the movie clip on the canvas layer. Give this movie clip the instance name `canvas_MC`. This will be used to hold the drawing.

5. Finally, give the submit button the instance name `submit_BTN` and the **NumericStepper** the instance name `strokeSizeControl`. You will notice the **NumericStepper** parameters have been set to a max value of 40, a min value of 1, and a starting value of 20.

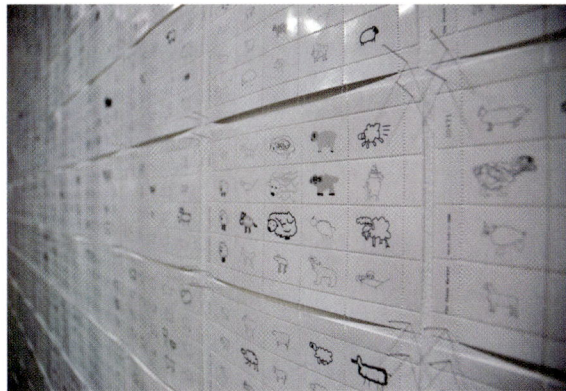

**Figure 8.10** A detail from the installation version of *The Sheep Market* (2006).

**Figure 8.11** An average sheep created from the aggregate of all the sheep graphics existing in *The Sheep Market*.

6. Now we are ready to code some functionality. Go to the first frame of the **actions** layer and open the Actions panel (F9). Add the following code:

```
var strokeSize = 20;

function setupCanvas() {
        drawClip = canvas_MC.createEmptyMovieClip("drawClip", 10);
        drawClip.lineStyle(strokeSize, 0x000000);
        drawClip.setMask(drawMask_MC);
}
setupCanvas();
stop();
```

Here we declare a variable to keep track of our stroke size. Because we have initialized our **NumericStepper** to 20 we need to reflect this value in the stroke size initially. We have created a function called `setupCanvas`, which will prep the canvas by creating an empty movie clip to hold our drawing. This empty movie clip can now be referenced as `drawClip` because of our declaration. We then set the drawing style for the `drawClip` movie clip to reflect our stroke size and the color black (`0x00000`).

---

**NOTE:** For the purposes of this tutorial all drawings will be in black and white, however it is very straightforward to add grayscale and color. The *drawingTool_End.fla* file for this chapter has plenty of comments to make this process easier.

---

At the end of the function, we set `drawMask_MC` to be used as a mask for the `drawClip` so that no drawing data will be visible outside of the drawing area. Finally, we call the function to execute when the frame is entered, and tell Flash player not to proceed to the next frame.

### Adding Functionality

Before we begin the fun of "making things work," lets quickly summarize the task algorithmically in an extremely casual pseudo-code explanation.

The recording process will involve saving the coordinate locations of the mouse while the mouse is pressed. In order to minimize the information being saved, we will only track the user's mouse position when the mouse position has changed. The format for recording the drawing will be kept minimally to line format (x1.y1.x2.y2) and all drawing commands will be separated by an underscore (_) character for easy parsing. Other commands will be listed by the character c followed by a character for the type (s for size) joined to the corresponding value by a dot (.). An example would look like this: `_67.97.68.98_c_s.21_55.89.56.90_`.

The code above would represent a user line from (67,97) to (68,98) followed by a stroke size change to size 21 and another line from (58,89) to (56,90).

Now let us turn this into real code!

1. In the same actions frame (we will maintain the excellent practice of keeping ALL code in a single frame), add the following code:

```
var positionOffsetX = canvas_MC._x;
var positionOffsetY = canvas_MC._y;
var drawCommands = "";
var penX;
var penY;
var penDown = false;
```

These variables will be available to multiple functions so we will declare them upfront (and outside other functions). The purposes of these variables will be explained for each use.

2. Add the following mouse movement code next:

```
onMouseMove = function () {
    mouseShow = true;
    if (drawMask_MC.hitTest
(_xmouse, _ymouse)) {
        theX = _xmouse-
positionOffsetX;
        theY = _ymouse-
positionOffsetY;
        mouseShow = false;
        pencil_MC._x = _xmouse;
        pencil_MC._y = _ymouse;
        if (penDown) {
            drawCommands +=
"_"+penX+"."+penY+"."+theX+"."+theY;
            penX = theX;
            penY = theY;
            drawClip.lineTo
(theX, theY);
        }
    } else {
        if (penDown) {
            drawClip.moveTo
(theX, theY);
            penX = theX;
            penY = theY;
        } else {
            pencil_MC._x = -
5000;
            pencil_MC._y = -
5000;
        }
    }
    if (!mouseShow) {
        Mouse.hide();
    } else {
        Mouse.show();
    }
};
```

This function will be executed every time the mouse position is changed. We start by assuming that the mouse is visible for our mouse check procedure (we will come back to this in a second). After determining if the mouse cursor is over the drawable area using ActionScript's `hitTest` method, we create position variables which reflect an offset. The reason for this is that we want to be recording mouse coordinates relative to the drawing area, as opposed to relative to the entire movie clip. If the user is within the drawing area, we want the mouse graphic to be replaced by our brush movie clip, `pencil_MC`; this is done by setting a flag, `mouseShow`, whose Boolean is used to call either of the two functions: `Mouse.hide`, or `Mouse.show`. Finally, if the pencil is down, we add the coordinates to the drawing variable.

If the `else` code added (setting the pencil to -5000, -5000) within the `hitDetect` fails, simply move the pencil location to the mouse location if the mouse is still down, so that if the mouse leaves the drawing area, it can resume drawing upon re-entry. If the pencil is not down, it moves the brush movie clip to an off-screen location (-5000, -5000).

The last portion completes the mouse check by hiding or un-hiding as specified earlier.

3. Add the following mouse down code:

```
onMouseDown = function () {
        if (drawMask_MC.hitTest
(_xmouse, _ymouse)) {
theX = _xmouse-positionOffsetX;
                theY = _ymouse-
positionOffsetY;
                penDown = true;
                drawClip.moveTo
(theX, theY);
                penX = theX;
                penY = theY;
        }
};
```

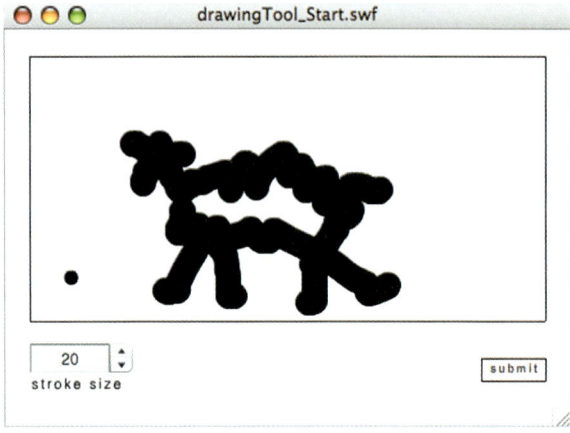

**Figure 8.12** I wonder if Koblin will pay me two cents for this? It is hard to draw a sheep with a brush size of 20!

This code will set the `penDown` variable when the mouse is down and within the drawable area. It will also move the ActionScript drawing point to the current location and set the pencil location variables for use in our mouse recording function above.

4. Add the following mouse up code:

```
onMouseUp = function () {
    penDown = false;
};
```

5. Run and test the project.

You should now be able to create a simple drawing (with a stroke size of 20) in your drawing area.

### Finalizing the Tool

1. Still working in the same FLA file, add the following code to add stroke size changing functionality:

```
var strokeSizeControl:mx.controls.
NumericStepper;

var nstepListener:Object = new
 Object();
nstepListener.change = function
(evt_obj:Object) {
        strokeSize = evt_obj.
target.value;
        drawCommands += "_c_s."+
strokeSize;
        updateStroke();
};
strokeSizeControl.addEventListener
("change", nstepListener);

function updateStroke() {
        drawClip.lineStyle
(strokeSize, 0x000000);
        pencil_MC.brush_MC._xscale
 = strokeSize*9+5;
        pencil_MC.brush_MC._yscale
 = strokeSize*9+5;
}
```

This code begins by creating a listener for the `numericStepper` component. The potential for listeners is outside the scope of this tutorial, but basically the listener will execute our function whenever the component is altered. Our function will add the stroke size change to our list of `drawCommands` and call the function `updateStroke`. The `updateStroke` function will change the drawing style for the `drawClip` to reflect our change and will scale the brush clip to approximately the size of our stroke (quickly approximated with the legendary guess and check routine to be a magical formula of: `(thesize x 9)+5`).

2. Run and test the project. You should now be able to change the size of the drawing tool!

### Adding the Save Functionality

We will now save the contents of our drawing variable to a file using `loadVars` and PHP by adding the following code:

```
var filename = "userDrawing.txt";

sendDrawing = new LoadVars();
sendDrawing.onLoad = sentDrawing;

submit_BTN.onPress = sendIt
function sendIt() {
        sendDrawing.drawing =
 drawCommands;
        sendDrawing.filename =
 filename;
        sendDrawing.sendAndLoad
("http://[yourWebsite]/save
Drawing.php", sendDrawing, "POST");
}
```

**Figure 8.13** With brush stroke variability, greater detail can be used.

The first variable declaration here specifies the filename on the server to which we want to save our drawing. For now this is a static value, but this could easily be set to take a value from the user or change over time.

Following the filename declaration, the code creates a `loadVars` object called `sendDrawing` for sending and receiving data. We declare that the function `sentDrawing` should be called when the `sendDrawing` object loads data (after having sent data to the server). We then attach the `sendIt` function to the submit button so that it will execute on mouse press. In the `sendIt` function we attach the `drawCommands` variable, containing our drawing, with the post name drawing to be sent to the server. We also include the filename and submit the object to the PHP file, which we will create next.

### Saving Files with PHP

Although sending data to a Web server may seem daunting, this tiny PHP script is extremely simple and will serve our purposes just fine. This file uses a function that requires PHP 5, so make sure the system that will be serving this file has the newest PHP version installed.

1. Create an empty text document titled *saveDrawing.php*.

2. Add the following code to the file:

```
<?Php
$drawing = $_POST['drawing'];
$filename = $_POST['filename'];

$theFileContent = "drawing=" .
 $drawing;
file_put_contents($filename,
 $theFileContent);
echo "response=Drawing Saved!";
?>
```

Believe it or not, that is the entire thing. After declaring the file to be a PHP file using `<?`, we create two variables for receiving the `POST` data being sent from our Flash file. We then create a new variable that contains the string `"drawing="` combined with the values from our drawing variable so that we can echo the data back to Flash and into the `drawing` variable. Finally, we save the contents of the new variable to the filename received from Flash and echo back to Flash the string `Drawing saved!` into the `response` variable.

3. Save your PHP file and upload to a PHP 5 enabled Webserver.

### Adding PHP to Flash

We are now ready to wrap it all up.

1. Return to your Flash project.

2. Go to frame 2 of the project and give the dynamic text box the instance name `responseText`.

3. Go back to frame 1 of the **actions** layer and replace `[yourWebsite]` in the `sendAndLoad` call, located in the `sendIt` function with the exact path to your PHP file.

4. Add the following function to your actions frame:

```
function sentDrawing() {
        gotoAndStop(2);
        responseText.text =
sendDrawing.response;
}
```

This will advance the application to frame 2 once the drawing has been sent and update the text response with the response from the server (you can add enhanced error handling here as well).

5. Run and test your application.

6. Jump in the air and smile! You should have a functional drawing tool.

### Oh... You Want to See Your Drawings Too?

The drawing player works exactly the same way the drawing recorder works, but backwards. I have included the file *viewTool.fla* for your convenience (located in the Chapter_08 folder on the DVD). To use the tool, simply edit the first line of code to reflect the path of your drawing file and run. I have included a few references to color implementation in this code as well.

### Where Could Things Have Gone Wrong?!!

If you are having trouble getting your application to work, make sure all instance names are correct and all functions are being called properly. Strategically inserting `trace("I got this far");` into your code is a good way of seeing if things are being executed.

If you can not see your images in the player, make sure the drawing files are being created successfully and that the content is being added. You can add the line `trace(sendDrawing.drawing);` to the end of your `sendIt` function to make sure that the drawing is being recorded properly.

If you are still having trouble, go ahead and open *drawingTool_End.fla*, update your Web server path in the `loadVars` call, then test with this version. If this file is not working properly, chances are you are having issues with your server: either the paths are not correct, or you are having some form of a permissions issue. Make sure that you are running your application on the same domain you are trying to save. Finally, you may need to grant your PHP script special privileges to allow write access, especially if your sysAdmin is crazy about security, in which case, you may have no choice but to beg. Good luck!

## ON YOUR OWN

Novices often regard Flash as merely a tool for creating discrete time based movies. Incorporating techniques with PHP, as Koblin has taken us through, provide a way of sharing and reviewing work created at various times, by various users. Try adding onto the drawing tool that you created in the DIY section with elements such as color and transparency. Think of other screen states you may want to save, like the end screen of a puzzle or game.

# ERIC SOCOLOFSKY

Creative Play with ActionScript

# ERIC SOCOLOFSKY

With education and work experience in the fields of architecture and digital media, Eric Socolofsky has a versatile, creative sensibility that strongly influences his production as an artist and designer. His background in architecture stretches back to his undergraduate studies at Washington University, where he earned a Bachelor of Arts in Architecture (cum laude) with a concentration in Music Performance. From there, Socolofsky went to Chicago where he practiced architecture for three years. His studies and research during this time provided a crossover into the realm of digital media, which he opted to pursue more thoroughly at New York University's Interactive Telecommunications Program, earning a master's degree in 2004.

**Figure 9.1** Here, an audience participates with Socolofsky's audio-visual installation *Aperture* (2006).

Socolofsky is a relative newcomer to the world of Flash, a testament to his natural ability as well as to his hard work over the past few years. His studies at NYU provided an introduction to programming and using multimedia software, taking courses that focused on programs such as Flash, Director, and Processing. This was the initial spark that propelled Socolofsky to explore space, interactivity, and perception through these types of tools. Since then, he has obviously made a great leap in becoming a master at his craft, relying quite heavily on procedural methods.

**Figure 9.2** "Creative play" is an important theme in Socolofsky's work; the formal elements in his projects, such as color, form, and sound, act as a means to this end.

Flash's flexibility for experimentation, as well as being a solid environment for rapid prototyping, are the main reasons Socolofsky employs this tool in his work. He has also made extensive use of Flash's increasing ability to connect with the external world through sensors, microcontrollers, and other software programs. *Salon*, a project of Socolofsky's that connects Flash with Cycling74's Max/MSP, is a prime example. Harnessing the superior audio capabilities of Max/MSP, Socolofsky uses a communication gateway called **flosc** (written by Ben Chun) as a pipeline for Max/MSP audio to communicate with Flash graphics and interface.

*Salon* represents very well what Socolofsky defines as "creative play," a concept he has identified as a primary research interest. Creative play goes beyond capturing the input of an audience to control audio and visuals. This notion of an interactive experience regards the artwork as a core mechanic for converting users into participants, adding significantly to the content of the artwork.

Socolofsky attributes the notion of artwork functioning as a core mechanic to Katie Salen and Eric Zimmerman. Their highly acclaimed game theory book, *Rules of Play*, has inspired many artists and designers, including Socolofsky. Besides being huge influences, Socolofsky works with both Salen and Zimmerman at Gamelab, *www.gamelab.com* (founded by Zimmerman and Peter Lee in 2000).

Socolofsky's other influences range from Flash based Websites, such as *www.sofake.com*, to artists not even using computers in their work, such as installation artist Olafur Eliasson.

**Figure 9.3** *Salon* (2004) invites the user to populate a room with famous twentieth-century personalities. Once selected, a representative icon floats through the salon, playing processed audio samples.

After finishing his master's degree at NYU, Socolofsky spent a year in residence at Eyebeam's Production Studio. Eyebeam *www.eyebeam.org*, based in New York City, is one of the leading centers for new media in the world. Socolofsky has also completed a variety of freelance and personal work using Flash, including work for Toyota, CourtTV, and Global Action Project.

In addition to his work at Gamelab, Socolofsky teaches interactive multimedia at NYU and Pratt Institute. Socolofsky constructively conveys his experiences developing highly detailed interactive environments to his students; many of the classes he teaches focus on Flash.

**Figure 9.4** Speaking of good examples of creative play... Socolofsky collaborated on quickcomic.com with Alex Eben Meyer and Ahmad Saeed. Visitors can make their own comic and save it to a database. Comics in the database can be viewed, rated, and e-mailed to friends.

**Figure 9.5** Socolofsky produced the Flash content for Global Action Project's Website. Other team members who worked on the site include, Ilona Parkansky, Ahmad Saeed, and Jasky Raju.

## DIGITAL DECONSTRUCTION: *VECTOGRAM*

*Vectogram* is one of Socolofsky's earliest projects incorporating Flash. In *Vectogram*, one of the first things you notice is the lack of a screen/keyboard/mouse environment where most Flash projects tend to reside. Borrowing from the 1980s era cocktail-style table, Socolofsky built a custom cabinet housing a computer, custom circuitry, and arcade-style interface.

Sitting before *Vectogram*, the user is greeted with a game that, in addition to stretching the boundaries of Flash based artwork, breaks many of the preconceptions of video game appearance and gameplay. The game is designed to be a two-player experience. Players strategically deploy "vectoids" to the screen in an attempt to cover it with abstract drawings. Each vectoid has a strength and a weakness relative to the other vectoids. The players can choose to either cooperate or compete for control of the electronic canvas, creating a collaborative multimedia experience in the process.

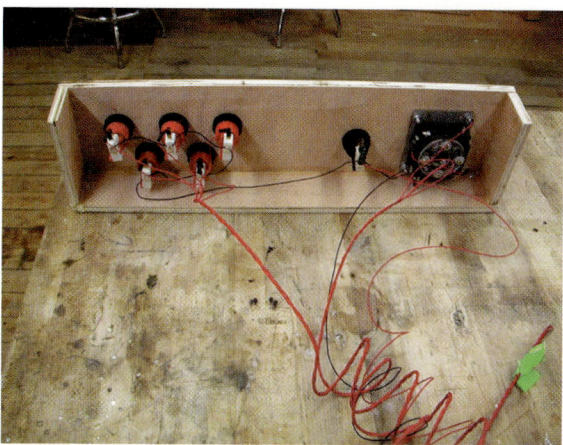

**Figure 9.6** Here is a look at some of the electronics and woodwork of *Vectogram* (2004).

**Figure 9.7** For Socolofsky, aesthetics and interface do not stop at the boundaries of the Flash Stage.

### DIGITIAL DECONSTRUCTION: *SILLY WALKS GENERATOR*

The *Silly Walks Generator* grew out of a request from Socolofsky's client (New Video Group based in New York City) to produce a promotional game for *Monty Python's Flying Circus* DVD release. Socolofsky began looking through Flying Circus sketches for inspiration and content, and the Ministry of Silly Walks sketch stood out as having a lot of potential for translating into Flash.

**Figure 9.8** Only by carefully marshaling your resources will you be able to generate a picture pleasing to your eye!

"Some of my favorite Monty Python content has always been Terry Gilliam's animations. I realized that John Cleese's walks could be even sillier if translated into a context similar to Gilliam's animations and that Flash would be able to present that translation quite successfully. After a bit more thought, I decided that a more open-ended, toy-like experience could be more successful in this context than a game, and the idea of creating one's own Silly Walks was born."

The *Silly Walks Generator* is a tool that allows users to generate simple keyframed animations of one of four Flying Circus characters. It also supports some simple application-level features, like the ability to save and load your walks and sample walks.

This piece had three main challenges: building the inverse kinematics (IK) engine, developing the keyframe animation engine, and designing a user interface around these two systems. Socolofsky has distilled a simplified version of the IK engine behind *Silly Walks Generator* into a tutorial, introducing a powerful system for interactivity and animation.

**Figure 9.9** A player enjoying the *Vectogram* (2004) experience.

CHAPTER NINE 151

**Figure 9.10** It is fun to interact with the *Silly Walks Generator*. By adjusting the various settings and creating keyframes, you can create a unique Monty Python sketch for the Internet.

**Figure 9.11** The user can also customize their own silly walk animation by choosing from different characters and scenes.

### DIY: *SILLY WALKS GENERATOR*: THE INVERSE KINEMATICS ENGINE

The IK system is a method used by animators to easily and quickly script lifelike motion. An IK system comprises a series of jointed limbs with one fixed endpoint and one movable endpoint. As the movable endpoint is repositioned, all other limbs in the system reposition themselves automatically.

---

**NOTE:** To demonstrate an IK system in real life, try placing a cup on a table in front of you. Without moving your shoulder, reach for the cup. Notice that your upper and lower arms and your wrist and elbow joints reposition themselves without having to think about it; your focus is only on the position of your hand. Animators use IK systems in the same way; by fixing one joint and moving another toward a target, all of the joints and limbs in between fall naturally into place.

---

The *Silly Walks Generator* makes use of a custom-built IK system to enable the user to create fluid animations with almost no knowledge of traditional animation processes. In this tutorial, we will step through the high-level elements of the IK system used in the *Silly Walks Generator*.

#### The Building Blocks of an IK System: The Joint and the Limb

The only two elements in an IK system are limbs and their joints. There are a series of rules that govern how all the limbs and joints interrelate, but at the core of the system are really just these two elements. The simplest limb is just a straight line (think of your upper arm, for example) and two points at either end (your shoulder and elbow).

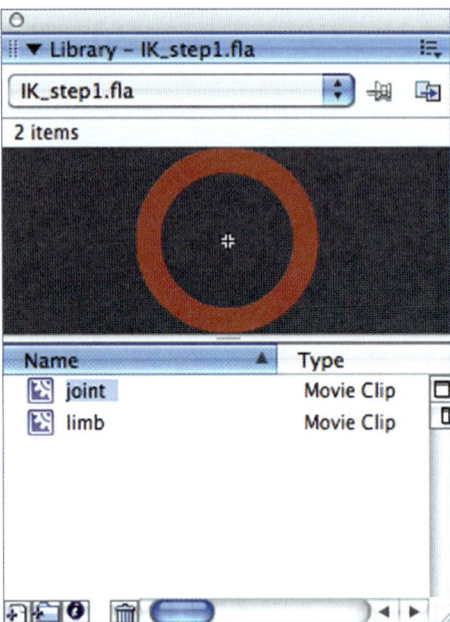

**Figure 9.12** In a moment, you will be inspecting the interrelationship of the joint and the limb.

Locate the folder on the DVD for chapter 9. Inside you will find three folders containing the files associated with each of the sections we are about to cover. To get started, go to the *step1_setup* folder and open *the IK_step1.fla*, *Joint.as*, and *Limb.as* files. This should open up three tabs in your Flash workspace.

---

**NOTE:** If you do not have Flash Professional, you will not be able to edit AS files inside the Flash work space. Instead, you can open them in any text editor. You will not have the same functionality and color-coding.

---

Click around on the Stage and movie clips, taking note of the instance names given to the Limb movie clips. Double-click one of the **limb** movie clips to enter its Timeline, and take a look at the instance names given to the **joints** (the small circle movie clips). The **joint** with the instance name of `jtHead` is centered precisely over the registration point (shown as crosshairs on the Stage) of the **limb** movie clip. Also notice how each joint has a registration point at its center. This registration point can either be manually adjusted by moving around the graphics inside a movie clip or established when you first create a symbol, as seen in Figure 9.13.

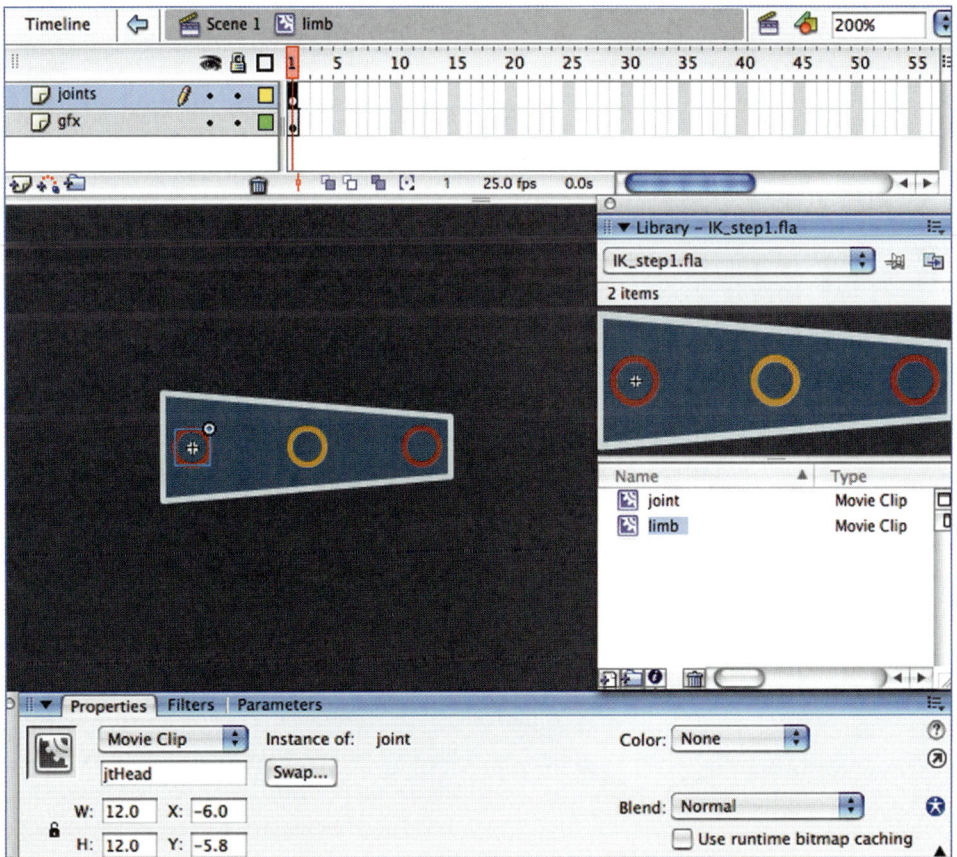

**Figure 9.13** Notice how the registration point for the joint named jtHead is centered exactly over the registration point for the limb.

The center joint (it has the `jtCenter` instance name) will act as a center of rotation when directly manipulating this limb. The head and tail joints will be used to connect these limbs into a skeleton. But to do that, we need to harness the powers of ActionScript.

### Activating the Joints to Create a Skeleton

Now let us look at the ActionScript classes driving these movie clips—the code responsible for allowing the limbs and joints to interrelate. Limbs rely on their joints for all of their translation and rotation. Our IK engine associates the **head** joint of each limb to move toward the **tail** joint of the limb in front of it. The Joint class is very simple; it basically just keeps track of the X/Y coordinates of each joint. Click on that tab, or open the Joint.as file if it is not already. Notice that the workspace for .as files are radically different than regular .fla files. Since .as files contain only ActionScript, there is no need for a Stage, Timeline, etc. Here is the code for the Joint class:

```
class Joint {
        public var x:Number;
        public var y:Number;
        private var mc:MovieClip;

        //this is the constructor
 function
        public function Joint
 (mc:MovieClip) {
                this.mc = mc;
                this.x = mc._x;
                this.y = mc._y;
        }
}
```

Simple enough, right? Pay special attention to the constructor function: `Joint`. It must be named exactly the same as the class at the top of the code, as well as the actual FLA file,

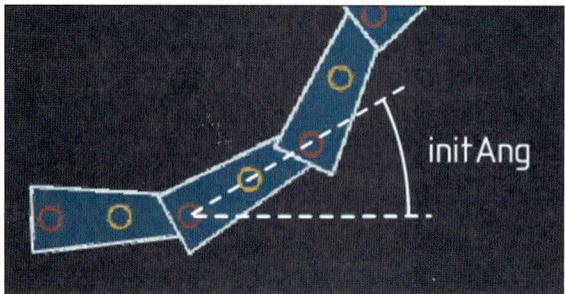

**Figure 9.14** initAng before rotation.

Joint.as. Tab over to the *Limb.as* file so we can run through this custom class.

The constructor for our Limb class is calling a few functions we have not written yet, so let us walk through them one-by-one.

```
public function Limb (mc:Movie
Clip) {
        this.initMC(mc);
        this.findJoints();
        Limb.storeLimb(this);
}
```

Function `initMC` is responsible for setting up the Limb's on-stage representation. This function is primarily responsible for copying properties of the movie clip (which we have already created in the .fla) into the Limb object for easier management. Without going into an involved discussion about the merits of composition vs. inheritance, I will just say that we are going to be doing a lot of tricky math with these movie clip properties, and it is best to separate them conceptually from the movie clip representation of this object before we start manipulating them. In other words, we should be thinking about the properties like x, y, and rotation as properties of the Limb object, not of its on-screen movie clip representation. That said, here is the initMC method which defines the Limb class:

```
private function initMC ↵
(mc:MovieClip) :Void {
    //store the MovieClip as a ↵
property of this Limb
    this.mc = mc;

    //store the MovieClip's ↵
properties in this Limb
    this.x = this.mc._x;
    this.y = this.mc._y;
    this.ang = this.mc._ ↵
rotation/360 * (2*Math.PI);

    //store a unique identifier ↵
 for this Limb
    this.num = parseInt(this. ↵
mc._name.substr(4));

    //initialize this Limb's ↵
user interface
    this.mc.onPress = Proxy. ↵
create(this, this.mcPress);
    this.mc.onRelease = this. ↵
mc.onReleaseOutside = Proxy. ↵
create(this, this.mcRelease);
}
```

The first few lines are simply storing a reference to the movie clip in the **Limb** object's mc property, and copying its _x and _y values into the x and y properties of the **Limb**. The next line converts the movie clip's _rotation value from degrees to radians and stores it in the **Limb's** ang property. The next line stores the Limb number by taking the number off the end of the **Limb** movie clip's name, and we

will use this number as a unique identifier. The last two lines are setting up Mouse event handlers for the IK system's user interface; we will revisit these lines later.

The findJoints function is a handy utility to scan through the limb instances we created in the authoring environment to find any joints that we have placed in each. It is added right after our initMC method, and it looks like this:

```
private function findJoints () ↵
:Void {
    //find and store head joint
    if (!this.mc.jtHead) {
        trace("ERROR:: no ↵
jtHead in " + this.mc);
        return;
    }
    this.headJt = new Joint( ↵
this.mc.jtHead);

    //find and store center joint
    if (!this.mc.jtCenter) {
        trace("ERROR:: no ↵
jtCenter in " + this.mc);
        return;
    }
    this.cenJt = new Joint ↵
(this.mc.jtCenter);

    //find and store all ↵
"child" (other) joints
    this.childJts = new Array();
    var nextJtNum = 0;
    while (this.mc["jt"+ ↵
nextJtNum]) {
        this.childJts.push ↵
(new Joint(this.mc["jt"+nextJtNum]));
        nextJtNum ++;
    }
}
```

This function takes advantage of our cleverly devised naming convention to enable the location of the head and center joints and an unlimited number of additional joints. It is critical that the joints are named exactly as specified by the code in this function: `jtHead`, `jtCenter`, and `jt0`, `jt1`, `jt2`, etc. As this function finds each joint movie clip, it creates and stores a new Joint object for each.

The last task performed by the constructor is to store this **Limb** in a list of all the Limbs in this skeleton. Limbs need a way to access each other, so they are placed in a static array of the Limb class, like so:

```
private static function storeLimb
 (limb:Limb) :Void {
        if (!Limb.instances) {
Limb.instances = new Array(); }
        Limb.instances.push(limb);
}
```

We will also need a static function to pull the Limbs out of storage:

```
public static function get
Instance (num:Number) :Limb {
        return(instances[num]);
}
```

At this point, the Limbs all have Joints, but we need to make the Limbs aware of their neighbors. The Limbs will come together to form a whole skeleton.

### Building the Skeleton

A skeleton in an IK system is really just a series of associations between limbs. An arm consists of the upper arm, the lower arm, the hand, and each of the fingers, each with their own series of finger bones. A torso is one large element (we can refer to this as a limb, too) with five limbs: the arms, the legs, and the head. Each of these associations between limbs has a hierarchy; the torso can be referred to as the parent of the head, arms, and legs; where the torso moves, the head, arms, and legs follow. If the torso is the parent, it follows that the head, arms, and legs are the torso's children. The same goes for the arm: the lower arm is a child of the upper arm, and the parent of the hand; the hand, in turn, is the parent of each of the fingers. A limb in an IK system can have only one parent, but can have as many children as it wants.

The skeleton for our example is a quite simple one; it looks something like a snake, or a human spine. Each Limb has at most one parent and one child Limb. There is a good chance that we will want to create something a bit more complex in the future, so we will keep that in mind as we write the Skeleton functionality. To establish these associations in our system, we will start with a function in the Limb class, called `initFamily`:

```
public function initFamily
(childLimbs:Array) :Void {
        this.numChildLimbs =
childLimbs.length;
        this.childLimbs = new Array();
        for (var i=0; i<this.
numChildLimbs; i++) {
            this.addChild
(childLimbs[i], i);
        }
}
```

`initFamily` calls a function `addChild`, which in turn calls a function `setParent`. These three functions together create on each Limb an array of child Limbs, a reference to this Limb's parent, and a reference to the Joint on the parent to which this Limb is attached.

```
private function addChild ↵
(childLimb:Limb, childNum:Number) ↵
:Void {
    this.childLimbs[cNum] = ↵
childLimb;
    childLimb.setParent(this, ↵
this.childJts[childNum]);
}

public function setParent ↵
(pLimb:Limb, parentJt:Joint) :Void {
    this.parentLimb = pLimb;
    this.parentJt = parentJt;
}
```

To initialize the skeleton, we have but to call `initFamily` on each of the Limbs. In order to initialize the skeleton, we have to place limbs on the Stage in the authoring environment (our .fla); as such, the skeleton initialization code will also live in the authoring environment. Tab back to the *IK_step1.fla* and take a look at the code placed on frame 1 of the **code** layer.

```
function initSkeleton () {
    //create Limbs
    for (var i=0; i<6; i++) {
        new Limb(this[↵
"limb"+i]);
    }
    
    //init limb families
    Limb.getInstance(0).↵
initFamily([Limb.getInstance(1)]);
    Limb.getInstance(1).↵
initFamily([Limb.getInstance(2)]);
    Limb.getInstance(2).↵
initFamily([Limb.getInstance(3)]);
    Limb.getInstance(3).↵
initFamily([Limb.getInstance(4)]);
    Limb.getInstance(4).↵
initFamily([Limb.getInstance(5)]);
    Limb.getInstance(5).↵
initFamily([]);
}
initSkeleton();
```

`initSkeleton` loops through all the limb instances on Stage, makes a Limb object for each, and creates the required associations between limbs. Note that `limb5` has no children—it is at the tail-end of the skeleton. Our skeleton is now fully initialized and ready to learn to move!

### Translation

Let us begin with getting the translation in place, then we will worry about the rotation. The basic concept of translation in an IK system is that the head joint of one limb always approaches the tail joint of the next limb. We can make this happen with a programmatic animation concept known as easing.

> **NOTE:** Easing, at its most basic, is an application of Xeno's Paradox, the situation proposed by the ancient Greek philosopher Xeno in which repeated steps covering half the distance remaining to a target will never quite get you there. While this is true, if one takes those steps each at the same speed, they will approach the target with a nice gliding motion that slows as they near the target.

The logic required to produce an easing effect is very simple: find the distance from a destination to a current location and move some fraction of that distance. Then do the same the next frame, and the next, until the object is close enough for horseshoes. In code, simple easing looks like this:

```
var easeSpeed:Number = 0.2;
var dx:Number = target._x - this._x;
this._x += dx * easeSpeed;
```

This code should be executed every frame, and should also be executed on the Y axis for two-dimensional easing. Varying the `easeSpeed` variable will vary the rate at which the object approaches its target; keep it between 0.0 and 1.0. Later, we will be adding the `translate` method in the *Limb.as* class file to ease our limb movement.

For now, we will enable this skeleton to be dragged around by clicking and dragging on any of its limbs. That means it is now time to implement the `mcPress` and `mcRelease` methods we stubbed out earlier. Find the *step2_translation* folder on the DVD and open the files: *IK_step2.fla, Joint.as* and *Limb.as*. Activate the *Lims.as* file and check out the `mcPress` and `mcRelease` methods.

```
public function mcPress () :Void {
      Limb.stopAllLimbs();
      this.findMovementJoints(null);

      //translate
      this.mc.onEnterFrame =
Proxy.create(this, this.update, 0,
 false);
      this.mc.onEnterFrame();
}

public function mcRelease () :Void {
      //store mouse coordinates
to complete easing animation
      this.lastX = _root._xmouse;
      this.lastY = _root._ymouse;

      //glide to a stop
      this.mc.onEnterFrame =
Proxy.create(this, this.update, 0,
 true);
}
```

**NOTE:** Regarding the Proxy class—You may have noticed the use of something called `Proxy` earlier, when assigning `mcPress` to `this.mc.onPress` and the same with `mcRelease`. Proxy is a very handy class written by Joey Lott *person13.com* that expands on Macromedia's Delegate class. It allows a function to be called with a specified scope, with parameters. If the code read: `this.mc.onEnterFrame = this.update;` any references to this inside the `update` function would resolve to the Limb's mc reference instead of to the Limb itself. Also, Proxy allows us to pass parameters to the re-scoped function call. For more information on the Proxy Class, and to download the source, please visit *www.person13.com/articles/proxy/Proxy.htm*. Without `Proxy`, creating this functionality would entail using a messy and not very object-oriented "hook."

The *Silly Walks Generator* IK engine is set up to allow what I call "dynamic reparenting," in which any Limb can become the top of the IK chain when dragged. As such, `mcPress` is responsible for establishing this hierarchy and for making the necessary calculations to support it. It first kills all previous Limb movement with a call to `Limb.stopAllLimbs`. It then calls `findMovementJoints` to determine which Joints will be used in the translation. Finally it sets off a function `update` that will be called every frame. For brevity's sake, `findMovementJoints` is not dissected in this text. In summary, this function establishes `this.movJt` and `this.tgtJt` for each Limb by recursing both up and down the skeleton's hierarchy from the Limb that was selected. `movJt` is the Joint on a given Limb that will approach (while dragging its Limb along with it) `tgtJt`; `tgtJt` is a Joint on this Limb's parent Limb.

Once we have established the Joints each Limb will use to follow its parent Limb, we can begin the Limb translation, which will happen every frame. The function `update` is responsible for executing the translation, which again, is in the `Limb.as Class`.

```
private function update 
(dAng:Number, auto:Boolean, bIs
Stopping:Boolean) :Void {
        var mpt = getMovementPoint();
        var tpt = getTargetPoint
(auto);
        translate(mpt, tpt);

        //update parent, and 
recursively update children
        if (this.parentLimb != 
this.prevLimb) { this.parentLimb.
update(0, true); }
        for (var i=0; i<numChild
Limbs; i++) {
                if (this.childLimbs
[i] != this.prevLimb) { this.
childLimbs[i].update(dAng, true); }
        }

        //flag for stopping, in 
Limb.checkForStop()
        if (!this.stopped && Math.
abs(tpt.x-mpt.x)<=Limb.TRANS_
THOLD && Math.abs(tpt.y-mpt.y)<=
Limb.TRANS_THOLD) {
                this.stopped = true;
        }

        if (bIsStopping) {
                Limb.checkForStop();
        }
}
```

The `update` function works as follows: find the current location of `movJt`, then find the location of `tgtJt`, perform the Limb translation, recurse through all the other limbs and do the same. Check to see if this Limb is close enough to its target to stop calculating its movement.

`getMovementPoint` is the simplest element in this process. In order to calculate distances between points within different Limbs, we need a common frame of reference for the points' coordinates. ActionScript has a built-in tool for just this purpose, `localToGlobal` can be used to transform the coordinates of a point in a movie clip into global (`_root`) space, and it is used in `getMovementPoint` to find the coordinates of this Limb's `movJt` in global space.

`getTargetPoint` has to handle a few different conditions and is a bit more complex than `getMovementPoint`. However, it serves a very similar purpose: it calculates the coordinates of the target point toward which Limb will move in global space. Let us walk through each of the three conditions.

```
private function getTargetPoint 
(auto:Boolean) :Object {
        var targetPt = {x:null, 
y:null};
        if (this.prevLimb) {
                //if this Limb has 
a Limb higher up in the IK 
chain, use tgtJt
                targetPt.x = this.
tgtJt.x;
                targetPt.y = this.
tgtJt.y;
                this.prevLimb.mc.
localToGlobal(targetPt);
        } else {
                if (!auto) {
                        //if the Limb 
is currently being dragged, 
use the mouse location as the target
                        targetPt.x = 
_root._xmouse;
                        targetPt.y = 
_root._ymouse;
                } else {
```

```
                //else use
the last location of the mouse
when dragging
                targetPt.x =
this.lastX;
                targetPt.y =
this.lastY;
            }
        }
        return targetPt;
}
```

The first conditional branch is used when calculating the target point of any Limb below the one being dragged (`prevLimb` refers to the first Limb above this one in the IK chain; in other words, the parent Limb). We calculated the target Joint to use in this circumstance in `findMovementJoints`, so we can use `this.tgtJt`, which is a Joint inside `this.prevLimb`, and then use `localToGlobal` to translate its coordinates into global space.

The other branch is used only by the Limb at the top of the IK chain. The `auto` parameter is true after the user has released the mouse to allow the IK chain to continue to resolve (slide into place), while freeing up the mouse for other tasks. When `auto` is `false`, this Limb will move toward the mouse. When `true`, this Limb will move toward the location of the mouse at the moment the user stopped dragging (when the mouse was released).

Finally, we come to the actual translation. After all of this setup, it is time to apply the easing technique described earlier. The translate function finds the distance from the movement point to the target point and translates this Limb's movie clip some fraction of that distance.

```
private function translate
(mpt, tpt) :Void {
        //ease from parent joint
toward target point
        var dx = tpt.x - mpt.x;
        var dy = tpt.y - mpt.y;

        //the farther the stretch,
the faster the follow
        var xSpeed = Math.abs(dx)/
(Math.abs(dx)+Limb.STRETCHINESS);
        var ySpeed = Math.abs(dy)/
(Math.abs(dy)+Limb.STRETCHINESS);
        this.x += dx * xSpeed;
        this.y += dy * ySpeed;
        this.mc._x = this.x;
        this.mc._y = this.y;
}
```

This code is almost a line-for-line adaptation of easing as described earlier; there is, however, one notable difference: our ease speed is not constant. In order to give a stretchy, somewhat realistic feel to the translation, the ease speed gets faster the farther a Limb has to travel. If the user drags a Limb very quickly, the other Limbs will quickly follow; if the user just nudges a Limb slightly, the motion will gently ripple through the other Limbs.

After the first Limb has been translated, `update` recurses through the rest of the Limbs in the chain and applies their translation as well. The last thing that `update` does is to tell a Limb to stop moving once it gets within a constant distance from its target, namely `Limb.TRANS_THOLD`. When the remaining distance in both the X and Y axes falls below this amount for all Limbs in the chain, the entire chain stops calculating its movement. Each Limb determines its own stopping point within `update`, the static function `Limb.checkForStop` checks all Limbs to see if they have stopped, and when they all have, fires the static function `Limb.stopAllLimbs`, which halts all translation calculation.

Tab over to the *IK_step2.fla* and test the movie. Now that we have a graceful, stretchy translation applied to our IK chain, we only need to apply rotation to make the IK system complete.

### Rotation

Rotation is conceptually quite similar to translation. When translating, a Limb eases itself toward its parent Limb; when rotating, a Limb eases its rotation to maintain the same rotation relative to its parent Limb as just before the rotation. Unfortunately, there are a couple of things that make executing rotation in a Flash IK system substantially trickier than translation. One of them is compensating for the fact that Flash thinks it is smarter than you, the other is trigonometry. (Do not be afraid! We will make it through that high-school nightmare—I promise.)

Before we can dive into the nuts and bolts of rotation, we need to enable the user to translate *and* rotate with some user interface modifications. In the *Silly Walks Generator*, a character is dragged by its torso by holding down the spacebar while clicking, and is rotated by simply click-dragging on any Limb. There are plenty of other UI (User Interface) options that may better suit a given project, but I found this to be a fairly effective interface for this project.

Close the step 2 files you were looking at in the previous section. Open the *step3_rotation* folder from the DVD and open up *IK_step3.fla*, *Joint.as*, and *Limb.as*. Let us start by looking at the code in the FLA file. Inside of `initSkeleton` in the Actions panel, take a look at the mouse handlers that have been added.

```
//enable dragging with spacebar+click
this.onMouseDown = function () {
        if (Key.isDown(Key.SPACE)) {
                translatingCharacter
 = true;
                Limb.getInstance(0).
mcPress.call(Limb.getInstance
(0), true);
        }
}

this.onMouseUp = function () {
        //if SPACE is down, stop
dragging
        if (translatingCharacter) {
                translatingCharacter
 = false;
                Limb.getInstance(0)
.mcRelease.call(Limb.get
Instance(0), false);
        }
}
```

With this code, when the user clicks anywhere on Stage with the spacebar held down the skeleton will start translating just as before, as though the first Limb was click-dragged. This frees up click-dragging directly on Limbs for our rotation functionality.

To enable this functionality, some changes were made to `mcPress` and `mcRelease` in the Limb Class. These changes are nothing more than branching the functionality of the press and release. If the user is translating, translation code will fire—if rotating, rotation code will fire.

```
public function mcPress (dragging:
Boolean) :Void {
        if (!dragging && Key.isDown
(Key.SPACE)) { return; }

        Limb.stopAllLimbs();
        this.translating = dragging;
```

```
            this.findMovementJoints(null);

    if (this.translating) {
            //translate
            this.mc.onEnterFrame
 = Proxy.create(this, this.
update, 0, false, false);
    } else {
            //rotate
            this.mouseAng = 
null;   //init inside userRotate
            this.mc.onEnter
Frame = Proxy.create(this,
 this.userRotate, false);
    }
    this.mc.onEnterFrame();
}
```

When the `dragging` parameter is true, `this.mc.onEnterFrame` will fire update every frame just as before. However, when the parameter is false, we will be calling a new function called `userRotate` every frame instead. The changes to `mcRelease` are similar, but deal with terminating rotation/translation processes rather than initializing them.

Please note in the included source code that we have also made some minor modifications to `findMovementJoints`, (for rotation re-initialization purposes), added some member variables, and added a new function called `stopNonChildren`. These changes are relatively tangential and will not be discussed here, but are commented on in the source files on the DVD.

With initialization behind us, let us move on to take a look at the main function responsible for executing the IK rotation, `rotate`. As mentioned earlier, our approach toward rotation will be quite similar to that of translation: each Limb will calculate the rotational distance toward a target angle and will move some fraction of that distance each frame until it is close enough. The target angle for a given Limb will be relative to its parent Limb; for example, if a child Limb is angled PI/4 radians (90 degrees) from its parent Limb, as its parent Limb rotates, the child Limb will continually rotate to maintain that PI/4 relative rotation.

However, the fact that the Limbs are all translating at the same time means that the rotation has to take that motion into account as well. In the end, we will find ourselves easing toward an average of two angles: the rotational offset just described, and the angle that keeps the child Limb's center point, its movement point, and its target point (on its parent Limb) aligned.

```
private function rotate (mpt:
Object, tpt:Object, dAng:Number) 
:Void {
    //ease rotation toward 
average of two angles:
    //aligning center joint, 
parent joint, and target point
 (atan2), and
    //initial rotation 
(initAng) relative to rotation 
of selected limb (+ dAng)
    if (!this.prevLimb) { 
return; }   //don't rotate top 
parent limb
    //correct dAng
    while (dAng-this.initAng 
< -Math.PI) { dAng += 2*Math.PI; }
    while (dAng-this.initAng 
> Math.PI) { dAng -= 2*Math.PI; }
    var endAng = dAng + this.
initAng;

    var cpt = this.getCenter
Point();
    var firstAng = Math.atan2
(cpt.y-tpt.y, cpt.x-tpt.x) + 
this.parentAng;
```

```
            //average and correct first
Ang and endAng
        while (firstAng-endAng < -
Math.PI) { firstAng += 2*Math.PI; }
        while (firstAng-endAng >
Math.PI) { firstAng -= 2*Math.PI; }
        var tgtAng = (firstAng +
endAng)/2;

        //keep tgtAng (-PI<>PI)
before calculating with ang
        while (tgtAng<-Math.PI) {
tgtAng += 2*Math.PI; }
        while (tgtAng>Math.PI) {
tgtAng -= 2*Math.PI; }

        //calculate follow angle
change
        var calcAng = this.
ang-this.getAngOffset(this.ang);

//remove additional rotations for
calculation
        if (calcAng>Math.PI/2 &&
tgtAng<-Math.PI/2) { tgtAng +=
2*Math.PI; }
        else if (calcAng<-Math.PI/2
 && tgtAng>Math.PI/2) { tgtAng
 -= 2*Math.PI; }
        tgtAng += this.getAngOffset
(this.ang);
        this.ang += (tgtAng - this.
ang) * Limb.ROT_SPEED;

        this.mc._rotation =
radToDeg(this.ang);
}
```

As with translate, rotate has movement point and target point parameters, calculated with `getMovementPoint` and `getTargetPoint`, which represent the point on a Limb that will move toward a target point on another Limb, respectively, and both in the global coordinate space. The third parameter, `dAng`, is how far the user has rotated the currently selected Limb since the mouse was pressed. We will see how this gets set when we look through the `userRotate` function.

The rotate function's first task is to calculate the angle of this Limb relative to the current rotation of the whole skeleton. When a Limb is pressed, `findMovementJoints` stores the current rotation of each Limb in its `initAng` property. As the user rotates the skeleton, every Limb farther down the skeleton, from the Limb the user is actively rotating, will rotate by the same amount (`dAng`). Therefore, the first angle we are looking for is `initAng` + `dAng` (Figure 9.15 and Figure 9.16). We will store that inside a variable called `endAng`.

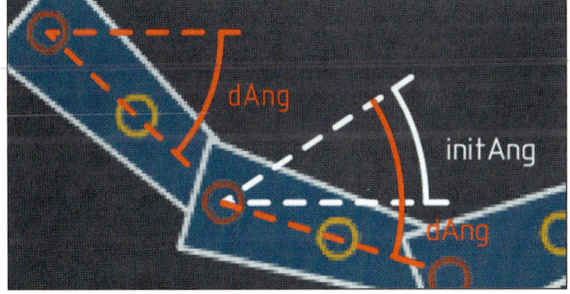

**Figure 9.15** `initAng` after rotation.

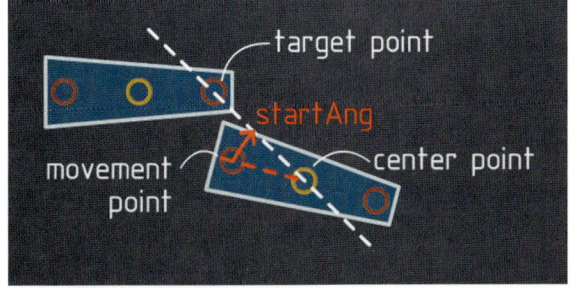

**Figure 9.16** Calculating the value for `startAng`.

The second task is to calculate the second angle, which is the angle at which the Limb's center point, movement point, and target point are all aligned. As Limbs translate relative to one another, the joints between Limbs start to slip. Easing toward this angle will keep the IK chain looking smooth. For example, if a parent Limb begins to move above its child Limb, the child Limb needs to rotate upwards in response to this movement. This angle is found by first using `Math.atan2` to find the angle between the center point and target point, and then by adding the rotation of this Limb relative to its parent Limb. This relative angle is calculated by `findMovementJoints` every time a Limb is clicked and rotation begins. We will store this angle inside a variable called `startAng`.

Once `startAng` and `endAng` are calculated, we simply find the average of the two, and ease toward that angle. Note that there is some angle correction happening in the `rotate` function; ActionScript has an annoying "feature" that locks angles between 180 and −180. If a movie clip's `_rotation` goes beyond those limits, 360 degrees are added or subtracted to bring it back in range. 181 degrees becomes −179, and −181 degrees becomes 179. In order to counterbalance the interpreter's activism, we make an effort to keep our own calculation angles within PI and −PI (180 degrees and −180 degrees).

Additionally, when easing, we run into the problem of easing across that boundary. A delta angle can jump from, say, 5 degrees (easing from 174 to 179) to −354 degrees (from 175 to −179), causing unexpected spins. To keep this unfortunate side effect under control, anticipate this condition with code that corrects angles before Flash Player can do it for you. This is the purpose of these lines:

```
if (calcAng>Math.PI/2 && tgtAng<-
Math.PI/2) { tgtAng += 2*Math.PI; }
else if (calcAng<-Math.PI/2 &&
tgtAng>Math.PI/2) { tgtAng -
= 2*Math.PI; }
```

Note also the use of the `getAngOffset` function, which accounts for any extra rotation value above 2 PI and below 0.

With the `rotate` function out of the way, all that is left is to give the user access to it. This is where the `userRotate` function comes into play. As a user clicks and drags a Limb to rotate it, `userRotate` implements that rotation. Note that `userRotate` is only ever called on the Limb the user is click-dragging; all other Limbs farther down the IK chain call `rotate`.

```
private function userRotate
(auto:Boolean, bIsStopping:
Boolean) :Void {
    var mpt = this.getMovement
Point();
    if (this.mouseAng == null)
{ this.mouseAng = Math.atan2
(this.mc._ymouse, this.mc._xmouse); }
    var dAng = this.ang - this.
initAng - this.getAngOffset
(this.ang-this.initAng);
//keep dAng b/w -PI and PI

    //calculate angle change
    var tgtAng;
    if (auto) { tgtAng = Math.
atan2(this.lastY-mpt.y, this.
lastX-mpt.x) - this.mouseAng; }
    else { tgtAng = Math.atan2
(_root._ymouse-mpt.y, _root.
_xmouse-mpt.x) - this.mouseAng; }
    var calcAng = this.ang-get
AngOffset(this.ang);  //keep
calcAng b/w -PI and PI
```

```
            if (calcAng>Math.PI/2 && ↵
tgtAng<-Math.PI/2) { tgtAng ↵
+= 2*Math.PI; }
            else if (calcAng<-Math.PI/↵
2 && tgtAng>Math.PI/2) { ↵
tgtAng -= 2*Math.PI; }
            tgtAng += this.getAngOff↵
set(this.ang);

            this.ang += (tgtAng - this.↵
ang) * Limb.USER_ROT_SPEED;
            this.mc._rotation = this.↵
radToDeg(this.ang);

            //only update children
            for (var i=0; i<this.↵
numChildLimbs; i++) { this.child↵
Limbs[i].update(dAng, true, false); }

            //flag for stopping, in ↵
Limb.checkForStop()
            if (!this.stopped && Math.↵
abs(tgtAng-this.ang)<Limb.↵
ROT_THOLD) { this.stopped = true; }

            if (bIsStopping) { Limb.↵
checkForStop(); }
}
```

This function is fairly straightforward conceptually, but is made a bit more complex by the extra math required to keep the rotation angles within a manageable range. It rotates the Limb the user is dragging toward the mouse, pivoting around the Limb's registration point. It also calculates the rotational difference between the current moment and the moment the Limb was clicked; it sends that value to all Limbs farther down the IK chain as the `dAng` parameter to `update`, where it is passed through to `rotate`.

When `userRotate` is first called immediately after a click, it calculates the angle from the Limb's registration point to the mouse (in the Limb's coordinate space), and stores that inside `mouseAng`. This value acts as a starting offset; as the mouse moves around the Limb's registration point, the Limb rotates relative to that starting offset. This makes the UI just a bit cleaner, as the Limb does not automatically rotate to the mouse when clicked. It rotates only when the mouse begins to move.

Next, we calculate the target angle toward which the Limb will rotate. Rather than snapping the Limb's rotation to the exact location of the mouse at all times when dragging, `userRotate` eases the Limb's rotation toward a target, in order to bring to the rotation UI the same fluid motion generated by the IK system. In short, easing the rotation produces a bit of play in the rotation UI.

To find the target angle (`tgtAng`), we first calculate the angle between the mouse and the Limb's registration point in global space, calculated with a call to `getMovementPoint` and stored inside `mpt`. We then have to remove that initial rotational offset, `mouseAng`. In order to avoid any unwanted extra rotations, we now have to do some number-juggling with `tgtAng` to get it within PI radians in either direction of `ang`. This is another unfortunate side-effect of ActionScript's annoying habit of limiting `_rotation` values between −180 and +180. Now that we have a usable `tgtAng`, we simply ease toward it.

As noted above, only the Limb actively being dragged by the user calls `userRotate`, so it propagates its rotation down through the IK chain by calling `update` on all its child Limbs. The `update` function then recurses down through the whole chain, until all Limbs below the Limb being rotated have updated their rotation and position as well.

At this point, testing your movie should provide a snake-like creature that can be dragged and repositioned with mouse clicks. If your version is not working, open the *step3_rotation* folder on the DVD and check out the files and code contained in there.

### Storing and Playing Back Animation

The IK system was definitely the most challenging element of this project. The solution I arrived at here came from a combination of intuition, trial and error, and even some dumb luck. I am certain that there are still refinements that can be made to this code, in particular in the areas that deal with angle correction. However, it seems to work pretty well for this application, and tying it to a keyframed animation recorder was not too difficult.

The data stored for each keyframe primarily comprises the X and Y location and rotation of each Limb in each keyframe. With that data, playing back an animation is just a matter of feeding that data back into the IK system and letting the system fill in the numbers in between each keyframe. While I would love to run through that part of the application as well, paper costs money! Besides, what fun is building an application if all of the problems are already solved for you?

CHAPTER NINE    167

### ON YOUR OWN

The IK engine has tremendous possibilities for creating your own interactive objects and creatures in Flash. In Socolofsky's tutorial, you created a snake-like form out of a string of limb/joint movie clips. Try creating your own graphics for these movie clips then string them together in various configurations to create unique IK-based creatures. Why stop at one IK skeleton? Try placing several together inside a movie clip for more complexity.

Another interesting variation would be to give these creatures their own behavior. Instead of waiting for the user to click and drag on a limb, make them self-propelled by recursively updating the X and Y properties of the head movie clip.

Design Engines and Social Networking

The best designers do much more than simply create design solutions for clients. Art projects and design experiments provide a testing ground for expanding formal and conceptual possibilities. Krister Olsson is a prolific designer whose commercial projects and experimental artwork exemplifies these notions. This body of work embraces a wide range of methods, from physical computing to interactive Web design and uses a variety of unsuspecting materials in their construction; eggshells, bone, grass, and animal gelatin are just a few things Olsson reuses in his creative projects. Conceptually, these works focus their experimental makeup to explore the roles of memorials and anti-memorials in contemporary society.

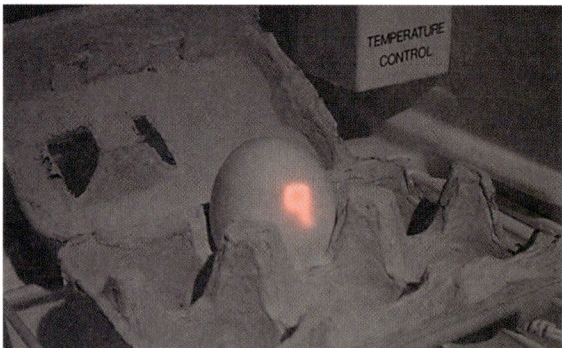

**Figure 10.1** *Memorial to Things Gone Bad* (2005) –Two eggs were carefully sawed in half and implanted with microcontrollers and LED displays. Each egg's display glows through its shell providing a visual indication of the number of days remaining before the egg goes bad. A pulsing dot at the bottom right of each display simulates a heartbeat. When an egg's number of days remaining reaches 0, its display and heartbeat fade out.

His screen-based work addresses issues of community and identity through the subversion of social networks and the creation of new collaborative creative tools.

Many of these projects were created using Flash. While Olsson enjoys many aspects of Flash, like the scalability of vector graphics and how it interfaces with other Web formats such as Ajax, XML, and PHP—he still has some concerns.

**Figure 10.2** Much of the technology in Olsson's *Snake In the Grass* (2005), remains hidden beneath an atypical, yet provocative, design material—grass.

"My one real problem with Flash, and other off-the-shelf software these days, is that it feels so incredibly bloated. Each version upgrade requires a computer upgrade just to handle the user interface (and in most cases, the UI has changed very little). The latest version of Photoshop has more functions than one can possibly fathom: I use maybe 10% of all available menus and dialogs."

Furthermore, Olsson points out that many works completed in Flash tend to have a homogeneous look. But he believes this is more of a problem of how this and other programs are taught. With this in mind, designers like Olsson certainly share at least this common trait: software does not make good work—designers and artists with good ideas do.

> "When I teach Flash or Processing I have students develop ideas for projects without regard for the skills required to build them. It is important that students not feel creatively inhibited by a lack of technical ability. Over the course of developing their projects, students learn what they need to learn, carving out their own comfortable space."

While still in the early part of his career, Olsson is actually very well established as a professional designer. His impressive résumé includes design work for MTV, Absolut, Sprite, Adobe, Sun Microsystems, CNET, Fujitsu, and AOL. Most of these works are part of the Tree Axis portfolio. Tree Axis *treeaxis.com* is a design firm based in Los Angeles, where Olsson is co-founder and principal designer.

Some of the prestigious awards and reviews highlighting Olsson's career include: the Japanese Agency for Cultural Affairs, *I.D. Magazine*, *Communication Arts*, Keio University, *The New York Times*, *Chicago Tribune*, *Los Angeles Times*, *Seattle Post-Intelligencer*, and *Wired*. The work recognized by these publications and organizations has been exhibited throughout the United States, Japan, Hong Kong, Australia, Singapore, Brazil, and Switzerland.

In addition to his work as a professional designer and artist, Olsson has also taught a number of courses in interaction design and

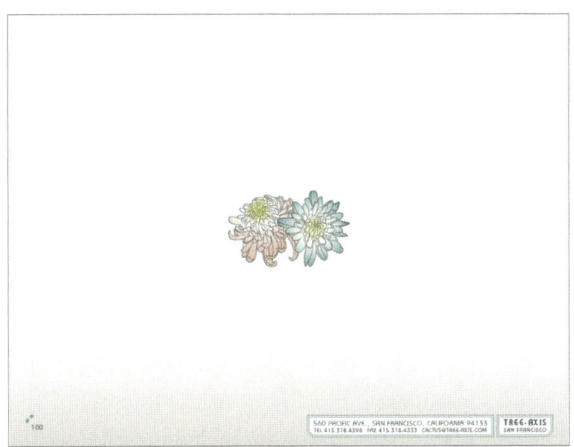

**Figure 10.3** The Tree Axis Website *treeaxis.com* houses many of the creative endeavors that will be covered in this chapter.

generative art at San Francisco Art Institute, California College of the Arts, and UCLA, often using Flash as the focal software. He notes a preference for these types of courses as it lends to his approach for building engines for creative expression.

Rounding out his professional experiences, Olsson is a former columnist for both *IdN* and *Shift* magazines. Even today, he still receives e-mails referencing or querying articles he wrote years ago.

Having recently finished his graduate degree from UCLA's Department of Design and Media Arts, Olsson is now focusing again on various design projects. Most notably, he has just completed the launch of the site showcasing the new Microsoft MP3 player, Zune.

When Olsson was a youngster in the early 1980s, during the height of the Atari 2600 boom, he can recall really wanting this early gaming console. His father did not want to buy him a game machine, so instead got him a TI-99/4A computer. Olsson spent a lot of time typing-in programs from books and magazines; one of these publications, *K-Power*, had music programs that played songs by the Talking Heads and the Ramones. At the time, his mind was still on the absent Atari system, but years later he understood how important it was to have worked with these early personal computers.

After a period of ambivalence towards computers, Olsson graduated with a B.A. in Computer Science from Swarthmore College. His studies focused on writing computer code in Lisp, Prolog, Java, and C. More important than the direct application of these coding languages, he discovered their deeper intrinsic value for problem solving and understanding a variety of system-based phenomena.

"I learned that in the same way that learning a foreign language can help one see the world differently, learning multiple programming languages allows one to attack problems from a variety of different perspectives."

**Figure 10.4** Olsson worked on the site for the new Zune media player *www.zune-arts.net/*.

Because of his father's line of work, Olsson was introduced at an early age to artists such as Rauschenberg, Christo, and Bill Viola. With these legendary figures as influences, Olsson found he did not have much interest for going into research or taking a traditional coding job after graduation. Instead, he began to explore multimedia development, at first using Director and later moving into Flash.

Within a relatively small community in the late 1990s, Olsson is someone who can claim he has been around to see the complete evolution of Flash. Somewhat excited by versions 3 and 4, it was not until the release of Flash 5 that he started to deploy this tool with commercial projects. As with many designers at this time, Olsson was morphing into Flash from Director, and many of his projects embedded Flash within Director. From this expertise he wrote an article for Webmonkey www.webmonkey.com that predicted a single unified multimedia platform within a year or two. This prediction never quite happened, but at this point, what is quite obvious is that Flash has come out on top as the leading interactive multimedia software tool.

### DIGITAL DECONSTRUCTION: PRETENDSTER

In 2002, a social networking Website called Friendster, *www.friendster.com* was launched. Quickly attracting millions of members (currently Friendster has over 36 million registered users), this Web service networks individuals by converting the "degrees of separation" amongst linked members into a virtual social conduit: adding a new "friend" automatically links to a larger community of friends. About the same time this Website was taking off, Olsson collaborated with some other artists to create a parody of Friendster called *Pretendster*.

**Figure 10.5** *Pretendster* (2003-2004) uses data mined from Friendster to create its own networks.

*Pretendster*, www.pretendster.com, uses Web robots (automated applications that retrieve data across the Internet) to mine data from Friendster, drawing connections between millions of people. Unlike limitations posed by Friendster, users of *Pretendster* have the freedom to explore connections unencumbered by degrees of separation.

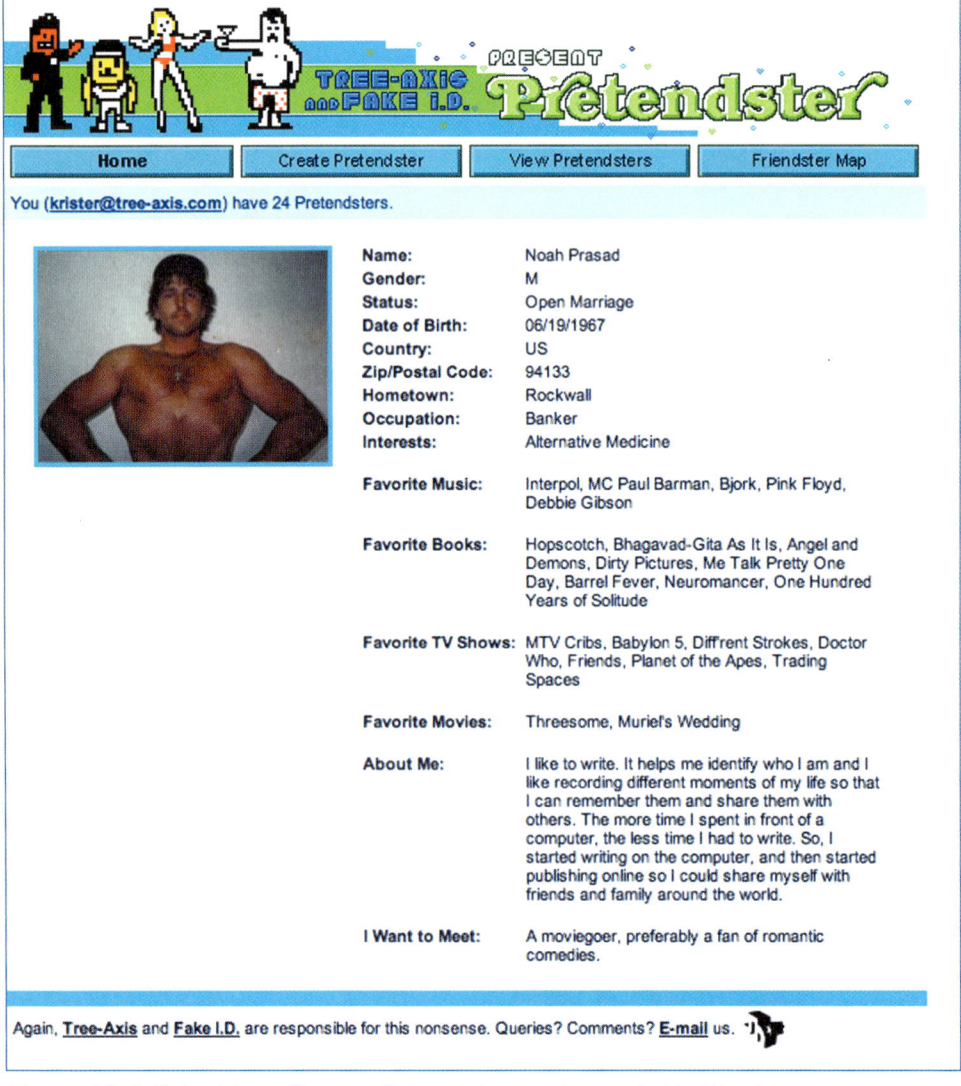

**Figure 10.6** A *Pretendster* profile: essentially, a data-puppet supported by Friendster.

The interface for exploring this spidered data was built in Flash. The *Pretendster* team overcame some design challenges by building a viewer that could present the data in a meaningful way. Profile images were not stored on the *Pretendster* site, but pulled from Friendster in real-time, requiring PHP code for both getting around the Flash sandbox as well as handling timeouts gracefully (something Olsson notes as being too-often overlooked when coding data-driven applications).

*Pretendster* was featured in a number of publications, including *The New York Times* and *Los Angeles Times*. It did not take long before Friendster killed off all "Pretendsters" and blocked their server from accessing the site. But a database was kept as a backup and was used to create *Friendster Pachinko* kristerolsson.com/?pachinko.

Also, two of the mascot characters on the *Pretendster* site found their way into a Zune-arts.net video.

## DIGITAL DECONSTRUCTION: ZUNE-ARTS

Launched just prior to the release of Microsoft's MP3 player (and updated roughly biweekly since), *Zune Arts* www.zune-arts.net showcases commissioned work exploring the notion of sharing. From a production perspective, the challenge was to create custom interactions between different pieces of content (both posters and videos). From a development perspective, what started small had to be flexible enough to accommodate numerous pieces of content as the number of commissions grew, so that Microsoft and the advertising agency, 72andSunny, could regularly push updates after the launch.

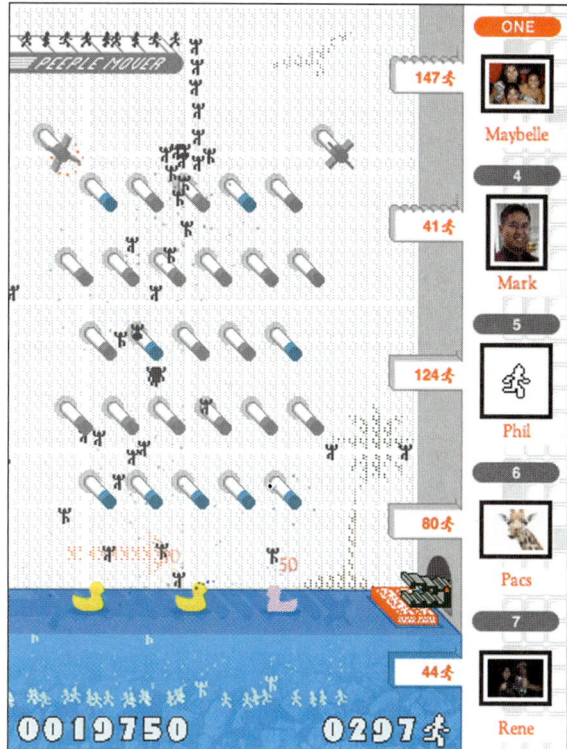

**Figure 10.7** *Friendster Pachinko* (2004) is an online game that uses the saved data from the *Pretendster* project.

**Figure 10.8** The *Zune-Arts* (2006) Website displays an array of interactive characters.

The variety of the commissioned works and the depth of information about their creators make the site very compelling. Videos featured on this site have found their way to other corners of the Web.

### DIY: A SCALING ANIMATED LINE-UP

When developing the navigation for *Zune Arts*, one of the ideas Olsson proposed was a line-up of characters arranged in reverse-bowling pin formation. The line-up would grow or shrink based on the width of the browser window, revealing or hiding characters as the window size changed. When clicked, a character would push aside the characters in front of it and walk forward. Olsson put together the following tutorial to explain a simplified version of that interactive line-up.

**Figure 10.9** Mini-animations are performed by the characters lined up across the site.

**Figure 10.10** The visitor can link to a variety of commissioned digital images, animations, and music videos.

Let us get started with the tutorial! Make sure you have launched Flash and have access to the DVD that came with this book.

To get started, open the file from the Chapter_10 folder titled *navigation.fla*.

When the file loads up in Flash, the first thing you will notice is that there is not much in the Timeline. A single script controls all the logic. A layer named **content** contains a single movie clip that has been given the instance name, content. Clicking into this clip, all you will find is a gradient, which is used for our movie background.

**NOTE:** One of the strengths of Flash is that it lets you mix pre-designed content with programmatically generated content. While this background could be generated entirely in ActionScript, it is much easier to simply draw it to the Stage, make it a movie clip, and give it an instance name. On the other hand, our character line-up will be programmatically generated from a single asset in our Library.

Encapsulating the background and our generated line-up inside the **content** movie clip gives us the freedom to modify all content in the future. For example, we may want to reposition everything, scale it, or even duplicate it and flip it to create a mock reflection. It is good to get in the habit of creating movie clip wrappers around key elements in your Flash movies.

Looking at the Library, you will see there are only 6 items. Two of those items are sounds that we use for rollover and click events.

We have our aforementioned **content** and **gradient** movie clips. The last two items in the Library are two ball movie clips: **ball** and **basic ball**. For the sake of simplicity the characters in our line-up are going to be balls,

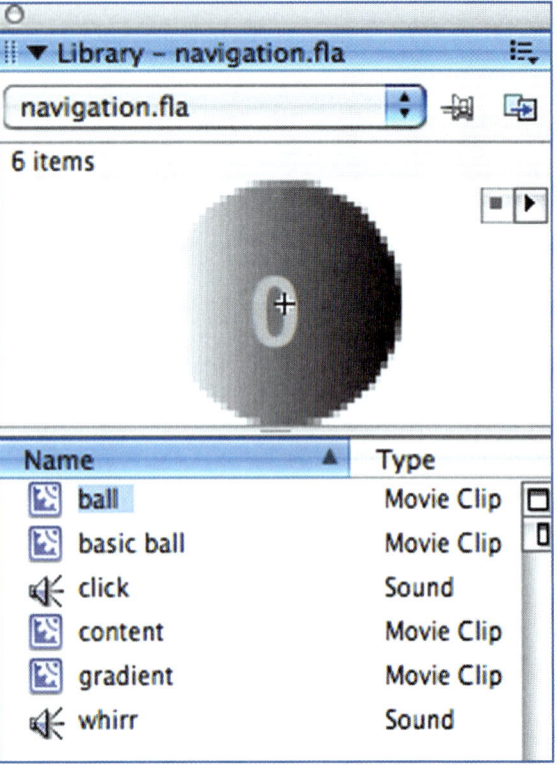

**Figure 10.11** Here is a peak at the Library for this file.

duplicates of a single movie clip differentiated by numbers placed on their surfaces. **Basic ball** is our atomic movie clip: it simply contains a centered gradient ball. **Ball** contains an animation of that ball in which the alpha changes over time. Also, a blur filter applied to the ball makes it appear that the ball is going in and out of focus. In a separate layer a dynamic text field will hold our ball's unique ID. The linkage for this movie clip is set to "Export for ActionScript," and it has been given the identifier `ball` so that we can use it with `attachMovie`.

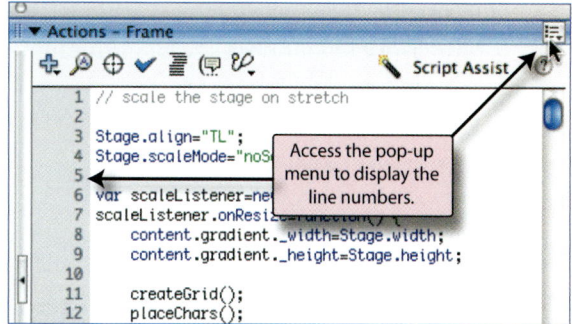

**Figure 10.12** The pop-up Menu contains a toggle for viewing the line numbers in the Actions panel. Make sure this is selected, as Olsson will be referring to his code by line number.

On to the ActionScript. There is a lot of code in our single script! Rather than going through it sequentially, we will hone in on different sections, referencing each by line number.

The first thing we need to do to is generate a grid on which we will place our characters. Think of this grid as a checkerboard. We do not want characters right next to each other; we need to make sure there is adequate space between them. Understanding that our grid will grow and shrink based on window size, we want to set a minimum width so things do not look strange if the window is too small. I have chosen a minimum width of 7, which will accommodate 3 characters horizontally (with empty spaces at the far left and far right). Also, for this example, we only want our grid to accommodate two rows of characters. So we will set an absolute grid height of 3 (empty space between the rows). We also need to set a pixel size for each square on the grid. For this example I have chosen 35, the size of our gradient ball.

This grid setup occurs in two locations. From line 17 we set our pixel size for each square:

```
// set up our grid

var squareWidth=35;
var squareHeight=35;

createGrid();
```

We break out our actual grid creation into a separate function, as it will need to be called when our window is resized as well. From line 107:

```
function createGrid() {
        // maintain an odd number
of rows and columns

        gridWidth=Math.max(7,Math.
floor((Stage.width/squareWidth)
/2-1)*2+1); // min 7 columns
        gridStartX=Math.floor
((Stage.width-(gridWidth*square
Width))/2);

        gridHeight=3; // no more
than 3 rows
        gridStartY=Math.floor((
Stage.height-(gridHeight*square
Height))/2);
}
```

Once we have our grid, we must generate our characters. Then we can place them. For each character we generate an empty movie clip, then attach the `ball` movie clip. From line 31:

```
var tMC=content.createEmptyMovie
Clip("char"+charStartDepth,char
StartDepth++);
        tMC.attachMovie("ball",
"ball",10000);

        charInstances[i]=tMC;

        tMC.ball.number.text=i; //
the ball identifier
```

```
        tMC.ball.gotoAndPlay(random
(tMC.ball._totalframes)+1); //
go to a random frame
```

After each character is generated it is added to an array, `charInstances`, used by the function `placeChars` to keep track of all our characters. Each ball is also given an ID (a reference to the order in which it was created) and begins playing its fade/blur animation from a different starting point. The remainder of the code gives each character a slight positional jitter (so they do not stand perfect order) and also sets up our event listeners. We will talk about those later.

To place the characters, we call our function `placeChars` on line 102. The first part of the function sets up variables for positioning the characters. For example, we want a space between the characters, so based on our grid width, we need to determine how many characters actually fit in a single row (line 119):

```
var tWidth=(gridWidth-1)/2;
```

On line 135 we check to see if the row we are currently generating is beyond our maximum number of rows:

```
if (tRow>gridHeight/2+1) {
```

If so, we make the characters from this point on invisible. Otherwise, we set character positions according to where they belong on the grid, scale them so that characters on the second row are smaller, and make sure they are visible. We also set custom properties such as `idleX`, `idleY`, and `idleScale`, as well as `mode`. These are properties we have set up to handle our animation.

Each time we place a character we check to make sure we have not gone beyond the maximum allowed per row. Starting at line 158:

```
if (++tRowChar>tRowNumChars) {
      tBaseX=Math.min((gridWidth↵
-1)/2,tBaseX+1);
      tX=tBaseX;
      tY-=1.5;
      tRow++;

      tRowChar=1;
      tRowNumChars—;

      tWidth=Math.max(1,tWidth-1);
      tScale=Math.max(.2,tScale-.2);
}
```

If we have, we need to move to the next row. Our `tBaseX` variable sets a starting point for the next row, allowing us to easily set up our reverse-bowling pin formation.

As with our function `createGrid`, we also call `placeChars` when our window is resized.

### Scaling to Window Size

With our `createGrid` and `placeChars` functions already in place, handling window resize events is a snap. Starting at the very beginning of our code we set up our Stage listener:

```
// scale the Stage on stretch

Stage.align="TL";
Stage.scaleMode="noScale";

var scaleListener=new Object();
scaleListener.onResize=function() {
      content.gradient._width=↵
Stage.width;
      content.gradient._height=↵
Stage.height;

      createGrid();
      placeChars();
}
Stage.addListener(scaleListener);
```

First, we are telling Flash that we want to anchor our Stage to the top left (hence, `"TL"`). Setting the `scaleMode` to `"noScale"` tells Flash that we do not want it to scale our movie when window size changes. We create our listener to handle `onResize` events, which occur whenever the window size changes.

Within the listener we set the size of our gradient background to the width and height of the Stage and call `createGrid` and `placeChars` to recreate our grid and place our characters on the new grid. That is all there is to it.

### Coming Forward

We want to add a little interaction to our line-up: clicking on a character will bring it forward. When we generated our characters we defined 3 events for each, starting at line 49: `onPress`, `onRollOver`, and `onEnterFrame`. `onRollOver` simply triggers a sound we have defined earlier. `onPress` starts our animation by calling the function `triggerChar`, passing the character to trigger. Let us look at our `onEnterFrame` handler first.

In a Flash movie, each `onEnterFrame` handler is called each frame. In our movie each character has an `onEnterFrame` handler assigned to it. This handler is responsible for animating its respective character. Starting at line 58:

```
tMC.onEnterFrame=function() {
      // animate?

      if (this.mode=="animating") {
            if (getTimer()>this.↵
startTime+this.duration) {
                  // done animating
```

```
                this.mode="idle";
                this._width=
this.baseWidth*this.destScale;
                this._height=
this.baseHeight*this.destScale;

                this._x=this.
destX;
                this._y=this.
destY;
                this.currScale
=this.destScale;

                if (this.
onDone!=null) this.onDone();
            } else if (getTimer
()>this.startTime) {
                // interpolate

                var tLerp=(get
Timer()-this.startTime)/this.
duration;

                this.curr
Scale=this.destScale*tLerp+this.
srcScale*(1-tLerp);

                this._width=
this.baseWidth*this.currScale;
                this._height=
this.baseHeight*this.currScale;

                this._x=this.
destX*tLerp+this.srcX*(1-tLerp);
                this._y=this.
destY*tLerp+this.srcY*(1-tLerp);
            }
        }
}
```

The handler first checks a property we have set up called `mode`. If we are animating, the handler then determines whether or not we should still be animating or if we should be finished by now by examining two custom properties: `startTime` and `duration`. There are a few other custom properties with source and destination counterparts: `srcX` and `destX`, `srcScale` and `destScale`, and so on.

Our animations are linear: a character moves or scales from a source location/size to a destination location/size over a predetermined duration. What we are doing each time the handler is called is linearly interpolating location and size based on the current time. If we are be done animating, but `mode` is still set to `animating`, we have a little extra code that sets `mode` to `idle` and places our character at the exact destination location, scaling it to the exact destination size.

We set `mode` and define our source and destination properties in our `triggerChar` function, starting at line 190. This is a large block of code that handles not only sending characters forward and bringing them back, but also determining if a character is already forward when another is clicked, making intelligent decisions about which characters to move out of the way and which to keep stationary.

We have a variable called `mode` that keeps track of our global state (not to be confused with the character property `mode`). This variable is set to `idle` when nothing is happening, `forward` when a character is coming forward or is holding a forward position, or `backward` when a character is moving back to its original position. The variable `activeChar` keeps track of the current active character so that once a character has been brought forward we know what to send back.

Whether bringing a character forward or sending it back, there is a chance there are characters in front that we want moved out of the way. From line 315:

```
// otherwise the ones in front
move over and then we move down

theChar.destY=theChar.idleY+square
Height*2.5;
theChar.startTime=getTimer()+250;
theChar.duration=calcDuration
(theChar);

for (var p=0;p<numChars;p++) {
      var tIC=charInstances[p];

      if (tIC.row==1) {
            // move out of the way

            tIC.mode="animating";

            tIC.srcX=tIC._x;
            tIC.srcY=tIC._y;
            tIC.srcScale=tIC.
currScale;

            if (tIC.col<theChar.
col) {
                  // move left

                  tIC.destX=
tIC.idleX-squareWidth*.75;
            } else {
                  // move right

                  tIC.destX=
tIC.idleX+squareWidth*.75;
            }

            tIC.destY=tIC.idleY;
            tIC.destScale=tIC.
idleScale;

            var tDur=calc
Duration(tIC);
            tIC.duration=tDur/
2+random(tDur/2);
```

```
            tIC.onDone=null;
      }
}
```

Here we are creating small animations for characters we want moved out of the way, setting up almost all the necessary properties for each affected character's `onEnterFrame` handler. We make liberal use of the function `calcDuration`, which returns the amount of time it will take for a character to move a specified pixel distance at a fixed speed. `calcDuration` is defined starting at line 393.

This code sets all necessary properties but one, the `startTime` property. We want our sidestep animation to cascade, so all our characters do not move at once. In order to do so we have to cascade our starting times. We do this starting at line 353:

```
// we've set up our required
animations, now set our start times
// first, lump our eligible elements

var tLeftArray=new Array();
var tRightArray=new Array();

for (var p=0;p<numChars;p++) {
      var tIC=charInstances[p];

      if (tIC.mode=="animating"
&& tIC.row==1) {
            if (tIC.col<active
Char.col) {
// add to the left array — assume
things are in order
                  tLeftArray.
push(tIC);
            } else {
// add to the right array — as above
                  tRight
Array.unshift(tIC);
            }
```

```
            }
        }

        var tTimer=getTimer();
        var currTime=0;

        for (var p=tLeftArray.↵
length-1;p>=0;p--) {
            currTime+=random(50);

            tLeftArray[p].start↵
Time=tTimer+currTime;
        }

        currTime=0;

        for (var p=tRightArray.↵
length-1;p>=0;p--) {
            currTime+=random(50);

            tRightArray[p].start↵
Time=tTimer+currTime;
        }
```

Setting up two temporary arrays, `tLeftArray` and `tRightArray`, we sort our characters based on whether they move to the left or right in order of proximity to the character coming forward. Once sorted, we simply set the start times of each character in order, adding a base start time to a random value, increasing the base start time by that random value, and so on. This creates the cascade effect.

Our behavior is very similar whether we are moving forward or backward, except that there is a chance that we are moving backward to bring another character forward. For this we need a special variable, `nextChar` and a special handler

`onDone`. `onDone` is triggered when a character has moved back into its place in the line-up (it is actually called by our `onEnterFrame` animation handler when an animation is finished). If nothing else is scheduled to come forward, `onDone` will have been set to `null`, otherwise it calls the function `triggerNextChar`, defined starting at line 182:

```
function triggerNextChar() {
    // can only be called by ↵
triggerChar()

    mode="idle";
    triggerChar(nextChar);
    nextChar=null;
}
```

This function resets `mode`, triggers the queued character, and sets `nextChar` to null.

Finally, there is a function `resetMode` called at the end of `placeChars`. This function resets the state of our line-up. There is a chance that when the window is resized and a character is forward characters will shift to different rows, creating awkward gaps and overlaps. It is essential that after a resize we reset our state: `placeChars` resets our character positions, but `resetMode` resets our `mode` and sets `activeChar` and `nextChar`to null, our virgin state.

Now open the file called *navigation-1.fla* from inside the Chapter_10 folder on the DVD. Test the movie from this file and also from the previous file you have been working through.

As you can see, *navigation-1.fla* reveals the beauty of parameterized design. Simply plugging in a few different numbers within the general structure of the code yields a design with a completely new scope. Working in this manner achieves a flexibility of design allowing for changing screen size, a number of graphical elements, and change of graphical style and/or size.

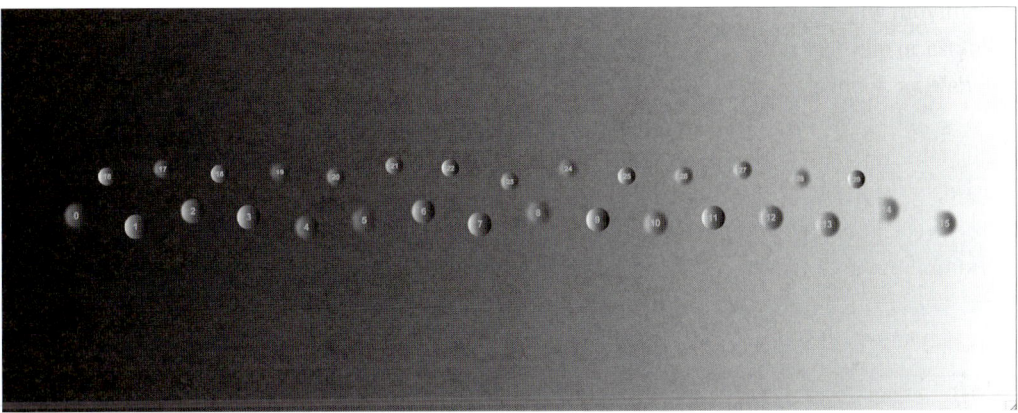

**Figure 10.13** *navigation.fla* is the file you have been working through.

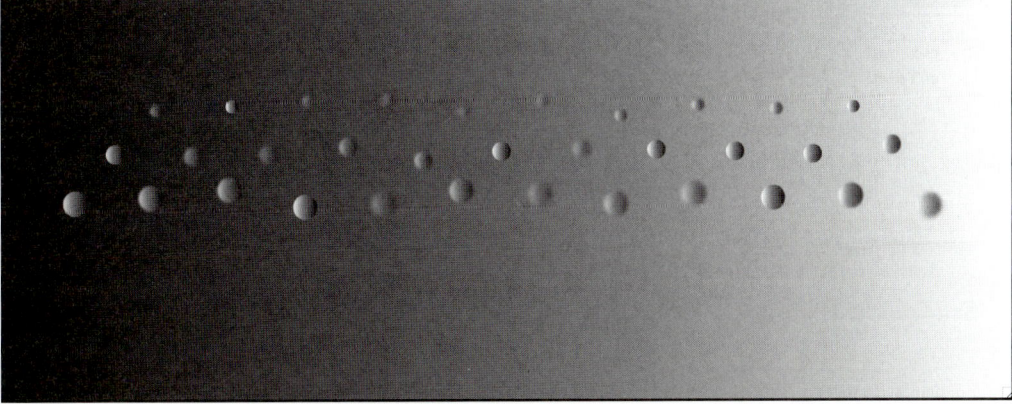

**Figure 10.14** *navigation-1.fla* –essentially the same code with different variables plugged-in.

## ON YOUR OWN

The possible uses of Flash's ActionScript go well beyond its obvious dynamic capabilities. As Olsson explores in the DIY section, creating modular structures with code can allow qualities like permutation and variation to play as important a role in the design process as scale, color, and composition. One interesting experiment would be to take this structure towards a logical conclusion; create a range of stylized characters to replace the stand-in ball graphics. Replace the generic sounds provided here with more unique sounds that relate to your character design.

While Olsson's example is an approach towards a specific design problem, try using this as a springboard for creating a similar technique that addresses a different design issue. These linear animations could easily be applied towards other properties besides positioning.

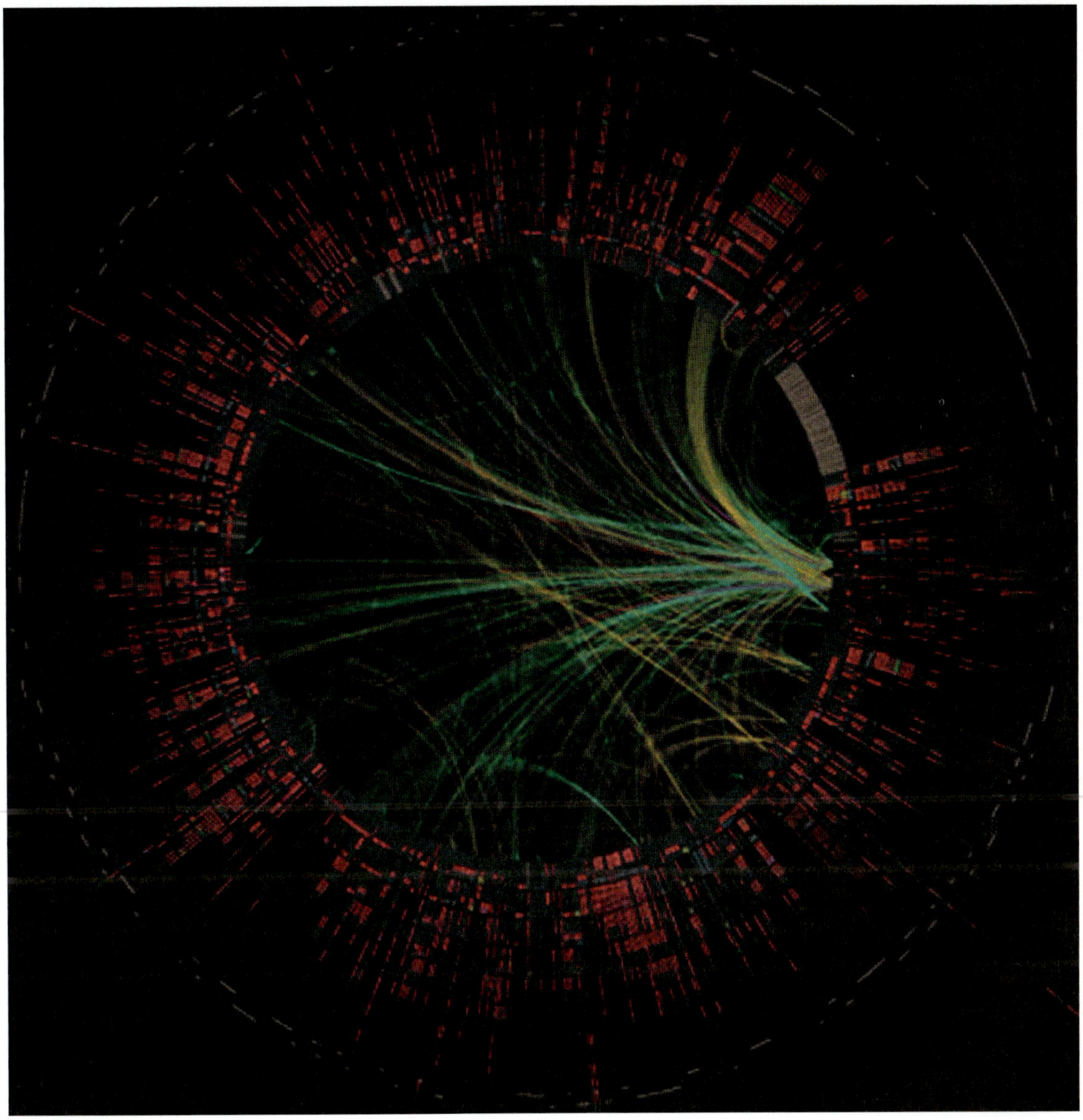

# SANTIAGO ORTIZ

---

Art and Artificial Life

# SANTIAGO ORTIZ

> "When I was 8, while playing ATARI, I came to the conclusion that human beings had invented those games, by figuring them out in their minds first, then by making them real somehow, and finally, and strangely enough, by placing them all in little black boxes. I mentally tried to find out how this process had developed, but a shade of mystery remained."

Santiago Ortiz grew up in Bogotá, Colombia, during the 1980s. At this time, there were only two places where you could get hold of American toys, appliances, and other commodities like Atari game systems. Wealthy Colombians flew to Miami, and the middle class went to San Andresito, a huge chaotic den located in the industrial zone of Bogotá. The Atari was Ortiz's first interaction with computer culture, closely followed by his first computer, a Casio PB1000. While immersing himself in the programs that could run on this computer, it was not long before he was learning how to create his own, using programming languages like BASIC.

Initially, Ortiz thought that making interactive graphics on the computer was all about drawing objects and teaching them how to behave by using other drawings. He was later shocked to realize that it was a rather abstract and linguistic procedure. At first, he stepped into this process by experimenting with his own games. Later, he was lured by a greater fascination: creating artwork by combining abstract graphic structures with audio—exploring the wonderful patterns and environments that could be wrested from the inner circuitry through code and math. This was especially enhanced when a friend of his parents (a physicist) gave Ortiz an advanced book on BASIC, from which he discovered how to create applications using controlled randomness and fractals. He has since perfected his artistic vision, creating forms that are intricate and perspicacious, oscillating between various states of complexity and coalescence.

**Figure 11.1** Ortiz sits before an installation of his artwork, *El Inventor de Historias (The Inventor of Stories)* (2004).

Ortiz has taught mathematics, art, and technology separately and cross-disciplinarily at institutions such as the Universidade do Porto in Portugal, the Universidad de los Andes in Bogota, and the European Universidad Europea de Madrid. He is also a co-founder of the magazine for digital art and culture called *Blank* and is a frequent collaborator with MedialabMadrid. Currently he works with Bestiario, *www.bestiario.org* a studio that creates interactive spaces based on complex information. His research has been featured at many reputable institutes such as the San Francisco Exploratorium, FILE, and the Ars Electronica Festival.

Committed to a form of systemic thinking that combines art, science, and other disciplines, it's no surprise to find that Ortiz has often collaborated with others on projects. He notes that collaborative projects increase the diversity of a work (thematically and in format), while also elevating the overall quality. *Microcosmos for Gaia* (with Lynn Margulis and Luis Rico) and *GNOM* (with Alfonso Valencia and Luis Rico) are a couple of recent projects that have combined Ortiz's skills and concepts along with those of others.

## DIGITAL DECONSTRUCTION: SONIDO Y ENERGIA (SOUND AND ENERGY)

*Sonido Y Energia* is a collection of interactive Flash environments that expand the possible relationships among sound, space, dynamics, energy, and interactivity. Ortiz has been updating these works for several years; each one in the collection addresses a new way for creating formal gestures through interaction.

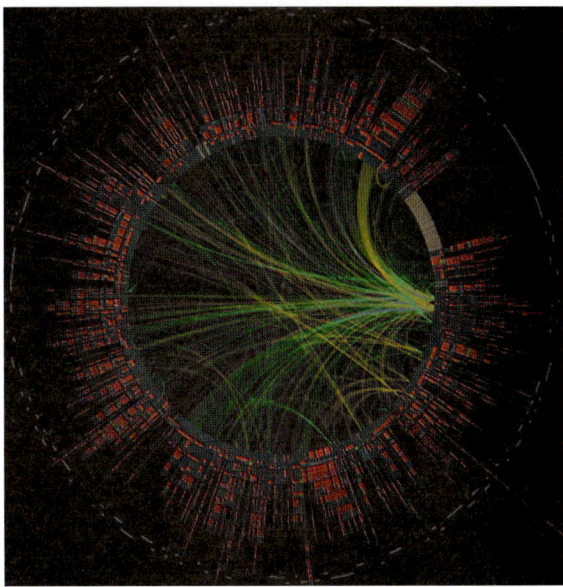

**Figure 11.2** *GNOM* (2005) was the collaborative effort of Santiago Ortiz, Alfonso Valencia, and Luis Rico.

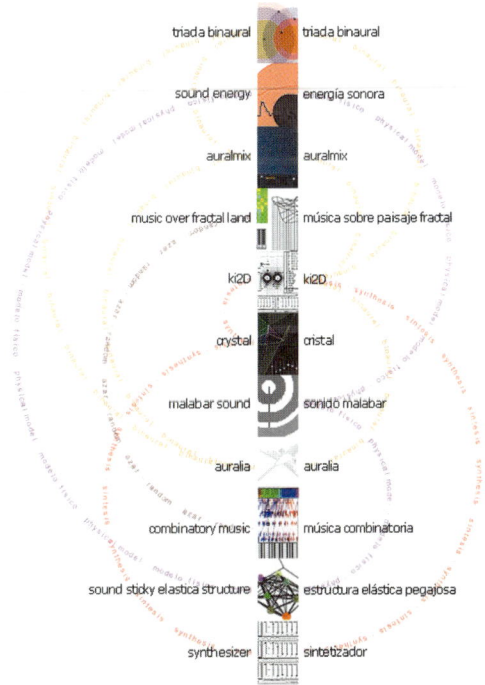

**Figure 11.3** This interface is the gateway for exploring all of the works in the *Sonido Y Energia* (2005) collection.

Some of the works in *Sonido Y Energia* are very simple, like *Cristal* and *Estructura Elástica Pegajosa*, where the interfaces for controlling the sound and graphics are readily understood. Others in the collection, such as *ki2D*, are harder to figure out, but the complexity of the interface lends to more intricate user-creations. *ki2D* is also educational; adjusting the waveform controls not only alters the audio, but the trajectory and motion paths for the objects. Equally revealing is *Música Sobre Paisaje Fractal*, where audio frequencies are used to model a virtual landscape.

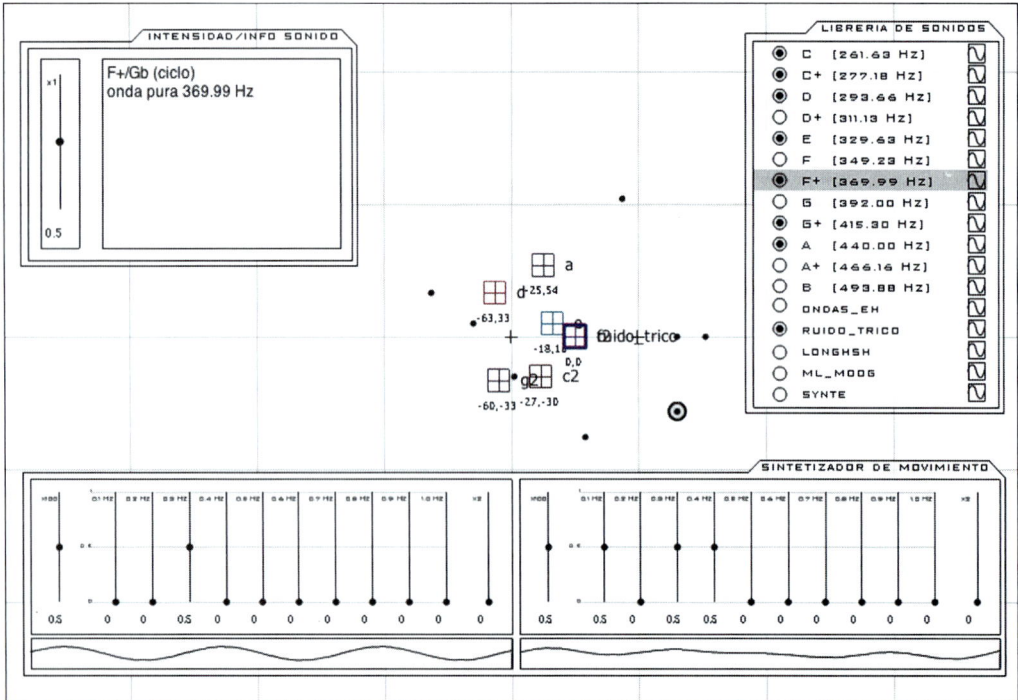

**Figure 11.4** *ki2D*

**CHAPTER ELEVEN**  191

**NOTE:** *Sonido Y Energia* can be broken down into several categories:
- Binaural: sounds in space—the intensity of each sound is in relation to distance
- Synthesis: wave synthesis is used to generate dynamics in space
- Physical model: gravity, elastics, bounding, friction, etc.
- Random: stochastic models are used to generate dynamic movement and sound

The *Sonido Y Energia* collection illustrates a powerful principle of code-driven generative art: algorithms generate a sequence of numbers, whose pattern can be manifested in movement, visual form, or audio frequency and sequence. Even simple high school level trigonometry can be quite valuable for generating interesting dynamics in the ActionScript sandbox.

Let's make a couple of Flash files that explore the elementary principles of sine and cosine: mathematical functions that are defined by properties of the unit circle. A unit circle is a mathematical model whose radius is 1 and is centered at 0,0 within a Cartesian coordinate system—the same coordinate system Flash uses. Since the 0,0 position in Flash is the upper left-hand corner of the Stage, we are going to reposition our unit circle so we can fully see what is occurring with the animation we are about to create.

1. Open a new Flash document that is 400 × 400 pixels in size.
2. Create a circle graphic (as pictured in Figure 11-07) that is 200 × 200 pixels and center it onto the Stage. Then draw a small circle on the Stage, placed on a separate layer. Make this small circle a movie clip with an instance name of `satellite`.

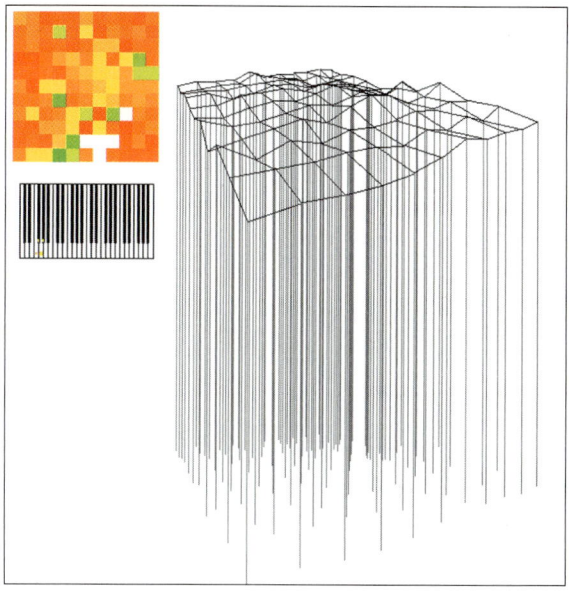

**Figure 11.5** *Música Sobre Paisaje Fractal (Music Over Fractal Land).*

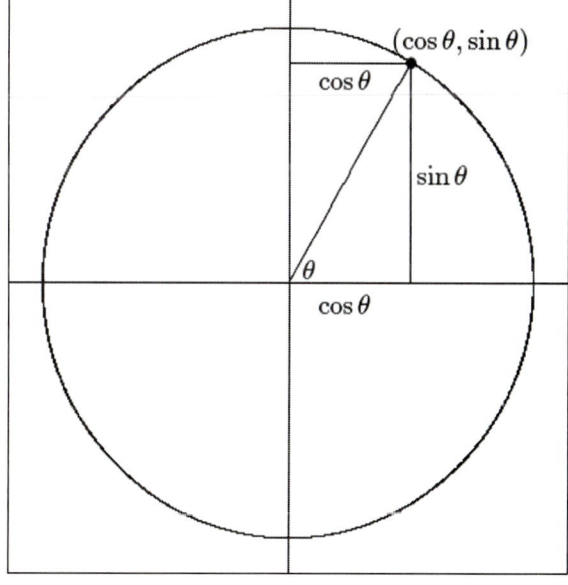

**Figure 11.6** Anyone remember this? It's the unit circle of trigonometry lore.

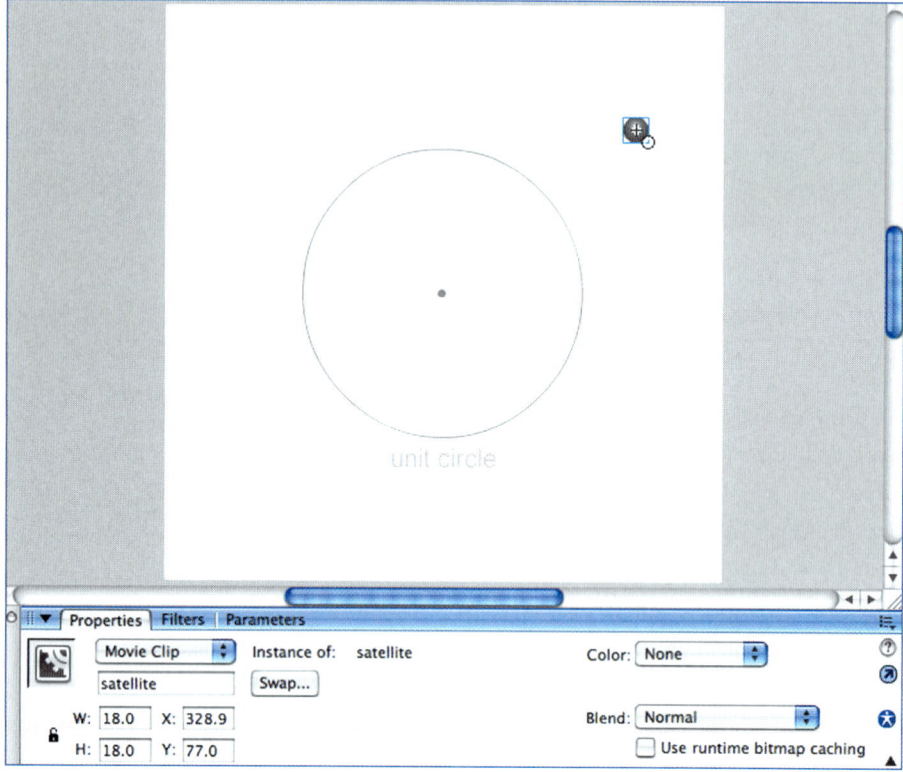

**Figure 11.7** This movie clip will soon animate around the circumference of the unit circle.

3. Select the `satellite` movie clip on the Stage, then type the following code in the Actions panel.

```
onClipEvent(load){
    var ucX:Number = 200;
    var ucY:Number = 200;
    var rad:Number = 100;
    var angle:Number = 0;
    var angleInc:Number = ↵
(2*Math.PI)/360;
}

onClipEvent(enterFrame){
    this._x = Math.cos(angle)*↵
rad+ucX;
    this._y = Math.sin(angle)*↵
rad+ucY;
    angle+=angleInc;
}
```

4. That's it! Test your movie and watch the satellite move around the unit circle.

In the `onClipEvent(load)` handler, we are setting a bunch of variables that will be established when the movie clip first loads. These variables are crucial for rotating this movie clip around the circumference of the unit circle. `ucX` (center X), `ucY` (center Y) and `rad` (radius) are all properties of the unit circle. To understand our `angle` variable, imagine a beam of light shooting out from a lighthouse, slowly rotating in a circle. But this beam will be invisible, providing the structure for placing the satellite as it orbits the unit circle.

The last line sets an amount that will be used for increasing the angle. Most non-mathematicians think in terms of degrees and how a circle is divided into 360 degrees. The way we divide a circle is quite arbitrary. Think of a clock, and depending on how detailed you want to be, you can think of a clock as having 12 or 60 subdivisions. Trigonometry in Flash (functions like `Math.sin` and `Math.cos` work in radians, not degrees. A circle is defined as having $2\pi$ radians (in Flash written as `2*Math.PI`). Our ActionScript code is taking this value, which equates to one revolution around a circle, and divides it by 360. But you could put any number here; it basically equates to how many subdivisions you want to divide the circle into. Try putting a different number (1000 for instance) in place of 360 and see how it effects the animation.

The final part of the code occurring in the `onEnterFrame` handler is quite simple. The X and Y values of the `satellite` movie clip are being reset every frame: this is the mechanism for the animation. Additionally, `angle` is being incremented on each frame load: this is the fuel for the animation. The _x and _y values are being set by basic trigonometry algorithms. The center point of the unit circle (`ucX`, `ucY`) is added to take into account that this unit circle is not sitting at 0,0, but at 200, 200. If you run into problems, open *circleTrig.fla* from the Chapter_11 folder on the DVD.

Other interesting things can be done with sine and cosine as well. Instead of thinking of time as cycling, like a classic clock, consider it to be a linear direction.

1. Create another Flash document with dimensions 800 × 200 pixels.

2. Draw a horizontal line in the center of the Stage and make another `satellite` movie clip as in our last movie.

3. Add the following code to the satellite movie clip.

```
onClipEvent(load){
    this._x = 0;
    this._y = 100;
    var rad:Number = 50;
    var angle:Number = 0;
    var angleInc:Number =
2*Math.PI/50;
    var pen:MovieClip = _root.
createEmptyMovieClip("temp", 1);
    pen._y = 100;
    pen.lineStyle(2, 0xEE0011, 50);
}
onClipEvent(enterFrame){
    this._x +=1;
    this._y = Math.sin(angle)
*rad+100;
    pen.lineTo(this._x, this.
_y-100);
    angle+=angleInc;

}
```

4. Test your movie. You should see a significantly different type of animation than the previous example.

This code moves the Y position of the satellite based on the same formula as the last example, but the _x position is being incremented by a constant value. A few extra lines of Drawing API code are used to trace the path of this sine wave. Open *circleTrig2.fla* from the Chapter_11 folder if you have any problems.

## DIGITAL DECONSTRUCTION: *MITOZOOS*

*Mitozoos* is a recent project of Ortiz's designed to function as an educational tool. Essentially, the mitozoo world is a mathematical model of artificial life. Flash is used as a tool for manifesting the enormous amount of data and calculations contained in this virtual world. *Mitozoos* came out the Bestiario studio, where Ortiz is a member.

*Mitozoos* simulates aspects of life: birth of individuals, nourishment, expending energy, reproduction, and death. In addition to representing these characteristics that illustrate the life of the individual, a broader simulation of life is represented through evolution. Generational patterns emerge through time, as natural selection occurs amongst prolonged reproduction choices and abilities among the individuals.

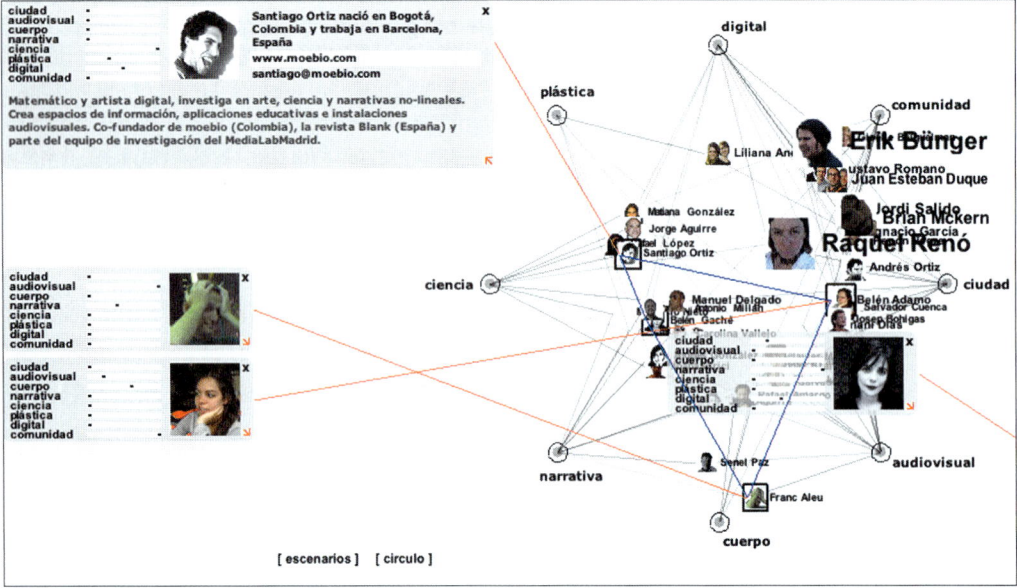

**Figure 11.8** Bestiario specializes in creating interactive spaces based on complex information.

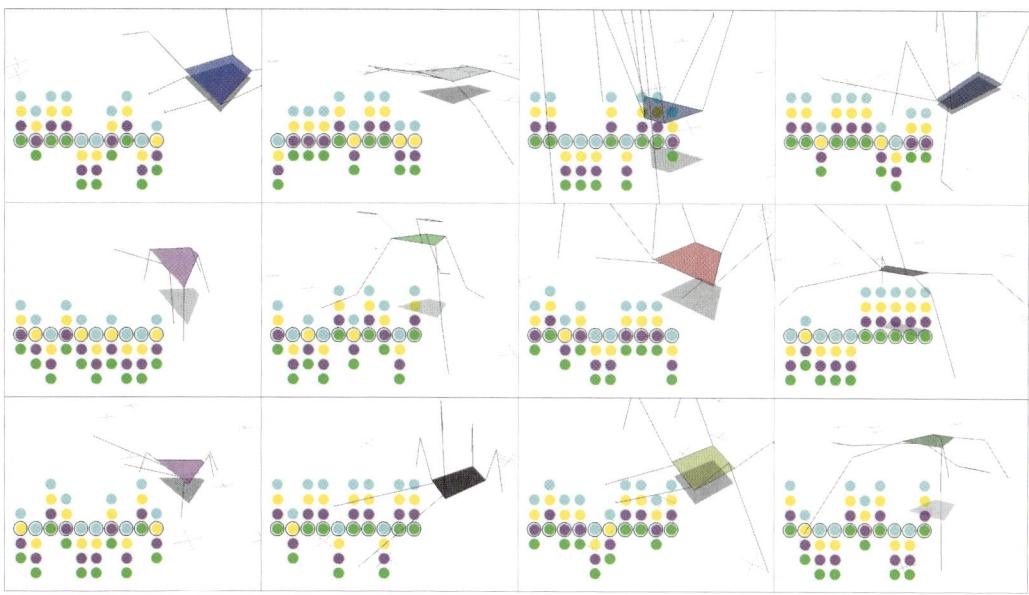

**Figure 11.9** Here we see *Mitozoos'* organisms along with their genetic blueprints.

Children, in particular, are delighted to interact with the *Mitozoos* environment. So much so, that during its inauguration they were creating so many mitozoos, and with such speed, that they managed to crash the system. Ortiz has gone on to alter some of his software and hardware to safeguard against another such event, while also enhancing the physical characteristics of the installation. Miguel Cardoso collaborated on the installation sound system that combines ActionScript with PureData (a program similar to Max/MSP). This combo was exhibited at the Sonar Festival in Barcelona in 2006.

**Figure 11.10** The *Mitozoos* installation was part of the Divulga Biotec exhibition.

## DIY: REPRESENTING LIFE: 4 STUDIES

Artificial life, when developed and focused through artwork, does not try to represent life in only a graphical way. Instead, such works strive to reveal meaning and form a discourse regarding the deeper qualities of life, such as reproduction, making strategic decisions, interaction in communities, morphology, cognition, metabolism, and a long et cetera. Ortiz's *Mitozoos* project bridges real and artificial life through the environment of code. Within this virtual space, the behavior of living organisms can be explored through simulation; graphical forms enact life-like permutations from within the limitless black box of the computer.

The following lesson combs through Ortiz's thoughts and experiments regarding organisms, society, reproduction, and artificial life through ActionSript. This will take the form of 4 studies: Reproduction, L-system, Social, and Evolution. In spite of being very simple, each one constructs a concrete example of an aspect of life found in the real world. Besides Evolution, each study has two FLA files on the DVD: one is simple and the other one is more advanced. Ortiz will explain only the first model in detail, giving points of consideration for understanding the more advanced FLA's on the DVD.

> "In the origin of modern man already existed the will to represent life."

### Reproduction

Open the *reproduction.fla* file from the Chapter_11 folder on the DVD. Before digging into the code, test the movie to see how it operates.

For many organisms, reproduction is the essential quality of life. This piece begins with an organism represented by a movie clip attached to the Stage. While the graphic for this movie clip is only a simple triangle, it is vitalized through ActionScript with the ability to move, and a slight probability of duplicating itself every instant. When this latter instance occurs, a new being appears, identical to the original one, inheriting the changeable parameters of angle and position.

**Figure 11.11** An outline of Altamira Cave paintings, Cantabria, Spain, painted around 13,000 years ago.

What I like about this example is how the code behaves like DNA for these simple organisms. By taking advantage of Object Oriented Programming (OOP), each object instance inherits internal code from a parent object. The graphical expression of this "genetic" code is a single triangle. To stress the concepts of artificial life in these models, I will sometimes refer to these graphics as bacteria. The function `drawBeing` (lines 1 to 9) receives a movie clip and draws inside it with methods from the Drawing API.

Here is the code for the `drawBeing` function:

```
function drawBeing(clip:MovieClip)↵
 :Void {
     clip.clear();
     clip.beginFill(0,60);
     clip.moveTo(-4, -4);
     clip.lineTo(5, 0);
     clip.lineTo(-4, 4);
     clip.lineTo(-4, -4);
     clip.endFill();
}
```

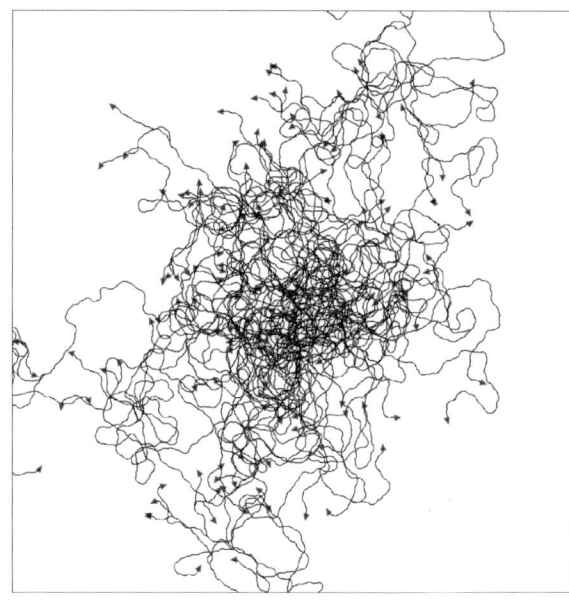

**Figure 11.12** Left on their own, these triangle-organisms reproduce quite rapidly.

In addition to their graphical representation, each bacterium can orientate and move their position. For this movement, three variable properties are altered: `_x`, `_y`, and `angle`. Bacterium also have the property v displacement speed that remains the same and invariable for all, making it a global property.

The environment these bacteria inhabit also has three properties that can be modified to change the model: `reproductionProbability`: which determines the probability of reproduction every bacterium has on each new frame; `beingSpeed` for the bacterium's displacement speed; and `angleVariation` defines how much bacteria spin on their random movement.

The most important section of this code occurs within the `onEnterFrame` function. Recursively executing whatever is assigned to it, this function is the machine for animating the bacteria. Even though there are many individuals, each one has its own behavior, independent from the others. Therefore, the `behavior` function is passed to the `onEnterFrame` function, so let's examine that section of code (lines 10 to 21):

```
function behaviour(){
        angleDeviation = (Math.random()-0.5)*angleVariation;
        this.angle +=angleDeviation
        this._parent.moveTo(this._x, this._y)
        this._x += this.v*Math.cos(this.angle);
        this._y += this.v*Math.sin(this.angle);
        this._parent.lineTo(this._x, this._y)
        this._rotation = this.angle*180/Math.PI;
        if(Math.random()<this._parent.reproductionProbability){
                this._parent.createBeing(this.angle, this._x, this._y);
        }
}
```

As this function is passed to the `onEnterFrame` function, the statements inside are executed on each frame of the individual. `angle` is updated by a random number between `-0.5*angleVariation` and `0.5*angleVariation`, which is later applied to the bacterium (remember that `this` indicates the movie clip that owns this code, hence `this._rotation` is changing the rotation of an individual bacterium). Notice how `this.angle` is also used to update the `_x` and `_y` coordinates; hopefully our unit circle review earlier in the chapter clarifies what is occurring here (Figure 11-14 illustrates the trigonometry of this case more specifically).

After a slight angle adjustment and reposition, `clip` is rotated (in line 17) so it will be oriented according to `angle`.

**NOTE:** While the angle is in radians, because that is the natural trigonometric mode for `Math.cos` and `Math.sin`, the movie clip property `_rotation` operates with degrees. Here are the formulas for converting back and forth:

```
radians = degrees * Math.PI / 180
degrees = radians * 180 / Math.PI
```

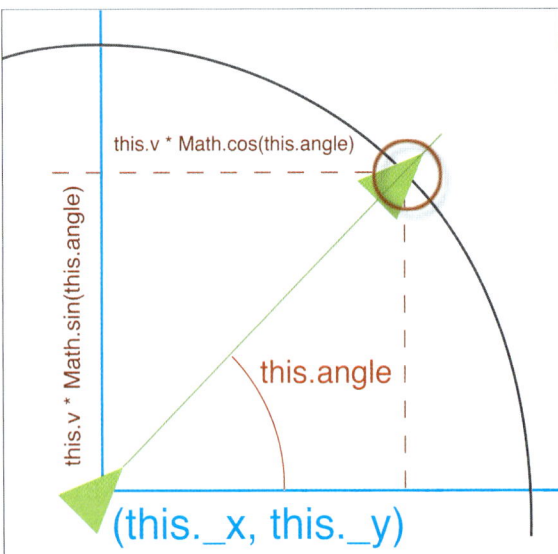

**Figure 11.13** The unit circle in this case is not a static structure; instead, it is a dynamic model that represents where an individual is currently positioned and the radius of possible displacement defined by the property `v`. Multiplying this value by the `sin` and `cos` of `this.angle`, finds where along this elliptical boundary our bacterium is to be repositioned.

The if statement on line 18 decides if the bacterium should reproduce. In order to do this, a random number is generated and compared to `reproductionProbability`; if the random number is lower, reproduction succeeds by invoking `createNewBeing`.

While the reproduction probability is really low, the longer the file runs, and the greater the population builds, you can see how reproduction builds exponentially. Many events along Earth's biological history, including the beginning of life, are very unlikely. But they had an extremely long time to develop—millions of years. If your program were to run for a million years, perhaps your virtual bacterium would find a way off the computer screen!

The function `createBeing` (lines 22 to 30) receives the parameters (`angle`, `x`, and `y`) from the parent, and passes them along to the new bacterium: `being._x`, `being._y` and `being.angle`. Here is the code:

```
function createBeing(angle:Number, 
 x:Number, y:Number):Void {
        var being:MovieClip = 
this.createEmptyMovieClip("being" 
+nBeings, nBeings++)
        being._x = x;
        being._y = y;
        drawBeing(being);
        being.v = beingSpeed;
        being.angle = angle;
        being.onEnterFrame = 
behaviour;
}
```

The moment this new bacterium is born, it has exactly the same properties as its parent: it is located in the same place, going at the same speed, and in the same direction. Nevertheless, immediately after that, both of them turn away due to the random component of their movement.

This next set of code sets the *origin of the organism*: the code that makes our very first bacterium and a set of global variables that defines its simple environment.

### Beginning

```
function begin() {
        //creates initial being
        createBeing(0, 350, 350);
        this.lineStyle(0, 0, 100);
}
//modificable paremeters
var reproductionProbability:Number 
 = 0.01
var beingSpeed:Number = 3;
var angleVariation:Number = 1.4;
//global variables
var nBeings:Number = 0;
//Low Quality for better performance
_quality = "LOW"
begin();
```

Bringing to life one bacterium—the ancestor of all the others—is enough to unleash reproductive madness. The function `begin()` is the line that sets it all into motion.

If you open the other file Ortiz prepared for this model on Reproduction (*reproduction2.fla* from the Chapter_11 folder on the DVD), you will see a version with a crop field that is constantly being regenerated. By moving, bacteria eliminate energy, and if they do not eat, they die. Reproduction requires a minimum energy level, and when reproduction succeeds, they give half their energy to their offspring. This variation of the Reproduction model introduces more complex facts of life: population is under the control of environmental conditions and in several ways are always at the risk of extinction.

**NOTE:** Observing the relationships in nature between space, food, community, and individuals led Darwin to elaborate his theory of evolution based on natural selection. Some bacteria, if they have enough food, can duplicate themselves every few minutes. If this process kept on going unchecked by food supply limitations, their population would grow until the moment when, a few days later, they would cover the whole planet!

### L-system

Open the **Lsystem.fla** from the DVD. This FLA is partly based on the file studied before, but introduces the grammar of L-systems. L-systems (Lindenmayer systems–after the Hungarian biologist Aristid Lindenmayer) are chains of characters that have a graphic rule associated to them. Besides the character chains (strings), an L-system has a rule that transforms the initial chain into a more complex one. *Lsystem.fla* is based on the following rule.

The initial chain is made of only one character: "F". And the rule is "F" > "F+F--F+F", which means every time there is an "F" it has to be replaced for a longer chain: "F+F--F+F".

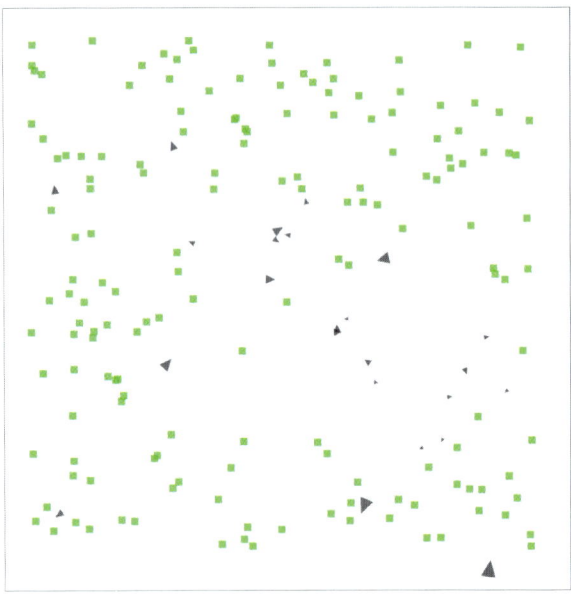

**Figure 11.14** In the more complex version (*reproduction2.fla* on the DVD) food is introduced to the environment. Rather than having the organisms reproduce automatically through time, a certain amount of food must first be eaten.

Below, the rule is applied three times, yielding three iterations:

```
F  >  F+F--F+F  >  F+F--F+F +F+F--F+F ↵
--F+F--F+F +F+F--F+F  >  F+F-- ↵
F+F  +F+F--F+F  --F+F--F+F  +F+F-- ↵
F+F   +F+F--F+F  +F+F--F+F  --F+F-- ↵
F+F   +F+F--F+F   --F+F--F+F  +F+F-- ↵
F+F  --F+F--F+F  +F+F--F+F   +F+F-- ↵
F+F  +F+F--F+F  --F+F--F+F  +F+F--F+F
```

**NOTE:** The following rules are applied to create a grammar for this L-system:

"**F**": advance and draw an outline

"**+**": turn 60 degrees (clockwise)

"**–**": turn –60 degrees (counter-clockwise)

L-systems are useful for (among other things) understanding the morphology of plants, creating artificial life, and generating fractal-like imagery. Here, we are performing the latter two: our organism's movement is based on the L-system we established above. Thanks to some commands to the Drawing API, the life of our organism is inscribed upon the Stage, revealing an ornate pattern that visually describes the behavior of our creature.

There are two particularly important functions in this example: `iteration` and `behavior`. `iteration` receives a character chain and applies the rule replacing a character for another chain.

```
function iteration(code:String) ↵
:String {
        var i:Number;
        var letra:String;

        for (i=code.length-1; ↵
i>=0; i—) {
                character = code.↵
substr(i, 1);
                textToIntroduce = "";
                switch (character) {
                case "F" :
                        textTo↵
Introduce = "F-F++F-F";
                        break;
                default :
                        //don't do ↵
 anything
                }
                if (textTo↵
Introduce != "") {
                        code = ↵
replaceCharacter(code, textTo↵
Introduce, i);
                }
        }
        return code;
}
```

The `behavior` function uses the L-system to define the behavior of the individual:

```
function behaviour(){
        this.indexCharacter++
        if(this.indexCharacter==↵
this.code.length){
                this.index↵
Character = 0;
        }
        this.character = this.↵
code.substr(this.indexCharacter, 1);
        switch (this.character) {
        case "F" :
                this._parent.↵
moveTo(this._x, this._y)
                this._x += this.↵
v*Math.cos(this.angle);
                this._y += this.↵
v*Math.sin(this.angle);
                this._parent.line↵
To(this._x, this._y)
                break;
        case "+" :
                this.angle += ↵
Math.PI/3;
                this._rotation += 60
                break;
        case "-" :
                this.angle -= ↵
Math.PI/3;
                this._rotation -= 60
                break;
        default :
                trace("UNEXPECTED↵
 CHARACTER!!!!!:["+character+"]");
        }
}
```

Notice that both functions must run through a chain of characters, and according to each one, an action is executed. The variation *Lsystem2.fla* creates several individual organisms with stochastic variation; working from an initial random chain and a random substitution rule, the code iterates the chain and the rule for a random number of times.

## Social

Communities are groups of individuals with a balance between autonomous behavior and collective behavior. For this example, every individual moves through two-dimensional space according to an angle. Additionally, individual behavior is designed not to go very far from the center: small random deviation is being constantly added to lend some diversity to individual movement.

The collective behavior influences the `angle` variable according to the angles of the other individuals around it. This way, when several organisms (we'll refer to them as birds) are around, they make a configuration. To create this collective behavior, every bird must know the position of the others. This is enabled through the global array, `arrayBeings`, which stores all of the individuals.

In the more advanced study, *social2.fla*, lines between individuals and movements are drawn, emphasizing strongest relations with opacity. Ortiz also made an ActionScript 3.0 version on the DVD, saved as *socialAS3.fla* and *socialAS3.as*.

## Evolution

To view our final artificial life model, open the *evolution.fla* file from the DVD.

This example actually has two models within the same FLA. The first one is a graphic of a random tree, with some restrictions laid out by a set of parameters. Selecting this creates eight new trees that inherit their appearance from the code of the selected tree, revealing the

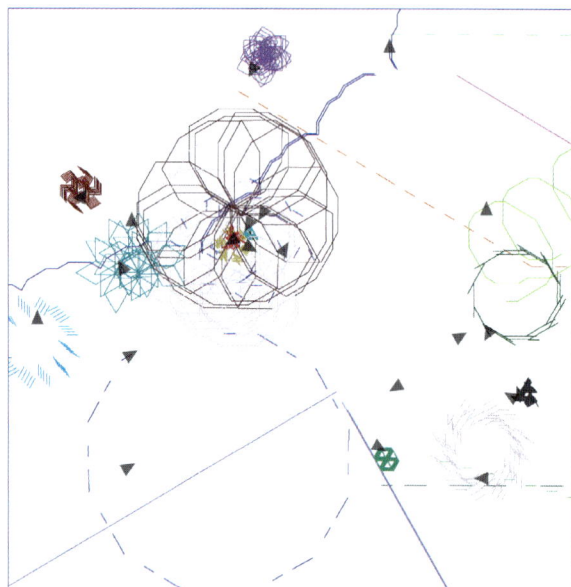

**Figure 11.15** Testing this movie creates quite a colorful display, not unlike peering into the emergent world of microorganisms.

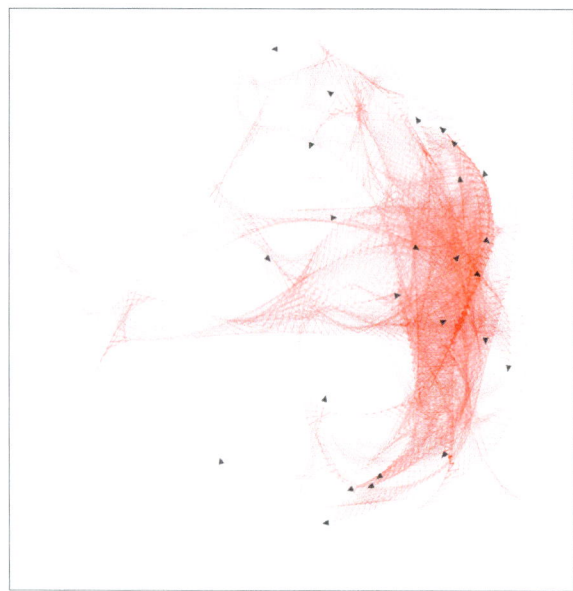

**Figure 11.16** Individuals from *social2.fla* leave a trail behind their movement.

second model in the process. Selecting any of these trees will place it in the center, becoming the visual and genetic focus for eight new trees. Consistently selecting a tree exhibiting certain traits (small, big, thick, leafy...) will create a series of new generations that perfectly illustrates the nature of evolution. Human civilization has been employing this type of genetic manipulation on plants and domestic animals for thousands of years.

An algorithm where criteria for selection are predetermined, although selection happens autonomously, is called a natural selection model. This is what is occurring in our FLA: every tree has a genetic code associated to it, on which the model is composed by a list of numbers.

**Figure 11.17** The evolutionary model is used here to rapidly progress through generations of trees. The animation that occurs is quite directed, as we see the genotype reinforced with each new inheritance.

In this file the key function is `randomMutation`, which receives a genetic code and transforms it, giving a variation to each of its values, increasing or decreasing it slightly. The global variation value `variationMagnitude` can be adjusted for more general or subtle results.

### References

Here are some good resources for further research on A-life.

http://www.levitated.net/notes/ECC
http://algorithmicbotany.org/papers
http://www.genarts.com/karl/evolved-virtual-creatures.html
http://www.alife.org

## DIGITAL DECONSTRUCTION: DEL MICROCOSMOS A GAIA

A more comprehensive display of Ortiz's interests, inspiration, and understanding of life and environment can be seen in his work *del Microcosmos a Gaia*. This project is largely based

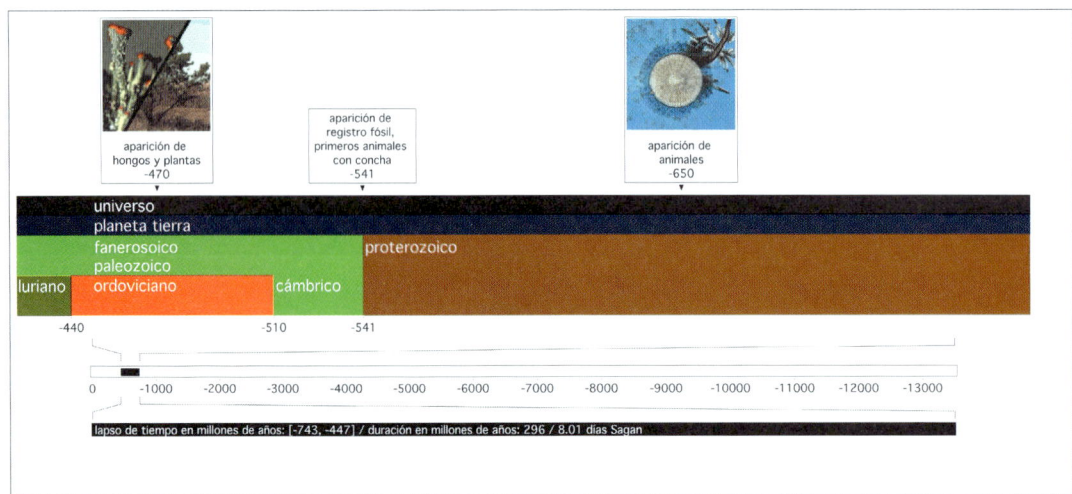

**Figure 11.18** *Del Microcosmos a Gaia* (2005) is a collaboration by Santiago Ortiz, Lynn Margulis, and Luis Rico.

on the theories of the microbiologist Lynn Margulis, whose work on endosimbiosis has been considered one of the greatest achievements in biology during the 20<sup>th</sup> century.

> "... we created a research project to build pedagogical experiences focused on communicating ideas such as Earth being a world rich in interactions, where every organism is as important as any other, and where the small organisms, as bacteria, for instance, are essential in the evolutive history; organisms have interaction with one another regardless of their scale, etc."

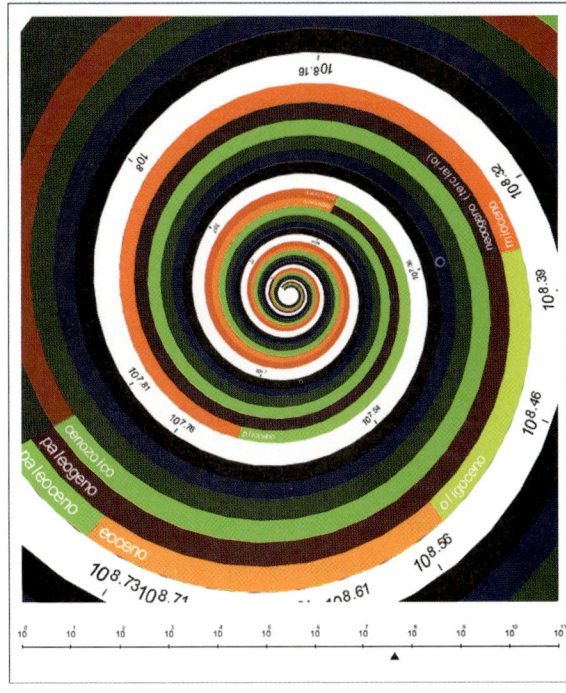

**Figure 11.19** Experimental navigation was used to reinforce concepts of proportion and scale in this work.

## ON YOUR OWN

Using Ortiz's artwork and technical examples as inspiration, see what you can create in terms of making your own organism(s) and evolutionary models. The key is to organize your code, and above all, to emphasize the difference between global effects and individual behaviors. A complex model may include different species acting reciprocally (symbiosis, parasitism, predator and prey, ...).

You should also give consideration to the relationship of the individual and surrounding environment. In real life, a being is inextricably linked to its environment—the same should be considered from a design viewpoint when building up a Flash movie that represents artificial life. Artificial life is a very wide field due to the interest it evokes on animation, video games, art and science, and above all else, because of the fact that life itself is an endless idea.

Generative Art with Flash

# JEREMY THORP

**A**former geneticist and part-time rock star, Thorp is a Flash designer and digital artist from Vancouver, Canada. He also acts as a consultant and trainer for a number of design agencies worldwide. Thorp's Website *www.blprnt.com*, hosts a unique collection of organic Flash experiments and generative artworks. It has won numerous awards and has been featured in many design magazines both online and in print.

Thorp describes his introduction to Flash as being "rooted firmly in panic." In the spring of 1999, he left the Vancouver Aquarium to take a job as a Flash designer at a local dot-com startup. While the job was ideal in many ways, there was only one problem—he did not know how to use Flash! So his entry into being a creative practitioner of Flash was of the proverbial trial-by-fire sort.

> "I would spend my days at work furiously trying to avoid looking incompetent and my evenings at home desperately trying to learn what I needed to know."

Before picking up Flash, Thorp studied biology and genetics at the University of British Columbia. These influences can be seen throughout his work and Flash experiments that certainly have a cellular/biological feel to them.

Thorp's first batch of Flash projects included dynamically generated trees, spiraling strings of DNA, and resonating sound waves. Over the

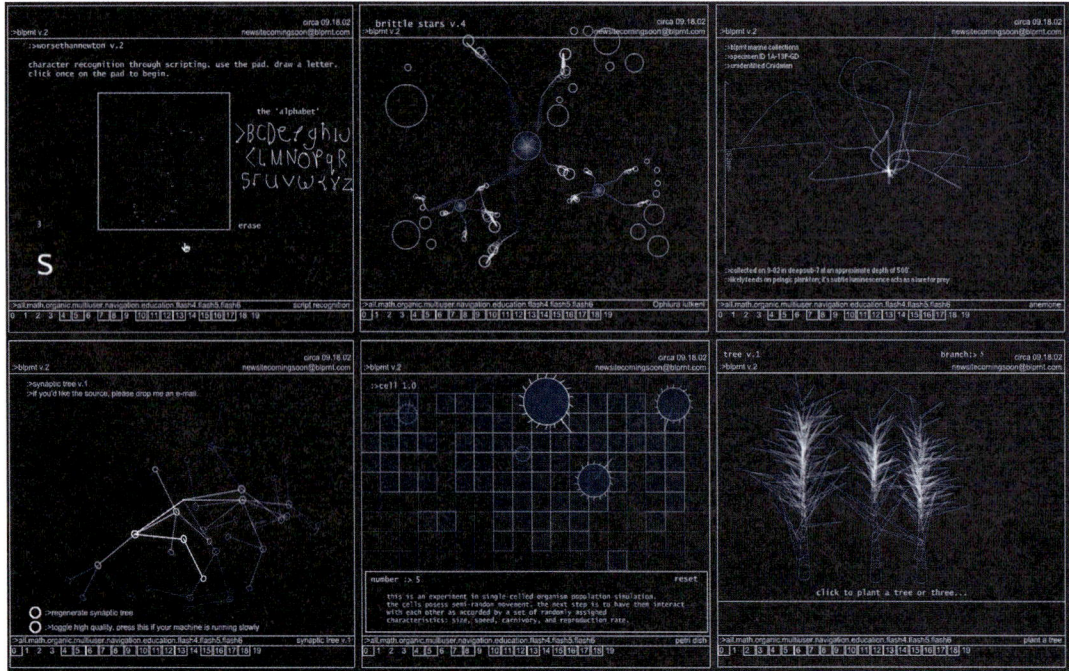

**Figure 12.1** Thorp started his Website, *www.blprnt.com*, in 1999. In addition to his Flash-based artwork and experiments, one can find links to his diverse interests and extensive client work.

next year, the site would grow to include 20 projects. As his work has evolved over the years, general themes related to science and biology have governed his Website, as well as the projects hosted there.

Not long after Thorp's first Flash job, he began working as a freelance ActionScript developer and Flash designer. Some of his clients include Honda, the Canadian Broadcasting Company, FOX, and the NHL. These works were primarily ActionScript-focused, involving prototyping of interface concepts, development of components, and creation of site architectures.

As with most of the people in this book, Thorp finds a comfortable overlap between his experimental art projects and design work. Lately this has been the result of exploring ways to apply concepts guiding his art into commercial work. Success has met this strategy through the development of experimental interfaces, commissions for interactive artwork, and conceptual consulting.

Thorp's work has also found form outside of the virtual space of the Internet. In 2006, he exhibited a collection of generative art prints in Budapest and in Vancouver, with several more shows and installations planned for 2007.

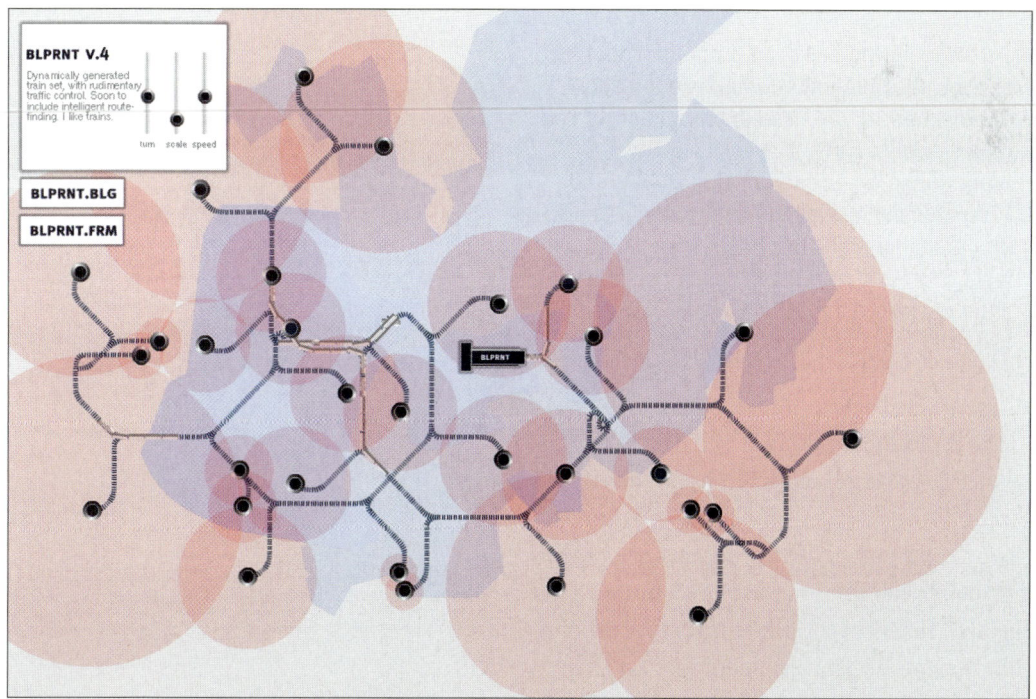

**Figure 12.2** Version 4 of *www.blprnt.com* has a randomly generated train system with variable compositional elements controlled by the user.

From a conceptual standpoint, Thorp incorporates evolutionary computing techniques into his methodology because several of his works employ such a process. He has also been researching pattern recognition and generation, sketching out future projects that harness these programmatic systems.

When he is not producing his own work, Thorp teaches Flash at Langara College's Electronic Media Design program, assisting up-and-coming designers with the development of their own creative projects.

**Figure 12.3** *tree.growth* (2005) was created using the Processing programming environment. The code Thorp wrote for this project grows digital trees, with final images exported as large format prints on canvas.

As an educator, Thorp attempts to do three things:
1. Introduce designers to basic programming principles.
2. Show students how to apply those principles to ActionScript projects.
3. And most importantly, introduce students to the idea of code as a creative medium.

"As we learn the basics of programming, I try to show the students how techniques and approaches can be used in both practical and creative ways. Over 14 weeks we cover a broad range of topics from Object Oriented Programming techniques to physics modeling and procedural animation. My hope is that at least a small number of my students will continue to explore the fields of code and generative art."

As mentioned before, Thorp is very interested in the evolutionary process and how it can be applied to creative media. He is convinced that evolution-based structures can be used to improve various creative processes, not only as a principle concept to be explored, but also through the incorporation into actual production. As a result, Thorp encourages his students to consider evolution when they are developing their own methods and techniques.

**"**Take a 'typical' design process, which might look something like Figure 12.4. Here we start with a set of possible design solutions, illustrated as colored blocks at the bottom of the diagram. There is a round of competition here, in which we generally choose two or three individuals from our population of solutions as the most fit. We then subject these individuals to another round of competition, resulting in one 'good' solution. Once we reach this point, there are typically a few rounds of optimization in which our solution is tweaked into its final form.

This process is generally good at finding a 'good fit' solution, but it is not well suited to finding a 'best fit' solution. It is a survival of the fittest process, but it neglects to include two of the most important elements of evolution—namely mutation and repeated hybridization.

An Evolutionary Design Process (EDP), then, might look like Figure 12.5. Here, we start with the same population of initial solutions, and we perform the same initial selection of our most fit individuals. However, rather than performing another selection on this small group, we instead perform a hybridization to create a new population of solutions. This process is repeated until we reach a solution that we are happy with.

During every generation, we also include some possibility of mutation. Here, mutation is illustrated by the brown block, which appears in the second generation. Mutation provides the opportunity to incorporate information that wasn't in our initial population into future generations. Ideally this mutation is stochastic—it should be a random, unpredictable change.

This process is better suited than the standard one for finding the 'best fit' solution.

I am in the process of building an evolutionary composition tool, Variance, which I hope will assist people in incorporating some parts of the EDP into their own process. More information about Variance comes later in this chapter.**"**

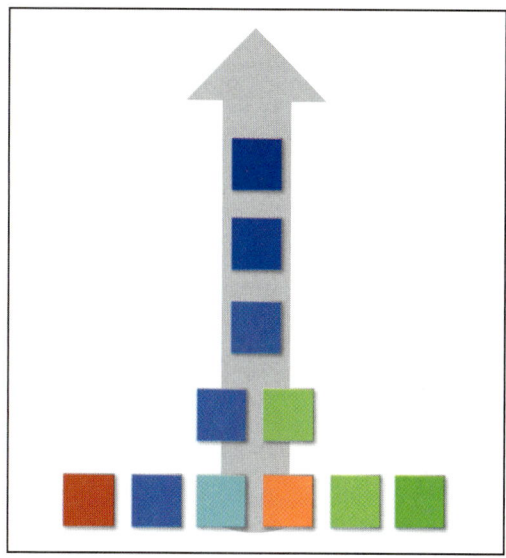

**Figure 12.4** This model reflects Thorp's notion of a traditional design process.

**Figure 12.5** Thorp's EDP model looks like this.

## DIGITAL DECONSTRUCTION: INDEX FOR X

In the fall of 2006, Thorp was asked to build a piece for the winter issue of *Born* Magazine. He set out to build a multimedia response to the poem, "Index for X and the Origin of Fires," a beautiful work by Ander Monson. The main goal was to respond to this poem through a visual composition that would avoid forcing the reader into one particular interpretation.

With this goal in mind, Thorp built a semi-intelligent engine that interprets the poem by accessing images from Flickr *www.flickr.com*, a social networking Website that is essentially a massive image database. As the engine runs through each line of the poem, images are gathered, then displayed semi-randomly, appearing just long enough for viewing before fading again into the background. As the viewer progresses through the poem, a collage of images and audio, along with the poem itself, builds a unique interpretation of the work.

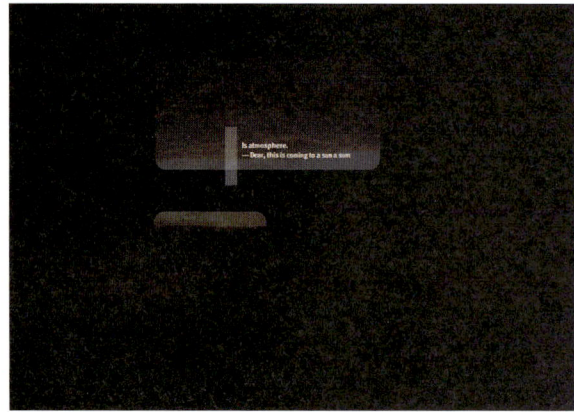

**Figure 12.6** *Index for X* (2006) is a multimedia interpretation of "Index for X and the Origin of Fires" by Ander Monson. It is viewable online at *www.bornmagazine.com/projects/indexx*.

**Figure 12.7** While randomness may be at play in the selection of the images, their formal treatment and aesthetic are not random. Thorp's style expressed through code captures a cohesive eloquence throughout the work.

*Index for X* can be thought of as a "collective interpretation," most obviously, because multiple artists combine to make a multimedia work live on the Internet, but more intrinsically, through Thorp's data-mining techniques that resources the creative eye of the massive Flickr community. The coding techniques add a sense of randomness to the site. Additional variance is added through the mercurial nature of Flickr; members of this community are constantly updating/adding/removing photos on their account.

## DIGITAL DECONSTRUCTION: DARWINSTRUMENTS

*Darwinstruments* are a collection of multi-tone sound toys that can be modified by the user. Each sound toy is a neural network with nodal virtual instruments. When the nodes are activated, they play a sound. To activate the nodes and hear the instruments, the user simply has to mouse over the graphical clusters. Each of the *Darwinstruments* will behave differently, and as such, will play a different composition

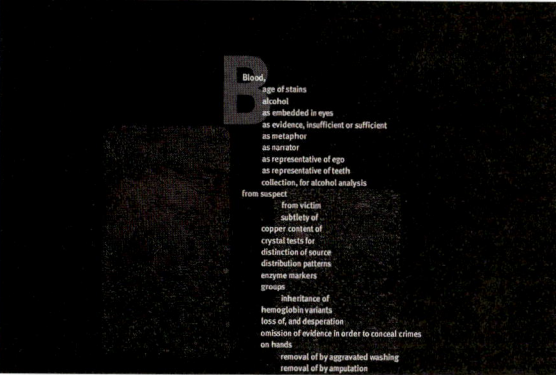

**Figure 12.8** This seems an appropriate entrance to *Index for X*, though each visit is a different experience.

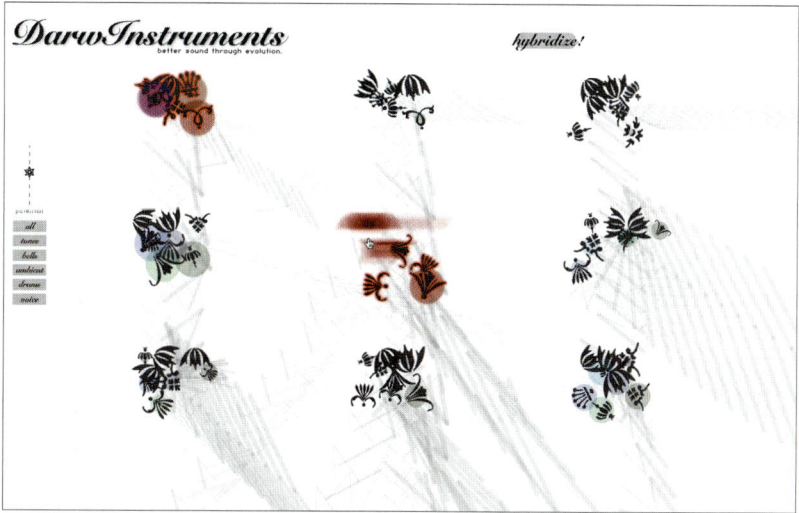

**Figure 12.9** The *Darwinstruments* (2006) behave as part instrument, part organism.

when activated. Selecting two instruments (they become red when selected) followed by hitting the "hybridize" button will engage the process of breeding a new population.

*Darwinstruments* was born out of Thorp's research on neural networks and how they could be applied in a creative way. Once the neural networks were successfully linked to the sound toys, he realized it would be difficult to consistently generate a lineage that produced pleasing results—there were simply too many variables to control. Adding genetic algorithms helped to corral and optimize these possibilities into a more stable direction.

### DIY: CREATING A GENERATIVE PARTICLE SYSTEM

Many of Thorp's Flash projects delve into the processes of *generative art*: a form of artwork relying heavily on coding techniques to formulate composition. The following tutorial he put together gives a nice introduction for applying these techniques via ActionScript.

#### Overview

Generative art and data-visualization projects typically involve rendering a lot of graphical information to the screen; often thousands of shapes are generated from a single composition. In previous versions of Flash, all dynamically drawn elements were vectors. This meant that Flash had to re-draw each element once every frame; a process that became very intensive when a lot of shapes were involved. This problem alone meant that Flash was rarely used for generative art projects or any work involving a lot of dynamic composition.

There is a solution for this in Flash 8. We can use the extraordinarily helpful BitmapData object to translate vector information into bitmap information, which is much easier to render. In this example, we will create a simple generative system and implement this new bitmap technique to render the result.

#### Setting Up the Project

Throughout this tutorial, we are going to be using a class-based approach. This means that most of our code will be written in separate AS files. I think there is a very strong advantage to this approach over the traditional "code in the FLA" method. Most importantly, all of the components of our project will be re-usable. If we use this strategy often, we will end up with a toolbox of reusable code that we can easily implement in future projects.

1. The first thing that we are going to do is to create a Flash Project file (FLP) that will manage the three files that we are going to be using and integrating. To do this, open Flash, and go to File ➡ New ➡ Flash Project. Save the project as *FlashArt.flp*. You will see the Project window with the title of our new project displayed.

2. Now we are going to create the files that will make up our project, and add them to our Project window. First, create a new FLA and save it as *FlashArt.fla*. Add it to your project by clicking the Add File to Project button at the bottom right of the project window.

3. Next, use the Add File to Project button to add the two AS files that are in the Chapter_12 folder on the DVD: *Mover.as*, and *Canvas.as*.

4. We are going to make the *FlashArt.fla* file our default project document, so that when we test our project, it is *this* file that gets launched. We do this by right-clicking (control-clicking if using a Mac) on the file in our project window and selecting Make Default Document.

**Creating the Particle System**

Now that the set-up is complete, we are ready to get started.

We are going to create a population of movie clips that use a simple set of actions to exhibit interesting behaviors when they act together in a group. In this case, the particles will be matched in pairs and will follow each other around the screen. These behaviors are defined in the *Mover.as* class file (we will look at the code in this file in detail a bit later).

1. Let us create a Symbol to represent our particles, and then we are going to link the Symbol to our class file. First, draw a box on the Stage and convert it to a symbol (Modify ➡ Convert to Symbol).

2. In the Convert to Symbol dialogue box, we need to link the Symbol to our class file. Click the Export for ActionScript checkbox in the linkage section. Now, we are going to give this symbol a linkage name so that we can attach it to our Stage dynamically. Let us call it `Block`. Next, we want to link the symbol to the class file, so we enter the name of the class file `Mover` in the AS 2.0 Class field. The dialogue box should look like Figure 12.11.

3. Press OK. Our symbol is now linked to the class file, and will automatically get any

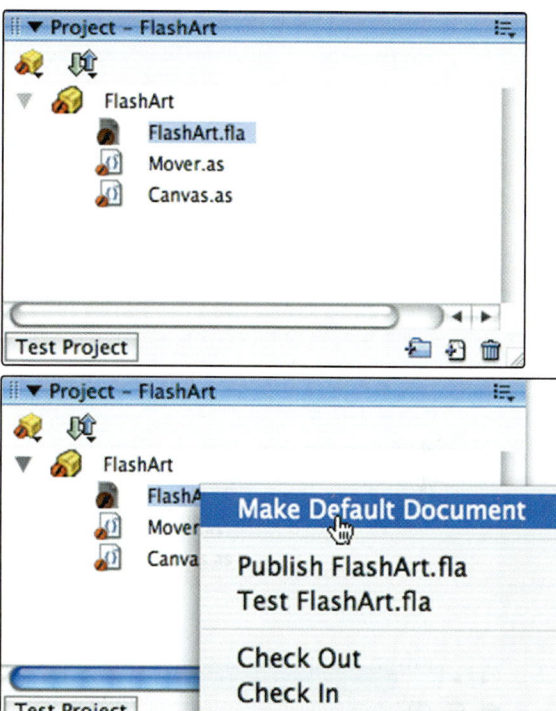

**Figure 12.10** This step will ensure that our .fla file is used when testing our movie.

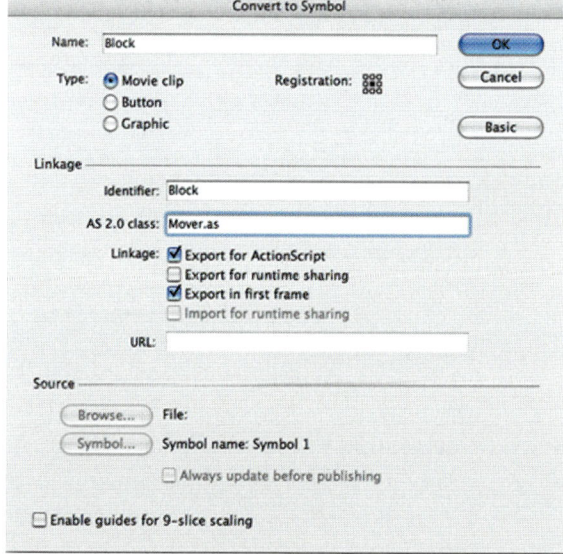

**Figure 12.11** You should be familiar with this box by now–but notice the AS 2.0 class we are supplying.

properties and behaviors that are defined in that file.

4. Next, we need to create a population of blocks on our Stage that will make up the particle system. Name the empty layer in your FLA **Actions**. Click on frame 1, and open up the Actions panel. Let us start by creating two arrays that will be used to manage the system:

```
moverArray = [];
availableTargets = [];
```

The first Array, `moverArray`, will be a list of all of the particles (blocks) on our Stage. The second one, `availableTargets`, will be used to match particles with one another.

5. Now, let us write a simple code for loop function that will create some particles on the Stage:

```
makeMovers = function(n:Number) {
    for (var i=0; i<n; i++) {
        var d = this.getNextHighestDepth();
        var m_mc = this.attachMovie("Block", "block" + d, d);

        m_mc._x = Math.random() * Stage.width;
        m_mc._y = Math.random() * Stage.height;

        _root.availableTargets.push(m_mc);
        _root.moverArray.push(m_mc);

        m_mc.init();
    };
};
```

This function uses the `attachMovie` method to attach instances of our `particle` movie clip to the Stage. It then uses the `Math.random` function to give the newly-created instances random `_x` and `_y` positions. Next, the function adds the new movie clips into the arrays that we built in the last step. Finally, it tells the particles to call their `init` method, which is defined in our class file.

6. We have a function that makes our particles. We now need one that pairs them up. This is relatively easy:

```
pairMovers = function() {
    for (var n in moverArray) {
        moverArray[n].chooseTarget();
    };
};
```

Again, the `chooseTarget` behavior is something that is defined in our class file. We will look closer at this function in a minute. For now, just know that this `pairMovers` function matches up all of the particles on our Stage with a random other particle.

7. We have written a fair amount of code on our Actions layer, but so far none of it actually does anything. To get the system running and see what it looks like, we need to execute our functions:

```
makeMovers(100);
pairMovers();
```

Go ahead and give the file a test!

### The Mover Class

You should see 100 squares on the Stage moving around in some interesting ways. Why are they moving like they are? Well, all of the behaviors of our blocks come from the code that is in our class file. Because the blocks are linked to this file, they automatically inherit all of the methods and properties that are inside of it. We can do this with any movie clip in any Library, provided the class file is available in the same directory as the FLA. Open the *Mover.as* so we can take a look at how it is set up.

Class files always start with a class declaration:

```
class Mover extends MovieClip {
```

In this case, we are naming our class, and telling Flash that it is a sub-class of an existing class: `MovieClip`. This means that objects created from the `Mover Class` will automatically get all of the helpful `MovieClip` properties (`_x`, `_alpha`, etc.) and methods (`play`, `stop`, etc.). This is called inheritance—our `Mover Class` inherits from the `MovieClip Class`. Inheritance is a nice way of structuring classes so that we do not have to repeat properties and methods over and over again.

In the next section of the class definition, we declare our variables. This is akin to a list of ingredients at the top of a recipe. We are simply telling Flash what variables we are going to use in our class so that Flash can warn us when we try to use something that was not expected:

```
var chasetarget:MovieClip;
var speed:Number;
var oldx, oldy:Number;
```

All of our variables are typed (as in data-type), telling Flash what type of data they should contain. Again, this is so that we can get a warning if we try to use the wrong data type. Once we have our variables declared, we get to the real meat of the class—the methods. In this case, there are three:

The `init` method sets values for our variables. This is important—declaring a variable does not mean that the variable exists; it just tells Flash to expect that variable. To actually create a variable, we need to assign it a value:

```
function init() :Void{

    speed = 5 + (Math.random() * 5);

    oldx = _x;
    oldy = _y;

    this.onEnterFrame = this.doMove;

};
```

The first variable, `speed`, is given a random value between 5 and 10. `oldx` and `oldy` are simply matched to the values of `_x` and `_y` respectively. In the last part of this function, we link the `onEnterFrame` event of the movie with its `doMove` function, so that it will move once per frame.

The `doMove` function is a simple easing function that moves the movie clip towards its chosen target:

```
function doMove() :Void{
    var xd:Number = chasetarget._x - this._x;
    var yd:Number = chasetarget._y - this._y;

        this._x += xd/speed;
        this._y += yd/speed;

        oldx = _x;
        oldy = _y;
};
```

In the first part of the function, we calculate the distance between this movie clip and its target. These values are stored in variables (`xd` and `yd`). We then move our clips a fraction of the way toward the target. The size of this fraction is dependant on our speed variable, so it will vary between 1/5th and 1/10th. Finally, in this function, we keep track of the last position values for X and Y (we will use this later).

We are left, then, with one more function in our class: `chooseTarget`. This function shuffles randomly through our list of available targets and chooses one to follow:

```
function chooseTarget() :Void{

    var loops:Number = Math.round(Math.random() * _root.availableTargets.length);
    for (var i=0; i<loops; i++) {
        _root.availableTargets.push(_root.availableTargets.shift());
    };
    chasetarget = _root.availableTargets[0];

};
```

The line inside the for loop combines the `push` and `shift` methods to advance our array by one index. The for loop runs a random number of times, so this simple function has the result of picking a random target from the available target list.

So, our completed particle system works like this: particles are created and paired up. Then, during every frame, they move towards their target. Because particles are unlikely to be paired to each other, they chase each other around a while before settling into a clump.

### Recorded History

The system that we have created is interesting, but it is hard to visualize what is actually happening. To assist in this, let us have the particles draw the path that they follow onto the Stage. In this way, we will get a visual history of the movement of the system. We are going to draw the paths using Flash's dynamic drawing methods.

1. First, let us create a movie clip in which to draw the paths. We can do this on the main Timeline, right after we activate the system. We will use the `lineStyle` method to set the drawing color of this new movie clip to be a transparent grey:

```
makeMovers(100);
pairMovers();

_root.createEmptyMovieClip("thecanvas_mc", _root.getNextHighestDepth());
thecanvas_mc.lineStyle(1,0,10);
```

2. We now have a "canvas" on which to draw. Now, let us teach the Movers to draw to that Stage. To do this, let us add a new method to the `Mover Class`. So switch over to the *Mover.as* file, and add the following code right after the `doMove` method:

```
function doDraw() {

    _root.thecanvas_mc.moveTo(oldx, oldy);
    _root.thecanvas_mc.lineTo(_x, _y);

};
```

3. This method draws a line on our canvas movie clip, from the last position of the Mover to the current position of the Mover.

Now we will get this method to run once every frame by adding it to the `doMove` method. If you look at the code for the `doMove` method, you can see where the call to the `doDraw` has been added. Update your code accordingly.

```
function doMove() :Void{

var xd:Number = chasetarget._x 
- this._x;
    var yd:Number = chasetarget.
_y - this._y;

    this._x += xd/speed;
    this._y += yd/speed;

    doDraw();
    oldx = _x;
    oldy = _y;
};
```

4. Test the movie again. What you should see is that your particles leave a trail, drawing on the screen and showing where they have been; it should look something like Figure 12.12.

You should also notice that the movie is running quite slow. This is because of the problem that we talked about right at the beginning of the tutorial: all of the lines being drawn are vectors, and Flash has to redraw them all once per frame. With 100 particles drawing 3000 lines per second, the Flash player is quickly brought to its knees.

Luckily, we can get around this problem in Flash 8. We are going to use a class that I have written, the `Canvas Class`, to convert all of those vector lines into bitmap data a few times per second. This will keep the system running smoothly.

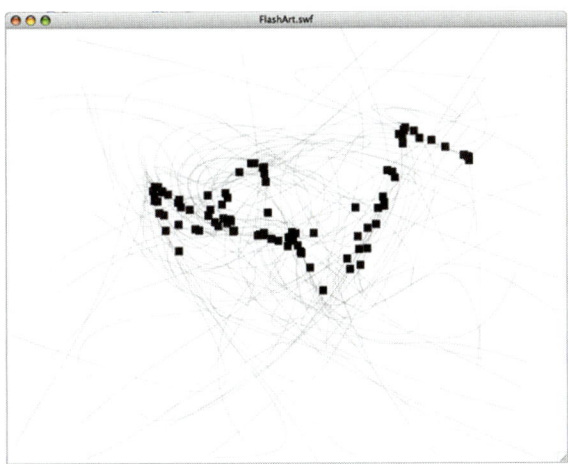

**Figure 12.12** Here is our project up to this point.

### Bitmaps Save the Day

The `Canvas Class` that we are going to use manages an instance of the `BitmapData Class`. It packages up some tricky code and makes it a bit easier to implement. You can use this class any time you want to convert a movie clip to a bitmap.

1. First, create an instance of the `Canvas` right after our last code on the Actions layer of the FLA:

```
_root.createEmptyMovieClip("the
canvas_mc", _root.getNextHighest
Depth());
thecanvas_mc.lineStyle(1,0,10);

var c = new Canvas(_root);
```

2. Now, let us set up a function that will draw our canvas movie clip to this canvas instance:

```
doDraw = function() {
    c.etch(thecanvas_mc);
    thecanvas_mc.clear();
    thecanvas_mc.lineStyle(1,0,10);
};
```

3. After we have copied the contents of `thecanvas_mc` into a bitmap, we clear `thecanvas_mc`, and reset its drawing color. The last thing to do is to get this function to run a few times a second. We do this using an interval:

```
setInterval(doDraw, 200);
```

4. Test your movie again. It should run a lot faster than before. Indeed, this movie can run indefinitely without having any processor slowdown at all.

If you get stuck, open up the *FlashArt.flp* file in the Chapter_12 folder from the DVD.

**Figure 12.13** Now we have a smoothly running generative artwork.

## DIGITAL DECONSTRUCTION: *VARIANCE*

After his work on *Darwinstruments*, Thorp became interested in how to apply genetic algorithms and evolution towards a visual design process. This led to his project called *Variance*—an evolutionary computing engine for evolving graphic compositions. *Variance* is a graphical environment that can be used to evolve compositions from any set of graphic elements. The ability to hybridize elements of a composition becomes part of the creative palette, somewhat like a Brush or Color Mixer, yet more powerful as aesthetic fancy gives way to a design ontology.

> "*Variance*'s intended use is as a brainstorming tool. It is also intended as a mechanism to enhance the design process, by leveraging evolutionary techniques. Currently I am building several commercial and non-commercial projects that use the *Variance* engine. Though it is currently limited to creating graphical compositions, I would also like to expand the engine to handle sound, video, and other media."

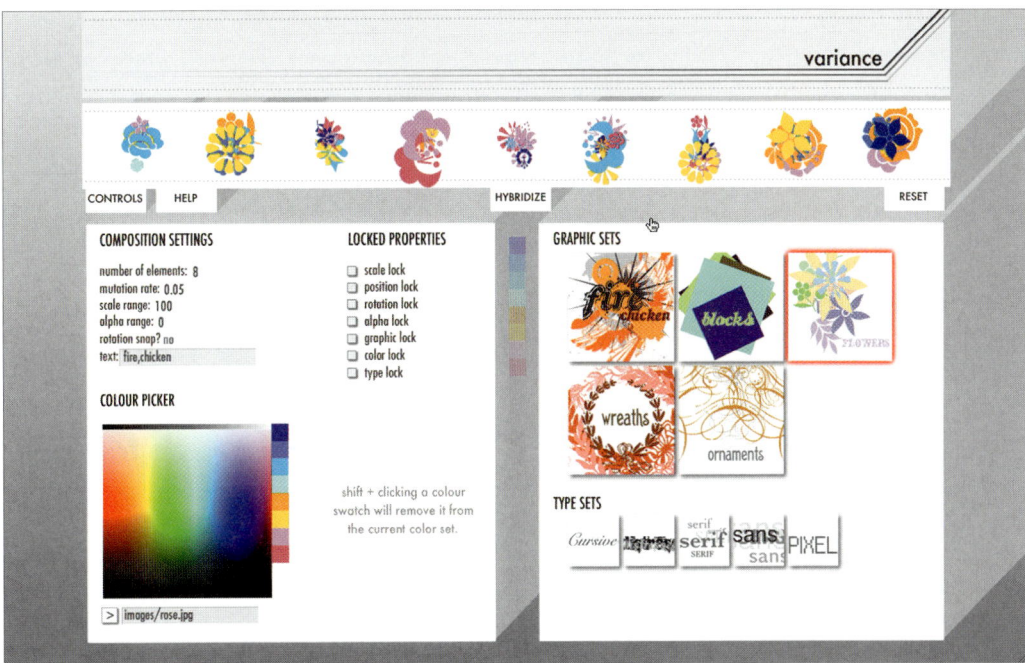

**Figure 12.14** The *Variance* environment.

**Figure 12.15** Forms being selected and modified through an Evolutionary Design Process (EDP).

## ON YOUR OWN

In this example we have seen how we can use evolutionary behaviors to create interesting visual compositions using Flash. There is a lot of room to experiment with this system. What happens if you add more particles? What happens if you make the particles themselves invisible? What about adding color? There are a lot of ways that this system could be adapted. If you are feeling particularly daring, you can extend this class by adding new properties and methods—give it a try!

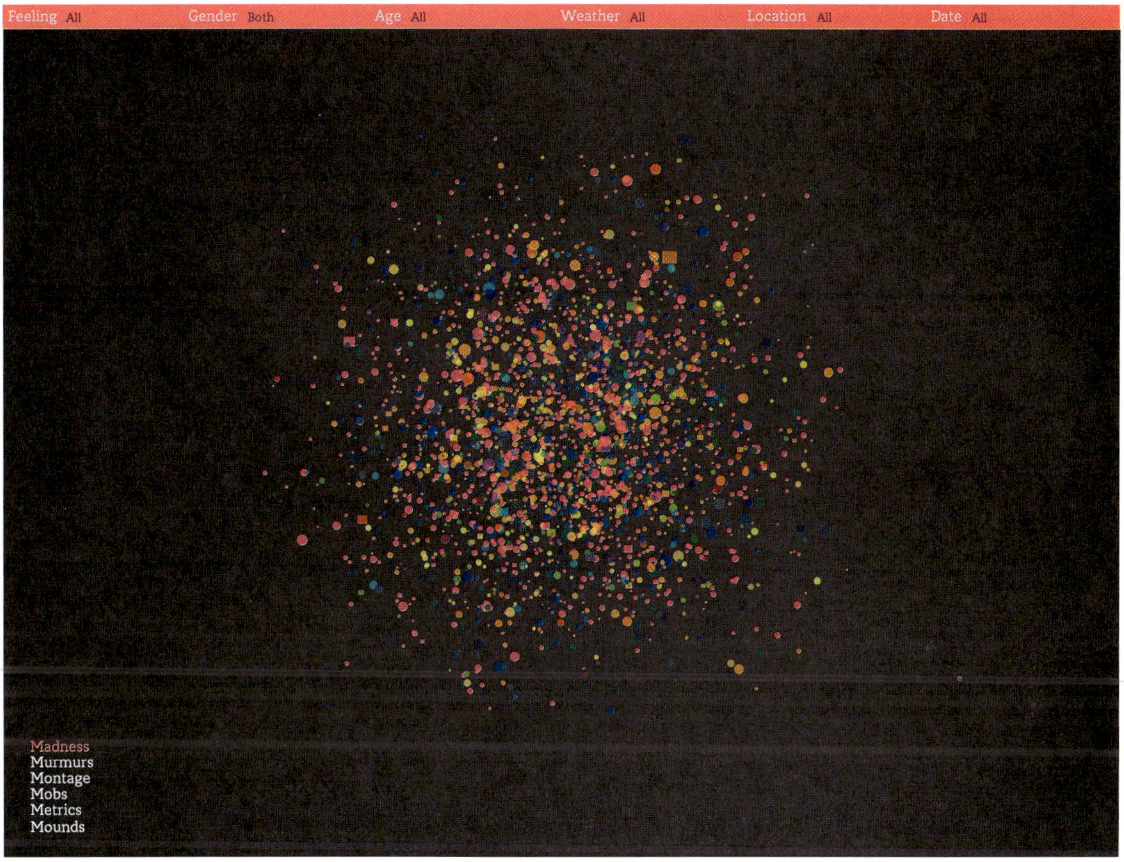

| Feeling All | Gender Both | Age All | Weather All | Location All | Date All |

**Madness**
Murmurs
Montage
Mobs
Metrics
Mounds

Visualizing Information

# JONATHAN HARRIS

Art and Design for the Web has rapidly transitioned from static displays to fluctuating visualizations of live data. Jonathan Harris is an artist who has not only taken notice of this trend, but is one of the leading innovators in creating data-driven projects that fully illuminate phenomena that are inherently amorphous. His work can be viewed from his Website *www.number27.org*.

Some of his recent topics of research in this vein include: social software networks like Flickr and MySpace, the frequency of language and events flowing through the Internet, and the presence and activity of multinational corporations like Starbucks and McDonalds. How these entities affect and shape our world cannot be summed up in a single snapshot or pie-chart. Harris's skill for gathering up data surrounding recent cultural trends and re-routing them through a carefully structured lens, finds form in his provocative works of art and design. The experience of engaging these works are not only fun and engaging, but educational as new perspectives are provided for our unfolding digital vernacular.

Although obviously quite skilled in the various crafts associated with designing elaborate multimedia projects, Harris was mainly focused on traditional art practices in his youth. In fact, he even held a certain disdain for computers and electronics until reaching college.

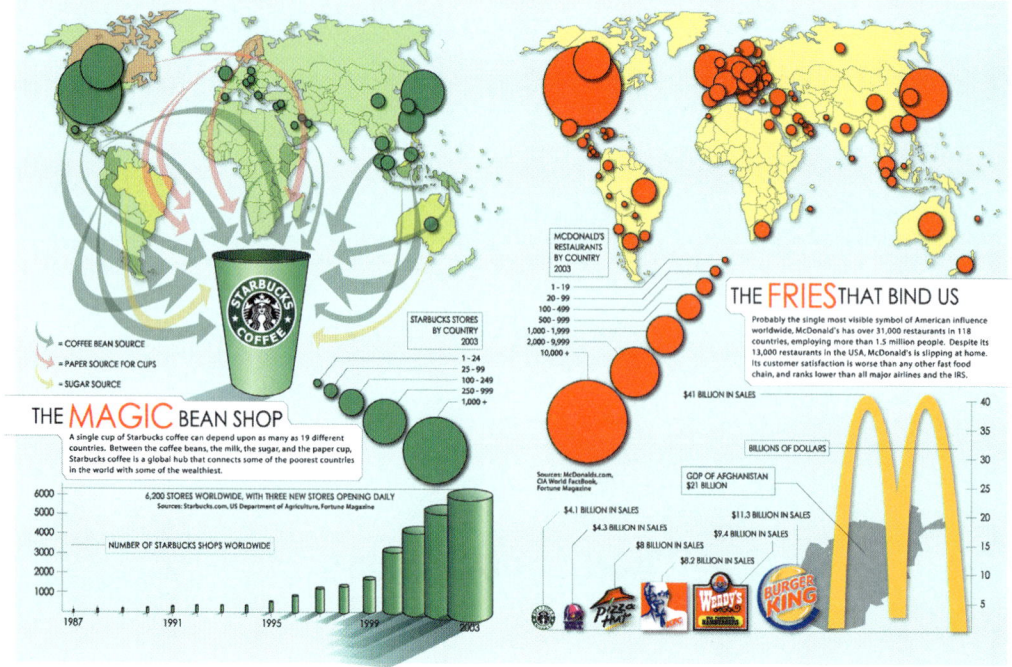

**Figure 13.1** Some of Harris's research while at Princeton includes this data visualization of multinational fast-food corporations.

"I tried video games but they didn't hold my interest. I always had a problem with the idea that entertainment could be centrally prescribed and consumed by anyone who would pay the price of admission. For this reason, I have never liked theme parks, blockbuster movies, or chain restaurants. I've always had the idea that entertainment should be a personal thing–full of uniquely crafted experiences."

As a freshman at Princeton, Harris reluctantly signed up for a basic computer science class to fill a core requirement. One of the assignments was to create a Web page and Harris put together a site containing some pictures of his paintings, images from his native Vermont, his class schedule, and some other assorted details. This class opened the door for his creative direction to address the Internet as a valuable resource.

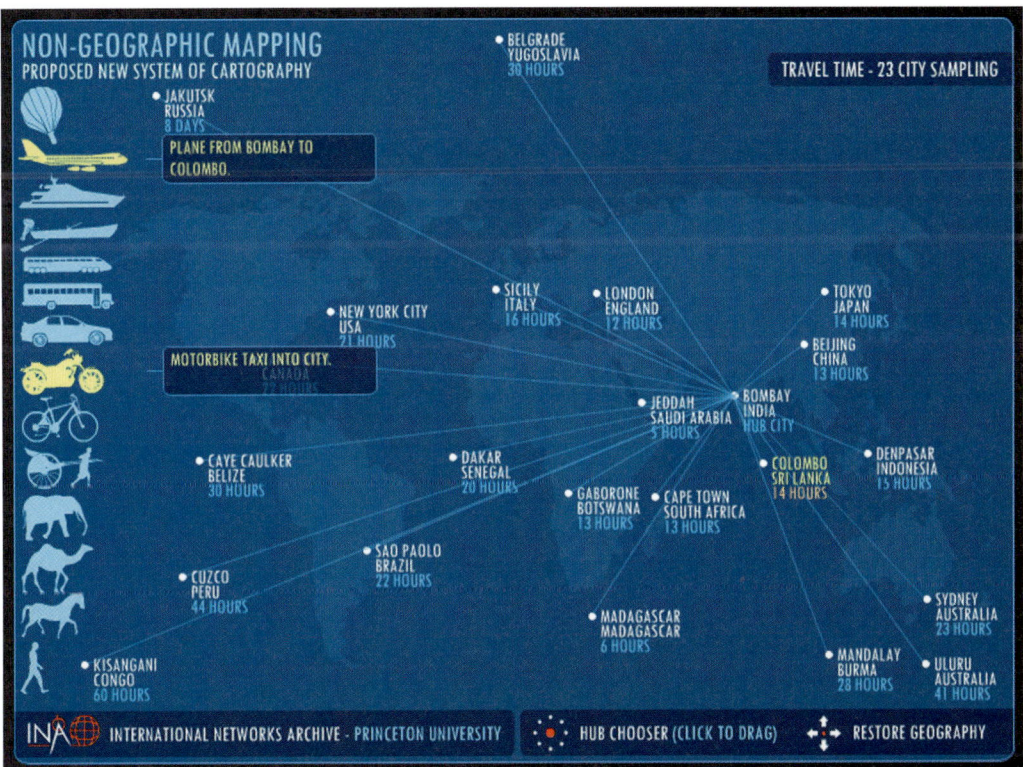

**Figure 13.2** One of the themes expressed by the International Networks Archive (where Harris was active in 2003) is that geography and physical space is becoming increasingly irrelevant.

> "The process made me realize that there were thousands of other people like me, putting up a Web page, putting their life online. For the first time, I saw the possibility of finding humans in the web of machines. I decided to change my major to computer science, curious to see what I could find in this new discipline."

Harris's thesis at Princeton was a program called ExtraExtra, which automatically scanned around 100 news sites every hour to find and cluster similar news articles, thereby providing multiple accounts of the same story. Also at Princeton, he founded *Troubadour Magazine*, a publication that explored world cultures using themed issues like "Empire," "Evildoers," and "Pirates!". The magazine enjoyed great success, winning two awards from the American Society of Professional Journalists.

> "I loved this chance to glimpse inside other people's minds. At this point there was a deep rift between the creative, highly experiential processes of traveling, keeping sketchbooks, and editing *Troubadour,* and the isolated detachment of writing computer code. The former felt so human, the latter so inhuman."

Harris began to bridge the divide between code and creativity at Fabrica, Benetton's highly reputed fellowship program and research center in Italy. During his residency there, Harris made computer programs that studied the human world using the Internet as a data source. He took notice that many traditionally offline activities were suddenly moving online. Photographs that used to be stored in scrapbooks are now being uploaded as digital files and shared on Flickr. Private diaries filed away

**Figure 13.3** A page from Harris's sketchbook reveals his talent for painting as well as some design inspirations.

on a nightstand are now expressed publicly in blogs and on socialware sites like LiveJournal and MySpace. Many of these sites are changing the way people meet and stay in contact with each other. These social developments have Web page facades, but behind this they exist as data coursing through the Internet and this is where Harris's work focuses.

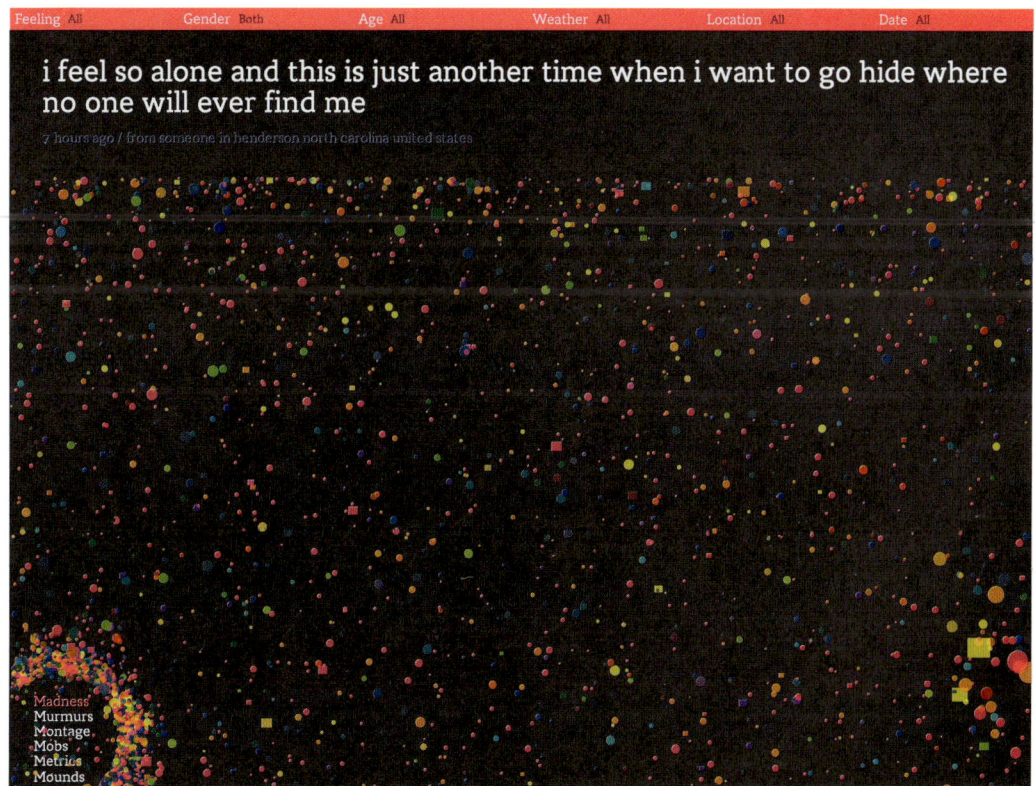

**Figure 13.4** *We Feel Fine* (2006) *www.wefeelfine.org* was created by Jonathan Harris and Sep Kamvar. The software behind this project draws from people's blog postings, examining the collection of human emotions as they are related through the massive collections of journals, blogs, and Web pages across the Net.

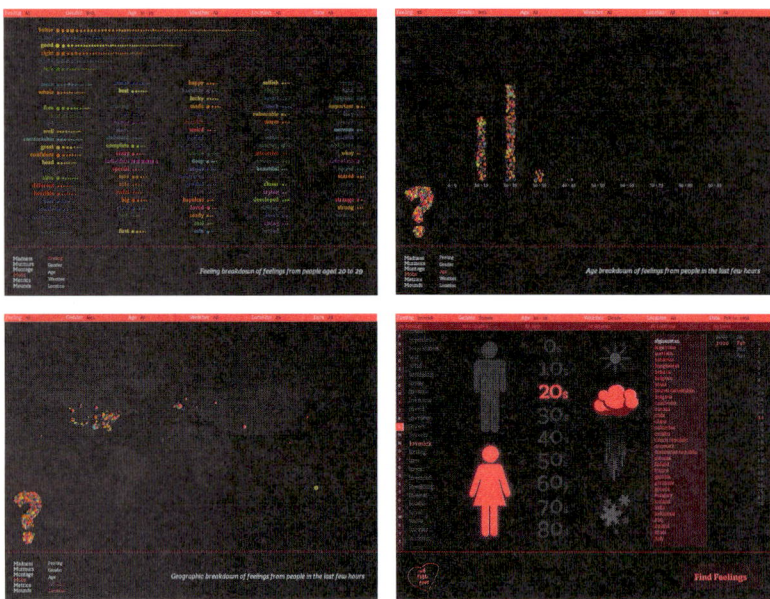

**Figure 13.5** There are a variety of ways to explore the current data of human emotions expressed on the Net. Each one reveals a new perspective regarding the statistical aspects of the retrieved data.

**Figure 13.6** The user can choose to view groups sharing a particular emotion (or place, weather, age, etc.).

**DIGITAL DECONSTRUCTION: *WORDCOUNT***

It was while working at Fabrica that Harris created *WordCount*, an interactive presentation of the 86,800 most frequently used English words, ranked and scaled in order of importance and arranged side by side as one very long sentence. The site utilizes a Flash front-end interface that retrieves data from server-side applications performing data mining routines.

When *WordCount* first loads, a long list of words are prominently displayed across the screen beginning with a huge "the" on the left, followed by successively smaller words trailing off towards the right. The position and relative size of each word is based on its frequency of occurrence.

There are four ways you can navigate through this list of words. Across the top are buttons that allow you to scroll back and forth by a single word. Below the list of words, a visual graph, representing the complete list, can be

**Figure 13.7** *Word Count* (2003) has won numerous awards, including a Webby award in 2005 and the Information Design award from AIGA in 2003.

**Figure 13.8** Typing in the word "America" will get this result.

manipulated for rapid scrolling. There is also a word rank search box. Directly typing into either of these, followed by a return-click on the keyboard, will activate the word list accordingly.

Tapping into the database of the British National Corpus, *WordCount* is able to generate its list of words. More common words (like "the") occur early in the list, while rare words appear later in the list. One unintentional result of this project was the amount of e-mails from avid conspiracy theorists—probably after examining the results of such searches as seen in Figure 13.8! These are, of course, examples of coincidence mixed with personal projection. But it is fun hunting for meanings across these analytical designed proximities.

While observing people interfacing with *WordCount*, Harris noticed that people always searched for uncommon words. After initially poking around the interface, users would be quick to look for their name, perhaps a few other words with personal relevance, but invariably the process would lead to searching for "dirty words." Harris was curious as to whether this was just a trait of his foul-minded friends or something more indicative of general human behavior.

To study this matter further, he created a corollary project, *QueryCount*. Where *WordCount* tracks the way humans use language naturally, *QueryCount* tracks the way we use *WordCount*. What words are people most interested in investigating for their degree of occurrence?

A quick glance at *QueryCount* www.wordcount.org/querycount.php will show a list of words in the order of frequency as actively queried in *WordCount*. Many of them prove Harris's hypothesis that, overwhelmingly, people seem to have dirty minds.

When *QueryCount* was first launched it was relatively easy to influence its form due to it is being a cumulative collection of searched words from *WordCount*. During this time, Harris noticed that people were purposefully adding queries on *WordCount*, in order to shape

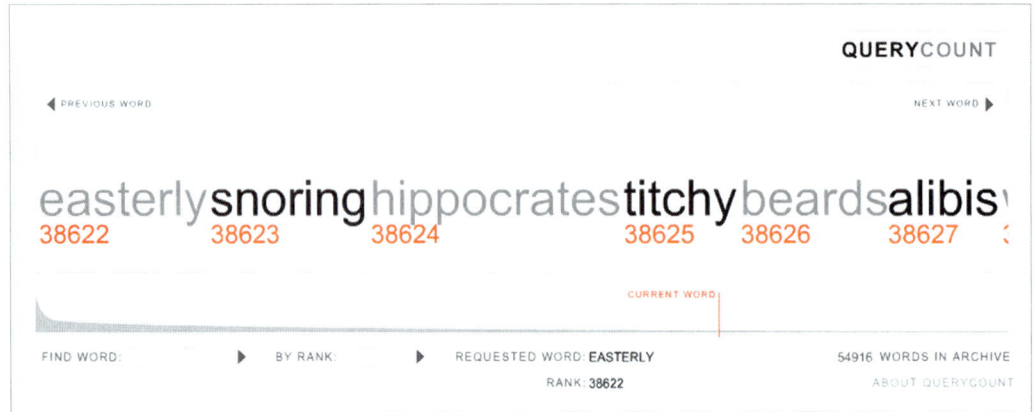

**Figure 13.9** Hopefully "snoring" will only be associated with my name on *QueryCount*!

the form of *QueryCount*. This was taking place around the same time that the U.S. had invaded Iraq. On the first day of the invasion, somebody was trying to force the phrase "this war is a mistake" in *QueryCount*, by searching incessantly for those five words, in that order, in *WordCount*! And it actually worked: for several hours during this period, the phrase "this war is a mistake" was displayed on the initial loading of *QueryCount*. After a brief poignant life, the traffic from other people's searches drowned it out forever.

> "It struck me how strange and beautiful it was that some anonymous soul was trying to communicate his political ideology through such an obfuscated medium. He could have picked up the phone and called a friend, or walked down the street and talked to a real person, but instead he chose to broadcast his anti-war sentiments through the linguistic meta-analytics of *QueryCount*. That was one of the clearest glimpses I have had of the human in the machine, the individual amidst the zeitgeist."

### DIGITAL DECONSTRUCTION: 10 × 10

Through *WordCount*'s success at revealing interesting relationships between words and the people using them, Harris moved onto new questions such as, "What does a single moment in our world look like?" In response to his own question, Harris created *10−10*: a project composed of the top 100 words and pictures in the world (according to Internet usage), updated and archived every hour from the heaviest trafficked Internet news sites. The results range from the frivolous to the shocking, but always resulting in a fitting snapshot of human civilization.

Along with Flash, *10−10* employs custom applications and scripts (in Perl, PHP, and MySQL) running on a server to determine the 100 most significant images. Each hour, these collective files, scripts, and applications snap into action, operating the retrieval processes to grab the required media and information, concluding with the Flash movie we experience on the site: www.tenbyten.org.

The Flash front-end carefully constructs an interface designed to present the results as a picture postcard window, composed of 100 different frames, each of which holds the image of a single moment in time. Clicking on a single frame allows us to peer a bit deeper, with several links available for exploring the actual news items associated with this image.

In a way, *10−10* functions as a scribe for human history. With each hour, a snapshot is preserved from this objective cybernetic vision, leaving a trail of visual statements that forms a continuous pattern of human activities.

**Figure 13.10** *10x10* (2004) has won awards of distinction from Ars Electronica, *ID Magazine*, and a Webby Award.

**Figure 13.11** Clicking on the image retrieves a detailed view, along with the headlines across the Web hosting it.

**CHAPTER THIRTEEN**  233

**Figure 13.12** Clicking on the image again brings up a larger view.

The Flash interface employs a space-saving "tsunami menu" to present 100 words in a 400-pixel vertical space. The images act as the principle interface, while beneath the grid are controls for searching the historical trail archived by *10−10*.

### DIGITAL DECONSTRUCTION: *PHYLOTAXIS*

*Phylotaxis* is another of Harris's data-driven Flash works; it was developed for *Seed Magazine* www.seedmagazine.com, a science and culture publication based in New York. The goal of this work was to develop a visual expression of the space where science and culture meet.

The Fibonacci Sequence was used as a structure for the media elements. This sequence is defined by a series of numbers where each number is the sum of the previous two numbers (1, 1, 2, 3, 5, 8, 13, etc.). As abstract as this concept may seem, it is actually related to many natural phenomena, such as the petal arrangement of roses, the breeding patterns of rabbits, and the shape of our galaxy. It is also found in man-made items, ranging from the design of the Great Pyramids to the construction of Stradivarius violins.

The name for *Phylotaxis* comes from "phyllos" (leaf) and "taxis" (order). In botany, it is the study of the ordered position of leaves on a

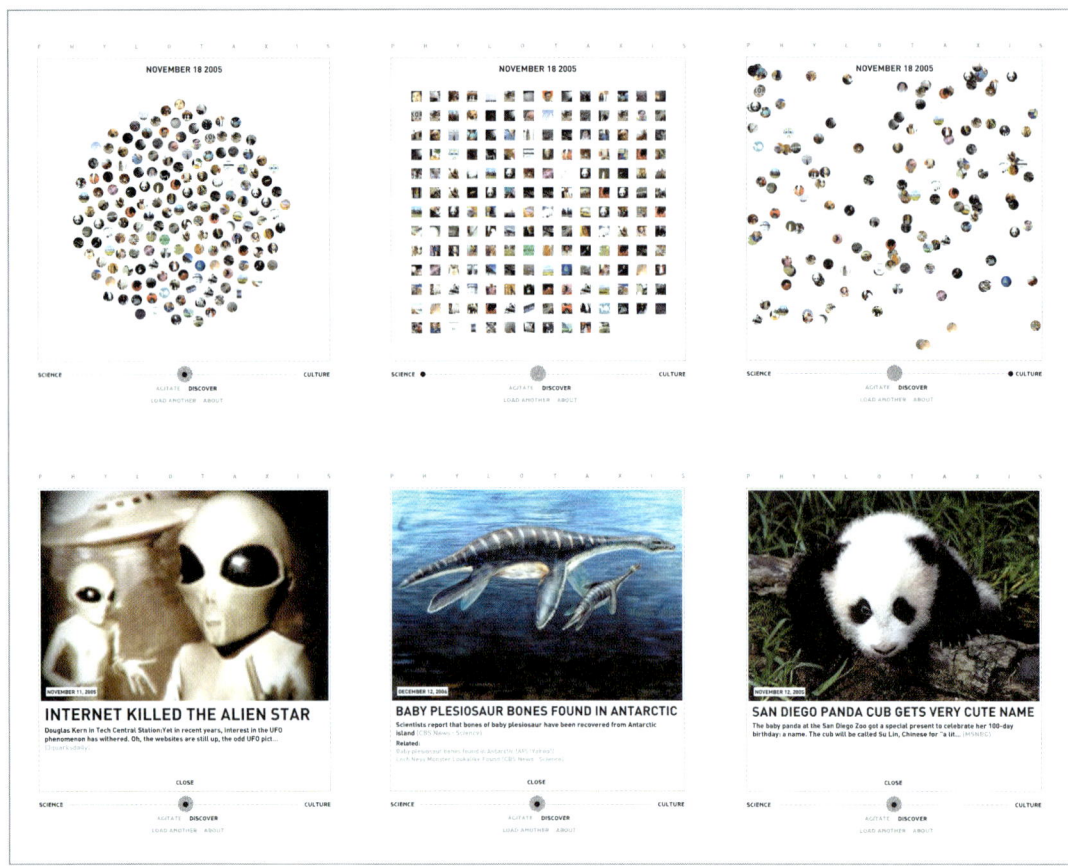

**Figure 13.13** *Phylotaxis* (2005) was a Webby Award nominee for the Best Navigation/Structure category.

plant stem, and also applies to the shape of pinecones and the dispersion of seeds on the flat head of a sunflower. Harris's *Phylotaxis* is used to illustrate the delicate balance between science and culture.

> "Without the randomness of culture, science becomes dry and predictable, imprisoned in a strict square grid. Without the rational thinking of science, culture quickly teeters towards chaos. Only when science and culture are recognized as peers can harmony be achieved, expressed through the astonishing *Phylotaxis* shape."

The individual nodes within this interface are updated every few hours by server-side applications that scour the Internet for data sources relating to science. In this way, the flow of content distributed across the *Phylotaxis* structure is automatically populated beyond the human aesthetics involved with editing.

Perl code lies at the core of the back-end programming, acting as the data-mining engine, analyzing and clustering science articles and images. On the Flash front-end of things, a complex particle system governs the nodes that make up the *Phylotaxis* structure. Sliding the controls towards "Science" gravitates the particles towards a grid arrangement. When the slider is pulled towards "Culture" the particles become more chaotic in their arrangement. When the slider is placed halfway between "Science" and "Culture," the particles are attracted to the *Phylotaxis* homeostasis.

## DIY: DATABASES AND FLASH

In this section, Dylan Moore, a graduate student at the Pratt Institute and talented ActionScripter, was brought aboard to dig deep into the technical layers that are involved when using Flash with MySQL and PHP. In particular, Dylan examined *Phylotaxis* as a source of inspiration for putting together this tutorial, which will describe how Flash can access MySQL databases via PHP. For those of you who are completely new to concepts of using databases with Flash, you may want to open the unabridged version of this tutorial from the DVD, titled *MySQL_PHPandFlash.rtf* in the Chapter_13 folder.

### Introduction

To begin, there are essentially four technical ingredients at work in a project like *Phylotaxis*:

1. Storing information in a database.
2. Requesting information.
3. Transferring that information into Flash.
4. And finally—an evocative interactive particle system to display information.

For the purposes of this tutorial, we need to set up all of these mechanisms (usually distributed across a server and local machine) onto your single computer. While this is not the standard for database-driven Flash projects, it is a good way to grasp what happens across the MySQL, PHP, and Flash environments. This requires setting up a MySQL database, and a PHP document, before wrapping everything up in the more familiar environment of Flash.

### MySQL and PHP Installation

To obtain MySQL, point your Web browser to *www.mysql.com* and click on the download section. You will want to download the MySQL Community Server. When you choose "Pick a mirror" you will be directed to the download page. Be sure you choose the correct download for your operating system and hardware.

When the download is complete, decompress the file and install the packages. You should also install the MySQL.prefPane so you can start and stop the MySQL server. For communicating with MySQL, I have chosen to work with the command line because it requires no additional software to be installed, and also because it is simple to use for beginning database management.

Obtaining PHP involves a similar process. Go to this Website: *www.php.net*, select the "downloads" link, and then find your operating system (Windows is the default page, but Macintosh can be selected from a list on the left). Once downloaded, install PHP on your system.

If you have never used Web sharing before (and are using a Mac), be sure to make a stop over to the System Preferences, then select Sharing. Turn on "Personal Web Sharing" under services. This will activate your Sites folder in your home directory as your active Web directory.

If you are not on a Macintosh, this is a good time to find out where your Web directory is located (where your computer places Web files to serve). If you are unsure about how to set up PHP or your Web server, I strongly suggest looking at the very well prepared tutorial on PHP.net's site *us2.php.net/tut.php*.

### Creating a MySQL Database

MySQL is a vast topic that has been covered in many books, with most numbering hundreds of pages. This section is only intended to get your feet wet if you have never worked with

**Figure 13.14** This is the download section for my computer: a G4 laptop (pre Intel), which is running Mac OSX 10.4.

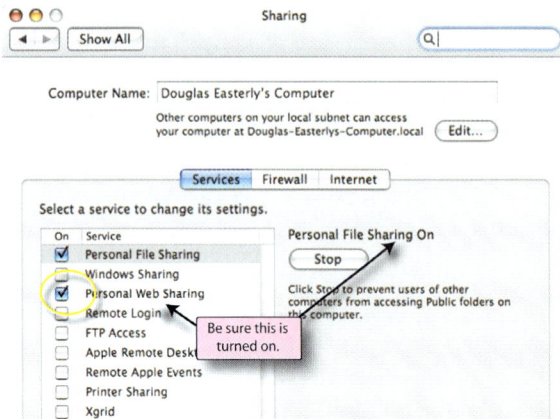

**Figure 13.15** Personal Web Sharing needs to be activated for this tutorial.

MySQL before so that we can get some data into Flash.

1. The first thing we need to do is establish the command line. This will be the channel of communication to our database. If you are using a Windows machine, launch the MySQL Command Line Client, which should have been installed with MySQL, then skip to step 3.

2. If you are using a Macintosh, launch Terminal, ▪ which is located in the Utilities folder inside the Applications folder. The following steps need to be done the *first* time you work with MySQL (you will need to do this only once). Type the following in the Terminal window, pressing enter at the end of each line, and provide your password when needed:

```
cd /etc
sudo pico profile
```

This will open up a text editor called Pico where you see a line that begins

```
"export PATH="...
```

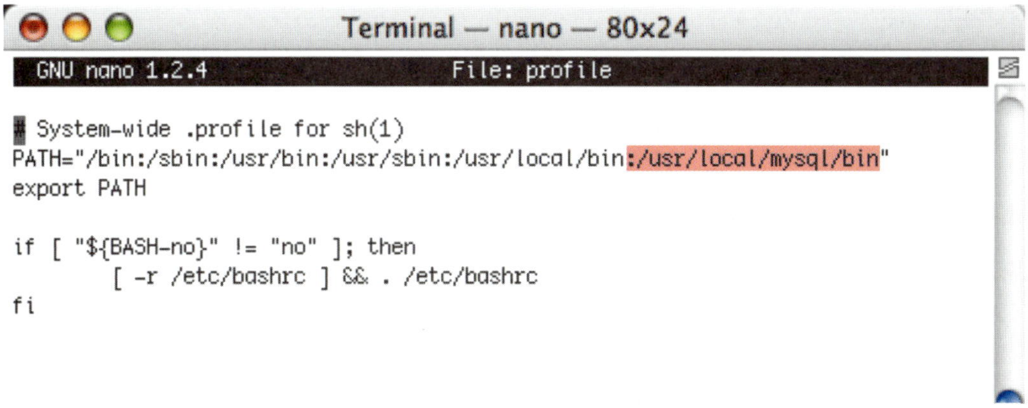

```
# System-wide .profile for sh(1)
PATH="/bin:/sbin:/usr/bin:/usr/sbin:/usr/local/bin:/usr/local/mysql/bin"
export PATH

if [ "${BASH-no}" != "no" ]; then
        [ -r /etc/bashrc ] && . /etc/bashrc
fi
```

**Figure 13.16** Do not worry if your Path profile does not look exactly like mine–just be sure this line gets added.

Add the following on the next line below this:

```
PATH=${PATH}:/usr/local/mysql/bin
```

Then, press ctrl-X to quit. Pico will ask you if you want to save. Press the Y key. Finally, it will ask you what file name you want to save the file as. Just press Enter to accept it as the same name. Easy enough, right? Now, close the Terminal window and re-open a new one. This is important for your changes to take effect.

What did we just do? We set up our Terminal to find all the MySQL commands, so when we ask for them later, Terminal will know where they are.

3. Whether you are using the Command Line Client in Windows or the Terminal from a Macintosh, I will simply refer to this as "the command line" from here on out. Now let us use our command line to open a connection to a MySQL database.

When you launch the command line on a Windows machine, you must put in your username and password to connect. On a Macintosh, put in the following line, press Enter, and then put in your password when prompted:

```
mysql -u root
```

That is it! You are connected to MySQL, but there is not a database yet, so let us make one now.

4. Type in the following at the `mysql>` prompt, hitting the return key after typing each line:

```
create database swarm;
use swarm;
```

The first line creates a new database named `swarm`, and the second line tells MySQL to use the swarm database.

5. Next, let us make a table and some fields in that table. Begin by typing the following at the `mysql>` prompt:

```
create table particle (id integer,
name char(10), size integer);
```

This line makes a `particle` table (think of it as a spreadsheet), and some fields (think columns in a spreadsheet) labeled `id`, `name`, and `size`. We can make this list of fields as long as we want by simply adding more labels and *data types*, separating each new field with a comma.

6. However, once you create a table, you have to do something a little different to add a new field afterward. Here is how to do it, because we want to include a label for an integer named `speed`:

```
alter table particle add column
speed integer;
```

7. Great. Let us see what our table looks like now. Do this by typing in the following at the `mysql>` prompt:

```
describe particle;
```

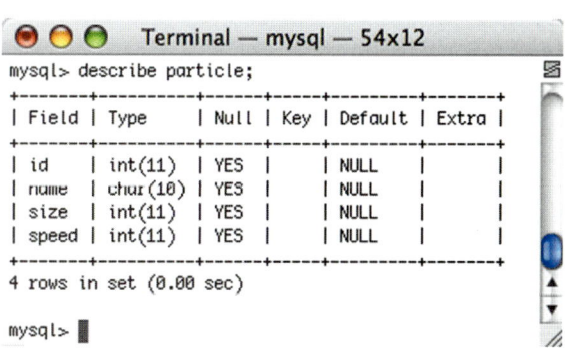

**Figure 13.17** Your output should look like this. You can see the listing of `id`, `name`, `size`, and `speed`. These all have the correct data type.

8. Now that we have our database schema set up—that is, the organization that all of our data will fit into—let us actually add some data. This is an important step to note, because MySQL databases are rarely populated with data manually. Usually a script or some Web app feeds information autonomously in. Jonathan Harris's *Phylotaxis* project, for instance, does this with an extensive back-end written in Perl. However, as this is our first time out and about with MySQL, I am going to stick to making some manual entries so we can first understand how the data is added, requested, and delivered.

9. Still at the `mysql>` prompt, enter the following, then hit Enter on your keyboard:

```
insert into particle (id, name,
 size, speed) values (1, 'first
one', 2, 5);
```

This makes a new particle entry, with an id value of `1`, a name of `'first one'`, size of `2`, and speed of `5`.

10. Let us make a few more entries and then take a look at our data. Remember to hit the Enter key after each line.

```
insert into particle (id, name,
 size, speed) values (2, 'second',
 2, 3);
insert into particle (id, name,
 size, speed) values (3, 'third',
 1, 1);
select * from particle;
```

11. Okay, it looks good, except for one thing: for our databases, we are going to avoid using spaces in our name field. So, let us learn how to edit a record after we have already made it:

```
update particle set name='first'
 where name='first one';
```

This will change our first entry's name record from `first one` to `first`:

Now let us check the output to make sure it worked:

```
select * from particle;
```

If you get lost, take a look in the Chapter_13 folder on the DVD. You will find a file called MySQL_listing.txt that contains each of these steps in order.

12. To quit the MySQL server, just type this at the `mysql>` prompt (followed by a hit on the Enter key):

```
\q
```

### Working with PHP

Now it is time to serve the information when it is requested. This will be switching gears a little bit from command line entry to using a text editor of your choice. Launch NotePad, TextEdit, or whatever is your personal favorite. If you get stuck at any part of this PHP section, the Chapter_13 folder on the DVD contains all of these example files.

**NOTE:** Whichever editor you use, be sure to be saving your file as "plain text." This is naturally done for you in something like NotePad on a PC. If you are in TextEdit, then choose "Make Plain Text" from the Format Menu.

1. In your blank text document, type the following:

```
<?php
phpinfo();
?>
```

2. Save the file as *testpage.php*. This file should go wherever your computer puts pages it serves; on a Macintosh, this would be in the Sites folder in the Home directory.

3. Let us test that our page loads. This is an important step to remember, because if you are like me, you will be tempted to just drag this .php file into a browser window. This will not work. Instead, open a Web browser (Firefox, Safari, etc.), and load the PHP file by typing the following URL: *http://localhost/~username/testpage.php*. *~username* should be replaced with the name of your Home directory. Figure 13.21 illustrates what I typed in for my computer.

If you do not see something like Figure 13.21, one of these likely happened: PHP did not get installed correctly, your PHP file is not in the right place, or, you are not asking for the right place to load it from.

4. Let us try a bigger PHP script. Make a new document, put in the following code, and save it to your Web directory as *date.php*.

```
<?php
$date=date("d M Y H:i:s");
printf("Test page loaded on: ");
echo($date);
?>
```

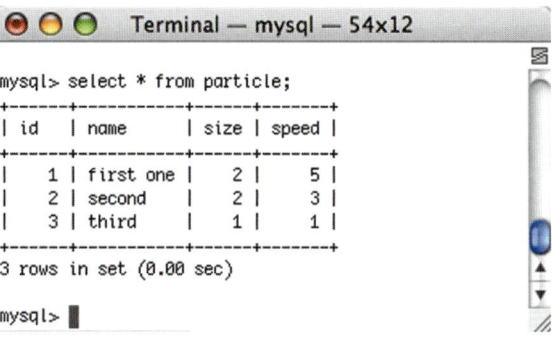

**Figure 13.18** The output should now look like this.

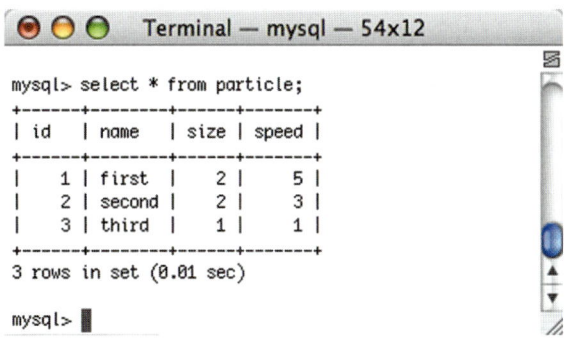

**Figure 13.19** Now we have consistent syntax for each of our name records.

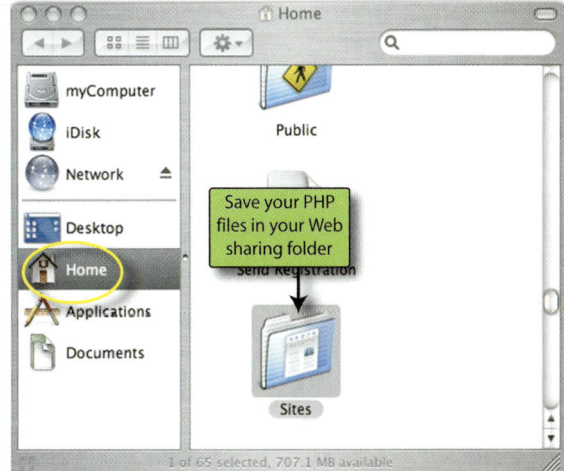

**Figure 13.20** This is where I placed my PHP files on my Mac.

5. Try loading *date.php* in your web browser like you did for the last .php file. This script is now using a *variable*. Variables in PHP begin with a $ sign. In this case, $date is being set to hold today's date. Next, we print out "Test page loaded on:" followed by whatever info $date is holding right now. If you reload this page, you will see the date and time change. It is not that exciting, but it is a start.

## Connecting PHP and MySQL

Now, for the moment we have all be waiting for: connecting PHP to our MySQL database.

1. Create a new PHP file, save it into your Web directory, and then add the following PHP code:

```
<?php

$connection = mysql_connect
("localhost", "root", "")  or die
("Can't connect to our database.");
$database= "swarm";
mysql_select_db($database);

$query= "select * from particle";
$result =mysql_query($query) or
die ("Sorry, that query doesn't
work.");

$data = mysql_fetch_array($result);
echo($data[1]);
mysql_close($connection);
?>
```

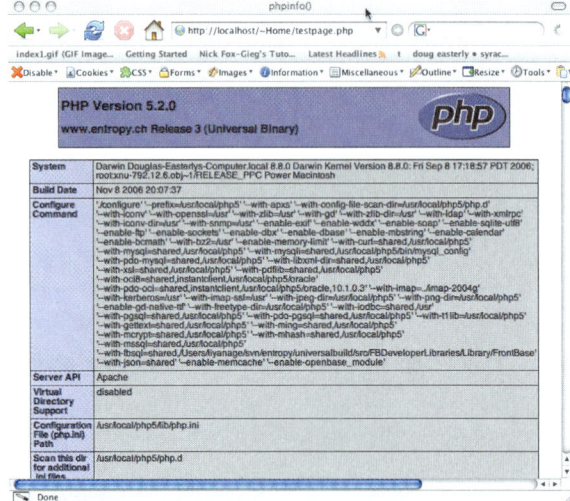

**Figure 13.21** You should see a page that shares what version of PHP you are using, plus a ton of configuration information.

A few highlights from this code:

We know what the first and last line of this script does. It simply tells the server that we are working with PHP in between the `<?php` and `?>` marks.

Moving down to `$database="swarm"`: we are making a variable called database and setting it equal to the word `"swarm."` It is very straightforward, especially with the next line that is telling our MySQL database to use `$database`, which is just `"swarm"`.

With the variable called `$query` we are setting it equal to the MySQL command to gather records. Next, we make a new variable called `$result`, which is set to all of the records inside our `particle` table. The `mysql_query` command passes the information back from the database and into `$result`.

`Echo` is a way of asking PHP to write something to the screen, and in this case, we want to write out some of our database info, specifically the second element in the array. If we look back to our database, this should be the `name` field in our first particle. Sure enough, if I load this page, I get `first` printed on the screen.

**NOTE:** If something is wrong, you may want to first make sure that MySQL is running on your computer: If you are using a Mac, open your System Preferences and launch the MySQL preference pane.

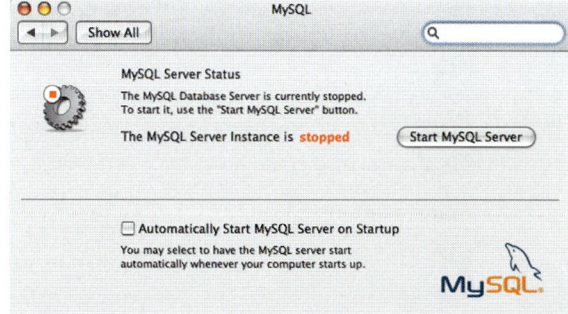

**Figure 13.22** If your MySQL preference pane looks like this, then you need to click the "Start MySQL Sever" button.

2. Remember, our ultimate goal is to get this data into Flash. Flash has the ability to load data from a URL, such as the output from this PHP file. However, Flash requires the data to come in as one line and it has to be formatted in a special way.

   Change your .php file to reflect the following code:

```php
<?php
$database= "swarm";
$connection = mysql_connect
("localhost", "root", "")  or die
("Can't connect.");
mysql_select_db($database);
//which database do we want?
$query= "select * from particle";
 //save our query to a variable.
$result =mysql_query($query) or
die ("No data!"); //'or die' if
the query fails.


$rec_count= mysql_num_rows
($result);    //How many records
are there?
 for ($i=0;$i<$rec_count;$i++)
// Run this for loop for as many
records we have
 {
    $data = mysql_fetch_array
($result);    //Put the current
line into $data.

    print("&id$i=$data[0]");
//Print out the spot 0—which is
the id.
    print("&name$i=$data[1]");
 //Print out spot 1, which is the
name.
    print("&size$i=$data[2]");
 //Next, print spot 2, the size,
    print("&speed$i=$data[3]");   //An
d finally, spot 3, which is the speed
.
 }
print("&rec_count=$rec_count");
// How many records
 mysql_close($connection);
//Close our MySQL connection

?>
```

   To help make the code more legible, I have added *comments*. A comment starts with a double slash mark (like this: //) –just like ActionScript!

3. Test your file and you should see the following:

   There are some interesting things happening in this string of characters. First of all, every variable has an ampersand (&) in front of it. Second, there are no spaces, or line breaks, or non-standard characters (aside from the strategically placed ampersands).

Now it is time to launch Flash for the last leg of this tutorial. There are not any platform differences at this point, just know where your .php file is located.

### Bringing PHP and MySQL into Flash

To begin, Flash is going to load the variables from an address (URL) that we specify. For each record Flash finds, we will attach a movie clip of a circle to the Stage. Each of these circles will look and move according to the properties of each particle record we load.

**NOTE:** The Flash files on the DVD for this tutorial will need one important change made before they will work. You will need to set your Web directory where your .php files are located. Each Flash file is set up to work with my computer, not yours.

1. Create a new Flash document. The default dimensions of 550 × 400 should be just fine, but change the frame rate of the document to be 30 fps (Modify ➡ Document).

2. Open the Actions panel by going to Window ➡ Actions. Put in the following code on frame 1 of **Layer 1**:

```
var baseurl = "http://localhost/↵
~Home/";
var dataReceiver = new LoadVars();
var dataSender = new LoadVars();

// Load data from database
trace("Retrieving Data!");
dataSender.sendAndLoad(baseurl+↵
"finalData.php",dataReceiver,"GET");

// Function to load word data
dataReceiver.onLoad = function()
{
     trace("loaded");
     for(i=0; i<3; i++)
     {
     trace(dataReceiver["name"+i]);
     }
}
```

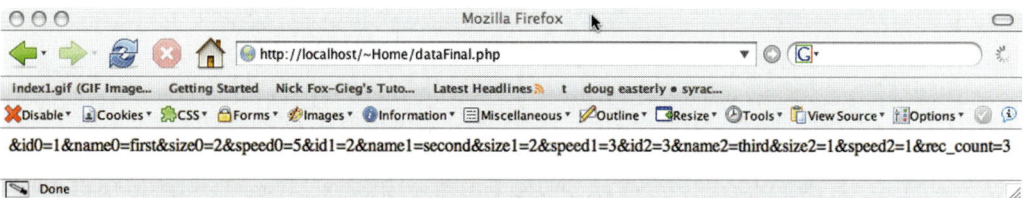

**Figure 13.23** While this PHP code uses the same data as before, it formats it so that Flash will like it.

3. The only part of this code you have to alter is this portion: *"http://localhost/~Home/"*. In the quotation marks, put the URL of where your .php document can be found without specifying the document itself. Be sure to keep the semicolon at the end of that line. This line essentially asks Flash to make a variable that stores a location, so we can call that location later.

Moving on, we have the following two lines:

```
var dataReceiver = new LoadVars();
var dataSender = new LoadVars();
```

These lines are creating objects that will eventually handle loading our data from the .php document. The first line is simply saying "please make a new object called `dataReceiver`, and make it from the `LoadVars` Class." The second line is also creating an object from the `LoadVars` Class named `dataSender`. These new objects we have made, like all objects, have properties and methods. I will show you how to use those soon.

Now we get to this crucial line:

```
dataSender.sendAndLoad(baseurl+
"finalData.php",dataReceiver,"GET");
```

This is the meat and potatoes of this ActionScript—the line that gets the data from our .php file! Let us break this line down into parts:

`dataSender` is our object we made earlier, and we will be using it to get the data.

`.sendAndLoad` is a method of the `LoadVar` Class (so our `dataSender` also understands it).

`baseurl+"finalData.php"` points to our .php file. It does this by concatenating our `baseurl` variable, plus the `"finalData.php"` filename.

`dataReceiver` is the object that we would like to receive the data from our .php file.

`"GET"` is the protocol that `sendAndLoad` will use to get this information.

Put this all together, and the line essentially says, "Please go to this address to fetch data, using the GET method, and put the received data into our `dataReceiver` object for later use."

Next up is the function to load data.

```
dataReceiver.onLoad = function()
{ ... }
```

It takes time to locate the database, ask for information, and load it into `dataReceiver`. In the meantime, Flash is going to be cranking through frames without any data to work with. If we try to do something with data that has not arrived yet, we will encounter an error. Thus, we have to use a method called `onLoad` that activates when our data has been received. This means that the code we put between the brackets will only be run once, and not until, the data is loaded. The technical name for this structure is a callback, since this method will be "called back" when the time is right.

The code that is called inside the brackets is:

```
trace("loaded");
    for(i=0; i<3; i++)
    {
    trace(dataReceiver["name"+i]);
    }
```

The code inside the for-loop is able to use the variable `i` to do something slightly different each time the loop is run. In this case, we are stepping through the names of our particles in the `dataReceiver` object. From these trace functions, and if you have your Home directory set properly in the first line, you will get the following output from Flash when you test your movie.

As our code stands right now, there are a couple of problems. First, it will only load the first three names of our particles, and nothing else. Secondly, and more importantly, it is not doing anything useful with this data! Let us fix that first problem.

4. In our `onLoad` callback, update your code inside the brackets to read like this:

```
trace("loaded");
var loop:Number = parseInt(data⏎
Receiver.rec_count);
for(i=0; i<loop; i++)
{
    trace(dataReceiver["name"+i]);
    trace(dataReceiver["id"+i]);
    trace(dataReceiver["size"+i]);
    trace(dataReceiver["speed"+i]);
}
```

Here, we have a new `loop` variable that will hold the number of records being passed into Flash. This all seems straightforward, except for maybe the `parseInt` function—this makes the `rec_count` data into a number. You might think that it is a number already, but you would be wrong: all of our data is coming in as characters. So, it might appear to be a 3, but it would be a character `"3"`, not the actual number 3.

Also notice how we are replacing the number 3 from our for-loop conditional, to the newly created variable called `loop`. This means that we can go back later and add records, or delete records, and our code will be able to handle any number of records, not just three.

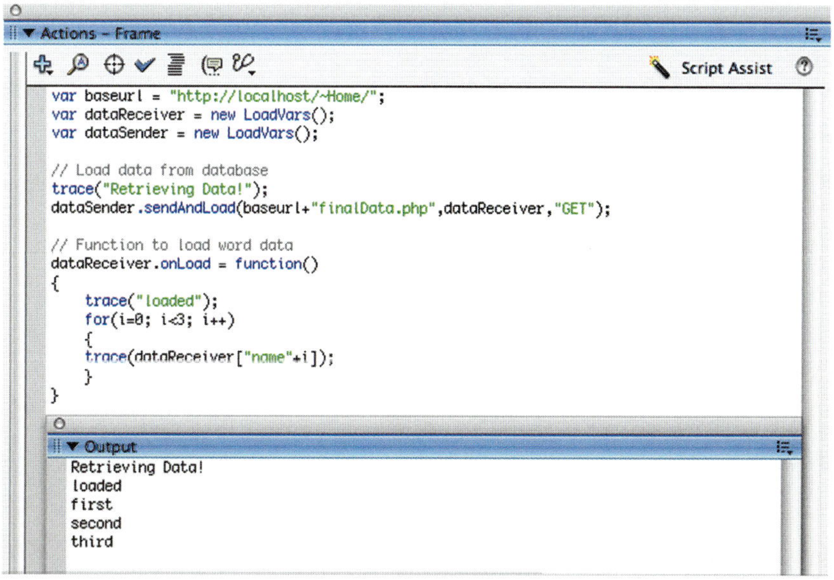

**Figure 13.24** Our output window is looking good. It is time to put this data retrieval into action.

The final change in our code is the inclusion of a bunch of trace functions in our for-loop. These all use bracket syntax, just as before, to display all of the data we have for each of the records. When you run this code, you will see the contents of Figure 13.25.

5. Now we can actually visualize this data by connecting it to movie clips. From the tool palette, select the circle tool and draw a small circle using only a fill color. Make sure the stroke is set to none.

6. Next, use the Select Tool to select the circle. In the Property Inspector you will see the height and width values. Set both of these to 24 pixels. Set the X and Y positions both to 12.

7. With the circle selected, go to Modify ➡ Convert to Symbol (or F8). In this pop-up dialog box, choose Movie clip, and give it the name `mc_particle`. Before clicking "done," be sure to check the box next to Export for ActionScript.

8. Take a look in your Library for **mc_particle**. Return to the main Timeline and delete the instance of `mc_particle`. We will be creating all of our instances programmatically with ActionScript.

9. Double-click on the **mc_particle** inside the Library. You will see your circle come back to the center of the Stage. Select the circle graphic on the Stage then convert this to a Symbol (Modify ➡ Convert to Symbol). When the dialog window comes up, leave it on the default Movie clip setting, give it the name `inside` and check Export for ActionScript.

10. Next, click on the **mc_particle** label above the Timeline, taking you from the **inside** Timeline, back to the **mc_particle** Timeline.

11. Select the circle on the Stage (the **inside** movie clip) and look at the Property Inspector. Type `inside` for the instance name then set the X and Y positions to zero.

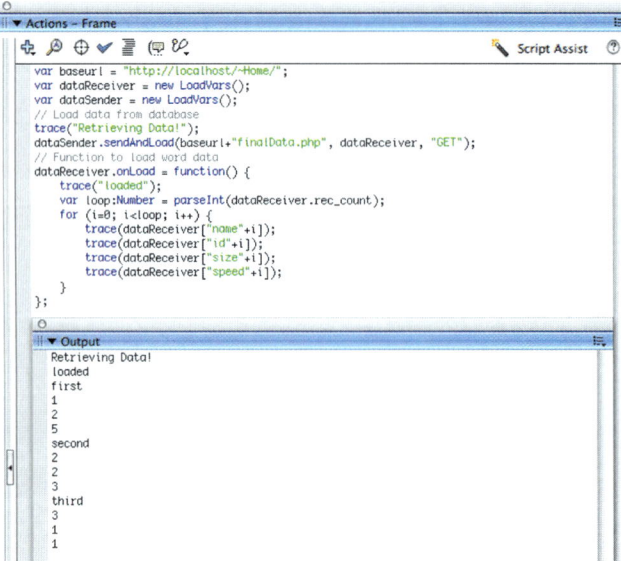

**Figure 13.25** Here are all of our records displayed in the output window.

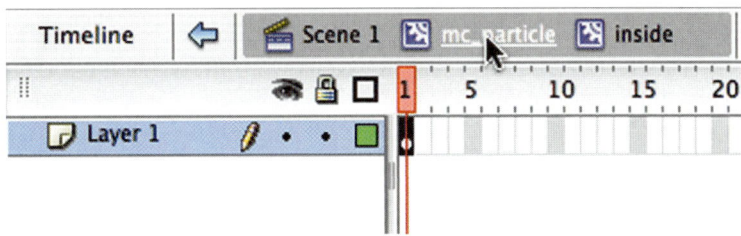

**Figure 13.26** By now you should be well familiar with navigating between nested Timelines.

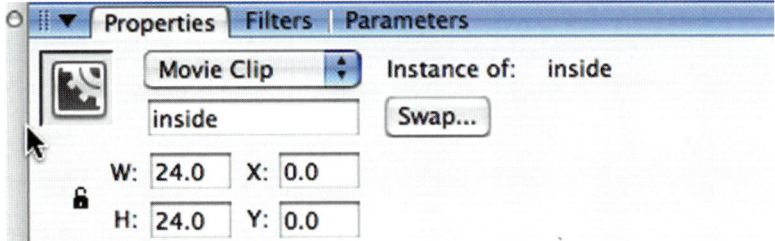

**Figure 13.27** Do not forget to add the `inside` instance name.

12. Click on **Scene 1** to come back to the main Timeline. You will not need to delete anything off of the Stage this time.

13. Bring back the Actions panel and select frame 1 of **Layer 1**. Replace the old for-loop with this one:

```
for(i=0; i<loop; i++)
    {
_root.attachMovie("mc_particle",
 "mc_particle"+i, i);
_root["mc_particle"+i]._x=250;
_root["mc_particle"+i]._y=200;
_root["mc_particle"+i].id=data
Receiver["id"+i];
_root["mc_particle"+i].particle_
name=dataReceiver["name"+i];
_root["mc_particle"+i].particle_
size=dataReceiver["size"+i];
_root["mc_particle"+i].speed=data
Receiver["speed"+i];
    }
```

Let us break this down, since there is a lot going on here:

```
_root.attachMovie("mc_particle",
 "mc_particle"+i, i);
```

This line simply attaches a movie clip from your Library to the Stage and gives it a name and a depth.

The next six lines are all setting some variables inside our new movie clip, such as its `_x`, `_y`, `id`, `particle_name`, `particle_size`, and `speed`. Most of these bits of data are not going to do much yet, so we will have to write some more code to make this interesting.

14. From the Library, double-click on **mc_particle** to open up its Timeline. Make a new layer called **actions**, select frame 1 of this layer, and then type the following code in the Actions panel:

```
this.onEnterFrame=function()
    {
    this._xscale=this.particle_
size*10;
    this._yscale=this.particle_
size*10;
    this._rotation+=this.speed*10;
    this.inside._x= _root.
xmouse-250;
    }
```

This should be the last bit of code you will need to enter in for this tutorial. There are not any surprises here, but let us break it down to be sure it makes sense:

This whole block of code is another callback. Instead of running when data is loaded, like our other callback from earlier, this one runs each time Flash draws a new frame. The four lines of code in the brackets set some object variables. `this._xscale` and `this._yscale` are internal variables that control how big this particular `mc_particle` instance should be drawn. `this._rotation` sets the number of degrees the movie clip should be rotated to.

The final line in this block moves the circle away from the center registration point. As the whole movie clip is rotating, this will have the effect of giving the circle's rotation a larger radius. In the end, as the mouse moves, the circle will begin to orbit around its central registration point, wobbling further and further away as the mouse's X position moves towards the edges of the screen.

15. At this point, go ahead and test this movie; be sure to move the pointer around and take a look at the results.

All of the hard work is done, so now it is time to play.

1. With your Flash file still open, launch your command line tool that you used earlier to set up the database.

2. Launch MySQL: `mysql -u root` and tell it to use the **swarm** database (`mysql> use swarm`). You are ready to start making new records:

```
insert into particle (id, name,
size, speed) values (4, 'fourth',
4, 1);
```

3. Test your Flash movie again to watch the visuals change. Try adding a few new particles to the **swarm** database, using different sizes and speeds, and watch what that does in the Flash file. If it is not working, compare your file against the *Final.fla* file located in the Chapter_13 folder on the DVD.

## ON YOUR OWN

Connecting your Flash files to databases can be a very powerful technique, not only extending the dynamics of your movies, but allowing them to take on whole new meanings and investigations. Jonathan Harris is certainly an ideal source of inspiration in this regard, as the data under analysis in his work provides both the visual and conceptual structure.

Try extending MySQL, PHP, and Flash from what Dylan Moore covered in the DIY section. If you have your own server, the next obvious step is to get MySQL and PHP running there so visitors to your site can take advantage of these dynamic data processors. As Moore mentions, databases are most valuable when they are dynamically set. In addition to researching Perl as a means of generating your own applications in this regard, you should also look up sites that offer API services such as Flickr and Google. There is also a really great GUI application for creating spiders and scrapers called Anthracite made by Metafy *www.metafy.com*.

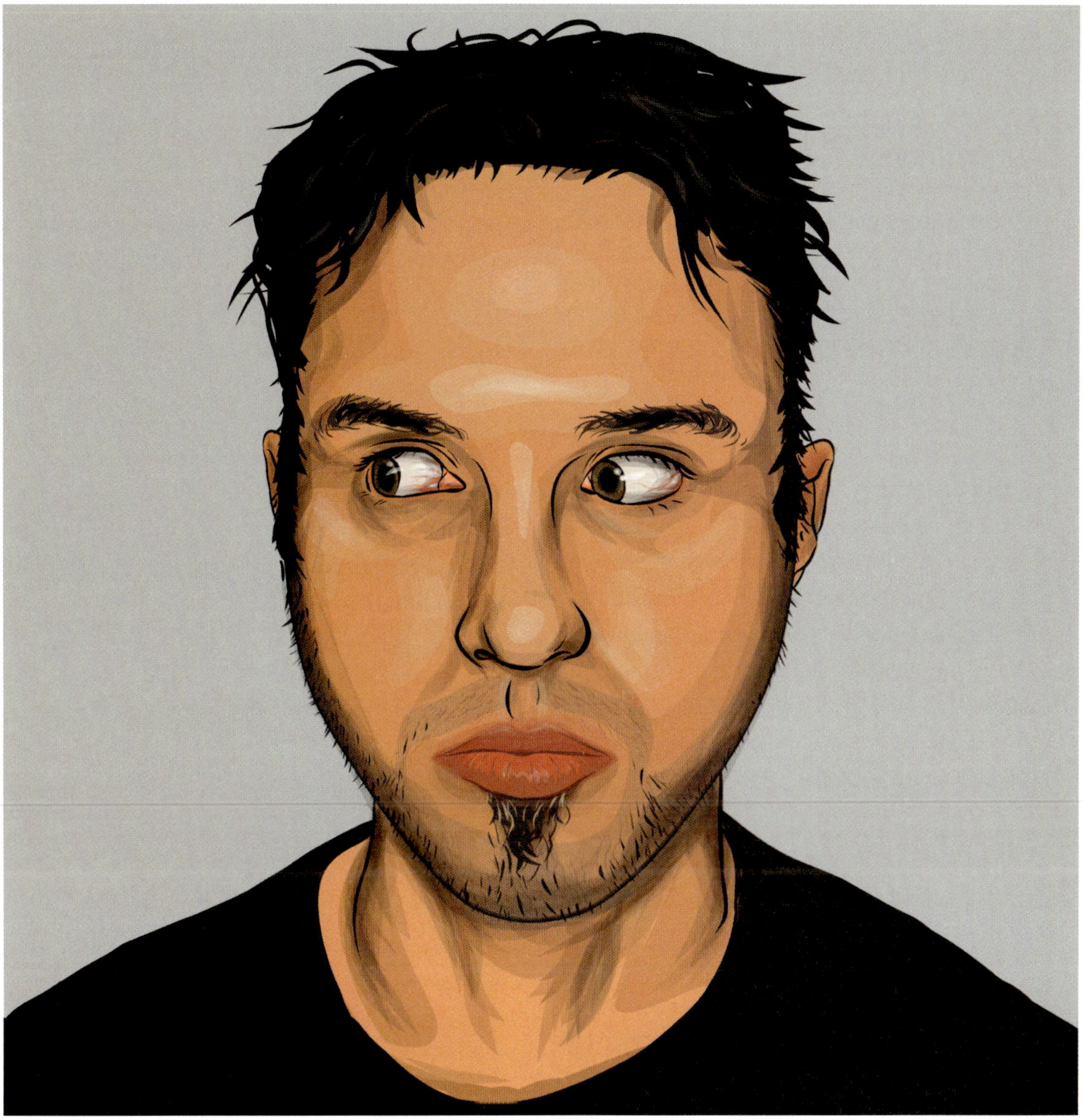

# 14 DAN SHUTA

Physical Computing with Flash

# DAN SHUTA

Dan Shuta hails from the wooded hills of upstate New York. During his childhood, without a neighborhood available for mischief or any nearby playmates to speak of, he resorted to spending a lot of time in the realm of his imagination. Most of these days consisted of drawing robots, beasties, and life studies of action figures. Reflecting on his childhood, he notes that it makes sense that he has turned out being a visual artist—even if he did not really know what that meant during these formative years.

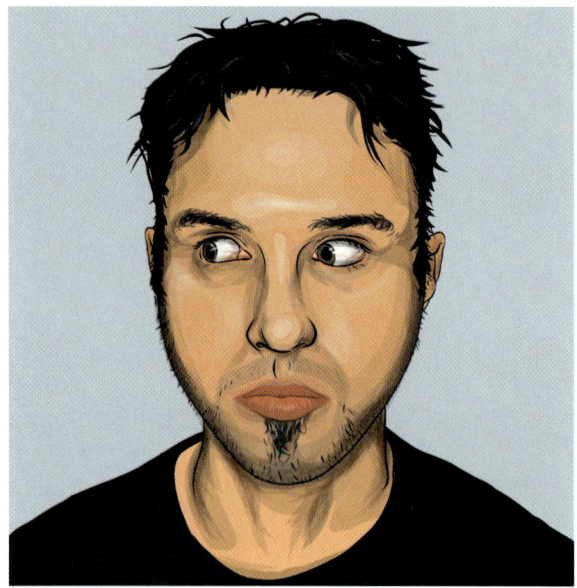

**Figure 14.1** Shuta created this self-portrait after he started working on Richard Linklater's film *A Scanner Darkly* wip.warnerbros.com/ascannerdarkly/.

Shuta maintained a tunnel vision of sorts throughout school. Like many Flash enthusiasts, Shuta now finds himself wishing he had applied himself more when it came to math. But his high school years were still valuable, throwing himself into his passions for drawing, sculpture, and other traditional media.

"I think that the scolding I received from teachers about doodling in class all over the edges of assignments and 'not applying myself properly' only fueled my passive rebellion."

With his family's first computer, Shuta was able to type a paper and even browse the Internet; but other than that, his computer experience was quite limited. For instance computer programming was an alien concept that he never once considered, certainly not as a creative endeavor.

**Figure 14.2** This painting is titled *A Victim of Heedless Excess* (2006). It was recently displayed as part of the Vulgar Display of Art exhibition at the Continental Club in Austin, Texas.

# CHAPTER FOURTEEN 255

"Over the years I had spent a large portion of time with video games, mostly because they were escapist entertainment and I appreciated the design of the character sprites and animation and sound. I wasn't really thinking about the gears at work behind the scenes. I would have loved to make my own game, and even planned many of them on paper without an inkling of how they would actually be constructed into working software. It never dawned on me that I would eventually have the knowledge and tools at my disposal to do just that."

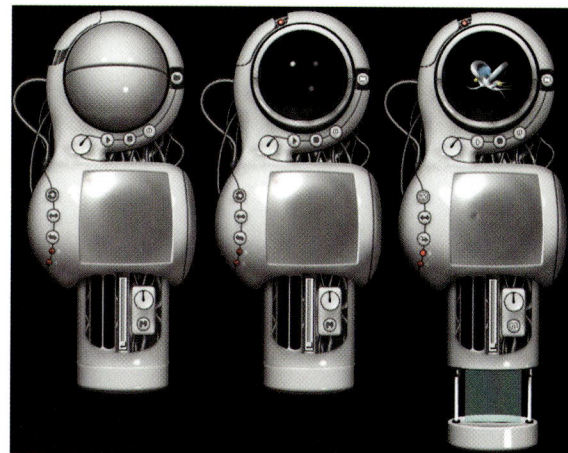

**Figure 14.3** It is easy to see Shuta's painting skills translate into his digital artwork: software cannot compensate for innate creativity.

During his sophomore year at Syracuse University, with the arrival of his first computer (a Power Mac G3), and in conjunction with some introductory courses using Photoshop and Director, Shuta arrived at a personal renaissance of creativity. There were so many new tools and opportunities to learn and new methods and modes for creating artwork, that he could no longer pursue only inks and pencils.

It was not too long after his initiation into digital art making that Shuta started to work with Flash. A summer job at a design firm (his first experience working with computers in a professional setting) gave him some freedom to thoroughly explore the software. He had to quickly learn Adobe Illustrator, Photoshop, and Flash to create technical drawings for an industrial air-space manufacturer. Flash 4 was the version he was using at this time. It was not until Flash 5 came out that he started to use ActionScript.

Although Shuta received his B.F.A. with honors in Computer Art, he completely explored all of the offerings of a liberal arts education. His transcripts display a very diverse range of

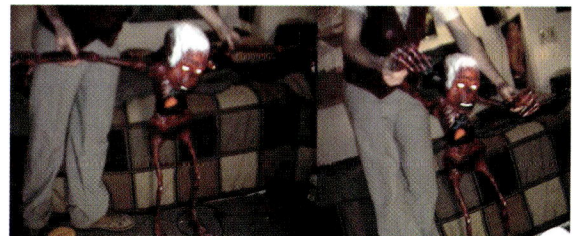

**Figure 14.4** You will see more from Shuta's interest in creatures like this one in the DIY section later in the chapter. This figure, *The Breather* (2002), is a kinetic sculpture/puppet. Its materials include: a Bondo and steel skeleton, melted plastic bottles, electrical tape, red tool dip, plastic wrap, plaster gauze, and bike inner tubes.

classes (like sculpture—see Figure 14.4) along with doing a lot of personally directed independent research.

Shuta's initial work out of college was as an adjunct instructor at Syracuse University and doing design and illustration for Cornell University's eLearning division. Both of these jobs were largely Flash-centric and extended his skills even further, especially with ActionScripting.

After two years in Ithaca, Shuta moved on to Austin, Texas, where he was offered a job as an animator for Richard Linklater's film *A Scanner Darkly*. Bob Sabiston is the founder of Flat Black Films, the studio that produced the animation for this film. Flat Black Films is famous for using the rotoscoping software that Sabiston created called Rotoshop. Rotoshop was also behind Linklater's other animated film *Waking Life*, as well as other notable works, such as Lars Von Trier's *The Five Obstructions*. Shuta thoroughly enjoyed working on *A Scanner Darkly*, and using Rotoshop in particular.

> "It was like nothing I had ever used, or have since. It was so incredibly smooth and fluid to draw with, probably about as close to the nuanced control of 'natural' media as vector shapes can get."

Although Flash has many features and uses that Rotoshop lacks (creating Web applications, etc.), it was a challenge for Shuta to return to its comparatively inferior drawing capabilities. This applies to Photoshop and pretty much any other computer-based drawing software that he has tried. *The Waking Life* DVD has a step-by-step demonstration of Bob Sabiston's displaying Rotoshop.

**Figure 14.5** This image from one of Shuta's Flash projects for Cornell was completed in 2003.

**Figure 14.6** These are obviously much funnier than the typical "Teamwork" motivational posters one sees in offices.

**Figure 14.7** Here is a sample from Rotoshop, a still from the film *The Even More Fun Trip* (2007) by Susan Sabiston.

Also, Sabiston's company has a podcast worth checking out: just search for "Flat Black Films" on iTunes.

### DIGITAL DECONSTRUCTION: AUDIORGANIC

One of the first projects Shuta created where things finally "clicked" was *Audiorganic*. In this work, Shuta's experiences with digital audio were spliced together with his increasing knowledge of ActionScript, creating a quirky sequencing device in Flash.

Featuring vibrant colors and unique characters, the project was directed by a concept that sought to deliver an interactive experience that would be fun for kids, as well as adults. Using little monsters that made funny noises seemed to be a good route to take, avoiding the typically abstract formal display most designers lean towards when visualizing sampled instruments.

The first step required drafting a menagerie of creatures, all of which possess a unique body design and sound from a particular range in the audio spectrum. Each creature was to be an instrument, and Shuta composed the FLA so each could be heard clearly when layered and sequenced. Since Shuta did not have a Wacom tablet at the time, he drew the brief animation frames for each creature's "screech" or "gurgle" or "poot" with ink on paper and scanned them in to Flash. He then recorded himself making noises into a microphone and manipulated the audio until it represented what he imagined each creature would sound like.

**Figure 14.8** This motley crew comes to life when cued by the sequencer, performing animations and expressing a unique sound.

**Figure 14.9** Take a look at the characters' gestures.

As with a basic sequencer or drum machine, small markers of color matched to each creature can be dragged to the sequencer grid. As the playhead runs over the marker, a corresponding creature utters its noise. The markers can be rearranged or deleted at will by the user. Overall, *Audiorganic* functions as a hybrid of a sequencer, toy, and experimental narrative.

### DIY: BUILDING A CUSTOM PHYSICAL INTERFACE FOR FLASH

By itself, Flash already is capable of some sophisticated live control of media and algorithmic work. However, you might want to expand the available tactile controls beyond the mouse and keyboard. In this section, Shuta will explore how to build your own electronic sensory input device to control a custom, real-time animated character. Physical computing techniques such as this are becoming more and more popular with Flash.

#### Hardware, Software, and Supplies

MakingThings *www.makingthings.com* has a series of electronic modules available that allow you to easily utilize various hardware sensors, buttons, and switches as control inputs for Flash creations. You can also connect components such as DC motors, solenoids, and lights that can be controlled and automated with ActionScript.

I am going to demonstrate how to build a sensor glove that will be connected to a computer running Flash via the Teleo MultiIO module set from MakingThings. We will use this hardware to animate a real-time puppet in Flash. I have provided a demonstration Quicktime video of the finished project on the DVD, *dshuta_videodemo.mov* in the Chapter_14 folder.

**Figure 14.10** Whenever someone mentions "puppet" in the context of multimedia, they usually mean metaphorically. In this DIY section, Shuta will address puppets in Flash, both real and virtually.

## CHAPTER FOURTEEN 259

You will need Flash MX 2004 or later to use the free software components that MakingThings provides, but this tutorial will be produced with Flash 8.

**NOTE:** MakingThings also supplies other modules that work with Flash. This tutorial should generally work for those microcontrollers as well: just follow their readme files for installing drivers and software, and locate their input terminals for connecting sensors.

Complete instructions for installing the required ActionScript libraries, USB driver, and XML server are available on the MakingThings site. Here is a summary of the simple installation process:

1. Download and install the Macromedia Extension Manager:

   *www.adobe.com/exchange/em_download*

   This is available for both Mac OS X and Windows.

2. Download and install the necessary items from MakingThings:

   *www.makingthings.com/teleo/products/downloads/flash_class_library.htm*

   - Teleo Flash readme
   - Teleo Flash class library extension package
   - Teleo FTDI USB driver (installing the USB driver may require a restart)
   - Telco XML server

3. Connect the USB cable to your computer and to the Teleo. Plug in the power source to the Teleo.

4. Decompress and run the XML server.

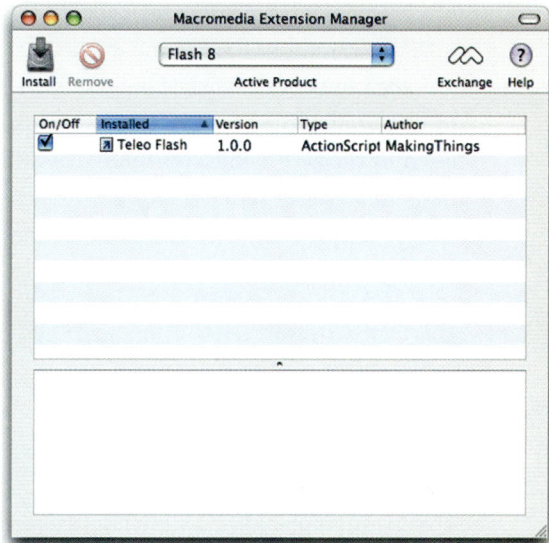

**Figure 14.11** The Teleo MultiIO module from MakingThings.com

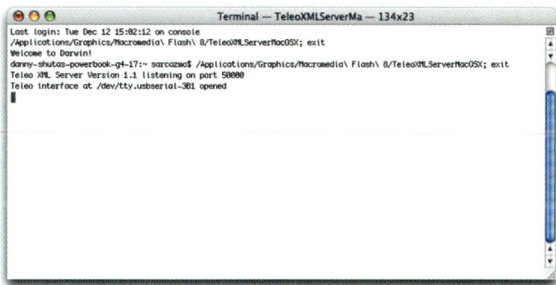

**Figure 14.12** Be sure you turn the Teleo Flash extension on, using the Macromedia Extension Manager.

5. I placed the UNIX executable file for the XML server into the Flash 8 application folder and double-clicked on it to open it in Terminal under Mac OS X. You can also enter the path name yourself. The process is similar for Windows and Linux operating systems, so follow the included readme files for your particular OS.

**NOTE:** It is convenient to have a clean table next to the computer running the Flash project while building and testing.

For this tutorial I will be using the following items:

- MakingThings Teleo MultiIO, USB translator and power adaptor modules with USB cable and included power adapter
- Roll of electrical tape
- At least 25 feet of stranded, 22-gauge wire. I am using three different-colored spools to help organize the wiring for this project.
- Wire stripper tool
- 2 bend sensors from MakingThings
- 2 photocells from MakingThings
- 2 10kΩ 1/4 watt resistors, supplied with the bend sensors
- 2 1kΩ 1/4 watt resistors, supplied with the photocells
- Mini alligator clip jumper leads. Multiple colors are useful for wiring organization. Mine are 14", factory insulated from RadioShack, but you can wrap your own insulation with electrical tape. You may choose to solder the wires and other components together, or solder your own jumper leads from clips and wires. I will not be covering soldering; there are several good tutorials online if you do a simple Google search for "soldering tutorial."
- Small, flathead screwdriver
- Sheet of plain scrap paper
- Scissors
- Source of bright, focused light; in my case a small halogen desk lamp
- Sacrificial sock (optional)

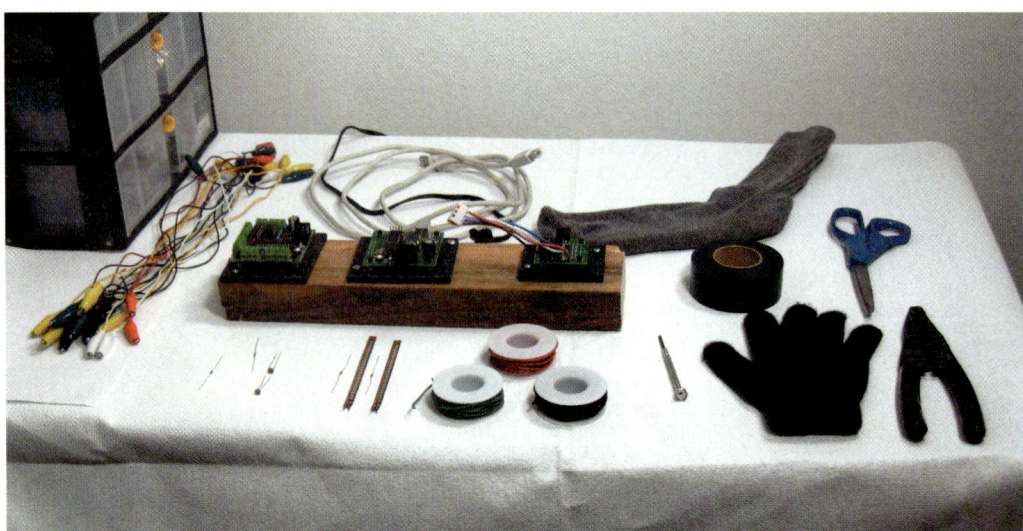

**Figure 14.13** Your terminal should look something like this, showing that the XML server that is allowing communication between Flash and the Teleo is operational.

**NOTE:** While I do not want to attempt an explanation of electrical theory for the tutorial, I do want to briefly describe what happens when a circuit is made on the Teleo MultiIO module using a variable-resistance sensor going into one of the analog inputs.

Resistance, which is measured in ohms ($\Omega$), limits the flow of electricity in a circuit. As electricity travels through a sensor, and as the sensor receives direct stimulus, its resistance changes. A resistor is added to create a voltage divider, which balances out the circuit for measuring the sensor's value and helps to provide a voltage to the analog input. The Teleo module will then translate this resulting voltage into numerical data that Flash can interpret and use via ActionScript. A thorough explanation of these concepts is available at the MakingThings Website.

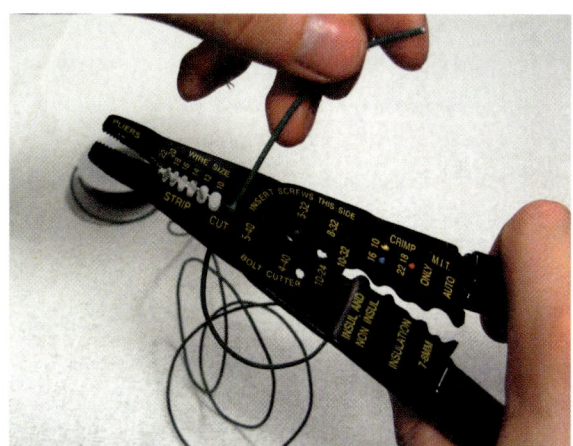

**Figure 14.14** Those are a lot of supplies, but the final payoff is going to be worth it!

### Constructing the Circuits

Now it is time to cut and strip some wires. You may choose different lengths/colors of wire to suit your needs, but here is what I will be making:

- 4 two-inch green wires
- 4 two-inch red wires
- 4 two-foot red wires
- 4 three-foot black wires

1. First, cut the wire lengths.
2. Measure about a quarter of an inch toward the end of the wire.
3. Then strip off that amount.
4. Twist the exposed strands into a more rigid tip.
5. Now we can wire up the sensors. The Teleo MultiIO board uses convenient screw terminals to connect wires with sensors and actuators. Simply slip the stripped end of a wire into the terminal, and screw it down with a small flathead driver.

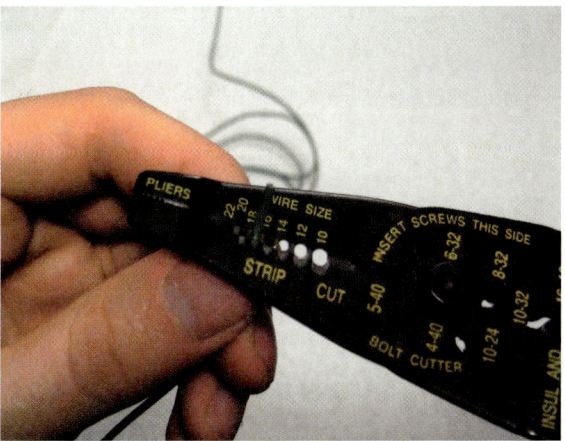

**Figure 14.15** Stripping wire is pretty simple. Just try not to be sloppy.

Before we start connecting wires to the MultiIO, let us set up the wiring system for our sensors. Each of the four sensors will have the same wiring setup as seen in Figure 14.17.

1. Connect one end of a long black wire to a jumper lead.
2. Connect the free end of this jumper lead to either connection point on one of the sensors.
3. Connect another jumper of the same color to the other connection point on the sensor.
4. Connect the free end of this jumper to one end of a long red wire.
5. Connect the opposite end of the long red wire to another jumper of the same color.
6. Connect the free end of this jumper to both a short red wire and one end of a resistor. Be sure that both the stripped end of the short wire and the resistor are firmly gripped by the jumper lead's clip. I will use the 1k resistor here for the photocell and the 10k resistor for the bend sensor.
7. Connect the free end of the resistor to another jumper cable.
8. Connect the free end of this jumper cable to a short green wire.

Once the sensor wiring is completed, we can connect everything to the MultiIO module.

Following the diagram in Figure 14.18, we just need to follow these steps:

1. Connect the long, black wires to the GND terminals. Two wires can easily fit into each terminal, and it is not important which GND terminal is used for any of these particular wires.

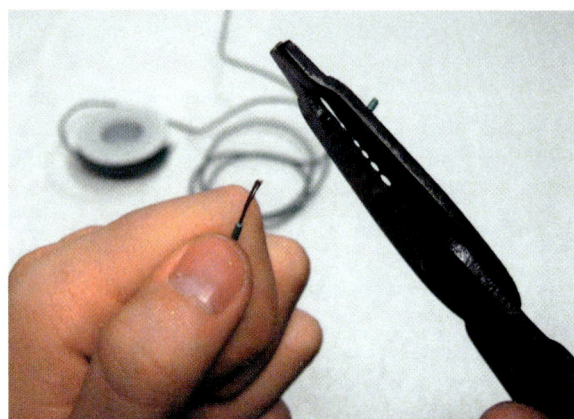

**Figure 14.16** Multiple wires can be connected to one terminal.

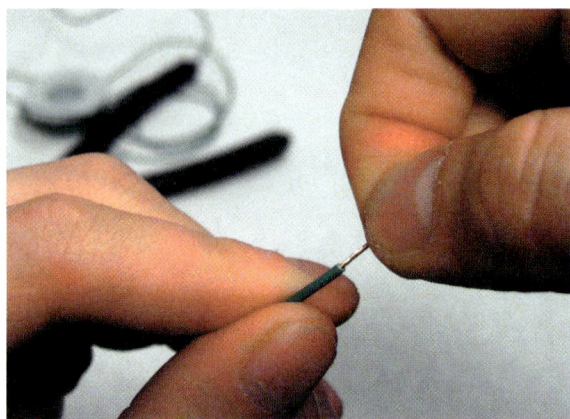

**Figure 14.17** Here is a diagram for wiring each sensor.

**Figure 14.18** This is how the sensors should connect to the Teleo board.

2. Connect the short, green wires into the 5v terminals. There is one 5v terminal on the same side as the Analog Inputs, and another on the opposite side of the board. Like the GND connections, any 5v terminal can be used for any of these wires.

3. Connect the short, red wires to the analog inputs. This time we need to connect the wires to specific terminals, and with only one wire going into each terminal. The wiring of the bend sensors must be connected to Ain0 and Ain1, and the photocells need to go into Ain2 and Ain3.

### Creating the Cyber Sock Puppet

Now we are ready to attach our wiring system to the knit glove. This process requires a hand to be in the glove for proper placement of the materials, and it is much easier if you have an assistant wear the glove while you attach

**Figure 14.19** Here is how my setup looks. If you use color-coded wires and jumper leads as I am using, it should be easy to keep track of the wired network. Be sure that the jumper lead clips on the sensor terminals are separated and insulated from one another.

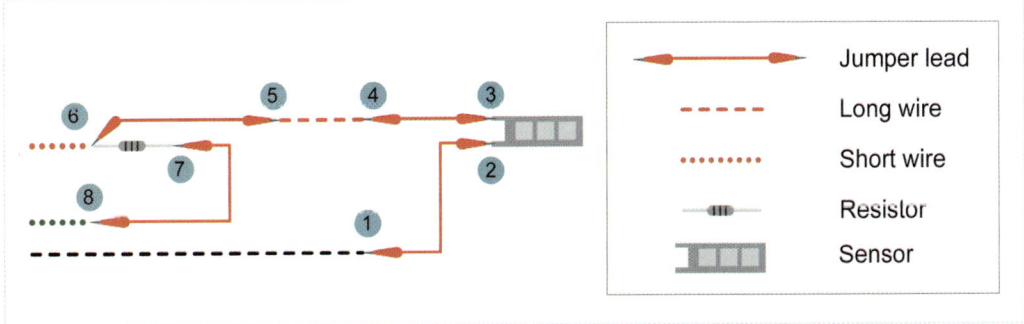

**Figure 14.20** If the clips are not firmly connected they might creep around and cause a short circuit. Be sure that there are no bare wires, resistor leads, or metal clips cross-connecting. It is not necessary that every single piece of exposed metal be covered or insulated, as long as you keep an eye on the wiring and components while you are testing.

the various components. Otherwise, put the glove on your own hand and carefully connect the pieces yourself.

1. First, we want to take the bend sensor that is connected to Ain0 and attach it to the glove's middle finger.

2. The flat end of the bend sensor should extend a wee bit beyond the end of the glove finger, with the strip of light-colored squares facing up.

3. Now we will cut a strip of electrical tape several inches long. Ensuring that the bend sensor remains centered along the length of the finger, take this strip and wrap it around the end of the bend sensor and the end of glove's middle finger.

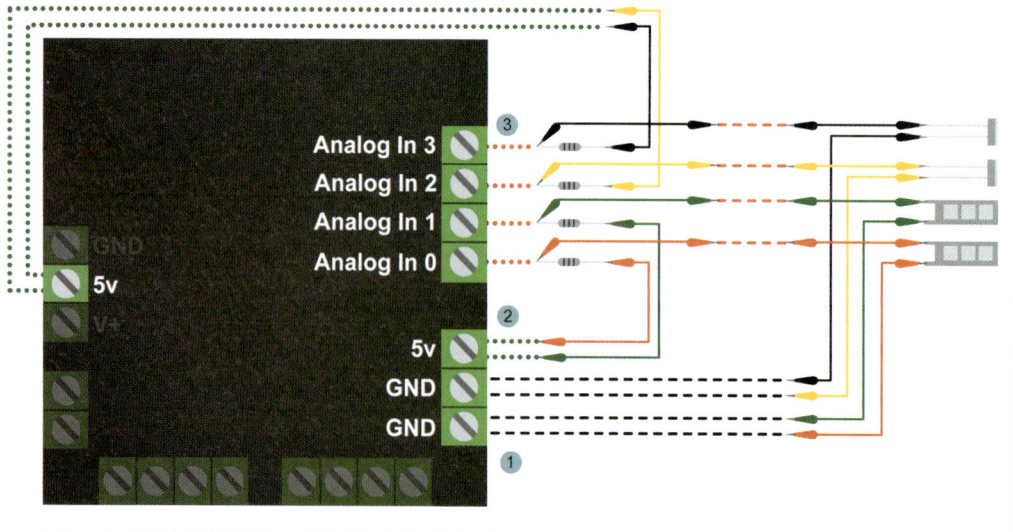

**Figure 14.21** A bend sensor is a form of resistor that changes resistance as it is bent in either direction. This type of sensor will detect subtle changes in its shape, which we will use to control the degree of opening and closing of our character's mouth as well as the tilt of their head.

The bend sensor is now anchored to the end of the middle finger. If you try curling your finger down, you will notice that the sensor easily bends along with the finger, however it tends to slip off to one side or the other due to the weight of the jumper clips and wire assembly. We need to create a bracing point that the bend sensor can slide through during its bend.

4. Cut another strip of tape, around 7 inches or so. Set the strip aside, then take the scissors and scrap paper and cut a rectangular shape of paper that spans the width of the electrical tape. Stick this strip of paper in the center of the electrical tape, as shown in Figure 14.23.

5. Then wrap this tape-and-paper combo around the middle finger, on top of and slightly behind the large joint in the finger, with the paper strip facing down over the bend sensor. Do not wrap it too tightly around your finger, or you will not be able to remove your finger from the glove.

Now when you bend your finger, the sensor should still bend freely, smoothly sliding through the narrow tunnel we have made instead of sliding off of your finger. The paper covering the tape acts as a tunnel that keeps the bend sensor from sticking.

6. We are going to do a similar attachment with the second bend sensor, but this time we will be anchoring the end of the sensor slightly behind the knuckle, in-line and behind the middle finger bend sensor. Place the new anchoring strip over the knuckles, across the back of the glove. It is not necessary for this strip to wrap all around the hand.

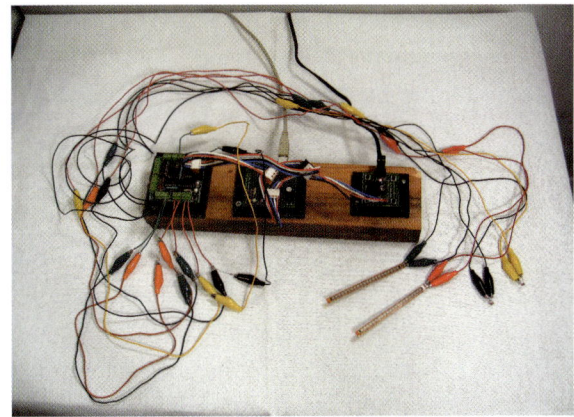

**Figure 14.22** After lining up the bend sensor, use electrical tape to keep it secured to the glove.

**Figure 14.23** This paper will act as a sleeve for the bend sensor to slide through, while keeping it in line with our finger.

7. Next create another tape-and-paper combo strip that is long enough to wrap about halfway around the wrist at the base of the glove. Be sure this bracing strip is not too tight, or it will be difficult to remove the glove or put it back on.

You should now be able to bend your wrist up and down while simultaneously opening and closing your fingers, as if miming with a puppet. The bend sensors should smoothly bend along with your hand and wrist motion, the jumper clips helping to keep the sensors flattened against the back of your hand. If they seem to snag a bit, be sure that the paper in the bracing strips is completely covering the area where the sensor needs to travel.

Now that we have our bend sensors connected, it is time to install the photocells.

8. Disconnect the jumper leads from the photocell connected to Ain2.

9. Take this photocell and carefully slip its lead wires through the glove in the valley between the knuckles of the index and middle fingers.

10. Then re-connect the jumper leads to the photocell. Be sure that only the wafer of the photocell is now visible. The photocell leads should be pulled completely though and grasped snugly by the jumper leads. This photocell is going to function as the light-sensitive eyes of our Flash character.

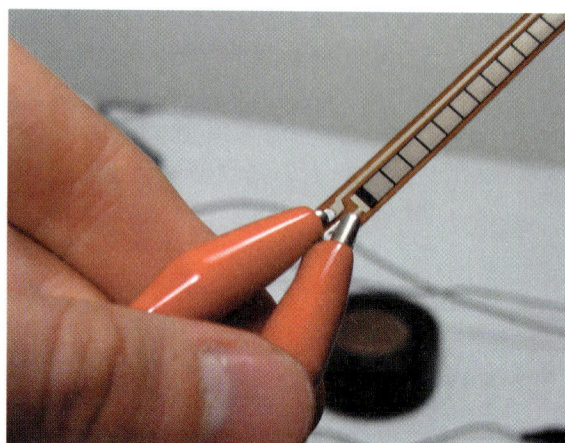

**Figure 14.24** Now your construction should be fairly sturdy.

**Figure 14.25** Photocells are also a form of variable resistor, but instead of detecting shape changes, they alter their resistance based on the amount of light striking their surface. Like bend sensors, photocells detect subtle changes and they can provide fluid ramps in value.

11. Next, we are going to install the second photocell. We'll use this one to determine when the character's mouth is completely closed. Install this sensor like the previous photocell, this time using the photocell connected to the Ain3 input and inserting it between the tip and the pad of the thumb.

12. Allowing some slack for free thumb movement, tape the wires of this jumper lead to the base of the glove thumb, just in front of the tape strip around the wrist. You can gently bend the photocells into a better angle once they are firmly connected to their respective jumper leads.

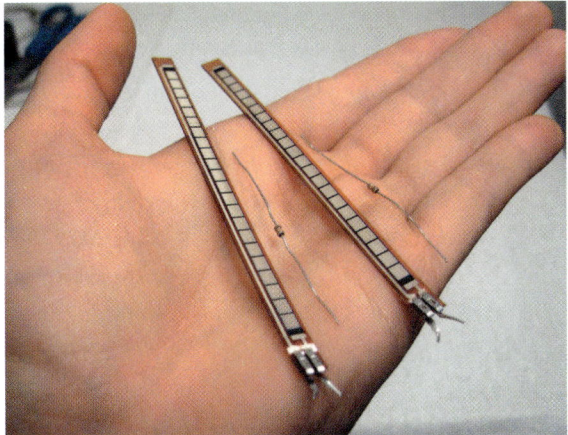

**Figure 14.26** After securing the photocell into the glove, reconnect the jumper leads.

**NOTE:** You may notice that all of the wires dangling about can get caught on things or pull and twist your bend sensors around. An easy solution to this is to cut off the elastic portion of a sock and pull it down over the assembled glove while you are wearing it. This will hold the wires against the arm, which keeps things tidier and allows you to focus on the experiment rather than making sure the wires are always where they should be.

Now we can go on to the Flash portion of the tutorial! You may want to take off your new, fashionable glove to follow along with both hands.

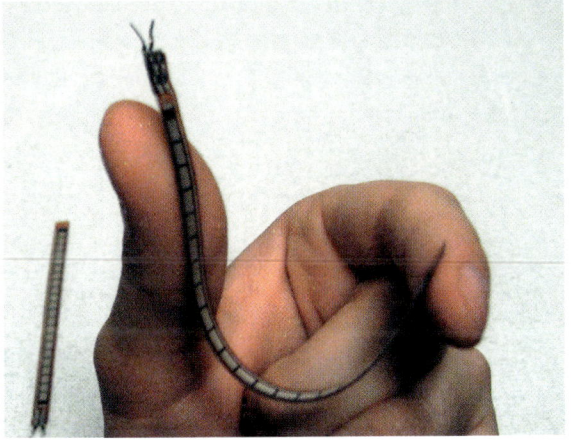

**Figure 14.27** Our cyber sock puppet is now complete!

### Creating the Flash Puppet

Open the Flash 8 file *puppet_complete.fla* from the Chapter_14 folder on the DVD. If you test the movie and view the resulting SWF, you will see that the mouth and eyes will slowly play through their animated frame range. We are going to apply the ActionScript that will allow this puppet to react to the sensor glove.

This character was constructed using simple shapes (with no outlines) that could be shape tweened, and layered on top of one another to create a seamless head and body. Dig down into the movie clips holding the shapes (by double-clicking on them) to explore how they were made. I used shape hints on most elements that utilize shape tweens such as the upper portion of the head, the lower jaw, and the mouth mask.

The entire head is in its own container movie clip to allow rotation based on wrist movement. All of the elements that make up the head and face are on separate layers within this movie clip that are all tweened over a range of 100 frames. Movement of the bend sensor on the glove's middle finger will determine which frames to jump to within this frame range.

The eyes follow the motion of the head, along with all of the other facial elements. Because we want the eyes to open and close independently of the facial animation, they are contained within their own movie clip inside the **puppethead** clip with its own range of 100 frames. The photocell on the glove's knuckle will determine the current frame within this **eye** movie clip.

At the top of the Stage, I have also put a set of text fields and some value sliders for testing purposes.

All of the following ActionScript is going to be placed on the first frame of the **actions** layer on the main Timeline.

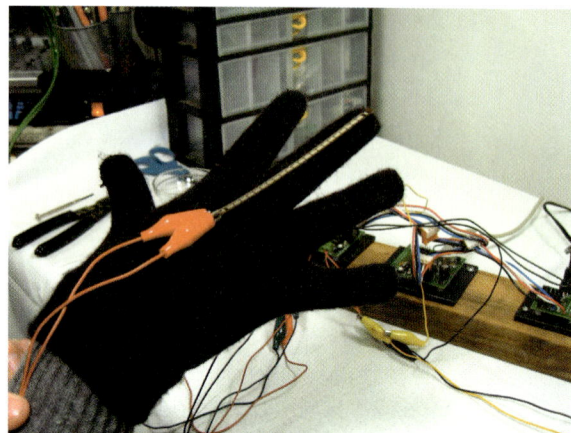

**Figure 14.28** This dinosaur Shuta created in Flash is going to mimic our sock puppet.

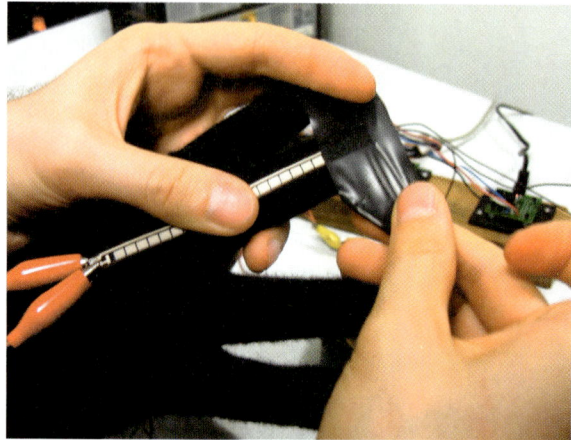

**Figure 14.29** Testing the SWF as it is will show the various states of this character. But we are going to add ActionScript to relegate these animations to user control.

1. First we will write the following lines to stop the mouth and eyes from animating on their own:

```
fullpuppet.puppethead.stop();
fullpuppet.puppethead.eyes.stop();
```

2. We will be using the photocell on the thumb to determine whether or not the mouth is completely closed. When the mouth is open, we want the Boolean variable `mouthopen` set to `true` and the red **led** circle up in the control panel to become visible. We will write the function to handle this photocell later on, but here we will initialize these elements to their "off" state:

```
var mouthopen:Boolean = false;
led._visible = 0;
```

3. Now we will set up the sliders in the control panel. The sliders are already built for you, but we need to apply the ActionScript to make them useful. Because there are some inconsistencies that may be present in our data glove, from the manner in which we open and close our fingers to the slight electrical differences in the seemingly identical sensors and resistors, we want to have a way to vary the range of values that are transmitted from the glove.

The resulting value from these sliders will later be used to invert the value received from the sensor glove and also set a total value range to apply toward the sensory input.

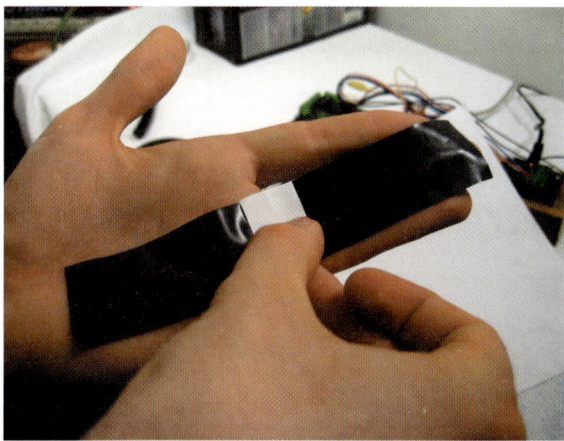

**Figure 14.30** These tweened frames are going to be mapped to the movement of the hand controlling the sock puppet. The wiring, Teleo MultiIO board and ActionScript, are going to negotiate real-world movement and gesture into virtual-world animation.

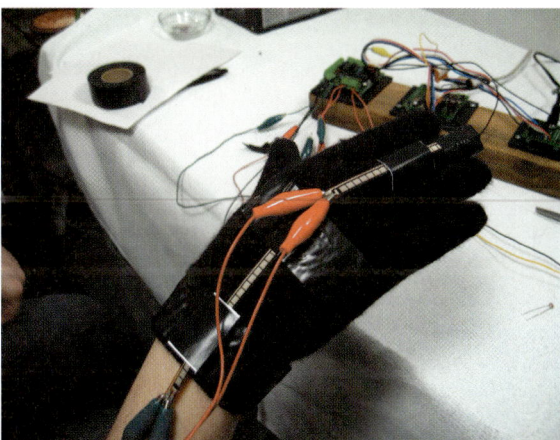

**Figure 14.31** In order to achieve independent control, the eyes are placed within their own movie clip.

```
var linelength:Number = mouthRange↵
Slider.sliderBgline._width;
var hStart:Number = mouthRange↵
Slider.sliderHandle._x;
var hEnd:Number = hStart + ↵
linelength;
var vBound:Number = mouthRange↵
Slider.sliderHandle._y;
```

Figure 14.32

Figure 14.33

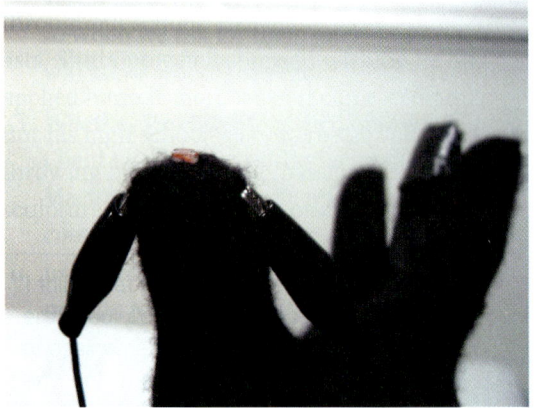

Figure 14.34

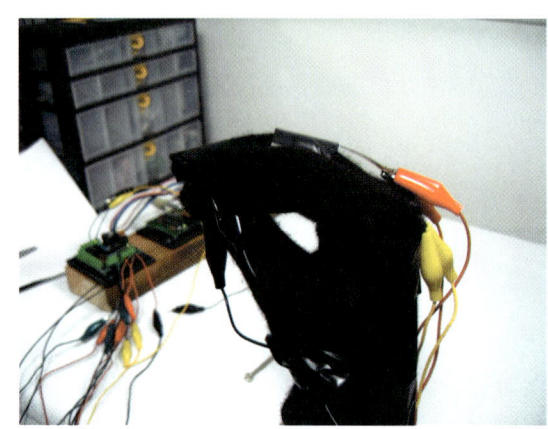

Figure 14.35

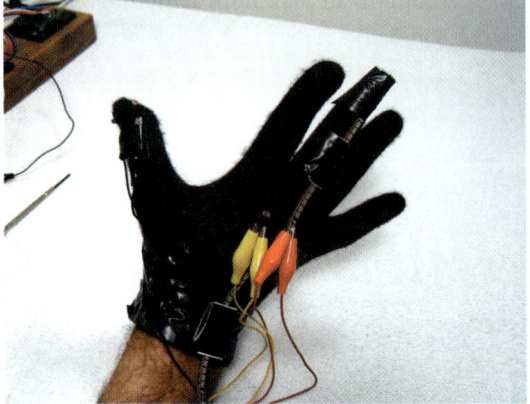

Figure 14.36

Figure 14.37

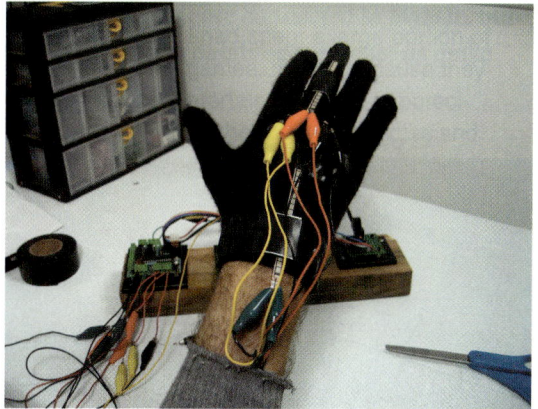

**Figure 14.38**

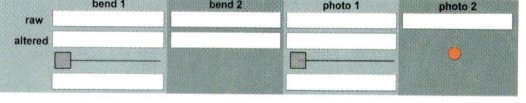

**Figure 14.39**

**Figure 14.40**

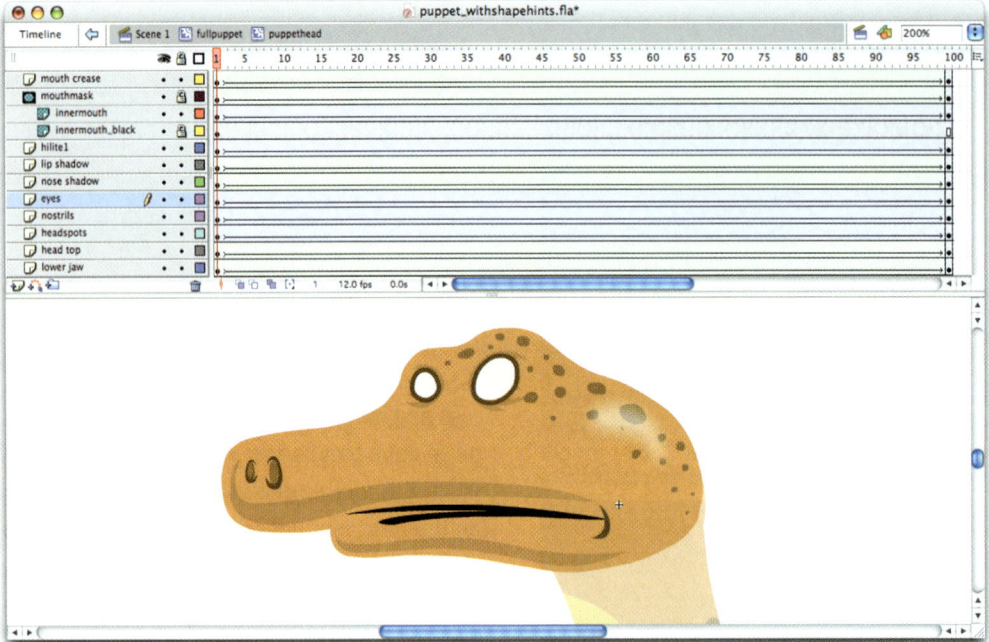

Figure 14.41

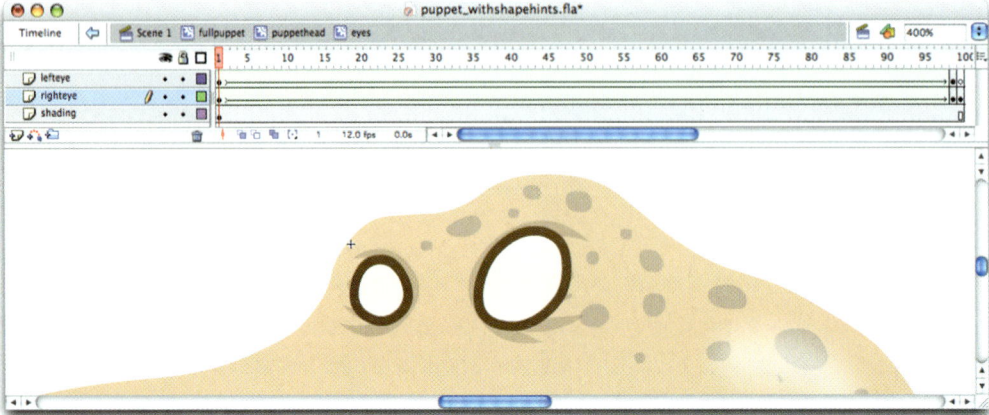

Figure 14.42

This block of ActionScript declares the sliding range and characteristics of the sliders. Since the `mouthRangeSlider` and `eyeRangeSlider` sliders are identical instances of the same movie clip, we will read the values of elements within `mouthRangeSlider` to determine the values for the `linelength`, `hStart`, `hEnd`, and `vBound variables`. These variables are then used to determine the boundaries and parameters for both sliders.

4. The next block of code will place the sliding mechanism for each slider in its initial position. We will take a starting number for each slider and use it in a percentage reversal formula:

```
var mouthStartrange:Number = 35;
var eyeStartrange:Number = 20;
mouthRangeSlider.sliderHandle._x =
 Math.floor((linelength * mouth
Startrange)/100);
eyeRangeSlider.sliderHandle._x =
 Math.floor((linelength * eye
Startrange)/100);
```

I arrived at the `mouthStartrange` and `eyeStartrange` values though some trial and error by testing the idiosyncrasies of the sensors and my own hand movements in the glove after all of the code to handle the data was written. These values give the most satisfying results within my range of hand motion, yet you may find that different values are optimal for your own arrangement. The percentage reversal is used to place `sliderHandle` at a relative location along its total range of movement. In the case of the mouth slider, I want the handle to start at 35 percent of the total 100 percent horizontal range of movement.

5. Now we will set up the functions that will handle interaction with the sliders:

```
var mouthPercentage:Number;
var eyePercentage:Number;
mouthRangeSlider.sliderHandle.
onPress = function (){
     var mouthSlidermover = set
Interval(mouthSlidermove,50);
     mouthRangeSlider.slider
Handle.startDrag(true, hStart,
 vBound, hEnd, vBound);
};
eyeRangeSlider.sliderHandle.
onPress = function (){
     var eyeSlidermover =
setInterval(eyeSlidermove,50);
     eyeRangeSlider.slider
Handle.startDrag(true, hStart,
 vBound, hEnd, vBound);
};
mouthRangeSlider.sliderHandle.
onRelease = mouthRangeSlider.
sliderHandle.onReleaseOutside =
function (){
     clearInterval(mouthSlidermover);
     mouthRangeSlider.slider
Handle.stopDrag();
};
eyeRangeSlider.sliderHandle.
onRelease = eyeRangeSlider.slider
Handle.onReleaseOutside =
function (){
     clearInterval(eyeSlidermover);
     eyeRangeSlider.sliderHandle.
stopDrag();
};
function mouthSlidermove(){
      mouthPercentage = Math.ceil
(mouthRangeSlider.sliderHandle._x/
linelength)*100);
     mouth_rangedisplay.text =
mouthPercentage;
}
function eyeSlidermove(){
```

```
        eyePercentage = Math.ceil(↵
(eyeRangeSlider.sliderHandle._x/↵
linelength)*100);
        eye_rangedisplay.text = ↵
eyePercentage;
}
```

As you can see, the ActionScript for each slider is pretty much identical. When the `mouthRangeSlider` slider handle is pressed, we use `setInterval` to continually check where the `sliderHandle` is via the `mouthSlidermove` function. This function generates the `mouthPercentage` variable using a normal percentage formula, `(mouthRangeSlider.sliderHandle._x/linelength)*100)`. This resulting percentage is then used by the function that handles the middle finger bend sensor input, which we will be writing a little later.

The boundaries of the slider are set by the arguments in `startDrag`, using the `linelength`, `hStart`, `hEnd`, and `vBound` variables that we declared earlier. When the slider handle is released, we end and remove the interval and call `stopDrag`. We will add the `onReleaseOutside` handler to the `onRelease` line for each slider, since the mouse pointer may be outside of `sliderHandle` when the mouse button is released.

6. Then call the `mouthSlidermove` and `eyeSlidermove` functions to set the`mouthPercentage` and `eyePercentage` variables based on the initial position of the sliders:

```
mouthSlidermove();
eyeSlidermove();
```

That is it for the slider code. If you test the movie at this point, you should see a range of 0 to 100 in the text field below each slider, though they do not really do much yet but slide around.

7. Now we will create the code to handle the data that the MultiIO module is going to throw at us. We are going to first import the MakingThings Flash class libraries that we downloaded and installed with the Macromedia extension manager:

```
import com.MakingThings.*;
```

This will import the entire package of custom classes from MakingThings that are required for communication between Flash and the XML server and are not supplied with the Flash application.

8. Next we will create a new MultiIO Analog In object for each of the analog inputs on the Teleo module:

```
var ain0:TMioAin = new TMioAin(0);
var ain1:TMioAin = new TMioAin(1);
var ain2:TMioAin = new TMioAin(2);
var ain3:TMioAin = new TMioAin(3);
```

Because we have imported the MakingThings Flash class libraries, Flash will recognize the `TmioAin` datatype as valid and allow us to store the new `TmioAin` instances in the variables `ain0` through `ain3`. We supply the number as an argument for each `TMioAin` instance so it will reference that particular number input on the MultiIO board.

9. Now we will declare the sample rate and data resolution values for the incoming sensor data. When we use the `setResolution` or `setPeriod` methods that are available via the imported

MakingThings class Library, Flash will write the supplied argument values to the Teleo module. The resolution value can range from 1 to 10 bits, and the period, or sample rate, can range from 1 to 32767 milliseconds. Using a for-loop, we will set the resolution to the maximum of 10 bits and the sample rate to a speedy 10 ms for all four of the analog inputs so we get a nice, fluid feed of data from the sensors:

```
for (var i:Number=0; i<4; i++){
    this["ain" + i].set
Resolution(10);
    this["ain" + i].setPeriod(10);
}
```

**NOTE:** Keep in mind that the more data you have traveling through the Teleo network, the more clogged and unpredictable it may become. Normally, it is best to try and set the resolution and sample rate as low as your project's parameters will allow.

10. We are now ready to write the functions that will handle the sensory input from our glove. Let us start with the bend sensor on the middle finger, which is connected to Ain0. This sensor will be controlling the opening and closing of our character's mouth:

```
ain0.onValue = function(val){
    var v:Number = Math.round
(val) - 7;
    valueText0.text = v;
    var useval:Number = Math.
round(((mouthPercentage-v)/mouth
Percentage) * 100);
    valueText0a.text = useval;
    if(mouthopen){
        fullpuppet.puppethead.
gotoAndStop(useval);
    }
};
```

I will step through this function:

`ain0.onValue = function(val){`

The `onValue` method, also supplied by the MakingThings class Library, will receive a new value whenever the connected sensor detects a change. Each time the bend sensor connected to Ain0 is bent in one direction or the other, it passes the new numerical data to the argument `val`, which is then used by the code within the function.

`var v:Number = Math.round(val) - 7;`

We declare the variable v as equal to the rounded number passed to `val`. Because we are declaring v within the function in this way, it keeps v only available from within this function, so we can also use a variable named v in the other functions for handling the other sensors. I am subtracting 7 from this resulting value since the 10k Ω resistor I am using with this bend sensor is not ideally matched for the voltage divider. I found this slight offset through some brief trial and error, and it provides a more satisfactory movement in my case. You may need to change this number or remove the subtraction completely to suit your needs.

`valueText0.text = v;`

This displays the value received from the input in the **raw** row under **bend 1** in the control panel at the top of the Stage before we apply the inverted percentage formula.

`var useval:Number = Math.round(`
`((mouthPercentage-v)/mouth`
`Percentage) * 100);`

This line takes the positional value from `mouthRangeSlider` and subtracts the value received from the analog input (`mouthPercentage-v`). This subtraction offsets the sensory input value based on our setting with `mouthRangeSlider` so that the resulting value will start under or around 0 when the fingers are in closed position and rise as the middle finger on the glove is straightened. After the offset, we divide this number by the value from `mouthRangeSlider` and then take this resulting quotient, multiply it by 100, and round it off to arrive at a final percentage value. We want to round the number because this final number, `useval`, is used to move the frames of the character's mouth animation forward as the glove's finger straightens, or backward as the finger is curled back into its closed position. Considering that we are referring to frame numbers, we want only integer values.

```
valueText0a.text = useval;
```

This displays the value used to control the mouth in the **altered** row under **bend 1** in the control panel.

```
if(mouthopen){
      fullpuppet.puppethead.gotoAndStop(useval);
}
```

Here we check to see if the Boolean variable `mouthopen` is set to `true`, and if so, we allow the mouth to animate. This helps avoid unwanted frame jumps if the value of the middle finger bend sensor happens to change while the mouth is supposed to be closed. We will control this variable with one of the photocells.

That is it for the finger bend sensor. If the value displayed for the **altered** text field under **bend 1** in the control panel goes below zero or above 100, it is alright because the mouth animation will move only between frames 1 and 100. Try to adjust the mouth slider to allow the most comfortable range of opening and closing motion with the glove. Let us move on to the wrist bend sensor, which will control the rotation of the head:

```
ain1.onValue = function(val){
      var v:Number = Math.round(val);
      valueText1.text = v;
      if(!mouthopen){
            rotVal = Math.round(v * -1.5)) + 20;
            fullpuppet.puppethead._rotation = rotVal;
            valueText1a.text = rotVal;
      }
};
```

This function is a bit simpler than the last one. Notice that we are calling the `onValue` method for `ain1` in this function, rather than `ain0`. Before we set the rotation of the head based on shape of the bend sensor on the glove wrist, we need to check the `mouthopen` variable. If `mouthopen` is `false`, we can rotate the head. If `mouthopen` is `true`, the head will not rotate. This is to ensure that the rotation of the wrist does not interfere with the bend sensor on the finger, and vice versa. If you look at the fields for the bend sensors in the first column of the control panel, you will notice that as you move your wrist, the raw value for the first bend sensor will also sometimes change, even when your fingers do not.

We do not need a percentage value this time because we are not stepping through a set number of frames to animate the rotation of the head. Instead, we are going to use a variable `rotVal` to control the rotation mathematically. First, we will take the sensor's input value `v` and multiply it by –1.5 to invert the resulting value and get a larger range of motion than we would normally get from the limited motion data generated from our wrist movement. You can experiment with this value if the range of motion you end up with is not satisfactory. We want to invert the value so that the head is rotating up and down when we do the same with our wrist. We take this inverted value and round it off, then add 20 to offset it into a more pleasing angle (you may want to experiment with this final added number, but 20 was best in my case). The resulting number is then used to rotate the head, with `fullpuppet.puppethead._rotation = rotVal;`.

11. We are done with the code for the bend sensors, so now we will move on to the two photocells. The first photocell, connected to Ain2, will control how much our character's eyes squint, as if they are in bright light:

```
ain2.onValue = function(val){
    var v:Number = Math.round(val);
    valueText2.text = v;
    var useval:Number = Math.round((((eyePercentage-v)/eyePercentage) * 100) / 4);
    valueText2a.text = useval;
    if(useval >= 1){
        fullpuppet.puppethead.eyes.gotoAndStop(useval);
    }else{
        fullpuppet.puppethead.eyes.gotoAndStop(1);
    }
};
```

This function uses the `eyePercentage` value taken from the `eyeRange` slider in the control panel. This code is very similar to the code we used for the bend sensor on the middle finger, except before rounding the final result of the offset/percentage formula to arrive at `useval`, I am dividing the value by 4 to get a more gradual change.

Remember that this is needed for my particular lighting situation, which is the halogen desk lamp I am using next to my computer. When I have the glove away from the light, the eyes are wide open. As I move my hand closer to the light, the eyes begin to narrow until they are squinting completely when I am right up next to the bulb. You might want to experiment with other values depending on your lighting situation.

Another difference in this function from the first bend sensor function is that instead of checking the `mouthopen` variable to allow jumping to different frames, we check whether `useval` is greater than 1.

12. Here we come to our final and simplest sensor handling function. The photocell on the thumb, which is connected to Ain3, is going to set the `mouthopen` Boolean variable to `true` when it detects even a small amount of light, then back to `false` in the absence of light. This works well with our glove design because the electrical tape that is anchoring the bend sensor to the tip of the middle finger acts as a very good

light inhibitor when it is pressed against this photocell:

```
ain3.onValue = function(val){
    var v:Number = Math.round(val);
    valueText3.text = v;
    if(v < 93){
        mouthopen = true;
        led._visible = 1;
    }else{
        mouthopen = false;
        fullpuppet.puppethead.
gotoAndStop(1);
        led._visible = 0;
    };
};
```

The logic statement here checks to see if the raw value received from the thumb's photocell is less than 93, and if so sets the `mouthopen` variable to `true` and makes the little red led circle in the control panel visible to indicate that the mouth is open. If v is greater than 93, it makes the led invisible, sets `mouthopen` to `false` and forces the mouth animation to jump to **frame 1**, where it remains closed.

This may seem different than how we handled our other sensors because we are not performing any data inversions or fudgy math hacks. The inverted value is not necessary here because we are simply using this photocell as a threshold switch to determine if the mouth is open or closed.

13. That is it! Don your sensor glove and test your Flash movie. The puppet should open its mouth fluidly as you open and straighten out your fingers and close its mouth as you close your fingers. You will find that certain hand positions and motions provide better results in the puppet. Cover the photocell on your thumb with the taped tip of your middle finger to ensure that the mouth is closed, and rotate your wrist up and down to tilt the head. Move the photocell on the knuckle close to a bright light source and watch the eyes narrow and squint. Try moving the sliders in the control panel to see if you get a more desirable response from the puppet.

If your puppet/Flash setup is not working, open the *puppet_complete_withcode.fla* file from the Chapter_14 folder on the DVD and check your code against mine. Also be sure to check that all of the wires and connection points on the glove and wiring assemblies and Teleo board are firmly connected. Something may have come loose during testing. Also be sure that there are no short circuits being caused by the stripped wire ends or resistor leads or jumper clips touching or crossing where they do not belong. If a short circuit occurs, it may manifest itself as harmlessly as the Flash puppet simply not working properly or as dramatically as smoking electronic components on the Teleo board. Be vigilant and careful when playing with electricity.

Also, consider the processing resources available when developing a Flash/Teleo application. You not only need to plan for your Flash application to run smoothly and within the limits of the host computer's abilities, but you also need to stay within the data bandwidth and processing capabilities of the Teleo hardware and network.

For further reading, *www.MakingThings.com* has an abundance of information, covering everything from their available hardware modules to electronic theory.

 ## ON YOUR OWN

Working with electronics, especially with analog sensors that detect forces or environmental changes, can be unpredictable. The more meticulously-controlled your installation environment, the more you can predict and plan what will happen as the sensors take in data or your application controls lights or motors. A group of electronic components that look the same and are labeled identically often have slightly different characteristics that must be compensated for. The lighting situation in a given area can change throughout the day and also depends on the types of lights installed in that area. Sensors can lose accuracy and require re-calibration.

Despite the possibility for unpredictable results, you now have in your hands a very rich and powerful way to interact with Flash that goes far beyond the limitations of the traditional keyboard and mouse. There are sensors available for detecting humidity, distance, pressure, rotation, radiation, and many other aspects of the real world. You can utilize a wide variety of buttons, switches, lights, motors, solenoids, potentiometers, and other tangible components.

This physical computing demo that Shuta covered in the DIY section is a good launching point. A lot of time and effort could be spent making a more detailed puppet and a more articulated Flash environment. The control panels are great for testing your system, but you may want to exclude these troubleshooting tools in a final artwork.

## A

ActionScript
   for animations, 69–71
   artificial life and, 196–204
   controlling color with, 92–98
   controlling sound with, 120–121
   creating Flash puppet, 267–278
   on frames, 111–112
   functions, 22–23
   IK system and, 154–166
   logic statements, 24
   movement and texture with, 78–83
   overview, 21–25
   placement, 25
   vs. Processing, 134
   scaling animated line-ups with, 179–185
   scrolling a movie clip inside a mask with, 110–112
   statements, 22
   with symbols, 13–14
   text files and, 91–92
   variables, 23–24
ActionScript version setting, 29–30
addChild function, 156–157
Adobe After Effects, 36, 44–45
Adobe Illustrator, 59–61
Adobe Illustrator (.ai) files, 20, 60–61
After Effects. *See* Adobe After Effects
algorithms, genetic, 220–221
Align tool, 65
alpha channels, video, 31
Alpha setting, 78
*Altar-ations* (Davis), 103–104
animated line-ups, 176–185
animation
   character, 69–72, 176–185
   creating, with IK system, 152–166
   creating tweened, 11–14
   easing effect, 157–158
   importing files for, 60–62
   interactive, 69
   motion tweens, 11–14, 66–68
   rotoscoped, 46–47
   scaling character line-ups, 176–185
   storing and playing back, 166
   working with layers, 64–66
   working with Timeline, 64–66
*Aperture* (Socolofsky), 146
arguments, 111
art, generative, 191–193, 209–220
artificial life, 196–204
Atari, 188
attachMovie method, 79, 83, 216
audio files
   *See also* sound
   blending, with graphics, 120–121
   importing, 26
*Audiophile* (Miranda Zúñiga), 51
*Audiorganic* (Shuta), 257–258
auto parameter, 160

## B

background color, 3
Bandwidth Profiler tool, 13
behavior function, 201
bend sensors, 264–266, 276–277
best fit solutions, 211
biology, 89, 205
bitmap caching, 31
BitmapData Class, 214, 219–220
Bitmap Properties dialog box, 63
bitmaps
   defined, 59
   importing, 26, 61–63
blend modes, 31
body-code, 22

*Breather, The* (Shuta), 255
Brush tool, 7, 17, 38
button symbols, 20–21

## C

callbacks, 246–247, 250
Canvas Class, 219–220
Cardoso, Miguel, 195
Center for Embedded Network Sensing, 133
character animation, 69–72, 176–185
    *See also* animation
chooseTarget behavior, 216, 218
Cinema 4D, 122
circles, drawing, 5–6
class-based code, 214
class files
    linking symbols to, 215–216
    Mover class, 217–218
*Codec* (Takeo Magruder), 87
code-driven generative art, 191–193, 209–220
collaboration, 43–44, 189
collective interpretation, 213
color
    background, 3
    controlling, with ActionScript, 92–98
ColorChange( ) function, 97
color gradients, 5
Color Mixer, 5, 9
color objects, 92–98
comments, 22
*Communion* (Takeo Magruder), 88
communities, 202
Convert to Blank Keyframes command, 39
Convert to Symbol dialogue box, 17, 215
Corel Painter, 36
cosine, 191–193, 198
createBeing function, 199
createGrid() function, 180

creative play, 146, 147, 148
creativity, 171, 255
cue points, 31
curly braces ({}), 22, 111
_currentframe value, 128
custom fills, 9
cyber-domestic aesthetic, 74
*Cyber-Kitchen* (Loseby), 75

## D

*Darwinstruments* (Thorp), 213–214
*Data_cosm* (Takeo Magruder), 89
databases, 235–251
    connecting PHP and, 242–244
    creating MySQL, 236–240
    installing MySQL, 235–236
    using with Flash, 244–251
data-driven projects, 134–135, 224
data-mining techniques, 213, 229–231
dataReceiver object, 246, 247
dataSender object, 246
data visualization, 212–220, 224
Davis, Juliet, 102–113
default settings, 2–3
Delegate class, 158
*Del Microcosmos a Gaia* (Ortiz), 204–205
*Dentimundo* (Miranda Zúñiga), 52–53
depth, 103
design issues, 117
design process, 211, 221
Diana, Carla, 116–129
*doc-u* (Loseby), 83–85
documents
    multiple, 2
    new, 2–3
    publishing, 29–30
    sizes, 37
doDraw method, 218–219

doMove function, 217–219
Download Settings, 85
drawBeing function, 197
drawCommands variable, 141
drawing
    data-driven, 134–135
    dynamic, 218–219
    with Flash, 37–39
    importance of, 118
    subtractive, 7
drawing recorder application, 137–143
drawing tools, 4–8, 38
duration variable, 125
dynamic drawing, 218–219
dynamic reparenting, 158

### E

easing effect, 157–158, 160, 164
Easing parameters, 31
electronic sensory input devices, 258–278
Eliasson, Olafur, 147
*El Inventor de Historias* (Ortiz), 188
end variable, 125
<*Event*> (Takeo Magruder), 88
event handlers, 22–23, 25, 71, 111–112
Evolutionary Design Process (EDP), 211, 221
evolutionary model, 202–204
evolutionary process, 210–211, 220–221
execute interval function, 126
experimentation, 117, 146
ExtraExtra, 226
Eyebeam, 148

### F

*Fallout* (Miranda Zúñiga), 54–55
[ *Fallujah . Iraq . 31/03/2004* ] (Takeo Magruder), 89–92
Fibonacci Sequence, 233

files
    default settings, 2–3
    exporting, 29–30
    importing, 26–28, 60–63
    loading external SWF, 106–109
    moving, 6
    multiple, 2
    opening new, 2–3
    PHP, 142
file types, 2, 26
fills
    custom, 9
    setting properties, 5
filters, 31
findJoints function, 155–156
findMovementJoints function, 160, 162, 163, 164
Flash, custom physical interface for, 258–278
Flash files
    embedding multiple, into HTML page, 76–77
    using with PHP and MySQL, 244–251
Flash puppets, creating, 267–278
Flash version setting, 29
Flash Video file format (FLV), 27
Flat Black Films, 256
Flickr, 212, 226
*Flight Patterns* (Koblin), 132, 133–135
flosc, 147
for-loops, 246–247, 248
forms, centering, 5
*Foxhole Manifesto* (Gieg), 34
frames
    adding, 42
    placement of ActionScript on, 111–112
Friendster, 173–175
Fry, Ben, 134
functions, 22–23, 80–81
    *See also specific functions*

## G

Gamelab, 147
generative art, 191–193, 209–220
generative particle system, 214–220
genetic algorithms, 220–221
getdistance function, 80
getMovementPoint function, 159, 163
getTargetPoint function, 159, 163
Gieg, Nick Fox, 34–48
Gilliam, Terry, 150
Global Action Project, 148
*GNOM* (Ortiz, Valencia, and Rico), 189
gradients, 31
graphics
    bitmap, 26, 59, 61–63
        blending audio with, 120–121
    vector, 4, 26, 59–61
graphic symbols, 20, 64–66
groups, making, 6
guide layers, 14–16
GUI (Graphical User Interface) tools, 92

## H

handlers. *See* event handlers
Harris, Jonathan, 224–252
hitTest method, 111, 139
homogeneous look, 170
HTML pages, embedding multiple Flash movies in, 76–77
HTML Publish setting, 30
hyp() function, 80

## I

if-else statements, 24
If statements, 24
if statements, 199
if-then statements, 124
Illustrator. *See* Adobe Illustrator
images
    bitmap, 26, 59, 61–63
    vector, 4, 26, 59–61
*Index for X* (Thorp), 212–213
individual experience, 87–88
initAng property, 163
initFamily function, 156–157
initMC function, 154–155
init method, 216, 217
instance names, 21–22, 108–109, 248–249
interactive environments, 102, 119–121, 189–193
interactivity
    with 3D models, 122–124
    creative play and, 147
    recording user, 137–143
International Networks Archive, 225
interval_id variable, 125
intervals, 125–126
inverse kinematics (IK) system, 150, 152–166
    building blocks of, 152–154
    rotation, 161–166
    skeleton creation, 154–157
    storing and playing back animation, 166
    translations, 157–161
Iraq War, 89–90, 231
iteration function, 201
*I Wanna Be Famous* (Gieg), 43

## J

*Jack* (Diana), 117
Johnson, Liz, 110
Joint class, 154
joints, 152–156, 158–159
JPEG images, settings for, 30, 62–63

## K

keyboard shortcuts, 3–4
keyframes
   defined, 66
   inserting, 15
   motion tweens and, 11–14
   placement of ActionScript on, 25
*ki2D* (Ortiz), 190
Koblin, Aaron, 132–144

## L

Layer Properties menu, 14, 15
Layer Property Inspector, 108
layers, 8–9
   creating, 8
   guide, 14–16
   hierarchy, 10
   mask, 16–18, 103, 108–112
   masked, 108–109, 112
   repositioning, 9
   working with, 60, 64–66
Layers section, 3
Library assets, 11, 20
Limb class, 155, 156
limbs
   in IK system, 152–166
   rotation of, 161–166
   translations, 157–161
Lindenmayer, Aristid, 200
line-up, scaling animated, 176–185
Linkage Identifier, 79, 83
Linklater, Richard, 256
LiveJournal, 134, 227
loadMovie command, 105, 109
LoadVars Class, 92, 246
loadVars command, 141
localToGlobal function, 160
logic statements, 24

Loseby, Jess, 74–85
Lott, Joey, 158
L-systems, 200–202

## M

Macromedia Extension Manager, 259
MakingThings, 258–259
Margulis, Lynn, 205
masked layers, 108–109, 112
mask layers, 16–18, 103, 108–112
mass media, individual experience of, 87–88
Math.cos function, 198
Math.random function, 216
Math.sin function, 198
Max/MSP, 146–147
mcPress method, 158, 161–162
mcRelease method, 158, 161–162
media
   exporting, 29–30
   importing, 26–28
Melody Assistant X, 127
*Memecry* (Koblin), 134
*Memorial to Things Gone Bad* (Olsson), 170
Miranda Zúñiga, Ricardo, 50–72
*Mitozoos* (Ortiz), 194–195, 196
mode variable, 182
*Monolith[s]* (Takeo Magruder), 87
Monson, Ander, 212
*Monty Python's Flying Circus*, 150
*Mood Threads* (Koblin), 134
Moore, Dylan, 235
motion
   with ActionScript, 78–83
   scripting, with IK system, 152–166
Motion Guide layer, 14
motion sensors, 124
motion tweens
   creating, 11–14
   working with, 66–68

mouse
    hovering over items, 3
    interactivity, 20–21
mouse handlers, 161
move function, 80–81
movement point parameters, 163
Mover class, 217–218
MovieClip class, 80–81
MovieClip.prototype.nameOfFunction, 80–81
movie clip symbols, 20
    ActionScript and, 21–25
    scrolling, inside a mask, 110–112
MP3 audio compression, 30
music compositions, 124–126
mutations, 211
Muybridge, Eadweard, 46
MySpace, 227
MySQL, installation, 235–236
MySQL databases
    adding to Flash, 244–251
    connecting PHP and, 242–244
    creating, 236–240

### N

neural networks, 213–214
news creation, 89–90
nextChar variable, 184
not equal (!=) operator, 24

### O

Object Drawing mode, 31
objects, grouping, 6
Olsson, Krister, 170–186
onClipEvent handlers, 111, 192
onDone handler, 184
onEnterFrame handler, 123, 181–184, 193, 198
onion skinning, 39
Onion Skin view, 18, 39, 42–43

onLoad method, 246–247
onPress event, 123, 181
onRelease event, 122–123
onReleaseOutside event, 122–123
onResize events, 181
onRollover event, 23, 181
onValue method, 275
Option key, 5
*Option of War, The* (Gieg), 35–36
Ortiz, Santiago, 188–206
OureData, 195
Oval tool, 4–5, 9, 31
Oven Digital, 51

### P

parameterized design, 185
parameters, 22, 158
Pencil tool, 14, 15
PHP
    connecting to MySQL database, 242–244
    installation, 235
    working with, 240–242
PHP files
    adding to Flash, 244–251
    saving, 142
*Phylotaxis* (Harris), 233–235
physical interface, custom, 258–278
*Pieces of Herself* (Davis), 105–106, 110
placeChars function, 180, 184
PLANETii, 117
*Polystyrene Dream* (Davis), 104–105
*Position/Disposition* (Loseby), 75
pre-designed content, 178
*Pretendster* (Olsson), 173–175
Processing, 134
programmatically generated content, 178
programming languages, learning, 172
Property Inspector, 3, 5, 7, 12, 93
prototype functions, 80–81

Proxy class, 158
Publish command, 29–30
Publish Settings, 62
puppets, creating Flash, 267–278

## Q

*QueryCount* (Harris), 230–231
quickcomic.com, 148
Quicktime, 26

## R

radians, 193, 198
randomness, 212
raster graphics. *See* bitmaps
Raw compression setting, 30, 128
Reas, Casey, 134
Rectangle tool, 31
registration points, 5–6, 153
*Repercussion* (Diana), 124–126
reserved words, 24
reset function, 80
resetMode function, 184
reusable code, 214
rotate function, 162–164
rotation, 161–166
_rotation property, 198
rotoscoping, 46–47
Rotoshop, 256
Ruler units, changing, 3
*Rules of Play* (Salen and Zimmerman), 147

## S

Sabiston, Bob, 256–257
Salen, Katie, 147
Salon (Socolofsky), 146–147
scaling animated line-ups, 176–185
*Scanner Darkly, A* (film), 256
scope, 158

screen dimensions, 37
Selection tool, 7, 9
sensory input devices, 258–278, 276–277
setInterval method, 125–126
setPeriod method, 274–275
setResolution method, 274–275
setTransform() method, 96
setVolume method, 127–128
shapes, converting to symbols, 17
shape tweens, 18, 66–67
*Sheep Market, The* (Koblin), 132, 136–137
shortcuts, 3–4
Shuta, Dan, 25479
*Silly Walks Generator* (Socolofsky), 150–166
Simulate Download, 85
simulations, 196
sine, 191–193, 198
skeletons, creating, 154–157
sketching, 106, 118
Smoothing adjustment, 7
*Snake in the Grass* (Olsson), 170
social communities, 202
social networking, 170, 173–175, 212, 226–227
Socolofsky, Eric, 146–167
*Sonido Y Energia* (Ortiz), 189–193
sound, controlling, 120–121
sound compositions, 124–126
sound objects, 120–121, 127
sound volume, 127–128
Stage, 3
Start panel, 2
startTime property, 183–184
statements, 22
*Street Fighter*, 56
strokes
    moving, 6
    new features, 31
    setting properties, 5

subtractive drawing, 7, 8
swatches, custom, 8
SWF files, loading external, 106–109
Symbol Properties window, 127
symbols
    ActionScript and, 13–14, 21–25
    button, 20–21
    converting shapes to, 17
    creating, 10–11
    graphic, 20, 64–66
    instance names, 21–22, 108–109
    linking to class files, 215–216
    movie clip, 20, 21–25, 110–112
    properties of, 13
    Timeline and, 19
    types of, 19–21

## T

tablet pressure button, 38
Takeo Magruder, Michael, 87–100
target point parameters, 163
technical issues, 117
technology-based art, 51
Teleo MultiIO module, 258–259, 261, 274–275
Template setting, 30
*10 × 10* (Harris), 231–233
*Terranium* (Diana), 119–121
text boxes, 31
text files, external, 91–92
texture, with ActionScript, 78–83
Thorp, Jeremy, 208–222
3D models, 122–124
Timeline, 3
    navigation, 66, 248–249
    symbols and, 19
    working with, 64–66
Tools panel, 3–7
_totalFrames property, 123

trace function, 24, 143, 246–248
{ *transcription* } (Takeo Magruder), 99
translations, 157–161, 198
Tree Axis, 171
*tree.growth* (Thorp), 210
triggerChar function, 182
trigonometry, 191–193
*Troubadour Magazine*, 226
tweens
    creating, 11–14
    defined, 12
    Easing parameters, 31
    guide layers, 14–16
    motion, 11–14, 66–68
    shape, 18, 66–67

## U

ungrouped objects, 6
update function, 158, 159, 160–161, 165–166
updateStroke function, 141
user input
    animations and, 69, 71
    creative play and, 147
    recording, 137–143
user interfaces, 149
userRotate function, 164–165

## V

*Vagamundo* (Miranda Zúñiga), 55–58, 69, 72
variables, 23–24, 217
*Variance* (Thorp), 211, 220–221
*Vectogram* (Socolofsky), 149
vector graphics
    creating, 4
    defined, 59
    importing, 26
    shape tweens and, 18
    working with, 60–61

Version setting, 29
*Victim of Heedless Excess, A* (Shuta), 254
video alpha channels, 31
video cue points, 31
video encoder, 31
video files, importing, 26–28
video import, 31
*Views from the Ground Floor* (Loseby), 76–77
visualization, 224
volume, 127–128

## W

Wacom tablets, 37
walk cycles, creating, 40–43
*We Feel Fine* (Harris and Kamvar), 227
window resize events, 181
*WordCount* (Harris), 229–231
workspace, 3
*World[s]* (Takeo Magruder), 89
*www.blprnt.com*, 208–209

## X

_x property, 71
Xeno's Paradox, 157

## Z

Zimmerman, Eric, 147
Zune, 171, 172
*Zune Arts*, 175–176

**IMPORTANT-READ CAREFULLY**: This End User License Agreement ("Agreement") sets forth the conditions by which Delmar Learning, a division of Thomson Learning Inc. ("Thomson") will make electronic access to the Thomson Delmar Learning-owned licensed content and associated media, software, documentation, printed materials and electronic documentation contained in this package and/or made available to you via this product (the "Licensed Content"), available to you (the "End User"). BY CLICKING THE "I ACCEPT" BUTTON AND/OR OPENING THIS PACKAGE, YOU ACKNOWLEDGE THAT YOU HAVE READ ALL OF THE TERMS AND CONDITIONS, AND THAT YOU AGREE TO BE BOUND BY ITS TERMS CONDITIONS AND ALL APPLICABLE LAWS AND REGULATIONS GOVERNING THE USE OF THE LICENSED CONTENT.

**1.0 SCOPE OF LICENSE**

1.1 Licensed Content. The Licensed Content may contain portions of modifiable content ("Modifiable Content") and content which may not be modified or otherwise altered by the End User ("Non-Modifiable Content"). For purposes of this Agreement, Modifiable Content and Non-Modifiable Content may be collectively referred to herein as the "Licensed Content." All Licensed Content shall be considered Non-Modifiable Content, unless such Licensed Content is presented to the End User in a modifiable format and it is clearly indicated that modification of the Licensed Content is permitted.

1.2 Subject to the End User's compliance with the terms and conditions of this Agreement, Thomson Delmar Learning hereby grants the End User, a nontransferable, non-exclusive, limited right to access and view a single copy of the Licensed Content on a single personal computer system for noncommercial, internal, personal use only. The End User shall not (i) reproduce, copy, modify (except in the case of Modifiable Content), distribute, display, transfer, sublicense, prepare derivative work(s) based on, sell, exchange, barter or transfer, rent, lease, loan, resell, or in any other manner exploit the Licensed Content; (ii) remove, obscure or alter any notice of Thomson Delmar Learning's intellectual property rights present on or in the License Content, including, but not limited to, copyright, trademark and/or patent notices; or (iii) disassemble, decompile, translate, reverse engineer or otherwise reduce the Licensed Content.

**2.0 TERMINATION**

2.1 Thomson Delmar Learning may at any time (without prejudice to its other rights or remedies) immediately terminate this Agreement and/or suspend access to some or all of the Licensed Content, in the event that the End User does not comply with any of the terms and conditions of this Agreement. In the event of such termination by Thomson Delmar Learning, the End User shall immediately return any and all copies of the Licensed Content to Thomson Delmar Learning.

**3.0 PROPRIETARY RIGHTS**

3.1 The End User acknowledges that Thomson Delmar Learning owns all right, title and interest, including, but not limited to all copyright rights therein, in and to the Licensed Content, and that the End User shall not take any action inconsistent with such ownership. The Licensed Content is protected by U.S., Canadian and other applicable copyright laws and by international treaties, including the Berne Convention and the Universal Copyright Convention. Nothing contained in this Agreement shall be construed as granting the End User any ownership rights in or to the Licensed Content.

3.2 Thomson Delmar Learning reserves the right at any time to withdraw from the Licensed Content any item or part of an item for which it no longer retains the right to publish, or which it has reasonable grounds to believe infringes copyright or is defamatory, unlawful or otherwise objectionable.

**4.0 PROTECTION AND SECURITY**

4.1 The End User shall use its best efforts and take all reasonable steps to safeguard its copy of the Licensed Content to ensure that no unauthorized reproduction, publication, disclosure, modification or distribution of the Licensed Content, in whole or in part, is made. To the extent that the End User becomes aware of any such unauthorized use of the Licensed Content, the End User shall immediately notify Delmar Learning. Notification of such violations may be made by sending an Email to delmarhelp@thomson.com.

**5.0 MISUSE OF THE LICENSED PRODUCT**

5.1 In the event that the End User uses the Licensed Content in violation of this Agreement, Thomson Delmar Learning shall have the option of electing liquidated damages, which shall include all profits generated by the End User's use of the Licensed Content plus interest computed at the maximum rate permitted by law and all legal fees and other expenses incurred by Thomson Delmar Learning in enforcing its rights, plus penalties.

**6.0 FEDERAL GOVERNMENT CLIENTS**

6.1 Except as expressly authorized by Delmar Learning, Federal Government clients obtain only the rights specified in this Agreement and no other rights. The Government acknowledges that (i) all software and related documentation incorporated in the Licensed Content is existing commercial computer software within the meaning of FAR 27.405(b)(2); and (2) all other data delivered in whatever form, is limited rights data within the meaning of FAR 27.401. The restrictions in this section are acceptable as consistent with the Government's need for software and other data under this Agreement.

**7.0 DISCLAIMER OF WARRANTIES AND LIABILITIES**

7.1 Although Thomson Delmar Learning believes the Licensed Content to be reliable, Thomson Delmar Learning does not guarantee or warrant (i) any information or materials contained in or produced by the Licensed Content, (ii) the accuracy, completeness or reliability of the Licensed Content, or (iii) that the Licensed Content is free from errors or other material defects. THE LICENSED PRODUCT IS PROVIDED "AS IS," WITHOUT ANY WARRANTY OF ANY KIND AND THOMSON DELMAR LEARNING DISCLAIMS ANY AND ALL WARRANTIES, EXPRESSED OR IMPLIED, INCLUDING, WITHOUT LIMITATION, WARRANTIES OF MERCHANTABILITY OR FITNESS OR A PARTICULAR PURPOSE. IN NO EVENT SHALL THOMSON DELMAR LEARNING BE LIABLE FOR: INDIRECT, SPECIAL, PUNITIVE OR CONSEQUENTIAL DAMAGES INCLUDING FOR LOST PROFITS, LOST DATA, OR OTHERWISE. IN NO EVENT SHALL DELMAR LEARNING'S AGGREGATE LIABILITY HEREUNDER, WHETHER ARISING IN CONTRACT, TORT, STRICT LIABILITY OR OTHERWISE, EXCEED THE AMOUNT OF FEES PAID BY THE END USER HEREUNDER FOR THE LICENSE OF THE LICENSED CONTENT.

**8.0 GENERAL**

8.1 Entire Agreement. This Agreement shall constitute the entire Agreement between the Parties and supercedes all prior Agreements and understandings oral or written relating to the subject matter hereof.

8.2 Enhancements/Modifications of Licensed Content. From time to time, and in Delmar Learning's sole discretion, Thomson Thomson Delmar Learning may advise the End User of updates, upgrades, enhancements and/or improvements to the Licensed Content, and may permit the End User to access and use, subject to the terms and conditions of this Agreement, such modifications, upon payment of prices as may be established by Delmar Learning.

8.3 No Export. The End User shall use the Licensed Content solely in the United States and shall not transfer or export, directly or indirectly, the Licensed Content outside the United States.

8.4 Severability. If any provision of this Agreement is invalid, illegal, or unenforceable under any applicable statute or rule of law, the provision shall be deemed omitted to the extent that it is invalid, illegal, or unenforceable. In such a case, the remainder of the Agreement shall be construed in a manner as to give greatest effect to the original intention of the parties hereto.

8.5 Waiver. The waiver of any right or failure of either party to exercise in any respect any right provided in this Agreement in any instance shall not be deemed to be a waiver of such right in the future or a waiver of any other right under this Agreement.

8.6 Choice of Law/Venue. This Agreement shall be interpreted, construed, and governed by and in accordance with the laws of the State of New York, applicable to contracts executed and to be wholly preformed therein, without regard to its principles governing conflicts of law. Each party agrees that any proceeding arising out of or relating to this Agreement or the breach or threatened breach of this Agreement may be commenced and prosecuted in a court in the State and County of New York. Each party consents and submits to the non-exclusive personal jurisdiction of any court in the State and County of New York in respect of any such proceeding.

8.7 Acknowledgment. By opening this package and/or by accessing the Licensed Content on this Website, THE END USER ACKNOWLEDGES THAT IT HAS READ THIS AGREEMENT, UNDERSTANDS IT, AND AGREES TO BE BOUND BY ITS TERMS AND CONDITIONS. IF YOU DO NOT ACCEPT THESE TERMS AND CONDITIONS, YOU MUST NOT ACCESS THE LICENSED CONTENT AND RETURN THE LICENSED PRODUCT TO THOMSON DELMAR LEARNING (WITHIN 30 CALENDAR DAYS OF THE END USER'S PURCHASE) WITH PROOF OF PAYMENT ACCEPTABLE TO DELMAR LEARNING, FOR A CREDIT OR A REFUND. Should the End User have any questions/comments regarding this Agreement, please contact Thomson Delmar Learning at delmarhelp@thomson.com.